ENCYCLOPAEDIAS:
THEIR HISTORY
THROUGHOUT THE AGES

ENCYCLOPAEDIAS:
THEIR HISTORY
THROUGHOUT THE AGES

A BIBLIOGRAPHICAL GUIDE
WITH EXTENSIVE HISTORICAL NOTES TO
THE GENERAL ENCYCLOPAEDIAS ISSUED
THROUGHOUT THE WORLD FROM 350 B.C.
TO THE PRESENT DAY

ROBERT COLLISON

SECOND EDITION

1966
HAFNER PUBLISHING COMPANY
NEW YORK & LONDON

First published 1964
Second edition 1966
Hafner Publishing Co. Ltd.,
1 Grange Road, Kingston-upon-Thames,
Surrey

©

Copyright 1963 and 1965 by Robert Collison

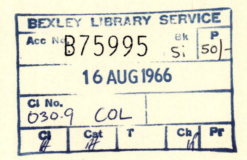
Printed in Great Britain by
Butler & Tanner Ltd., Frome and London

To

RUSSELL MUIRHEAD

explorator viae

ACKNOWLEDGMENTS

It is with profound gratitude that I acknowledge the encouragement and practical help given me by the following, though I must at the same time emphasize that they are in no way responsible for the text of this book: Professor W. S. Heckscher of the Kunsthistorisch Institut der Rijks-Universiteit, Utrecht; Mr John Armitage, Mr C. H. W. Kent, and Mr R. M. Goodwin, of the *Encyclopaedia Britannica*; Dr Karl Pfannkuch, Chefredakteur of *Brockhaus*; Mr G. C. E. Smith of *World Book Encyclopaedia*; Mr K. C. Ilmer, of The Hague; Dr Louis Shores, of Florida State University; Mr F. L. Kent, of the American University, Beirut; Mr W. R. Le Fanu, of the Royal College of Surgeons; Mr E. Simpson, City Librarian of Coventry; Mr G. Edward Harris; Professor L. J. Woodward, of the University of St Andrews; Mr C. F. Rae Griffin; Messrs H. K. Elliott, Ltd; and Mr F. Liebesny. And to Dr J. H. L. Pafford, of the University of London; Mr D. MacArthur, of the University of St Andrews; Mr S. Gillam, of the London Library; Mr S. P. L. Filon, of the National Central Library; Mr W. R. Maidment, of Camden Public Libraries; and Mr G. F. Osborn, of Westminster Central Reference Library, I offer my sincere thanks for the way in which they and their staffs made me welcome during my searches in their libraries.

R. C.

Hampstead
2nd July 1964

Advantage has been taken of the early issue of a new edition of this book to effect the following changes. The Appendices have been rearranged. Some fifty entries have been added to Appendix 4, and some annotations to other items have been amplified. The new Appendix 1 constitutes an essay on the *Encyclopaedia Metropolitana* incorporating some information on its financing that has come to light during the past year. Additional material on this important encyclopaedia is published in a special number (1966) of the *Journal of world history* devoted to the subject of Encyclopaedias. I am greatly indebted to Dr Guy S. Métraux, Secretary-General of Unesco's International Commission for a History of the Scientific and Cultural Development of Mankind, for drawing to my attention the project (unrealized) for the *Encyclopédie Péreire* in which Sainte-Beuve played an important rôle.

New encyclopaedias continue to appear: the latest are the one-volume *Penguin encyclopedia* (edited by Sir John Summersale), and the four-volume *Newnes Family encyclopaedia*—the former being perhaps the cheapest (12s. 6d.) encyclopaedia ever issued, while the latter is notable for its lavish colour illustrations.

R. C.

Hampstead
10th *January* 1966

CONTENTS

		page
Acknowledgments		(vii)
List of Illustrations and Charts		(xi)
Chronology		(xiii)
Introduction		I
I	The Beginnings	21
II	The Middle Ages	44
III	Bacon to the Encyclopédistes	82
IV	Diderot and the Encyclopédistes	114
V	The Encyclopaedia Britannica	138
VI	Brockhaus	156
VII	The Nineteenth century	174
VIII	The Twentieth century	199

Appendices

1	The *Encyclopaedia Metropolitana*	229
2	Samuel Taylor Coleridge on 'Scientific Method'	238
3	General Bibliography	296
4	List of Encyclopaedias not mentioned in the text	298
Index		315

ILLUSTRATIONS AND CHARTS

facing page

Title-page of the first volume of R. G. Löbel's *Conversations-lexikon,* 1796   104

Title-page of the first Hebrew Scientific encyclopaedia, the *Ma'aseh Tobiyyah* of Tobias Cohn (1653–1729) which, in addition to science, included theology and cosmography. It was published at Venice in 1707 (2nd edn. 1721)   105

Title-page of the first volume of the first edition of the *Encyclopaedia Britannica,* 1771   152

John Kay's caricature of Andrew Bell and William Smellie   153

Title-page of the first volume of the fourth edition (1817) of *Brockhaus,* considered to be the first edition completely attributable to F. A. Brockhaus   168

The bindings of two famous editions of *Brockhaus*   169

Charts   *page*

Chiu T'ung   36

Matthias Martini's classification of knowledge   83

CHRONOLOGY

Pre-Christian Era

c. 370   The first encyclopaedia work, compiled by Speusippos

c. 183   The first Roman encyclopaedia: Cato's *Praecepta ad filium*

c. 50   The first illustrated encyclopaedia: Varro's *Disciplinarum*

Christian Era

77   The first major encyclopaedic work: Pliny's *Historia naturalis*

c. 220   The first Chinese encyclopaedia: the *Huang Ian* (no longer extant)

c. 880   The first recorded Arabic encyclopaedia: Ibn Qutaiba's *Kitāb ʿUyūn al-Akhbār*

c. 940   The first Royal encyclopaedia, compiled by the Emperor Constantine VII

c. 980   The first example of collaboration in encyclopaedia-making: The Ikhwān al-Safā's *Rasā'ulu Ikhwān al Ṣafā*

1080   Alphabetical arrangement introduced in *Suidas*

1120   The first breakaway from tradition: Lambert of St Omer compiled his *Liber floridus*, in which he discards practical matters in favour of metaphysical discussion

c. 1130   The first successful attempt to describe in detail the techniques of the various crafts: 'Theophilus's' *De diversis artibus*

c. 1130   Honorius Inclusus's *Imago mundi* compiled

c. 1140   Probably the first British encyclopaedia: the Scottish monk Richard of St Victor's *Liber excerptionum*

c. 1180   The first encyclopaedia compiled by a woman: the Abbess Herrad's *Hortus deliciarum*

1244   Vincent of Beauvais's *Speculum maius* completed

c. 1246   Probably the first encyclopaedia in verse: Gautier de Metz's *Mappemonde* (written in French) *c.* 1264   The first real breakaway from Latin: Brunetto Latini's *Li livres dou trésor*

1273   Ma Tuan-lin's *Wên hsien t'ung k'ao* completed

c. 1315   The concept of the modern scientific encyclopaedia reached in the anonymous *Compendium philosophiae*

c. 1350   Increasing interest in the provision of biographical material exemplified in Guglielmo da Pastrengo's *De originibus rerum libellus*

c. 1410   The cross-reference comes into its own with Domenico Bandini's *Fons memorabilium universi*

c. 1520   Gregor Reisch achieves the ideal of the compact, readable encyclopaedia in his *Margarita philosophica*

1503   Domenico Nani Mirabelli's *Polyanthea nova*: the prototype of the Conversationslexicon

1531   Humanism exemplified in Juan Luis Vives's *De disciplinis*

1541   Ringelbergh uses the word 'Cyclopaedia' in the title of his *Lucubrationes*

1553   The first indigenous French encyclopaedia: Estienne's *Dictionarium*

1559   The word 'Encyclopaedia' first used in Paul Scalich's *Encyclopaedia, seu Orbis disciplinarum*

1606   Matthias Martini publishes the first book on encyclopaedia-compilation: his *Idea methodicae*

1620   Francis Bacon published his plan for *The great instauration*, and lays down the modern principles of encyclopaedia-making

1630   The last of the great Latin encyclopaedias arranged in systematic order: Johann Heinrich Alsted's *Encyclopaedia*

1653–   The first Hungarian encyclopaedia: János Apácza
1655   Cseri's *Magyar encyclopaedia*

1674   Louis Moréri's *Le grand dictionnaire historique* published

1690   Furetière's posthumous *Dictionnaire universel* published: the first example of the modern encyclopaedic dictionary

1694   Probably the first encyclopaedic work for women: John Dunton's *Ladies' dictionary*

1695   Probably the first encyclopaedia for children: Johann Christoph Wagenseil's *Pera librorum juvenilium*

1697 Pierre Bayle's influential *Dictionnaire historique et critique* published

1701 Vincenzo Maria Coronelli introduces the italicizing of quoted book titles

1704 Publication of the Jesuits' encyclopaedia, the *Dictionnaire de Trévoux*
      Publication of the first purely English general encyclopaedia, John Harris's *Lexicon technicum*
      Publication of the first truly German encyclopaedia, Sinold von Schütz's *Reales Staats- und Zeitungs-Lexikon*
      The Emperor K'ang Hsi orders the compilation of a series of Chinese encyclopaedias

1728 Publication of Ephraim Chambers's *Cyclopaedia*

1731 Johann Heinrich Zedler starts publishing his enormous *Grosses vollständiges Universal-Lexicon*—the first encyclopaedia to include biographies of living people

1746 The first serious encyclopaedia in Italian: Gianfrancisco Pivati's *Nuovo dizionario*

1751 Publication of the first volume of Diderot's *Encyclopédie*

1765 The Rev. Temple Henry Croker's *The complete dictionary of arts and sciences* issued. Possibly the first and only English provincial encyclopaedia

1771 The first edition of the *Encyclopaedia Britannica* completed

1773 Johann Georg Krünitz's gigantic *Oekonomisch-technologische Enzyklopädie* begins publication

1782 Panckoucke & Agasse's *Encyclopédie méthodique* begun

1793 The first real Russian encyclopaedia begun (but not completed): V. N. Tatischev's *Leksikon rossiiskoi*

1802 The first parts of Abraham Rees's *The new cyclopaedia* issued

1808 The first volume of Sir David Brewster's *The Edinburgh encyclopaedia* published

1809 Friedrich Arnold Brockhaus begins issuing his *Conversations-Lexikon*

1817 Based on Samuel Taylor Coleridge's plan, the first volumes of the *Encyclopaedia metropolitana* appear

1818   Ersch & Gruber commence publication of their vast (and never completed) encyclopaedia: the *Allgemeine Encyclopädie*

1828   The first edition of Noah Webster's *American dictionary*

1829   The first edition of the *Encyclopaedia Americana*

1840   The first edition commenced of Josef Meyer's *Der grosse Conversations-Lexikon*

1853   The first edition of an encyclopaedia designed to provide a specifically Catholic viewpoint: Herder's *Konversations-Lexikon*

1860   The Scottish firm of W. & R. Chambers issue the first edition of their *Chambers's Encyclopaedia*

1865   Pierre Athanase Larousse commences publication of his *Grand dictionnaire universel du XIXe siècle*

1868   Publication of the first edition of the Dutch encyclopaedia now known as *Winkler Prins' encyclopaedie*

1869   Publication commences of the first (and probably only) American German encyclopaedia: Alexander Jacob Schem's *Deutsch-amerikanisches Conversations-Lexicon*

1875   The first edition of the Swedish *Nordisk familjebok*

1876   The first volume issued of the Lebanese Butrus al-Bustani's *Da'irat al-Maarif*

1886   The first volume published of *La grande encyclopédie*

1892   *Hagerups Illustrerede konversations leksikon* first published

1893   *Salmonsens Konversations leksikon* first published

1895   The popular Russian 'Granat' encyclopaedia (*Entsiklopedicheskii slovar'*) starts its first edition

INTRODUCTION

*The impossible dream of intellectual order is at
least a dream of respectable antiquity*

REGINALD A. SMITH:
Towards a Living Encyclopaedia

A butler in a once-famous series of detective stories asked, as his reward for prowess in one of the earliest of his master's adventures, for a set of a well-known encyclopaedia. Methodically he started with page one of volume one but, such was his active part in various investigations, it is uncertain whether he ever got further than *Aaron* in his pursuit of knowledge. That butler probably epitomizes most people's efforts in this direction; we have all sat down to read an encyclopaedia at one time or another, but it is doubtful whether anyone has ever completed a thorough reading of any modern compilation of this nature. Whoever it was who defined an encyclopaedia as a book that is never read had more than a smattering of truth on his side. An encyclopaedia is frequently consulted, but is hardly a bedside companion in these days.

Between the two world wars a custom sprang up by which the public was persuaded to buy one mediocre novel by its being included with two or three others in a bumper 'omnibus' book. These thousand-page volumes were regarded as very good value for money, and there is no doubt that many a poor work got a better and wider hearing by its being sustained on either side by its abler companions in the sea of literature. This art of persuading people to buy something they do not want by offering it to them in one large package with something else they do want, is a system that has since been developed to amazing lengths (and with corresponding increase in strategic skill) through supermarkets and trading-coupons, but it is almost certain that encyclopaedias were the first to introduce the practice more than two thousand years ago. For example, it might prove impossible to sell to a man

B

I

engaged in the world of finance even a very well-written book on physics and its related subjects. And yet it may be comparatively easy to sell to the same man a set of an encyclopaedia that includes several hundred pages on these subjects, and for which he will have to pay handsomely in the total cost of the work! Thus it has always been: in the quest for complete digests and compendia of knowledge people have always and unquestioningly paid for millions of words they would probably never read. And it is ironic to think that in *their* quest for completeness, teams of encyclopaedia-compilers must sometimes have expended considerable effort in producing entries on minor subjects which not one of their readers has ever had the inclination or occasion to consult.

Nevertheless, it would be wrong to condemn the energy with which the encyclopaedia-makers pursued the will-o'-the-wisp of completeness, for this is a comparatively modern policy. For example, up to at least the end of the eighteenth century it was considered undesirable to include entries for living people in encyclopaedias, and many other features that we now take for granted in the modern encyclopaedia are quite recent innovations. But the chief mirage that hovered tantalizingly before so many generations was the belief that it was possible to compile a work that would supersede all other books and render them unnecessary. Not only did some compilers of encyclopaedias believe that this could be done, but there were also publishers and booksellers who believed it too, and therefore put powerful obstacles in the way of issuing encyclopaedias through fear of being deprived of their livelihood. In other words, there was a widespread belief that the whole of knowledge could be digested and codified into a few volumes, and that knowledge either stood still or made so little progress that the revision of one comprehensive work could easily cope with the results. And the booksellers who thought that any encyclopaedia could stop or reduce their sales of other works were as misguided as the newspaper proprietors of the 1920's who feared that the introduction of broadcast news could put them out of business. Rather did the newer medium stimulate the popularity of the older and, in both cases, their fears proved groundless.

One of the controversies that has never been cleared up satisfactorily is the question of the best method of arrangement of the contents of an encyclopaedia. Broadly speaking, there are three accepted methods;

A Systematically
B Alphabetically
    (*a*) by broad subjects
    (*b*) by specific subjects.

There is much to be said of behalf of each of these, and each can also be criticized adversely. Systematic arrangement prevailed for some hundreds of years during the early history of encyclopaedias —to the true scholar its appeal is very great for it is the only satisfactory way of bringing into juxtaposition closely related topics. This however at least partly assumes that the encyclopaedia will be read as a whole, or certainly that considerable sections will be treated in this way. Such a system of arrangement did not in any case suit those people who wished to make quick reference to a specific subject, for reference of this kind is dependent on good indexes, and thorough indexing has a history of less than a hundred years. The history of alphabetical arrangement is quite a thousand years old, but it did not come into general use until the eighteenth century and, even now, has not completely won universal allegiance.

The two differing types of alphabetical arrangement have continued parallel to each other and, until recently, the adherents of each were practically equal in numbers. At the present time alphabetical arrangement by specific subjects (as popularized by the Conversationslexicon) seems to be gaining in popularity—with some concession to special subjects (such as natural history) that particularly benefit from detailed and lengthy treatment—in spite of its artificiality. In fact, all alphabetical arrangement is artificial, just as the alphabetical roster of workers in a factory will separate men working at the same bench and people in the same department, so in an encyclopaedia alphabetical arrangement will, *e.g.*, separate COW from CALF, and SPINET from PIANO, at the same time that it places AARVAARIC next to AARON, and

TRIGONOMETRY close to TSETSE FLY. Clearly the answer is to provide a strong cross-reference system in any encyclopaedia arranged alphabetically, but this again is a comparatively modern adjunct whose full exploitation is not always appreciated by either editors or readers.

The distinction between a dictionary and an encyclopaedia is one that can easily be made by most people, even if the encyclopaedia happens to be a one-volume affair or the dictionary has spread to several volumes; even, moreover, if an encyclopaedia is called a 'dictionary', or a dictionary an 'encyclopaedia'. But there is an intermediate stage, now referred to as an encyclopaedic dictionary, whose history is longer than is perhaps generally appreciated. In a way, its first appearance may be termed accidental, for it was Furetière who, in 1684, completed his rival effort to the Académie Française's first edition of its dictionary. (Incidentally, Furetière's dictionary was arranged alphabetically, while the Académie's was arranged systematically.) But Furetière, in his attempt to show what a dictionary should include and how it should be arranged, produced a work that was midway between an encyclopaedia and a dictionary and thus provided the proto-type of a distinctive reference tool that has since had a long and distinguished history, proceeding through Noah Webster's immortal works to the latest example—*The Oxford Illustrated Dictionary*. While dictionaries have therefore been excluded from this little bibliographical account, the encyclopaedic dictionary has not, for it has contributed considerably to the life and progress of the true encyclopaedia.

Earlier, reference was made to selling people things they do not want. This may also include selling people expositions of opinions with which they disagree. In fact, it is almost certain that any thorough reader of any encyclopaedia would sooner or later dis-cover passages of this nature. Encyclopaedias have in truth long been convenient vehicles for unpopular or advanced opinions and ideas, and have long been the bugbear of censorship. While a monograph advocating seditious or irreligious or treasonable ideas might easily be seized before it left the press, the discovery of similar thoughts slipped in to various articles in an encyclopaedia might very well be delayed until copies had been distributed too numerously for their withdrawal ever to be achieved—a point of which Diderot took full advantage. Even when discovered, the offending encyclopaedia always appears to have enjoyed a privilege of comparative immunity that no individual author would have gained. Both church and police have at various times winked at the revolutionary style of some encyclopaedic articles, while individual court favourites and officials have given shelter to the rasher contributors.

Thus the encyclopaedia seems to have acquired a mystique of its own—in much the same way that the unsigned review in a modern literary journal has a power all of its own—which has given it an advantage it has not always deserved. For example, many encyclopaedias have, in their earlier issues, included old wives' tales and sheer nonsense among other articles full of sober fact—and these have been repeated in edition after edition, *and* copied by the more unscrupulous imitators and pirates! There is clearly a long-standing desire on the part of the user to invest the encyclopaedia with the qualities of comprehensiveness and accuracy, as witness the modern television quizzes that quote one or another encyclopaedia as their infallible authorities.

Bias—religious, political, etc.—has of course always been present in encyclopaedias. In the early monastic products there was a tendency to ignore or to play down classical scholarship. Later the laity took their revenge, and encyclopaedias tended to become excessively secular. More recently, nationalism has had its influence and effect; both Lenin and Mussolini wrote tendentious articles in the contemporary encyclopaedias produced in their respective countries, while Brockhaus eluded and Meyer fell victim to Nazi pressure. In subject-fields well known to them, experts are often heard to criticize the choice of one of their colleagues as a contributor to an encyclopaedia on the score of his or her opinions or prejudices, and it may be taken for granted that even under the most careful editorship there will always be the danger that some distortion of fact may appear here and there. But this will never be reason enough to condemn a whole encyclopaedia—no matter how much of a piece of hackwork it may be, it nevertheless probably includes some information that is elsewhere unobtainable, and so deserves its place on the shelves of the more comprehensive libraries.

In fact *any edition* of an encyclopaedia is worth preserving. Partly owing to their bulky nature, there has hitherto been a tendency to get rid of earlier editions of encyclopaedias as soon as a later issue is received. But the older edition is never entirely 'superseded'—rather, an older edition may well include more detail and better balanced information on some subjects, for encyclopaedias are very much slaves of fashion and, in order to insert an article on POP MUSIC, they will cheerfully chop off one of the paragraphs of an article on Alexander Pope. Given the room, there can be no better intellectual investment for a library or for a scholar than to store as many different encyclopaedias and their various editions as can be brought together. Consider the reason: since the middle of the eighteenth century there is hardly a man or woman of note throughout the western world who has not been asked to contribute to one or other of the hundreds of encyclopaedias an article on a subject on which he or she was an expert. Many of them have been people of action who never wrote books or articles in journals, many more have been the Einsteins and Churchills of their country and generation—but locked away somewhere in an encyclopaedia perhaps long since forgotten is some of their wisdom and mature understanding of the events of their times. Unfortunately, since the custom of signing encyclopaedia articles has never been universal, and since the contemporary records of publication of so many encyclopaedias have been destroyed, we shall never know the full extent of the literary wealth that has survived in them.

Revision of encyclopaedias is not of course always carried out by such drastic methods as that just mentioned, though it is a more frequent resort of desperate editors than one would care to tolerate. But the problem of the editor is a very hard one, for sales very largely depend on skilful revision, and this is as difficult as turning the dress of ten years ago into today's latest fashion, particularly since an expert may threaten to withdraw his text rather than submit it to abbreviation in any way. The various means that have been invented for bringing encyclopaedias up-to-date are remarkable and ingenious. The straightforward supplement was the earliest method adopted, and it has a history of at least three hundred years. But while a first supplement may be welcomed, a second is scarcely tolerated, and a third positively resented. Sooner or later the editor is faced with the necessity for thorough revision. A system which, theoretically, has great appeal, is the loose-leaf method, by which new pages (and sometimes new maps and illustrations as well) are substituted for out-of-date articles. There have been several carefully planned and admirable attempts to utilize this system in the service of speedy encyclopaedia revision. Unfortunately, not one of them has proved a publishing success, and the reason may well be that the general reading public has an aversion to extracting and inserting leaves in machine-like books, and that the method gives them a feeling of insecurity in that they are conscious of never having the final product. Certainly, loose-leaf encyclopaedias have suffered heavily from the intervention of wars and civil unrest, and there seems no special reason to believe that future efforts in this direction will be any more successful than were their predecessors. Nevertheless, at the time of the exposure of the Piltdown Man hoax, many an editor and many a proud owner of an encyclopaedia must have wished that it had been so constructed that a corrected entry could have been substituted for the original article on this subject!

Revision by means of the publication more or less regularly of new editions has prevailed among the more successful encyclo-paedias for at least the past two hundred years, and it is to the credit of Brockhaus, for example, that he was not only diligent in preparing new editions but also looked after the interests of his customers by enabling them to purchase only the supplementary material if they already possessed the previous edition. In fact, one might say that where an author confirms his literary position with his second book, an encyclopaedia declares its serious intent by the degree of thoroughness of its revision for the second and later editions. Even so, the man who regularly turns in his car for a new model every two or three years is hardly disposed to be so keen to exchange his encyclopaedia for a new edition even once in a lifetime, and this creates a financial problem that has defeated the publishers of several fine encyclopaedias in the past.

Of recent years, however, for the process of issuing new editions has in some cases been substituted the system of 'continuous revision'. The method of financing encyclopaedias has partly forced this change in policy on the part of the more highly organized encyclopaedias. With the innumerable developments in knowledge that take place nowadays, it is essential that the editorial staff of an encyclopaedia should be retained intact and should be employed permanently on the work of revising entries and securing new ones. But the sales of encyclopaedias are very uneven: they are highest in the first year of issue, and after that they decline quite as steeply as those of a new model of a motor car. Similarly, they almost cease on the announcement or even hint of the publication of a new edition being projected for the near future. To overcome this, some encyclopaedias have made a habit of publishing yearbooks that help to keep the basic encyclopaedia up-to-date and at the same time pay something towards the cost of keeping their editorial staff together. But 'continuous revision' goes further in this direction: in general terms, the system is to issue a new printing of the whole encyclopaedia at least once a year. Advantage is taken of each new printing to revise a proportion (perhaps as much as 10 per cent) of the articles. With such frequent issues, the likely purchaser is disinclined to hold back for the next issue, and so it is possible for the publisher to employ a permanent editorial staff and to organize his sales on a more equable footing. But there are drawbacks; the revision can prove unequal—there is naturally greater necessity to revise frequently articles on science, technology, politics, etc., where changes are bewilderingly numerous, than on the humanities where advances in scholarship are not nearly as familiar to the man-in-the-street. With the continuous revision system it is not easy to determine where revisions have been made without a page-by-page—and sometimes a line-by-line—scrutiny, but it is simple enough to discover those articles that are long overdue for re-writing. The feature that always betrays them very quickly is the appended bibliography where the absence of any new work published since (say) 1902 is circumstantial evidence that the original article by a great man of that period remains almost untouched! There are many distinct advantages relating to the method of continuous revision that renders it quite the best system for the editors and staffs of the modern encyclopaedia, but every scholar and research worker would be their more fervent admirer if they consented to add to each article the year in which it was last revised.

But however much continuous revision can help the sales force, the individual salesman still has a task that is formidable. The man who buys a car has no great difficulty in justifying his spending to his family—he has only to take them all out for a spin to have them all on his side. But even if both husband and wife see eye to eye on the purchase of an encyclopaedia on the score that it will help their children with their homework, they still have to sell the idea to the latter, and this is no easy task. I know of two children who, treated in this fashion, made a point of *never* consulting the encyclopaedia, so that when *their* children came to use it (as they did, eventually) some thirty years later, much of it was out of date but its physical condition was perfect! I know of another case where a well-paid technician, persuaded to buy an encyclopaedia on the strength of a cleverly planned specimen volume, found the complete work well beyond his comprehension or intellectual level, so that he gladly sold it a week later at a loss of £30. The fact is that, to sell encyclopaedias, one must be tough, thick-skinned, and convinced that the encyclopaedia in question will benefit people in spite of themselves. Nevertheless, the cost of the larger encyclopaedias puts them out of the range of many people who could profit from their possession, and there is a tendency to buy the cheaper and smaller sets that are nothing but uninspired hackwork turned out by the more general publishers, complete with various selling gimmicks. These catchpenny methods do no-one any good and cause the legitimate encyclopaedia-publishing industry great and lasting harm. Since the British Isles appear to be on the point of being invaded by some of the worst excesses of the American encyclopaedia market, it may not be amiss to offer to householders beset by eager salesmen, the classic response: 'Son, we got two 'cyclopaedias awreddy!'

But the hackwork production of encyclopaedias for a mass unin-
formed market is no new phenomenon: it is a sobering thought
that since 1800 new encyclopaedias (*not* counting new editions,
re-issues, etc.) have been appearing throughout the world at the
rate of more than one a year. It was at the beginning of the nineteenth century that publishers and booksellers began to appreciate
the very great profits that could be made from issuing encyclo-.
paedias, and they made their plans accordingly. A typical situation
is reflected in Olinthus Gregory's account of the origins and
fortunes of the *Pantologia* (see page 177), and an extreme example
may be seen in the issue of two rival encyclopaedias both edited by
the same man (see page 175). In fact, the alternative to Grub
Street methods, where the compiler was kept in poverty or drink
until he had completed his work, was to employ a scholar who
would probably write many of the more general articles himself.
The point is, of course, that the originators of encyclopaedias have,
since the introduction of printing in Europe, almost always been
business men of little or no scholarship, who have provided the
necessary finance and sales organization. It is understandable that
the editors could not in most cases have furnished either, and the
formula even nowadays for promoting a successful encyclopaedia
appears to be the establishment of a first-class team of editors
allied to a vigorous publishing house with world-wide contacts.
The absence of either of these partners—but most certainly the
second—seems to ensure eventual disaster for the encyclopaedia.

In this connection, it is interesting to note the changing fashion
in the size of encyclopaedias. Those we have today are comparatively small compared with many of the encyclopaedias produced
up to the end of the nineteenth century. Thus, the average substantial encyclopaedia nowadays comprises some sixteen to
twenty-four volumes—a small number compared with even some
of their own earlier editions, and even more insignificant in comparison with the occasional giants of one or two hundred volumes,
such as Ersch and Gruber's magnificent but uncompleted effort.
In fairness, however, it must be admitted that the introduction of
thin tough paper has enabled editors in many cases to reduce the
number of volumes without cutting the amount of text. On the

whole, however, the tendency has been to confine the modern encyclopaedia to some three or four feet of (quarto) shelf space. On the other hand there has been little demand for the size of the ordinary volume to be reduced from the familiar quarto volumes which have predominated over the centuries since the Middle Ages. There were quite a number of octavo, and a few duodecimo encyclopaedias issued in the nineteenth century, and there were a number of pocket-size editions in the eighteenth century. Although these were quite successful in their time, they have no imitators nowadays. The truth of the matter seems to be that, since an encyclopaedia represents a sizeable investment for most families, the purchasers want to see 'something for their money', and small volumes, handy though they are, fail to impress or to establish that intangible air of authority. From the editor's point of view, the larger format makes compilation easier, and gives greater scope for including both good illustrations and maps of a reasonable size.

The latter item raises an interesting topic. The inclusion of geographical information in encyclopaedias dates from the earliest period, but the current practice of including an atlas and a gazetteer is a fairly modern innovation which, if not strictly justifiable as a true ingredient of an encyclopaedia, is eminently acceptable. Just as some encyclopaedias include the function of a dictionary—even to providing the equivalents, in some cases, of words in foreign languages—so their insertion of an atlas and a gazetteer helps to make them 'all-purpose' tools that are especially suited to the restricted book space available in the modern home.

Just what are the full ingredients of a good encyclopaedia it is very difficult to say. Like the sausage, the quality of the encyclopaedia tends to vary greatly according to the contents and to the skill with which they are arranged and presented. Certainly, users expect the encyclopaedia to be strong in biographical information and this is fortunate for their compilers who, throughout the history of encyclopaedias, have shown themselves more adept in this department than in any other. On a wider basis the same situation exists; there is both a demand for considerable coverage in the humanities—particularly history, geography, religion and philosophy—and a tendency to supply information on this department of knowledge in good measure. Provision of information on the theoretical aspects of the sciences has also been a feature of encyclopaedias since very early times, but practical matters have been less fortunate. The successors to Theophilus and his *De diversis artibus* (see page 50) were thinly scattered throughout the centuries until the time of Furetière, and though he was defining technical terms at the end of the seventeenth century, and John Harris and Diderot gave much information on industrial machines and processes in the eighteenth century, most encyclopaedias ignored the trend until the early nineteenth century when at last it was generally accepted that articles on such subjects as candle-making and carriage-building, looms and forges, etc., were legitimate candidates for inclusion. The real fillip however was given by the Great Exhibition of 1851 that made industry respectable and incited curiosity in the way things are made among that very section of the population which was in a position to buy encyclopaedias. Today, the process has gone further still, and many encyclopaedias base part of their sales campaign on the large quantity of practical articles—on house-building, medical matters, legal advice, etc.—that have been included. With this has come a tendency to cut down on the humanities, and the long-winded articles on religion and philosophy and the principles of political economy that graced every encyclopaedia of the past, have given place to shorter—and often more readable if rather less scholarly—articles, with a more international viewpoint.

It is clear that the national encyclopaedia is already a thing of the past: the great days of the national encyclopaedia covered barely the 150 years from Diderot to the *Enciclopedia italiana*, and there is no place for it in the modern world. There was a brief period—approximately from 1850 to 1930—when a national encyclopaedia was a symbol of prestige, and to this we are indebted for a number of excellent items, but the dangers inherent in excessive nationalism showed themselves in the quality of much of their material.

The days in which articles on subjects so diverse as Nō plays, Mexican archaeology, citrus fruits, and Zen Buddhism, could all

be written by the nationals of one country, were already over when
the post-World War I supplement to the *Britannica* printed articles
on wartime operations by the chief military and political leaders
of the participating countries. Today, any good encyclopaedia will
try to obtain an article on any given subject from its chief exponent,
whether he be American or Japanese, South African or Polish.
Nevertheless, even with such a liberal policy, problems will continue to arise when, for example, the decision must be taken as to
who should write the article on the Suez affair—an Englishman,
a Frenchman, an American, or an Egyptian? And, it is very
difficult in the more abstruse subject-fields, where the number of
experts is extremely limited, to get a first-class brief article on a
specific topic—the experts are too busy, and are unwilling in any
case to allow themselves to be limited by questions of space or of
editorial policy, and the people who can spare the time are usually
not the best equipped for the job.

Thus the task of the editor of a modern encyclopaedia is a hard
one. He has a strict publication schedule to observe; he must keep
his eye on his rivals' efforts; and he must watch his own staff and
his outside contributors to ensure that wittingly or unwittingly
they do not plagiarize material already published elsewhere. (It is
a common practice in the editorial offices of encyclopaedias to
limit the access of staff to their own encyclopaedia—permission to
use other encyclopaedias must be sought from the editor.) And the
editor must co-operate with editors' offices in other countries (for
most great encyclopaedias are international nowadays), and with
the demands of the sales force who know that scholarship must be
tempered with popularity and a due regard for current interests
however ephemeral, if the sets of the encyclopaedia are not to lie
unused on the warehouse shelves. And the editor must keep up-to-
date with modern scholarship, with political trends and controversies (an encyclopaedia was once stopped at the docks of a
country that objected to a single map in one of its volumes), and
with the new topics and names that spring into fame overnight in
accordance with the journalists' feverish efforts to discover something new to whet the appetites of the readers of the evening
newspapers. Unprejudiced himself, the editor must be cognizant

of prejudices in others, and temper his contributors' opinions—
sometimes after considerable diplomatic effort—to safeguard his
readers' susceptibilities. And all this must be done, too, without
lowering his own standards, for an editor who has no standards is
lost. An encyclopaedia, if it is to be any good, must be based on
a philosophy that, roughly speaking, seeks to create a work that
will inform and stimulate, help and advance, promote discussion
and curiosity, explain and not baffle. It is a heavy responsibility
and one which, in spite of all the editorial boards and conferences,
an editor must ultimately bear on his own shoulders—and one
which today, at any rate, is increasingly borne in an admirable
fashion.

But editorial policy and editing do not imply censorship. Certainly Diderot deserved to be censored by Le Breton and his chief
proof-reader (see page 130), for Diderot was using his encyclopaedia as a means of conveying his own partisan views. On the
other hand, the suppressing of encyclopaedias that has occurred in
the past in Austria, in France, in Russia, in Germany, and elsewhere, was quite unjustifiable. A government represents, or should
represent its people, and the nation is able to exert its own informal censorship by not buying an encyclopaedia that does not
conform to its current outlook. After all, if the viewpoint of an
encyclopaedia is unpopular, it is either unpopular with the government and popular with the people (in which case the government
is unrepresentative, and the encyclopaedia is but one of many
ways of showing this), or it is popular with the government and
unpopular with the people—in which case, the people will not buy
it. Where it is likely to be unpopular with both government and
people, it is also unlikely to find any publisher.

Any burning of books is a sign of sickness in a nation, and any
attempt to influence the editorial policy of an encyclopaedia is but
another sign of the same disease. It is doubtful whether any
encyclopaedia of the future will be subject to quite the same pres-
sures as some of its predecessors, for international comment is
quick to perceive the slightest indication of censorship, and individual nations have shown themselves increasingly sensitive to
universal opinion. A more hidden danger is the total omission of

controversial subjects, or their treatment in an inadequate and superficial way; this can never happen where there is a good editor, and thus sudden and inadequately explained changes of senior editorial staff are worthy of scrutiny where there is any reason to suppose or to suspect that pressure still exists.

There are more mundane difficulties too that beset the modern editor, some of which are hard to overcome. Each encyclopaedia has its own policy with regard to consistency in spelling, in capitalization, in italicizing, in the form of bibliographical references, and so on. But statements of fact may vary. One contributor may name Truro as the capital town of Cornwall, another Bodmin. One contributor in one article may say that a piece of machinery was invented in such-and-such-a-year, another in a different article on some related subject—with equal justification—may quote a year or two earlier or later. These inconsistencies are very difficult to discover where some millions of words, supervised by a large staff of subject editors and specialists, are involved. The most careful collaboration between everyone concerned may still result in some ambiguities or contradictions slipping through into the text, and there is only the possibility that at the last moment they may be exposed by the indexers.

Encyclopaedias did not always have indexes, and the first good encyclopaedia indexes did not appear until the 1830's. The very function of indexing had hardly been understood many years previously, and yet it was an essential complement to the text of any good encyclopaedia. Although quite a number of encyclopaedias nowadays devote a whole volume to the index, one never hears a complaint from the users on this score, though any inadequacy of the index will quickly be resented. The reason is that for the great majority of its users, the encyclopaedia is a poor tool without its index. The compilation of indexes for encyclopaedias is a highly skilled task, for if it is to do its work properly, it must analyse every name, every topic, every idea, every illustration, map, and diagram, etc. (For example, Arthur Mee's *Children's encyclopaedia* owes much of its immense success to its excellent index.) The references, moreover, should always be to a fairly exact part of the page for it is difficult to find a single allusion among some hundreds of words on a closely printed page unless some system of page division is utilized. And with it must be included a strong system of cross-references. Encyclopaedias grapple with the problem of cross-references in various ways, and some of the best methods are employed by American children's encyclopaedias though, for sheer brevity and efficiency, Brockhaus's excellent signs are hard to beat. In the modern world of interdependence between the various branches of knowledge, no article can be self-sufficient: it must be qualified, elaborated, heightened and illuminated by what is contained in the articles on related topics. This is of course an argument in favour of the systematic rather than the alphabetic arrangement of subjects, but even this would not overcome the problem completely, and the need for cross-references would still exist to a large extent.

Nor is any encyclopaedia complete in itself. For one thing, it is in some measure out-of-date as soon as it is issued, for there is a time-lag between the moment it goes to press and the time it is in its users' hands. Moreover, the lengthiest encyclopaedia provides but an introduction to the various subjects of which it treats. Thus the need for good comprehensive bibliographies is clear. Nor should these bibliographies be confined to works in the language of the individual encyclopaedia: this would result in the best items being ignored in some cases. For example, the finest—perhaps the only—comprehensive book on the rearing of fish on a commercial basis in artificial lakes is in French, and probably the best works on several aspects of some minor oriental languages and cultures are in the same language. To omit these in favour of less worthy books in another and more easily read language is unjustifiable. A bibliography must be international in scope if it is to achieve its task of indicating to the reader the wider horizons beyond the limits of the article he has just read.

Continuity in encyclopaedias has been achieved in various ways. Some of the classical and mediaeval encyclopaedias survived hundreds of years without very much change—later editions sometimes suffered at the hands of inexpert revisers—but this indicated an undue reverence for the infallibility of ancient authority and a lack of critical approach and ignorance of the development of thought. From the time of Furetière's *Dictionnaire universel* and John Harris's *Lexicon technicum* onwards there was a greater tendency to preserve the larger encyclopaedias by subjecting them to fairly informed revision from time to time, but this was often done indifferently well and it was not until the *Britannica* and *Brockhaus* invented a more scholarly and business-like system of preparing new editions that we can say some degree of lasting continuity had been achieved. Nowadays, continuity has been firmly established in the case of nearly every major encyclopaedia, but the West can show no encyclopaedia to compare with some of the Chinese examples that have traversed a period of more than a thousand years. The Chinese contribution is truly remarkable; closely allied to the needs of the Chinese civil service system, the Chinese encyclopaedias carefully digested, revised, amplified and redigested knowledge (within, it is true, a very formal framework) throughout the past fifteen hundred years, and the history of encyclopaedia-making in the eighteenth century, for example, is quite as impressive in China as it is in Europe.

What is the future of encyclopaedias? The last word on the subject may well lie with H. G. Wells. In a series of speeches and essays written in 1936 and 1937—and subsequently collected in his *World brain* (Methuen, 1938), the seventy-year-old genius pointed out that there is a need for a new type of encyclopaedia to cope with the intellectual and practical needs of the twentieth century. He goes so far as to state that unless adequate steps are taken fairly soon to organize and codify human knowledge on some such lines as he indicates, the world faces disaster. Wells emphasizes that there is no necessity for encyclopaedias to be composed of 'special articles rather hastily written, in what has been the tradition of Encyclopaedias since the days of Diderot's heroic effort'. Instead, he suggests that that day is past and the World Encyclopaedia, as he terms it, of the future should comprise 'selections, extracts, quotations, very carefully assembled with the approval of outstanding authorities in each subject, carefully collated and edited and critically presented. It would not be a miscellany, but a concentration, a clarification and a synthesis.' He envisaged the combined efforts of the scholars and the learned institutions of the

c

world collaborating in the production and constant revision of a summary of human knowledge, the whole being strongly supported and amplified by carefully graded bibliographies suitably annotated.

Ten years later a professional journalist, Mr Reginald A. Smith, wrote an interesting little book *Towards a living encyclopaedia: a contribution to Mr Wells's new encyclopaedism* (Andrew Dakers, 1948), in which he enthusiastically supports and develops Wells's theme. Mr Smith felt that Wells did not go far enough in that the great general World Encyclopaedia he proposed was both overwhelming and at the same time insufficient for modern needs. He suggested that what was principally wanted was a very adequate series of graded and annotated bibliographies—lucid guides to what already existed in the way of published information, plus a series of specialized encyclopaedias, and a small general encyclopaedia. Supplementing these would be news digests and current, regularly revised, surveys of the progress of knowledge in broad subject-fields. The units of what Mr Smith renamed as the Living Encyclopaedia would be quite small—shorter than the average novel—so that the whole compilation would remain infinitely flexible, with the advantage that units could be assembled in a large variety of patterns to suit different individual needs. These units would all be linked by an elaborate cross-reference system, rendering unnecessary any repetition of information in any of the component sections.

These are powerful dreams and meanwhile the conventional encyclopaedia as we know it has gone on from strength to strength. Nevertheless, at least one experiment corresponding to these ideas in some measure exists in the University of Chicago Press's *International encyclopaedia of unified science* (see page 19), which has followed the pattern of small units (sold pre-war at one dollar each), forming parts of a projected series of volumes. Probably Wells was not consciously aware that his idea had been anticipated at the First International Congress for the Unity of Science, held at Paris in 1935, where Otto Neurath had read a paper on 'An international encyclopaedia on unified science' (*Actes du congrès international de philosophie scientifique*, Paris, Hermann, 1936, Part II).

Neurath had followed this up with an article on 'L'Encyclopédie comme "modèle" ' (*Revue de synthèse*, October, 1936), and then followed the Third International Congress for the Unity of Science, held at Paris in 1937, which was devoted to the project for compiling an *International encyclopaedia of science*. Action followed swiftly: the first unit-pamphlets were being published by 1938 and, in the first of these entitled 'Unified science as encyclopaedic integration', Otto Neurath described the motives that lay behind the creation of a new encyclopaedia and the policy to be followed by the editors and contributors. 'The *Encyclopaedia* is to be constructed like an onion. The heart of this onion is formed by twenty pamphlets which constitute two introductory volumes. These volumes, entitled *Foundations of the unity of science*, are complete in themselves but also serve as the introduction to what will follow. The first "layer" of the onion which will inclose this "heart", consisting of the first two volumes, is planned as a series of volumes which will deal with the problems of systematization in special sciences and in unified science' (*International encyclopaedia of unified science*, edited by Otto Neurath, Rudolf Carnap, Charles Morris, volume I, nos. 1–5, University of Chicago Press;Cambridge University Press, 1955, page 24). This encyclopaedia is still in course of publication, and is planned on a large scale: its specialized nature however prevents its inclusion in this work, though the principles on which it is based are clearly relevant to the concept of the general encyclopaedias of the future, and the parts so far published are an interesting example of the possibilities offered and the problems involved in this remarkable plan of what may perhaps be termed the three-dimensional encyclopaedia. Probably the complete Wellsian vision of the perfect encyclopaedia will never eventuate in the form he proposed, for it already exists in the more imperfect form of each of the great library collections in the different countries of the world. Here we have already the millions of unit-books on various subjects, carefully arranged by classification, indexed and cross-referenced in massive detail in vast catalogues, and serviced and exploited by a devoted band of librarians and bibliographers, and made available singly or in any choice of groups without fee to the public of their individual lands. Each day, a large number of authors and publishers put forth still more books and periodical articles that attempt to summarize, explain and develop existing ideas, and still more booksellers, librarians, and bibliographers work to make these publications available with the least hindrance to the readers who want them.

In all this system there is of course some waste, some duplication, some unnecessary writing and publishing. But its parallel is in nature's own proliferation, and no sensible being would restrict one or the other in the cause of economy. Too much is at stake— survival itself, whether it be of life or of knowledge. Both must survive, and extravagance in propagation is one way of ensuring this. The encyclopaedia of today is admittedly a very imperfect instrument, but it has its part to play in the recording of essential information and in the instruction of mankind.

This book has necessarily been restricted to the field of general encyclopaedias only. Complementing them is a far larger number of specialist encyclopaedias covering a great range of subjects, and the tendency is to produce still more such works on still more specialized topics. Their story is an interesting one, but remains to be investigated and told by historians better equipped to grapple with the chronicling of the development of knowledge in its innumerable branches.

Room has however been made in the Appendices for a reprint of the complete text of Samuel Taylor Coleridge's famous essay on Scientific Method from the first volume of the *Encyclopaedia metropolitana*. Little has been written on the philosophy of the planning and construction of encyclopaedias and the theories underlying their arrangement. Coleridge's ideas deserve to be rescued from the neglect which the comparative failure of the *Metropolitana* earnt them: he had much to say that is still very much to the point, and he gives a clear idea of the problems that beset the editor of any major encyclopaedia as he embarks on his formidable task.

Let them have that Encyclopaedian, all the learning in the world.

BURTON: Anatomy of Melancholy

Chapter *I* THE BEGINNINGS

Orbis ille doctrinae quam Graeci ἐνκύκλιον παιδείαν vocant.

QUINTILIAN: Institutio Oratoria

When encyclopaedias were first introduced, it is quite clear that the intention was to provide an all-round education within the bounds of a single work. Certainly the derivation of the Greek word which took so lengthy a period to come into fashion implies this, but by the time it had come into general use the function of the encyclopaedia had long implied that of a reference work intended for consultation rather than for continued reading. But at the beginning of its history the encyclopaedia was often planned to be read right through from the first page to the last and, in this way, it performed a very useful service for members of remote or enclosed communities, and for the vast majority of educated people who had no ready access to a library or, in fact, to more than a small number of books.

Nevertheless, confusion concerning the intention of the encyclopaedia was not long in making its appearance. Mr Geoffrey Grigson has called Pliny's *Historia naturalis* a gigantic 'Enquire Within', and indeed by the year A.D. 77 the first of the vast encyclopaedias suitable only for consultation had already come into being in the shape of Pliny's enormous and uncritical anthologies. And yet over fourteen hundred years later Gregor Reisch produced his little *Margarita philosophica* for 'Ingenuous Youth' to be read in its entirety, just as two hundred years previously Brunetto Latini's *Li livres dou trésor* had become one of Dante's favourite reading books.

If there were a father of encyclopaedias whose claim could be generally acknowledged, it would almost certainly be Plato, for it was he who set out to provide through his Academy at Athens (which survived under the same name for nine centuries at least) the full education that he believed every intelligent young man should possess. But he wrote no encyclopaedias of his own, or at least none has survived and there is no record of any having been made. The fragments of the first encyclopaedic combination are the work of his nephew, but the words are Plato's. Speusippos was the son of Plato's sister Potone, wife of Eurymedon. He was born at Athens after 408 B.C. A disciple of Plato's, he became his immediate successor at the Academy as Scholarch. To help in his teaching he compiled an encyclopaedic work of which only a few fragments of writings on natural history, mathematics, philosophy, etc., are now extant. These have been published in Paul Ludwig Friedrich Lang's dissertation *De Speusippi academici scriptis; accedunt fragmenta* (Bonn, C. Georg, 1911). Speusippos died about 338 B.C.

Again, though Aristotle (*c.* 384–*c.* 322 B.C.) was no encyclopaedist, there is no doubt that he had an encyclopaedic approach in his great series of didactic writings. These were really the record of his lectures in his own school, the Lyceum, which he had set up in Athens, and where the ideas he taught were at variance with those of Speusippos and his Academy. Aristotle's writings cover the following fields:

Philosophy, psychology, ethics, metaphysics
Politics, government, education
Most branches of science
Aesthetics
Poetics, rhetoric.

In addition, he commissioned his associates to compile works on mathematics, astronomy, medicine, and the history of science. His conception therefore of the scope of an all-round education was considerably more liberal and wider than that of most later encyclopaedists for nearly two thousand years. Nevertheless, his influence on encyclopaedia-making was felt somewhat earlier through the writings of William de Conches and Hugh of St Victor, and his own works provided inexhaustible quarries for many of the encyclopaedists throughout the Middle Ages.

If the Greeks were the fathers of the encyclopaedia, it must at the same time be admitted that this was an accidental and practical development from their early form of a mediaeval

university. Their contribution was a written record of the spoken
word. With the Romans the approach was entirely different.
The Latin world desired to epitomize the advance of knowledge
and to present it in the shape of letters or books that could be
read independently of any series of lectures or of any instructor.
Thus the first effort from the Italian peninsula came in a series
of letters, the *Praecepta ad filium*, written about 183 B.C. by the
great Roman consul Cato the Censor—Marcus Porcius Cato
(234–149 B.C.) to his son Marcus Porcius Licinianus. The work[1]
is now lost, but it is known to have included sections on agriculture, medicine, rhetoric, and possibly law and warfare as well.
The emphasis was on practical matters and on a high standard
of conduct, since Cato regarded with great suspicion the growing
influence of Greek thought that, to him, represented the unhealthy
example of a decadent world.

The contribution of the voluminous writer Marcus Terentius
Varro (116–27 B.C.) to the development of the encyclopaedia was
important. He had a very clear conception of the organization of
knowledge. In spite of the fact that only fragments of his work
have survived, it is possible to reconstruct to a certain extent his
approach to the problems of conveying a straightforward summary
of the existing state of knowledge in those troubled times. Thus
his *Disciplinarum libri IX*, like his later works, devoted each book
to a separate subject—in this case, the seven liberal arts:

(*a*) grammar   (*d*) geometry   (*f*) astronomy
(*b*) logic   (*e*) arithmetic   (*g*) music
(*c*) rhetoric

plus medicine and architecture. His *Rerum divinarum et humanarum
antiquitates* devoted the first 25 of its 41 books to human affairs,
and the remainder to those of the gods. Thus the arrangement
of the first part runs:

Books
I   Preface
II–VII   Man

---

[1] Which is also an early example of the type of literature that comes under the heading of 'Advice to a Prince' or, as in German, 'Fürstenspiegel'.

VIII–XIII   Geography: Rome, Italy, and the provinces
XIV–XIX   History, and Time
XX–XXV   Government and the State; Law.

An additional interesting point about this work is that the order of contents, in putting temporal affairs first, is in direct contra-distinction to that of the mediaeval encyclopaedias of the Christian Fathers which invariably started with things divine (the creation of the world; God and the angels; the Devil and his fiends; etc.), followed by mundane matters. Varro reflected therefore the con-temporary Roman attitude which was essentially a practical one of government and law and order, in which religion had a part to play but remained an organized section of the State. Biography was covered by Varro's *Imagines* which dealt mainly with out-standing Greeks and Romans, and was published with some seven hundred portraits. As Varro's work was one of the last to be published on papyrus, these portraits are unfortunately lost.

Varro's influence was immense for at least six centuries after his death: his works were copied, plagiarized and pillaged by later writers, and as time went on some authors appear to have been unaware that Varro was the original source of some of the material they were writing into their books.

The work of Aulus Cornelius Celsus, a Roman patrician of the first century, has continued to attract attention throughout the centuries, mainly owing to the survival of his detailed treatment of the subject of medicine. The *Artes*, written during the reign of the Emperor Tiberius (A.D. 14–37) comprised 26 books:

Agriculture	5 books
Medicine	8 books
Rhetoric	6 books
Philosophy and jurisprudence	6 books.
Warfare	1 book.

There is no evidence that Celsus was a physician, but he had a gift for the clear exposition of the ideas of the experts, and his work has remained a major source-book for the medical knowledge of his period, and it is clear that his work was intended to comprise a general encyclopaedia. The medical part of his writings has received most attention from modern editors, the chief editions being:

Charles Victor Daremberg. *A. Cornelii Celsi De medicina libri octo*. Leipzig, Teubner, 1859.

Friedrich Marx. *A Cornelii Celsi quae supersunt*. Leipzig and Berlin, Teubner, 1915 (Corpus medicorum latinorum, I).

Walter George Spenser. *Celsus: De medicina*. 3 volumes. London, Heinemann, 1935–38 (Loeb Classical Library).

to which Max Wellmann's *A. Cornelius Celsus: eine Quellenuntersuchung* (Berlin, Weidmann, 1913; Philologische Untersuchungen, Hft. 23) adds useful source material.

The *Historia naturalis* was written in A.D. 77 by Pliny the Elder (Gaius Plinius Secundus, A.D. 23–79). This vast work, comprising some 2,500 chapters in 37 books, could never have been designed for continuous reading. Pliny was no expert in any field of pure knowledge: rather was he a spare-time anthologist—he drew on the works of about five hundred authors from many countries— with a remarkable instinct for arranging things in an orderly fashion. Moreover, like many other early encyclopaedists, Pliny was an administrator accustomed to seeing the world in terms of divisions and sub-divisions. Thus his 37 books are arranged on the following plan:

Books

I	Preface; contents; sources
II	Cosmography; astronomy; meteorology
III–VI	Geography; ethnography; anthropology
VII–XI	Zoology; Man; inventions
XII–XIX	Botany
XX–XXXII	Medicine; pharmacology; magic
XXXIII–XXXVII	Metallurgy; mineralogy; the fine arts.

Pliny dedicated his encyclopaedia to the Emperor Titus, but the manuscript (in 160 volumes) was left to his nephew Pliny the Younger (Gaius Plinius Caecilius Secundus, A.D. 62–114). Pliny was inclined to be credulous and, as a result, many 'old wives' tales' became enshrined in his work and had as a result a direct influence on the works of his successors in encyclopaedia-making for at least the next fifteen hundred years, during which quite forty editions were published in addition to numerous epitomes, plagiarisms, etc. No self-respecting mediaeval library was without a copy. Major modern editions of the text include that of L. Jan and K. Mayhoff (6 volumes; Leipzig, Teubner, 1892–1933; Bibliotheca scriptorum graecorum et latinorum Teubneriana), and that of Detlef Detlefsen (6 volumes in 3; Berlin, Weidmann, 1866–82), while the text and translation, by William Henry Samuel Jones and L. F. Newman is included in the Loeb classical library (10 volumes; London, Heinemann).

Perhaps the prototype of the encyclopaedic dictionary—of which the prime example nowadays is the work of Noah Webster —was the *De verborum significatu* of Sextus Pompeius Festus, a second-century grammarian. Festus was in fact drawing the bulk of his dictionary from the larger work (now lost) of the first-century grammarian Marcus Verrius Flaccus (*fl.* 20 B.C.). Even of Festus's work only the sections comprising the letters M to V have survived, though Paulus Diaconus made a brief summary of the whole work in the eighth century. The Latin text of Festus has been edited by Wallace Martin Lindsay (Leipzig, Teubner, 1933; Bibliotheca scriptorum graecorum et latinorum Teubneriana), and in the fourth volume of the British Academy's *Glossaria latina* (5 volumes; London, 1926–31). A critical edition was also made by Karl Otfr. Müller (2nd edition, 1880).

It is known that the first Chinese encyclopaedia, the *Huang Ian*, was prepared by order of the Emperor about 220, but no part of this work, nor of several of its successors, has survived. The *Po wu chih* of Chang Hua (232–300) was revised about 1607 by Tung Ssŭ-chang under the title *Kuang po wu chih* and reprinted in 1761.

Little is known of Gaius Julius Solinus, the compiler of the third-century *Collectanea rerum memorabilium*. It is probable that he was a native of Rome or of its environs. Internal evidence seems to indicate that this encyclopaedic work was written about the middle of the century. Solinus gave his work a geographical basis into which he interpolated historical, natural historical, and other matters. He drew heavily—and without acknowledgement—on Pliny's *Historia naturalis* (about 90 per cent of his work comes from

Pliny), and on Pomponius Mela's geographical survey *De choro-graphia* (A.D. 37–41), as well as on other sources which can no longer be identified. His work was copied in the thirteenth century by Pierre in his *Mappemonde* (see page 63). In later years his work has frequently been referred to as the *Polyhistor*. Isidore of Seville copied freely from Solinus with confidence, and the *Polyhistor* was translated into several other languages notably English.[1] The standard modern edition of Solinus is Theodor Mommsen's *C. Iulii Solini Collectanea rerum memorabilium* (2nd edition; Berlin, Weidmann, 1895).

Quite the most fanciful form of all encyclopaedias of classical times was adopted by the Carthaginian Martianus Capella. Martianus, or Felix Capella (Martianus Minneus Felix Capella) was born in the second half of the fourth century. Between 410 and 429 he wrote an encyclopaedia in a strange mixture of prose and verse, sometimes known as the *Disciplinae* or the *Satiricon* or the *Satyra*, but which is more usually referred to as the *Liber de nuptiis Mercurii et Philologiae*—the title quoted by Fabius Fulgentius Planciades in 520.

The wedding of Philology to Mercury is an elaborate allegory in which the first two books are devoted to a description of the nuptials. The following seven books are devoted to the seven bridesmaids, *i.e.*, the seven liberal arts:

Books
I–II   The nuptials of Mercury and Philology
III   Grammar
IV   Dialectic: metaphysics and logic
V   Rhetoric
VI   Geography and geometry
VII   Arithmetic
VIII   Astronomy
IX   Music and Poetry

this arrangement thus foreshadowing (see page 44) the later concepts of the Trivium (Books III to V) and the Quadrivium (Books

[1] *The excellent and pleasant worke of Julius Solinus Polyhistor . . . translated out of Latin into English by Arthur Golding . . . London, I. Charlewoode, for Thomas Hacket, 1587 (reprinted: Gainesville, Florida; Scholars' Facsimiles and Reprints, 1955).*

VI to IX). In Books III to IX the allegory largely disappears and the treatment of the subjects is straightforward. The high-faluting style, the confident but comparatively ignorant and pedantic approach of the author, and his somewhat unselective (and often unacknowledged) borrowing from Pliny, Solinus, Varro, etc., did not prevent his work from having a lasting effect over a very long period.[1] In the sixteenth century, for example, there were at least eight published editions. A German translation was prepared by Notker Labeo (died 1028), an instructor at St Gall. The text has been edited in modern times by Adolphus Dick (Leipzig, Teubner, 1925; Bibliotheca graecorum et latinorum Teubneriana), and by Franciscus Eyssenhardt (Leipzig, Teubner, 1866).

Though Boethius (Anicius Manlius Torquatus Boethius, c. 480– c. 524) was not himself a compiler of encyclopaedias, he undoubtedly influenced the history of encyclopaedia-making both by his own philosophy and by his insisting on the fundamental importance of arithmetic, music, Euclid's geometry and astronomy as the basis of all learning. Thus Cassiodorus, who was possibly related to Boethius, was greatly influenced by him. So far the Romans had been busy interpreting and epitomizing the knowledge of the ancient world for the benefit of their own people. The rôle of Cassiodorus (Flavius Magnus Aurelius Cassiodorus Senator, c. 480–575) was quite different. A distinguished statesman, and secretary to Theodoric, he early realized the necessity for providing a new interpretation of Latin knowledge for the Goths, the new masters of Italy. As a bridge between the two worlds which were now living uneasily side by side in Italy and gradually coming to some compromise on their ideas and aims, Cassiodorus found his task by no means easy, and it was not till his voluntary retirement in 551 to the monastery of the Vivarium—which he had founded on the bay of Squillace in his native Bruttium—that he was able to compile his notable encyclopaedia. Cassiodorus dedicated his monastery to sacred and classical learning. A writer of distinction, his encyclopaedic work the *Institutiones divinarum et humanarum lectionum* became one of the outstanding works of his own

---

[1] Even on such diverse personalities as Copernicus, Leibniz, Boccaccio, Albericus, and Gregory of Tours!

times and 'one of the formative books of the Middle Ages' (Momigliano). The *Institutiones* are arranged in 36 chapters divided very unevenly into two books:

Book I. *Institutiones divinarum lectionum*

Chapters

I–XVI	The Holy Scriptures and commentaries
XVII–XXIV	Historians of Christianity, and the Fathers of the Church
XXV	Cosmography
XXVI	Cassiodorus's own critical system
XXVII	Figures of speech and the liberal arts
XXVIII	Readings for unlettered monks
XXIX	The Monasteries of the Vivarium and Castellum
XXX	The Scriptorium: spelling, bookbinding, lighting, timekeeping, etc.
XXXI	Medical works
XXXII	Admonition for the Abbot and the Community of monks
XXXIII	A concluding prayer.

Book II. *Institutiones humanarum lectionum*

Chapter

I	Grammar
II	Rhetoric
III	Dialectic
IV	Arithmetic
V	Music
VI	Geometry
VII	Astronomy.

This was not a book designed for the learned, but for 'the instruction of simple and unpolished brothers'. Cassiodorus was a clear- and far-sighted man, and had perhaps his eye on the more troublesome times ahead and on the necessity for providing for the certain preservation of the knowledge so far accumulated. As

Momigliano points out:[1] 'the task he set himself was to make pagan learning the servant of Christian knowledge. . . . Classical scholarship would contribute to monastic life. The cloister would replace the Court as a centre of culture.' And thus Cassiodorus emphasized in his encyclopaedia not only the priority of place of Christianity, by ranking it first in his book, but by degree of detail as well, for his second book, on the liberal arts, is but a brief account, drawn in the main from the works of Boethius, and only added since it would be useful for interpreting the Scriptures.

At a later date Cassiodorus added bibliographical notes in the margins of his manuscript, for part of his purpose was to introduce the monastic community to the extensive resources of the great library he had collected for them.

In spite of Cassiodorus's preference for the subject-matter of Book I, it was his second book that was more closely studied in the Middle Ages and which served as one of the principal sources for so many later encyclopaedias. In addition his *Variae*,[2] a collection of his official correspondence written in the time of Theodoric and Athalaric, served also as an informal contribution to encyclopaedic learning.

It is worth noting, also, that Cassiodorus's founding of his monastery of the Vivarium followed closely on the foundation in 529 by Benedict of Nursia (480–*c*. 542) of the famous monastery of Monte Cassino: the very year when, as Josef Pieper points out, 'the Christian Emperor Justinian closed the Platonic School of Athens, which had functioned there for nine hundred years' (*Scholasticism: personalities and problems of medieval philosophy*; translated by Richard and Clara Winston; London, Faber, 1961, pages 16–17). From the one came the most famous encyclopaedia of those days, while the latter was to shelter the first of the world's illustrated encyclopaedias. To these two bastions of early culture in an increasingly barbaric age we owe much of our present

---

[1] Arnaldo Momigliano. 'Cassiodorus and Italian culture of his time.' *Proceedings*, of the British Academy, volume XLI, 1956, pages 207–45. Also published separately in the same year.

[2] An important work on this collection is Joseph Jacobus van den Besselaar's *Cassiodorus Senator en zijn Variae*, Nijmegen-Utrecht, Dekker, 1945 (Academisch Proefschrift, 1945).

knowledge of the state of learning in their own and former times.

No edition of any part of the *Institutiones* was published until it was included in Johannes Sichardus's *Disciplinarum liberalium orbis, ex P. Consentio et Magno Aurelio Cassiodoro* (Basle, Bebelius, 1528). Jacobus Pamelius edited Book I (Antwerp, Christopher Plantin, 1566), and both books were first edited together by Gulielmus Fornerius (Paris, Sebastian Nivellius, 1579: reprinted 1589). Petrus Brosseus edited Book I as 'De divinis lectionibus in *Opera omnia quae extant* [*Cassiodori*] (Geneva, P. J. Choüet, 1650), and Johannes Garetius included both books in his *Cassiodori opera omnia* (2 volumes; Rouen, A. Dezallier, 1679).

Modern editions include that in J. P. Migne's *Patrologia cursus completus*, Latin series, volume LXX (1865); *Cassiodori Senatoris Institutiones*, edited from the manuscripts by Roger Aubrey Baskerville Mynors (Oxford, Clarendon Press, 1937); and, *An introduction to divine and human readings, by Cassiodorus Senator*, translated, with an introduction and notes, by Leslie Webber Jones, in the series Records of Civilization: sources and studies (no. XL; New York, Columbia University Press, 1946). Attention is also drawn to the following works which include important material on Cassiodorus's contribution to learning:

Joseph Jacobus van den Besselaar. *Cassiodorus Senator: leven en werken van een staatsman en monnik uit de jesde eeuw*. Haarlem-Antwerp, J. H. Gottmer, 1950.

Adolf Franz. *M. Aurelius Cassiodorus Senator: ein Beitrag zur Geschichte der theologischen Literatur*. Breslau, Aderholz, 1872.

R. Helm. 'Cassiodorus.' *Reallexikon für Antike und Christentum*. Volume II, 1954, pages 915–26.

Edward Rennard Rand. 'The new Cassiodorus.' *Speculum*, volume XIII, 1938, pages 433–47.

August Thorbecke. *Cassiodorus Senator*. Heidelberg, 1867.

A. van de Vyver. 'Cassiodore et son œuvre.' *Speculum*, volume VI, 1931, pages 244–92.

Without labouring unduly the influence of classification on encyclopaedia-making, it is well at this point to mention the close association of the ideas of the philosophers and those who arranged the contents of the encyclopaedic works. The basic theory of classification in early times stemmed from the *Categories* of Aristotle.

These were expounded by Porphyry of Tyre (*c.* 232–*c.* 301), a pupil of Plotinus, in his *Eisagoge* (*i.e.*, Introduction) to that work. Boethius translated the *Eisagoge* into Latin. Cassiodorus was, as has been mentioned, heavily influenced by Boethius. In turn, the whole of the later field of encyclopaedias for many centuries was influenced by Cassiodorus. Thus, from the time of Boethius onwards, no encyclopaedia-maker remained uninfluenced—though mainly unwittingly—by the classification theories of Aristotle as transmitted by Porphyry through Boethius and Cassiodorus. Bearing this in mind, the clear division of things divine from secular matters, which recurs so often in encyclopaedias of those times, becomes comprehensible when Porphyry's Tree is recalled:

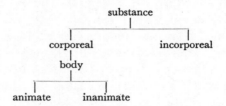

and it is easy to see how a man of Cassiodorus's background could devote one book to incorporeal matters and a second (and much smaller) to mundane themes. The inter-relation of philosophy, the classification of knowledge, and encyclopaedia-making is never far below the surface[1]—for example, Hugh of St Victor (see page 47) quite clearly divides linguistic logic as follows:

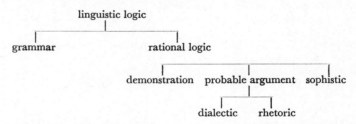

while St Augustine divided pagan knowledge (*De doctrina christiana*, II, XIX, 29*ff.*) as follows:

---

[1] Canon Joseph Mariétan. *Le problème de la classification des sciences d'Aristote à St-Thomas*, Paris, Alcan, 1901 (Thesis at Fribourg University).

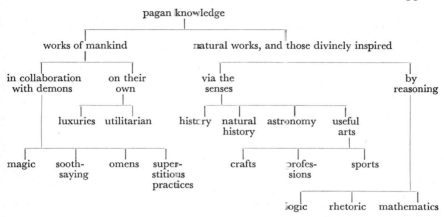

About the turn of the century, the Chinese encyclopaedia *Pien chu* was prepared: of this, part of the original compilation has survived. A little later (*c.* 620) the *I wên lei chü* of Ou-yang Hsün (557–641) was compiled in 100 chapters divided into 47 sections. Yü Shih-nan's encyclopaedia *Pei t'ang shu ch'o* was compiled about 630; it comprises 160 chapters in 19 sections, with emphasis on questions of public administration. An annotated edition, edited by K'ung Kuang-t'ao, was published in 1830.

Nevertheless, the first Christian encyclopaedia to be compiled for the benefit of the newly converted population of Spain failed to reflect the division between sacred and profane so categorically. St Isidore (*c.* 560–636), known also as Isidorus Hispalensis, became Archbishop of Seville in the Visigothic kingdom in 599 on the death of his brother Leander. Here he stayed until his death and, in spite of his heavy duties, worked on his encyclopaedia the *Originum seu Etymologiarum libri XX* for many years, the work being largely completed by the time he died. Some of the completed parts were circulated during his lifetime. The encyclopaedia was dedicated to his friend and disciple Bishop Braulio of Saragossa who edited and corrected the text. There is no single standard text, the arrangement of the twenty books varying, but one thing is clear—the starting point is never theology. Isidore always considered the liberal arts and secular learning as the true basis of a Christian's education. In fact, though its compiler was a leading

D

figure in contemporary Christianity, the source of much of the material in the encyclopaedia is pagan in origin. It was in truth 'an impersonal digest of universal knowledge, an encyclopaedic source book' (Jerome Taylor).

Isidore had been educated in the classical tradition, but his sources are invariably Latin instead of Greek. Although he did not consistently name his sources, it is known that he drew his geographical information from the works of Solinus and, more occasionally, from Varro, Orosius, St Jerome, St Augustine, Pliny, etc.; his authorities on other matters are Lactantius, Boethius, Lucretius, Caelius Aurelianus, Sallust, Vitruvius, Suetonius, etc.

Bearing in mind that no standard form is available, the contents of Isidore's encyclopaedia can be described as follows:

Books
I–III   The liberal arts
IV   Medicine
V   Jurisprudence; time; and a brief world chronicle
VI   The Bible
VII   The Heavenly hierarchy
VIII   The Church and heresies
IX   People; language; statecraft
X   An etymological dictionary (alphabetically arranged)
XI   Man
XII   Zoology
XIII   Heaven; the atmosphere; seas and oceans
XIV   Geography
XV   Cities and towns; building
XVI   Geology; weights and measures
XVII   Agriculture and horticulture
XVIII   Warfare; public games
XIX   Ships; houses; costume
XX   Food; tools; furniture.

The popularity of Isidore's encyclopaedia was great and lasting:[1] about one thousand manuscripts of the whole or part have sur-

[1] Carlos Cañal. *San Isidoro: exposición de sus obras e indicaciones a cerca de la influencía que han ejercida en la civilización española.* Seville, Imp. de la Andalucia moderna, 1897.

vived even to the present day. It appears almost certain that the better copies were illuminated and illustrated. As a source book its influence was immense and can be traced in works as different as Sir John Mandeville's travels and Gower's *Confessio amantis*.

A photographic reproduction of the Codex Toletanus (now the Codex Matritensis)—one of the best manuscripts—was edited by Rudolph Beer. F. Orevalo edited all of Isidore's works (7 volumes; Rome, 1797–1803), and this was reproduced in J. P. Migne's *Patrologia cursus completus*, Latin series, volumes LXXXI–LXXXIV. A more recent edition was edited by Wallace Martin Lindsay (2 volumes; Oxford, Clarendon Press, 1911; Scriptorum classicorum bibliotheca Oxoniensis). It is curious that Isidore, who had been born in Cartagena and had devoted his life's work to Spain, had to wait nearly thirteen hundred years for his first complete Spanish translation, based on Lindsay's text, by Luis Cortés y Góngora, as no. 67 of the series Biblioteca de autores cristianos (Madrid, La Editorial Católica, 1951), under the title *Etimologías: versión castellana total, por vez primera, e introducciones particulares*.

The Chinese encyclopaedia *Ch'u Hsüeh chi* ('Entry into learning') of *c.* 700 was the work of Hsü Chien (659–729); it comprised 30 chapters in 23 sections. A more important Chinese encyclopaedia is that of Tu Yu (735–812), a writer on government and economics, whose encyclopaedic work *T'ung tien* comprised nine sections:

Economics
Examinations and degrees
Government
Rites and ceremonies
Music
The Army
Law
Political geography
National defence.

This, which was completed about 801, is primarily concerned with administration—the subject Tu Yu knew best—and is classed with the *Wên hsien t'ung k'ao* (see page 65), and the historical encyclopaedia *T'ung chih* (see page 46), as one of the three T'ung, *San T'ung*, the latter forming the first part of a larger group of nine T'ung, the *Chiu t'ung*. The work was printed in 1747, and there have been several modern reprints. It was supplemented by the *Hsü t'ung tien*, which was compiled about 1767 in 150 chapters, and was itself continued by the *Huang ch'ao t'ung tien* or *Ch'ing ch'ao t'ung tien* (in 100 chapters) of *c.* 1786. This was followed by the *Po shih liu t'ieh shih lei chi* (in 30 chapters) of the poet Po Chü-i (772–846), which was supplemented by K'ung Ch'uan's *Po k'ung liu t'ieh* or *T'ang sung po k'ung liu t'ieh* (*c.* 1150).

CHIU T'UNG

N.B. The nine Chinese encyclopaedias listed here, covering the past twelve centuries were gathered together and published under the collective title *Chiu t'ung*. This diagram shows their collective names and their relation to each other.

Magnentius Hrabanus Maurus (also known as Hraban and as Rabanus) was born at Mainz about the year 776. He was educated at Fulda and then proceeded to Tours where he became one of Alcuin's favourite pupils, and from whom he earned the name Maurus. When Hrabanus returned to Fulda he soon became Abbot there and made his monastery the centre of Isidorian thought in Germany. In 847 he became Archbishop of Mainz. He died in 856.

His background and his interests made almost inevitable the compilation of his great encyclopaedic work *De universo*, which was in effect a plagiarism of Isidore's encyclopaedia. Hrabanus's work was in 22 books; every chapter begins with a suitable text from Isidore, followed by an allegorical or mystical explanation, for his approach was always strictly theological. Items (in particular, the liberal arts) which he felt were not relevant to the Scriptures he omitted. He described his themes as 'de rerum naturis et verborum proprietatibus, nec non etiam de mystica rerum significatione'. He dedicated his work to the king of Bavaria, Louis I.

Isidore had been careful in his arrangements of his subjects; Hrabanus, by omitting at least five of Isidore's books and mutilating the rest, produced an untidy mass whose chief claim to study is that he started his encyclopaedia with God and the angels— a pattern for a great many later works of the Middle Ages. The first printed edition was issued at Venice in 1473, followed by another (by Mentelin) at Strasbourg (about 1474), and by Colvener at Cologne in 1627. It was also included in J. P. Migne's *Patrologia cursus completus*, Latin series, no. CXI. At Monte Cassino there is a fully illustrated copy, made in 1022–23, at the wish of the Abbot Theobald. This magnificent copy, whose 265 leaves contain 361 illustrations, is described and illustrated in Fritz Saxl's 'Illustrated mediaeval encyclopaedias' (F. Saxl's *Lectures*; 2 volumes; London, The Warburg Institute, 1957: volume I, pages 228–54; volume II, plates 155–74); and in Adolph Goldschmidt's 'Frühmittelalterliche illustrierte Enzyklopädien' (*Vorträge der Bibliothek Warburg, 1923–24*; Leipzig, 1926, pages 218*ff.*). Readers will be interested in Saxl's theory that this manuscript is good circumstantial evidence that earlier encyclopaedias (particularly Isidore's) were also illustrated.

About 805 the Chinese scholar Su Mien compiled his encyclopaedia *Hui yao*; this, together with a supplement of 853, was revised by Wang P'u to form the *T'ang hui yao*. He completed this work in 100 chapters in 961. Wang P'u also completed in the same year the smaller (30 chapters) encyclopaedia *Wu tai hui yao*.

The first recorded Arabic encyclopaedia is the work of Ibn Qutaiba (Abū 'Abd Allāh Muḥammad ibn Muslim ibn Qutaiba), often called Ibn Ḳutaiba or al-Ḳutaibī or al-Ḳutabī, who was born at Kufa in 828. Both teacher and philologist, he was responsible for a number of important works, among which his encyclopaedic compilation is outstanding. The *Kitāb 'Uyūn al-Akhbār* is divided into ten books:

Book
I   Power
II   War
III   Nobility
IV   Character
V   Learning and eloquence
VI   Asceticism
VII   Friendship
VIII   Prayers
IX   Food
X   Women

the subjects being dealt with by the quotation of traditional aphorisms, historical examples, and old Arabic poems. Ibn Qutaiba wanted to make the knowledge of his times available to ordinary educated men, and particularly to the growing ranks of the administrative classes. The encyclopaedia was issued in a critical edition by Carl Brockelmann in 1903 (4th edition; Berlin, E. Felber).

There are also some supplementary works of Ibn Qutaiba's, which are apposite to the present history:

Kitāb al-Sharāb—of which a critical edition was prepared by A. Guy and printed in *al-Muktabas*, volume II, 1907, pages 234.*ff.*
Kitāb al-Ma'ārif (an historical handbook)—of which a critical edition by Ferdinand Wüstenfeld was issued in 1850 (Göttingen, Vandenhoeck and Ruprecht).
Kitāb al Shi'r (on poets and poetry)—of which a critical edition by Michiel Johannes de Goeje was issued in 1904 (Leiden, E. J. Brill).
Kitāb Ta'wīl al-Ru'ya—no longer extant.

The Byzantine Emperor Constantine VII (Constantine Porphyrogenitus) was born in 905. He was the son of Leo VI and succeeded his father at the age of seven. Until 945 his reign was purely nominal, so that it was natural that he should have become a scholar of considerable ability. Among his many writings was a series of encyclopaedias of special subjects, covering History, Jurisprudence, Agriculture, Medicine, Veterinary Surgery, and Zoology. They were unimportant in themselves, being nothing but anthologies (in Byzantine Greek) for the most part, though the work on jurisprudence was adopted as a basic textbook for law students. Some extracts from Constantine's works have been published, notably the *Excerpta Peiresciana*, the *Excerpta historica iussu Imperatoris Constantini Porphyrogeniti confecta* edited by U. Ph. Boissevain, C. de Boor, and I. Buttner-Wobst (4 volumes in 3; Berlin, Weidmann, 1903–10), and *Le Livre des cérémonies*, Tome I, livre I, chapters 1–46 (37), edited by Albert Vogt (2 volumes; Paris, Belles Lettres, 1935; Collection Byzantine). Constantine died in 959.

Not long after, another Chinese encyclopaedia was compiled. The author, Wu Shu (947–1002), dealt with celestial and terrestrial phenomena, mineralogy, botany and natural history. The original work was divided into fourteen sections, comprising one hundred articles. In 169c Hua Hsi-min supplemented Wu Shu's *Shi lei fu* by a work of twenty-seven sections containing 191 articles, under the title *Kuang shih lei fu*; Wang Fêng-chieh's *Hsü kuang shih lei fu* (1798), and Wu Shih-chan's *Kuang kuang shih lei fu* (1808), constituted two further supplements. Wu Shu also compiled the literary encyclopaedia *Shih lei fu* in 30 chapters, which was supplemented in 1846 by Huang Pao-chên's *Shi lei fu t'ung pien* or *Tsëng pu shih lei fu t'ung pien*, a revised edition of three earlier supplements.

For many years the oldest Muslim encyclopaedia was claimed—by people who did not recognize Ibn Qutaiba's earlier effort—to be that of the Persian scholar and statesman al-Khwarizmī (Abū 'Abdallāh Muḥammad ibn Aḥmad ibn Yūsuf al-Ḥwārizmi) who lived in the second half of the tenth century. His *Mafātīḥ al-'Ulum* ('Key to the Sciences') was compiled in the years 975–997. The author, who is sometimes referred to as al-Balḥī and who has been called 'The Scribe of Khwarazm', was clearly aware of the main lines of Greek thought, drawing on the works of such writers as Philo, Nicomachus and Euclid for some of his material. His encyclopaedia is divided into two groups:

1. *Indigenous, or Arab knowledge*

Chapters

I–XI	Jurisprudence
XII–XVIII	Scholastic philosophy
XIX–XXX	Grammar
XXXI–XXXVIII	Secretarial duties
XXXIX–XLIII	Prosody and poetic art
XLIV–LII	The history of Persia, Arabia, Islam, Greece and Rome.

2. *Foreign knowledge*

Chapters

I–III	Philosophy
IV–XII	Logic
XIII–XX	Medicine
XXI–XXV	Arithmetic
XXVI–XXIX	Geometry
XXX–XXXIII	Astronomy
XXXIV–XXXVI	Music
XXXVII–XXXVIII	Mechanics
XXXIX–XLI	Alchemy.

A critical edition of the *Mafātīḥ al-'Ulūm* edited by G. van Vloten, was issued in 1895 (Leiden, E. J. Brill).

Another Chinese encyclopaedia was compiled about the same time by the statesman Li Fang (925–996), or rather he played the principal part in the compilation of the *T'ai p'ing yü lan* under the orders of the second Sung emperor T'ai Tsung. The work was undertaken about 977 and was completed in 983. It is known that Wu Shu (see page 39) helped in this vast work. The original edition was divided into 55 sections comprising 1,000 books, and was a collection of extracts from some 1,690 works, of which a list is given at the beginning of the encyclopaedia. As scarcely one-fifth of these works are now extant, the list and the encyclopaedia are of special value. Contemporary with this, Li Fang and his collaborators compiled a rather more popularly written encyclopaedia, the *T'ai P'ing Kuang Chi*, comprising biographical and other information. These works were closely followed by the *Ts'ê fu yüan kuei* (*c.* 1013), a work of 1,000 chapters in 31 sections which is particularly strong in historical subjects. In 1568–72 the *T'ai p'ing yü lan* was revised and printed from movable type, and a new revised edition—by Yüan Yüan—in 1,000 chapters appeared in 1812. William Hung has provided it with an index, the *T'ai p'ing yü lan yin tê* (1935; Harvard-Yenching Institute Sinological Index Series, no. 23).

Collaboration in encyclopaedia-making first made its appearance as a result of the formation of the religious or political party which has become known as the Brothers or Brethren of Purity or the Sincere Brethren, or the Pure and Faithful. The Ikhwān al-Ṣafā' was founded at Basra in the tenth century and was particularly active from 980 to 999. The Brethren's aim was to harmonize authority with reason, and to construct a universal system of religious philosophy. Included in their endeavours was the purification of knowledge and, to this end, they published an encyclopaedic compilation usually referred to as the *Rasā'ulu Ikhwan al ṣafā*, comprising 52 pamphlets (the work of five authors):

Pamphlets

1–13   Arithmetic; geometry; astronomy; geography; music; arts and crafts; the human character; the Eisagoge, or introduction; the categories; the Hermeneutics, or principles of interpretation; and logic

14–30   Physics; the Universe; the four elements; meteorology; mineralogy; nature; botany; zoology; physiology; man —body, soul; philology

31–40   The senses; the origin of life; reason; the stars; love; resurrection; motion; cause and effect; definitions

41–52   Doctrine and religion; personal salvation; immortality of the soul; social life; faith; divine law and prophecy; spiritual life; spiritual beings; government; the order of the Universe; magic; divination and astrology.

The Brethren were well aware of the trend of Greek thought and philosophy concerning which they had pronounced aversions and likings. A complete edition of the *Rasā'ulu Ikhwan al ṣafā* was published in 1887–89 (4 volumes; Bombay, Nūr al-Dīn Jtwa Khān). Attention is also drawn to the edition of Friedrich Heindrich Dieterici: *Die Abhandlungen der Ichwán es Safâ in Auswahl* . . . (3 volumes; Leipzig, Hinrichs Verlag, 1883–86). An abridgement was made in Persia; and al-Majrīṭi made a Spanish recension.

Thus the first fourteen hundred years of encyclopaedia-making had seen the development of almost all the features we recognize in the modern version: the reliance on published authority (always a dangerous thing to do); the attempt to give overall coverage, and the intense preoccupation with classification; the introduction of the encyclopaedic dictionary and the use of alphabetic arrangement for this purpose; and, finally, the use of collaboration—a feature which rarely occurred again for the next seven hundred years. While the Arabs seem to have made a close study of classical and Byzantine thought and philosophy, there is practically no sign that the Western encyclopaedia-makers knew much of the resources of Arab thought and invention—a situation which prevails even today in the exchange of culture between East and West. And the development of the Chinese encyclopaedia was remote and mostly uninfluenced by either Arab or Christian. And so it has continued to the present day: the three great streams of encyclopaedias have developed independently and almost in complete ignorance of each other's methods and policies.

BIBLIOGRAPHY

C. Daremberg and E. Saglio. *Dictionnaire des antiquités grecques et romaines.* 5 volumes, and index. Paris, Hachette, 1873–1919

W. Engelmann. *Bibliotheca scriptorum classicorum* . . . *1700–1878.* 8th edition. 2 volumes. Leipzig, Engelmann, 1880–82

R. Klussmann. *Bibliotheca scriptorum classicorum et graecorum et latinorum* . . . *1878–1896.* 2 volumes in 4. Leipzig, Reisland, 1909–1913

S. Lambrino. *Bibliographie de l'antiquité classique, 1896–1914.* Volume I: *Auteurs et textes.* Paris, Belles Lettres, 1951

P. de Labriolle. *Histoire de la littérature latine chrétienne.* 3rd edition. 2 volumes. Paris, Belles Lettres, 1947

A. F. von Pauly and G. Wissowa. *Pauly's Realencyclopädie der classischen Altertumswissenschaft.* New edition. Stuttgart, Metzler, 1893 to date

Sir J. E. Sandys, editor. *A companion to Latin studies*. 3rd edition. Cambridge University Press, 1921 (reprinted, London & New York, Hafner Publishing Company, 1964)

Sir J. E. Sandys. *A history of classical scholarship: volume I—From the sixth century BC to the end of the Middle Ages*. Cambridge University Press, 1903 (reprinted, London & New York, Hafner Publishing Company, 1958)

L. Whibley, editor. *A companion to Greek studies*. 4th edition. Cambridge University Press, 1931 (reprinted, London & New York, Hafner Publishing Company, 1964)

Chapter *II* THE MIDDLE AGES

*The attempt to exhibit all Science in one body
the attempt to exhibit all Science to one mind,
which are the two forms of the attempt to
encyclopedize knowledge.*

Blackwood's Magazine, XVI, 32

The concepts of the *Trivium* and the *Quadrivium* as a basis of educa-tion in the Middle Ages had been foreshadowed by both Varro and Martianus Capella in their encyclopaedias. The *trivium* and the *quadrivium* between them represented the seven liberal arts which comprised the normal syllabus of the mediaeval student. For most students the *trivium*, or *scientiae sermocinales*, comprising grammar, logic, and rhetoric, was regarded as a sufficient train-ing, grammar being the most essential. In any case, grammar was considered the essential preliminary to all the liberal arts, since it was correctly judged that these could only be studied when the use of language had been mastered. For the more advanced students a course in the *quadrivium*, or *scientiae reales*, was con-sidered desirable; this comprised:

(1) geometry, (2) arithmetic, (3) astronomy, (4) music. But both the *trivium* and the *quadrivium* were regarded in the Middle Ages as subservient to the study of the Holy Scriptures and theo-logy, just as they themselves were considered superior to the study of the actual works of the classical and Byzantine authors— mainly through an intense fear of possible contamination from heathen ideas. Thus St Augustine strongly criticized Varro's arrangement of the contents of his encyclopaedia on the grounds that he placed secular matters before things divine. The arrange-ment, therefore, of so many mediaeval encyclopaedias was based on the idea of the liberal arts as defined in the *trivium* and the *quadrivium* which, in this way, artificially limited to some extent the effectiveness of these works both in respect of their arrangement and of their subject coverage. Thus it remained for

Hugh of St Victor to add ethics and theology, the crafts, and physics.

After Hrabanus Maurus there was an interval of more than two hundred and fifty years before any notable new encyclopaedia appeared in the West. Even when one was eventually issued, it is quite evident that the contribution that could have been made by Arabic scholarship was completely lacking: in this sphere, at any rate, there was no point of cultural contact between East and West.

In 1009 at-Tauḥīdī ('Alī b. M. b. A. at Tauḥīdī as Ṣūfī Abū Haijān) died. Shortly before his death he had completed an encyclopaedic work called the *Kitab al muqābasāt*: this comprised 103 sections of questions on various branches of knowledge.

Michael Constantino was probably born at Nicomedia in 1018. Later he adopted the name of Michael Psellus by which he is known today. He came of a wealthy family and, in the reign of Constantine Monomachus he was appointed in 1045 the first Professor of Philosophy at the newly founded University of Constantinople. A scholar, he achieved the position of Prime Minister in his 'fifties, and he pursued a classic career—for those times—of intrigue and ruthless conduct.

Psellus's encyclopaedic *De omnifaria doctrina Διδασκαλία παντο-δαπή* was dedicated to the Emperor Michael VII Ducas (or Parapinaces) (reigned 1071–73) who had once been his pupil. The *De omnifaria* comprised 193 questions and answers. Beginning with God and the nature of divinity—in which Psellus attempts to make some kind of compromise between Greek philosophy and Christianity—the work continues through most of the humanities and such scientific thought as was then available. Shortly after the Emperor's abdication in 1078, Psellus died. His encyclopaedia was printed in incomplete form by Johann Albert Fabricius (1668–1736) in his great series *Bibliotheca graeca* (volume 5; Hamburg, 1712), and reprinted in J. P. Migne's *Patrologia cursus completus*, Greek series, volume CXXII, pages 687–784, but was only included in outline in volume 10 of Gottlieb Christoph Harless's revised edition of that work. A critical edition of the text and an introduction by L. G. Westerink of the *De omnifaria doctrina* was published in 1948 (Nijmegen University thesis, 1948) at Utrecht by J. L. Beyers. After detailed study of the surviving manuscripts, Dr Westerink suggests the following arrangement for the text:

Chapters	
I–XX	Theology
XXI–LXV	Psychology
LXVI–LXXXI	Ethics
LXXXII–CVII	Physics
CVIII–CXIX	Physiology
CXX–CXXXVIII	Astronomy
CXXXIX–CLXXVIII	Meteorology and cosmography
CLXXIX–CCI	Miscellaneous

which, if correct, demonstrates a remarkably different idea of the encyclopaedia from that of the Western Christian Fathers.

Kao Ch'eng's encyclopaedia *Shih wu chi yüan* was compiled in 10 chapters of 55 sections about 1080, and was revised in 1806 under the title of *Shih wu chi yüan pu* (12 volumes). The Chinese encyclopaedia *T'ung chih* was compiled by the historian Chêng Ch'iao (1104–62). It comprised 200 chapters; the printed edition of 1747 was in 118 volumes. Chêng Ch'iao's approach was original throughout and he made a notable contribution to the subjects traditionally covered in encyclopaedias. It was supplemented by the *Hsü t'ung chih*, which was prepared about 1767 in 640 chapters of 48 sections, and by the *Huang ch'ao t'ung chih*, or *Ch'ing ch'ao t'ung chih*, in 126 chapters, of c. 1786. Yeh T'ing-kuei's literary encyclopaedia *Hai lu sui shih* was compiled in 22 chapters by 1149, and Jên Kuang's *Shu hsü chih nan* was prepared about the same time.

The dictionary which is known by the name of *Suidas* was completed some time in the tenth or eleventh centuries. It is an early example of the encyclopaedic dictionary and has been called the forerunner of the *Conversationslexicon*. But its main importance is that its arrangement was alphabetical—few books had previously adopted this system even for inset glossaries, and the arrangement did not have the immediate appeal for contemporary scholars that it has today.

Although the *Suidae lexicon* (standard edition, edited by Immanuel Bekker, Berlin, Reimer, 1854—now being superseded by

Ada Adler's edition, Leipzig. Teubner, 1928 to date) relied greatly on the works of Hesychius, it incorporated much new material and also quoted copiously from the works of the Greek writers.

The arrangement of the *Suidae lexicon* had no influence on the philosopher and theologian Hugh of St Victor (*c.* 1096–1141). Hugh was probably the nephew of Reinhard, the Bishop of Halberstadt. He was educated at the newly founded Augustinian house of St Pancras, at Hamersleben, and subsequently went to Paris. There he taught at the Abbey of St Victor, ending his life as master of the school there. His brief *Didascalicon: de studio legendi* was written in Paris in the late 1120's, and ever since that date its influence has been profound and widespread.

Hugh of St Victor's conception of the classification of knowledge may be demonstrated as follows:

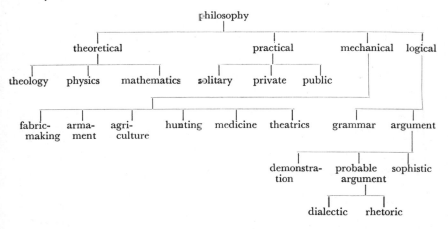

The *Didascalicon* comprises a preface, six books, and some authentic appendices:

Preface

The Origin of the arts

Book I

Philosophy, the pursuit of wisdom. The threefold power of the soul; man's unique possession of reason. Matters pertaining to philosophy. The rise of the theoretical, the practical, and the mechanical. Three 'manners' of things. The superlunary and sublunary world. How man resembles God. The three works—*i.e.*, of God, of nature, and of the craftsman. Nature. The origin of logic.

Book II

The distinguishing of the arts. Theology. Mathematics. The soul. The body. The quadrivium. Terms—arithmetic, music, geometry, and astronomy. Arithmetic. Music. Geometry. Astronomy. The definition of the quadrivium. Physics. The rôle of each art. Comparison of each art. Mechanical sciences. Fabrics. Armaments. Commerce. Agriculture. Hunting. Medicine. Theatrics (*i.e.*, entertainment). Logic. Grammar. Argument.

Book III

Study and discipline. Founders of the arts. The hierarchy of the arts in education. The arts and their appendages. The teaching of the arts. Qualities necessary to study. Exposition. Meditation. Memory. Discipline. Humility. The inquiring mind. Four remaining precepts—quiet, scrutiny, parsimony, and travel.

Book IV

The study of the Scriptures—the order and number of the Books; their authors; etc. Libraries. Translators. Apocryphal scriptures. The names of the Scriptures. The New Testament. The Canons of the Gospels. The Canons of the Ecumenical Councils. The principal synods. Librarians. Authentic writings. Apocryphal writings. Etymology of words relating to libraries and study.

The Scriptures and their study
Book V

The properties of the Scriptures. Threefold understanding. The implications of divine utterance. The seven rules. Hindrances to study. The fruit of sacred reading. The Scriptures as an aid to morality. Study, and action. The four steps to future perfection. Three types of student.

Book VI

Method of reading the Scriptures. Order of the disciplines. History. Allegory. Morality. The order of knowledge in books. The order of narration. The order of exposition. The construction and continuity of writing. The sense of scriptural writings. Divine deeper meaning. Expounding a text. A final prayer.

Appendices

A   The division of the contents of philosophy.
B   Magic, and its parts.
C   The three subsistences of things.

The *Didascalicon* was immediately popular and its influence has been lasting: nearly one hundred manuscripts prepared in the succeeding four centuries have survived today. Intended to counterbalance the growing influence of metropolitan and secular learning, Hugh's work renewed the argument for the preservation of the age-old system of monastic education and its recommendations were reinforced by the success of his own Abbey school and by his clear and cogent style. Heavily influenced by the works of St Augustine, Hugh drew also on those of Boethius, Plato, Macrobius, Remigius of Auxerre, John the Scot, and Cassiodorus, among many others.

The complete Latin text appears in *Hugonis de Sancto Victore Didascalicon de studio legendi: a critical text*, edited by Charles Henry Buttimer (Washington, D.C., Catholic University of America Press, 1939; Studies in Mediaeval and Renaissance Latin, X); and the first complete translation into English, with very full notes and critical apparatus, in Jerome Taylor's *The 'Didascalicon' of Hugh of St Victor: a mediaeval guide to the arts* (New York and London, Columbia University Press, 1961; Records of Civilization: Sources and Studies, no. LXIV).

Lambert,[1] a canon or prebendary of St Omer, compiled in 1120 a miscellany of the most interesting items that had come to his notice. The *Liber floridus*—sometimes called the *Floridum*—

[1] Not to be confused with his contemporary Lambert, Abbot of St Bertin (1095–1125).

E

comprised historical, theological, literary, astrological and scientific items, both in prose and verse. (From a map of the world as he knew it, Lambert appears to have thought of the earth as a sphere.) In spite of the fact that it deals with most of the subjects covered in the earlier encyclopaedias, it is hardly an attempt at an orderly conspectus and the subjects follow each other without any clear reason as to their progression. Though Lambert gives no sources for his extracts and paraphrases it is obvious that his principal influences were Isidore and Hrabanus Maurus.

Nevertheless, the *Liber floridus* occupies an important place in the history of encyclopaedia-making. It is a break with tradition. Perhaps influenced by the pseudo-Dionysian writings, Lambert discards practical matters in favour of metaphysical discussion, and a very marked interest in magic, astrology, and other such subjects. In addition Lambert gives much attention to history in general, and to local history in particular—such as that of his own diocese and family. Ten manuscripts of the *Liber floridus* have survived and are described (with extracts from the text) in Léopold Delisle's *Notice sur les manuscrits du 'Liber Floridus' de Lambert, chanoine de Saint-Omer* (Paris, Imprimerie nationale, 1906), which is a reprint from the *Notices et extraits des manuscrits de la Bibliothèque nationale et autres bibliothèques* (volume 38). Attention is also drawn to an important article 'The Liber floridus' by Eva Matthews Sanford in *The Catholic historical review* (volume 25, no. 4, 1941, pages 469 *ff.*).

Under the pseudonym of Theophilus, a man who was probably a German Benedictine monk and craftsman with the religious name of Roger, who may have been Roger of Helmarshausen—a Benedictine abbey, famous as an artistic centre in north-west Germany—wrote *De diversis artibus*, possibly some time during the early twelfth century. It was divided into three books:

Book
I   The materials and art of painting
II   Glass, and glass techniques and decoration
III Metal-working; bone-carving; the working of precious stones.

This work is unique for its times: no part has been proved to have been copied from any other and, for the most part, it avoids the old wives' tales that marred its contemporaries. Though this was not a general encyclopaedia, its significance in the history of encyclopaedia-making is great, for it is the first successful attempt to describe in detail the techniques of the various crafts—in contrast to Lambert who ignored them entirely—and foreshadows John Harris's and Diderot's similar ventures into the practical world six hundred years later. It is an original work by a writer who obviously had very considerable practical experience in metal-working. It is also a very personal document drawing freely on the writer's own reactions to his craft and, as such, has an engaging and simple tone which makes a direct appeal to the reader. His approach is very practical and orderly, always beginning with the tools and conditions necessary for successful operations, and proceeding in a logical way through the various processes. Incidentally, it includes the first direct references to European paper-making and to oil-painting. Gotthold Ephraim Lessing published the editio princeps in 1781 under the title *Theophili Presbyteri Diversarum artium schedula*—or, at least, it was published after his death in that year by Christian Leiste in his *Zur Geschichte und Litteratur aus den Schätzen der Herzoglichen Bibliothek zu Wolfenbüttel*, volume VI. Count Charles de l'Escalopier's *Théophile prêtre et moine: Essai sur divers arts* (Paris, 1843) followed but was eclipsed by Robert Hendrie's *An essay upon various arts in three books, by Theophilus, called also Rugerus, priest and monk, forming an encyclopaedia of Christian art of the eleventh century* (London, Murray, 1847) which described a newly discovered and more complete manuscript. Dr Charles Reginald Dodwell's *Theophilus: the various arts, translated from the Latin, with introduction and notes* (London, Nelson, 1961; Medieval Texts), at last establishes the Latin text on the direct authority of all manuscripts known at the present time. Another translation, *On divers arts*, has been made by John G. Hawthorne and Cyril Stanley Smith (University of Chicago Press, 1963).

The great achievement of the twelfth century was however the *Imago mundi* of Honorius Inclusus (*fl.* 1090). The description of Honorius as Honorius Augustodunensis, Honorius Solitarius,

Honorius of Autun or Honorius the Scholastic, and thus having some connection with Autun is very misleading: many modern scholars are convinced from the internal evidence of Honorius's writings that he was most likely to have been an English Benedictine monk, though others believe him to have been a priest and teacher in a monastery at or near Regensburg in southern Germany. (His work has even been attributed to St Anselm, 1033–1109.) The *Imago mundi* was undertaken at the request of Christian, later Abbot of St Jacob, whose desire for a 'mirror of the world' was faithfully carried out, though Honorius accurately predicted public criticism and private plagiarism in the centuries to follow. More than a hundred manuscripts survive. Honorius was the bridge between Hrabanus Maurus and Vincent of Beauvais. More original, realistic and far-sighted than the former, he drew on a wider range of authorities than any of his predecessors, and he did much to revive the encyclopaedic tradition which had almost lapsed since the Carolingian era. The immediate popularity of this, his best-known work, was enormous and copies were made for religious foundations all over Europe, while innumerable historians, scientists and geographers translated, incorporated or plagiarized the appropriate sections in their own works for many years to come.

Like his predecessors, Honorius relied on the works of the great scholars including St Augustine, Orosius, Isidore of Seville, Solinus (Polyhistor), Hyginus, Bede, and the mediaeval German chroniclers, from whom his own copying is usually accurate, and he did not neglect the writings of the classical authors such as Homer, Hippocrates, Plato, Virgil, Horace, Ovid, Lucan, Statius, and Josephus, even where their outlook was unequivocally pagan.

The *Imago mundi* was revised five times during Honorius's life, the first edition being completed about 1122, and the last some time after 1152. To this later writers and copyists continued to add for almost two hundred years. The work was divided into three books:

Book I. *Geography, astrology, and astronomy*

For the geographical section, Honorius, like Isidore, drew on Orosius and, to a less extent, on Solinus, St Augustine, and Bede.

The book begins with the creation of the world, and proceeds through an orderly description from the original divine conception to traditional accounts of the origin of countries and even of individual cities. Tradition and legend are faithfully recorded, and a specific reference to Regensburg accounts for one of the attributions named in the first paragraph above.

Book II. *Chronicle*

This includes chronological method.

Book III. *History*

A very short list of important events, beginning with the fall of Satan and proceeding through the traditional six ages of the world. Particular attention is paid to German cities and events in German ecclesiastical history.

In connection with the last Book, it is noteworthy that shortly after the issue of the first edition Honorius published his well-known *Summa totius de omnimoda historia*. Later issues of the third Book of *Imago mundi* to some extent complement the *Summa*.

The *Imago mundi* was translated into French, Italian, and Spanish, and considerable traces of its influence can be found in German chronicles from that time onwards, in the popular German *Lucidarius* (*c.* 1195), and even in the Saga of Olaf Trygvason. The text is printed in J. P. Migne's *Patrologia cursus completus*, Latin series, volume CLXXII. Attention is drawn to two important contributions on the subject of Honorius's life and works: Josef Endres's *Honorius Augustodunensis: Beitrag zur Geschichte des geistigen Lebens im 12. Jahrhundert* (Munich, Kempten, 1096), and Eva Matthews Sanford's 'Honorius, presbyter and scholasticus' (*Speculum*, volume XXIII, 1948: pages 397–425).

A popular Arab encyclopaedia by the Persian scholar al-Qazvīnī (Gamalāddīn Abu 'Abdallāh Muḥammad ibn Ahmad al Qazwīnī or al-Kazwīnī al-Shāfi'i) was published in 1135. This was called the *Mufīd al 'ulūm wemubīd al humūm*—'the giver of knowledge and the destroyer of cares'—and covered in 32 sections religion (*i.e.*, Islam), ethics, politics, the curiosities of nature,

geography, and history. It has sometimes been attributed to Abū
Bekr al Hwārāzmī (or Abu Bakr al-Khuwārazmi). This was later
translated into Persian by Adschaibol-Machlukat.

About this time the Scottish monk, Richard of St Victor (died
1173), Prior of the Abbey of St Victor in Paris, compiled his *Liber
excerptionum*. Richard had been a pupil of Hugh of St Victor, and
his book is an abridgement of part of his master's *Didascalicon* (see
page 47). Its principal importance is in the field of mystical theology and its history. It was printed in J. P. Migne's *Patrologia cursus
completus*, Latin series, volume CXCVI.

Ar Rāzī (Fahraddin Abū 'Abdallāh Muhammad ibn 'Omar ibn
al Hosain ibn al Hatīb ar Rāzī), known also as Fakhr al-Dīn al
Rāzī and as Fakhru'd-Dīn Rāzī, was born at Rai (the ancient
Rhages) near Teheran in 1149 and died in 1209. About 1178 he
compiled his *Gāmi' al 'ulūm*—'encyclopaedia of the sciences'. This
was followed shortly afterwards by al-Jauzī's *Kitab al mudhiš*. Al-
Jauzī—'Abd al-Rahmān ibn. Alī ibn al-Jauzī, or Gamāladdīn
Abū 'l farāg 'Abdarrahmān ibn abī 'l Hasan ibn 'Alī al Gauzī—
was born in Baghdad in 1116 and died in 1200. His encyclopaedia
was divided into five books, dealing with the Koran and Islam,
language, tradition, and history.

A foster-brother of Richard Cœur de Lion's compiled a notable
encyclopaedia. Alexander Neckam (1157–1217) was an Augustinian of St Albans. The first two books of his *De naturis rerum* comprised—owing to his didactic and critical but lively treatment—a
popular encyclopaedic work in the thirteenth century, and one
of the many sources of Albericus's *Liber ymaginum deorum*. The
contents, which drew freely and without acknowledgement on
Adelard of Bath and Isidore of Seville, were carefully planned:

Book I

Chapters

1–15   The Creation; angels, time, and the study of the planets
       (with which a direct concordance with human virtues
       is established)

16–22 Fire, and air

23–80 Birds.

Book II

Chapters

1–47   Water
48–98   The Earth; metals; plants
99–151   Animals
152–156   Man
157–172   Domestic animals; gardens; buildings
173–174   Learning
175–192   Society and sin.

The manuscripts of this work were collated by Thomas Wright and issued in a critical edition *Alexandri neckam de Naturis rerum libri duo, with the poem of the same author, De laudibus divinae sapientiae* in the 'Rolls Series', *i.e.*, Chronicles and Memorials of Great Britain and Ireland during the Middle Ages (no. 34; London, Longmans, Green, 1863).

Probably the first encyclopaedia compiled by a woman was produced by the Abbess Herrad towards the end of the twelfth century. Herrad was elected Abbess of Hohenburg in Alsace in 1167 where she remained until her death in 1195. During this period of her life she worked on the compilation of the finest illuminated manuscript encyclopaedia ever produced. The *Hortus deliciarum*, comprising some 650 pages, was illustrated with about nine thousand figures in 636 miniatures. Though not an original work—Herrad plundered the works of her predecessors—it is encyclopaedic by nature, describing in didactic fashion the history of the world (with emphasis on biblical stories) and its content, with commentaries designed to help and edify the nuns in her charge. Incidentally, all of the nuns are depicted and named in one of her illustrations. A small number of the illustrations were reproduced in Christian Moritz Engelhardt's *Herras von Landsberg, Aebtissen zu Hohenberg, und ihr Werk: 'Hortus Deliciarum'* (Stuttgart, 1818). During the nineteenth century many copies of some of the illustrations were made, and the whole (of those surviving) were listed—and many traced—by Comte Auguste de Bastard (Paris, Bibliothèque Nationale; Cabinet des Estampes, Ad. 144a). But at least 23 illustrations were never copied, and the representation of many others is of indifferent quality. During the preparation of a more adequate edition, the original manuscript was destroyed by fire in the siege of Strasbourg, and only a travesty of the superb quality of the illumination was reproduced in Alexandre Straub and Gustave Keller's edition of the *Hortus deliciarum* (Strasbourg, Schlesier & Schweikhardt, 1901), which had previously been issued in fascicles.in Strasbourg in the years 1879 and 1899 (Canon Straub died in 1891, and his work was completed by Canon Keller). A more recent and elaborate edition, Joseph Walter's *Herrade de Landsperg . . . 'Hortus deliciarum'* (Strasbourg and Paris, 1952), is selective. Otto Gillen's *Ikonographische Studien zum 'Hortus Deliciarum'* (Berlin, 1931; Kunstwissenschaftliche Studien, IX), is a noteworthy contribution to the subject.

Gervase of Tilbury (*c.* 1150–*c.* 1220), an Englishman who spent most of his life on the Continent, eventually became Marshal of the Kingdom of Arles under the Emperor Otto IV. It was for the Emperor that Gervase wrote his encyclopaedic work *Otia imperialia*, also known as the *Solatio imperatoris* or the *Liber de mirabilibus mundi* or the *Descriptio totius orbis*. This was completed about 1211: it is a miscellany of history, politics, etc., with a goodly mixture of legend from which Ralph de Coggeshall's *Chronicon anglicanum* (*c.* 1224) was taken in part. The *Otia*, which is very unreliable, is divided into three 'Decisiones' or parts:

I   The Creation of the world; fairies; the origin of music
II   Geography (particularly Rome); politics; history (especially Britain)
III Marvels.

Large portions of the *Otia imperialia* were printed in G. G. Leibnitz's *Scriptores rerum Brunsvicensium* (volumes I and II; Hannover, 1707–10). The third part was issued in an edited edition by Felix Liebrecht (Hannover, Rümpler, 1856). Ralph de Coggeshall's *Chronicon* has been issued in the 'Rolls Series' (no. 66, 1875) edited by Stevenson, and extracts from the *Otia* are included. Portions of the *Otia* were also included in André Duchesne's *Historiae francorum scriptores coaetanei* (5 volumes; Paris, S. and G. Cramois, 1636–49; volume III), and in J. J. Mader's *De imperio romano et gothorum, langobardorum, brittonum, francorum anglorumque regnis commentatio* (Helmstadt, 1673).

About the turn of the century T'ang Chung-yu's *Ti wang ching shih t'u p'u* (strong in matters concerning administration), the *Chin hsiu wan hua ku* (a general encyclopaedia), and P'an Tzŭ-mu's *Chi tsuan yüan hai* (revised by Wang Chia-pin, 1562), were issued.

The Spanish king, Alfonso X (1221–84), *El Sabio,* was not only learned but a poet as well. In a fashion reminiscent of the Emperor Constantine Porphyrogenitus three centuries earlier, Alfonso set himself to codify knowledge in a series of substantial compilations. His practice was to summon his collaborators who comprised three types: translators, compilers, and 'original' writers. He then supplied them with all the necessary books in four languages—Hebrew, Arabic, Latin, and Romance—and set them to work. Once the manuscripts were ready, he entered into committee (there are many miniatures extant of his sitting at a table with his collaborators), and the form of the book in hand was discussed and planned. In his *Grande e general estoria,* one of the King's hacks explains this system: 'el rey face un libro no porque el escriba con sus manos, mas porque compone las razones del e las enmienda e yegua e endereça e muestra la manera de como se deben facer e desi escribelas qui él manda, pero decimos por esta razon que él face el libro'. Alfonso's methods were truly modern: accounts given in one work were carefully compared with those in others, authority weighed, and decisions taken in the light of all the available written knowledge and the advice of his experts. In addition, the King paid careful attention to the language and style in which his books were written, and in particular made a notable contribution to the establishment of a scholarly tradition in the writing of Spanish history. It is unfortunate that much of his later life was occupied with political and fiscal troubles, ending in his defeat and desertion at Seville, abandoned by his own son Sancho.

Bartholomaeus Anglicus—often mistakenly referred to as Bartholomew de Glanville—was an English Franciscan scholar and lecturer who became a lector at Magdeburg in 1230. His *De proprietatibus rerum* (1220–40) was the most popular encyclopaedia in Europe for three centuries. Although his work was arranged in systematic order, it is interesting to note that within each book alphabetical order was introduced wherever possible—as in the case of lists of animals, places, etc. His plan was:

Books

I–II	God and the angels
III	The soul
IV–VII	The body and its anatomy, diseases, etc.
VIII–IX	Astrology, astronomy, time
X–XI	Matter, form, air
XII	Birds and insects
XIII	Water and fishes
XIV–XV	Geography
XVI	Geology
XVII	Trees and herbs
XVIII	Animals
XIX	Colours, scents, flavours, liquors
XX	Weights and measures, numbers, sounds

his principal and acknowledged sources being Isidore of Seville and Pliny.

Translations followed quickly: John of Trevisa (or John of Treves) translated it into English by 1398, and his translation was printed—with omissions—by Wynkyn de Worde (London, 1491), by Berthelet (London, 1535), and by Batman (London, 1582).

A copy of John of Trevisa's manuscript in the collection at Helmingham in Suffolk has been photographically reproduced by the Modern Language Association of America (no. 317; 1935). The king, Charles V, commanded Jehan Corbichon to make a French translation for him (Paris, A. Vérard, c. 1481), and Pierre Bersuire (see page 69) adapted it one hundred years later. Father Vicente de Burgos made a translation into Spanish (Toulouse, H. Meyer, 1494), and there was also a Dutch translation (Haarlem, J. Bellaert, 1485). Vivaldo Belcazer vulgarized it in Italy at the end of the thirteenth century. It was also one of the many sources of Richard Rolle's *The pricke of conscience* (*c.* 1348) and the second part of *The travels of Sir John Mandeville* (*c.* 1350).

Of the printed editions, the Latin text was first issued by Koelhoff at Cologne about 1470 (reprinted 1481), followed by Koberger's editions at Nüremberg in 1492 and 1519, and by numerous others until 1601.

Hsü T'ien-lin's encyclopaedia *T'ung han hui yao* was compiled in 40 chapters about 1226.

The Dominican friar Thomas of Cantimpré (or Thomas Cantimpratensis), who was certainly living during the years 1200 to 1270, compiled a similar work but one less able than that of his contemporary Bartholomaeus Anglicus. His *De natura rerum*, which was written in France about the years 1228 to 1244, had—like the *De proprietatibus rerum*—the object of preserving and explaining the Christian faith. It is interesting to compare the plans of the two works. Thomas, whose principal sources were Pliny, Adelard of Bath, Solinus, St Ambrose's *Hexaemeron*, and Jacques de Vitry, arranged his material thus:

Books	
I–III	Man; anatomy, soul, monsters
IV–IX	Animals: quadrupeds, birds, ocean monsters, fresh- and salt-water fish, snakes, worms
X–XII	Botany; trees, aromatic trees, aromatic herbs
XIII	Sources of water
XIV–XV	Metals and precious stones
XVI	The atmosphere
XVII–XVIII	The seven planets; the motion of the spheres
XIX	The four elements.

It is notable that neither work, even at this late period, treats of the subject of ethics. Though credulous and less comprehensive and scholarly in character than Bartholomaeus, Thomas's encyclopaedia was well received and much read. A Flemish translation was made by Jacob van Maerlant in the second half of the thirteenth century. It was also freely translated into German as the *Buch der Natur* about the middle of the next century by Konrad von Megenberg (died 1374) and was printed in translation at

Augsburg in 1475 and on six subsequent occasions in the same century. The original Latin text has never been printed, though some extracts are included in volume 3 of Cardinal Jean Baptiste Pitras' *Spicelegium solesmense* (4 volumes; Paris, F. Didot, 1852–58).

In the field of encyclopaedia-making, Vincent of Beauvais's *Speculum maius* was undoubtedly the outstanding achievement of the Middle Ages. Vincent was born about 1190, became a Dominican at Paris by 1220, was appointed a lector at the monastery of Royaumont by Louis IX about 1248, and died at Beauvais in 1264. The *Speculum*, a vast conspectus of the knowledge of the Middle Ages, was the last major work of its kind: after this, encyclopaedists began to compile for a wider public than the very limited world of religious communities, and it would also be true to say that the latter no longer retained the almost complete monopoly in scholarship which had been responsible for the theological framework within which each devout and monastic encyclopaedist had naturally felt obliged to work. It must be added that Vincent relied heavily on the research of his colleagues for many of his quotations from the outstanding works of the past (such as Adelard of Bath's *Questiones naturales*), plagiarized Isidore of Seville at times, and imitated Bartholomaeus Anglicus.

Vincent's great work must not be confused with his *Speculum vel imago mundi* which he had written some time before, though it is possible that he used the earlier work as a starting-point. The *Speculum maius* was first completed in 1244, and was continually subject to revision by Vincent until his death. It comprises four books, of which the last—the *Speculum morale*—was added early in the fourteenth century by another and unnamed author. The four books are:

I. *Speculum naturale*

Books	
I	God, divinity, angels, devils
II–VIII	The Creation: the first three days—used as a vehicle for physics, geography, geology, agriculture, alchemy
IX–XIV	Botany

XV–XXII	The Creation: fourth to sixth days— astronomy, weather, birds, fishes, animals (in the order in which they appeared on earth according to the Book of Genesis), and animal husbandry
XXIII–XXVIII	Man: soul and body
XXIX–XXXI	God and man
XXXII	A resumé of the *Speculum historiale*

II. *Speculum doctrinale*

Books	
I–III	Language (including a glossary), grammar, logic, rhetoric
IV–X	Ethics, family life and economics, politics, law
XI–XII	Crafts, architecture, war, sports, navigation, hunting, agriculture, applied medicine
XIII–XVII	Medicine, physics, mathematics, metaphysics, theology

III. *Speculum historiale*

Books	
I	Summary of the *Speculum naturale* and of the *Speculum doctrinale*
II–XXXI	A world history to 1244, based mainly on Pierre le Mangeor's *Historia scholastica* (c. 1160), covering Biblical, secular and cultural matters

IV. *Speculum morale*

Ethics, astrology, and theology (based principally on St Thomas Aquinas).

The *Speculum doctrinale* was originally planned to form part of the *Speculum naturale*, but the size of the work—and the demand for copies of specific sections—convinced Vincent that the formation of a separate division for the arts and sciences was advisable. In the same way, the inclusion of summaries of the individual Specula in each other enabled the requests for complete sets to be reduced somewhat—Vincent even published a separate epitome of the *Speculum historiale* which he called the *Memoriale*.

The *Speculum maius* served as the world's only major encyclopaedia for many years afterwards, and even today it remains of inestimable importance as the only repository of excerpts from some works which no longer survive, as a mirror to the state of knowledge during the thirteenth century, and—what is equally important—as a record of the cultural tastes and prejudices[1] of those times. It was responsible for the introduction of many quotations now in common use, and constituted the main source of such classics as the *Roman de la rose*, the Alexander romances, Colonna's *Liber de viris illustribus*, and of the lives of the saints as they are known, as well as one of the many sources of Boccaccio's *Genealogia deorum*, and *The travels of Sir John Mandeville*. In addition, it is invaluable for the history of Vincent's own lifetime.

Translations of parts of the *Speculum maius* were made into French, Spanish, German, Dutch and even Catalan, and innumerable epitomes, borrowings, plagiarisms and plunderings were its inevitable lot for the next two centuries at least.

Johann Mentelin of Strasbourg and his son-in-law Adolf Rusch (the 'R' printer), printed the first editions about the years 1472 to 1476. Mentelin printed the first, third and fourth *Specula*, while Rusch printed the first three, complete sets being made up from the combined products of the two printing-houses. The *Speculum historiale* was also printed at the monastery of Saints Ulrich and Afra at Augsburg in 1474; the *Speculum naturale* by the Printer of the Golden Legend at Strasbourg about 1481; and the *Speculum morale* by Winters at Cologne about 1477. The earliest editions are best: during the next 150 years the text became increasingly corrupt as the scholars of the day amended—not always for the best— the excerpts from Vincent's 550 sources in accordance with the contemporary editions of these works.

Even so, the earliest printed editions are all based on a fourteenth-century manuscript and there is need for a new critical

---

[1] It is notable that pagan and Christian legends are rarely mentioned by Vincent de Beauvais.

edition which is now being undertaken by Professor Berthold Louis Ulman on behalf of the Mediaeval Academy of America.

About 1246 a kind of encyclopaedic work in French octosyllabic verse, based on Vincent of Beauvais and Honorius Inclusus, entitled *Mappe monde* or *L'Ymage du monde*, deriving from Latin sources, was compiled by Gautier de Metz,[1] according to some authorities, and by Gossuin or Gossouin according to others. It was in three parts:

I   Cosmography
II   Geography
III   Astronomy, and astrology.

It proved very popular and edited versions in prose were published in Paris by Michel le Noir (*c.* 1495), in Geneva (edited by Francois Buffereau) by J. Vivian (1517), and again in Paris by Alain Lotrian (*c.* 1520) and—under the title *Le livre de clergie, nommé l'Ymage du monde*—by J. Treper. It was translated by William Caxton under the title of *The Mirrour of the world, or thymage of the same* and published (in black letter) by him (London, 1481), another revised edition being issued later under the title *The myrrour and descrypcyon of the worlde with many meruaylles and the vii scyences . . . with many other profytable and plesant comodytes* (London, L. Andrewe, 1527). Modern editions and critical works include:

L'*Image du Monde de Maitre Gossouin. Rédaction en prose. Texte du manuscrit de la Bibliothèque Nationale, fonds français no. 574. Avec corrections d'après d'autres manuscrits, notes et introductions par Oliver Herbert Prior.* Lausanne and Paris, Payot, 1913.
L'*Image du Monde, poème inédit du milieu du XIII* siècle, étudié . . . par Carl Fant.* Uppsala University, 1886. (Uppsala Universitets Årsskrift, 1886, Filos., språke. o. hist. 4.)
Caxton's Mirror of the World. Edited by Oliver Herbert Prior, London, Milford, 1912 (Early English Text Society, extra series no. CX).
The image of the world: essays in criticism. By Benjamin Harrison Lehman and others. Berkeley, California University Press, 1955 (University of California Publications, English Studies, no. 11).

But the first real breakaway from Latin as a medium for encyclopaedias was achieved by the master of Dante and Guido Cavalcanti. Brunetto Latini was born about 1220 near San

---

[1] In one of the incipits it is given as the 'Maistre Gauthier de Més en Loherains'.

Giusto. From 1254 onwards he practised as a notary, and was sent in 1260 by the Commune of Florence to seek a leader to oppose Manfred. In this he was unsuccessful and he took refuge in France during 1263. There is no foundation for the story that during this period he visited England to see Roger Bacon. During his exile, Brunetto compiled his *Li livres dou trésor*—not to be confused with his brief poem *Tesoretto* which was written in Italian—and in 1266 he returned to Italy with his own copy, the first edition having already been published. From 1282 until his death in 1295 Latini took a prominent part in the government of Florence. In that city he added his chapters on Frederic II and Manfred. But before the second edition had been given to the copyists, two passages of natural history (about four pages of the original manuscript) had disappeared—thus, none of the earliest manuscripts comprise *all* the known chapters. Fourteenth-century copies were completed by collating the various editions.

Latini wanted to reach the Italian cultured classes: he therefore used French, their common language, as his vehicle. His audience was secular, and thus his plan of arrangement was different:

Book I

Chapters	1–5	Plan
	6–18	Theology
	19–98	Universal history
	99–120	Physical sciences
	121–124	Geography
	125–129	Agriculture
	130–200	Natural history

Book II

Chapters	1–101 (first part)	Ethics
	101 (second part)—129	The virtues
	130–132	Sins

Book III

Chapters	1–72	Rhetoric
	73–105	Politics

Latini's approach was concise and accurate and had an immediate and wide appeal. This was the first vernacular encyclopaedia with a basis of Cicero rather than Aquinas, and a public of merchants and officials rather than scholars and theologians. It was translated into the French of France by Jehan de Corbichon under the title *Le trésor qui parle de toutes choses*, and into Italian by Bono Giamboni (*fl.* 1264). Three Italian editions were published between 1474 and 1533. The Modern Language Association of America have published photographic reproductions of three of the manuscripts in the Bibliothèque Nationale (1934–36) which demonstrate the variations in the different copies. The French text of the encyclopaedia has been printed twice in France: at Lyons in 1491, and in Paris in 1539. The first Italian edition was printed by G. de Flandre at Trevisa in 1474, and another printed by N. Garanta, was published at Venice in 1533. Based on the collation of some forty-two manuscripts, P. Chabaille (1796–1864) produced a standard edition—originally inspired by Napoleon I—of the French edition in the Collection des Documents inédits sur l'Histoire de France, 1re série, Histoire littéraire, page xxxiv (Paris, Imp. imperiale, 1863). The original text had been critically edited by Francis James Carmody as volume 22 of the Publications in Modern Philology (Berkeley, University of California Press, 1948).

The first issue in 1246 of the Chinese encyclopaedia variously known as the *Ku chin shih wên lei chü* or *Shih wên lei chü* or *Hsin pien ku chin shih wên lei chü*, Hsieh Wei-hsin's *Ku chin ho pi shih lei pei yao*, and the *Ku chin yüan liu chih lun* (or *Yuan liu chih lun* or *Hsin chien chueh k'o ku chin yüan liu chih lun*), all preceded the completion in 1273 of Ma Tuan-lin's main work, the *Wên hsien t'ung k'ao* known as the *T'ung k'ao* a vast encyclopaedia in 348 books, published in 1319. This was an extension of Tu Yu's *T'ung tien* (see page 35), Tu Yu's original nine divisions being expanded into nineteen and five new divisions being added (including bibliography, uranography and phenomena). It was reprinted in 1341–68, and published again in 100 volumes in 1524. A supplement, the *Hsü wên hsien t'ung k'ao*, comprising 254 books, was compiled by Wang Ch'i in 1586, and printed *c.* 1603; a revision of this supplement, the

F

Hsü wên hsien t'ung k'ao, ch'in Ting, was ordered by the Emperor Ch'ien Lung in 1747 and completed in 1772, and further supplements, the *Huang ch'ao wên hsien t'ung k'ao* (*c.* 1786), and the *Huang ch'ao hsü wên hsien t'ung k'ao* or *Ching ch'ao hsü wên hsien t'ung k'ao* (1905; revised and enlarged 1922). A further extension of the work in 266 volumes was compiled during the same reign. Another and very important Chinese encyclopaedia, the *Yü hai* ('Sea of Jade'), was compiled about 1267 by the educationalist Wang Ying-lin (1223–92). The work was published in 1351, and reprinted in 240 volumes in 1738. The original work comprised 200 books, divided into 21 sections, and containing about 250 articles and a number of appendices.

At the beginning of the fourteenth century the Egyptian historian and civil servant en-Noweiri—Shihāb al-Dīn Aḥmad ibn 'Abd al-Wahhāb al-Bakrī al-Kindī al-Shafi'i al-Ṅuwairi (1279–1332)—compiled one of the three best-known encyclopaedias of the Mameluke period (the others were those of al-'Umari and al-Kalkashandī—see pages 66–72). This was the *Nihāyat al-Arab fī funūn al-aadab*—'the aim of the intelligent in the arts of letters'—which took twenty years to write, and which runs to nearly nine thousand printed pages. Its plan is:

1. Geography: heaven and earth—astronomy, meteorology, chronology, geology, geography
2. Man: anatomy, folklore, conduct, politics
3. Zoology
4. Botany, including economic botany, herbs, etc.
5. History: with special emphasis on oriental and Islamic history

of which the fifth part comprised almost half the work. A complete edition was issued under the title *Dār al-Kutab al-Miṣrāya* (1923), in 18 volumes, edited by Aḥmad Zakī Pāshā (died 1934).

The anonymous *Lumen animae*, compiled about 1300, comprises two books of 75 titles and 267 chapters respectively. These chapters are arranged in rough alphabetical order. The materials collected in them are drawn chiefly from patristic sources or moral writers, and there are few items dealing with the natural sciences. The

75 titles of the first book include moral and didactic items, and some attention is paid to scientific information. Some thirty years were required for the compilation of this encyclopaedic work which was addressed to Pope John XXII. The *editio princeps* was issued by Matthias Farinator, a Carmelite of Vienna, under the title *Light of the soul, or Book of the moralities of great natural things* (Augsburg, Anton Sorg, 1477), and was reprinted in the same year. Further editions were issued by Michel Greyss (Reutlingen, 1479), and by the Printer of Legenda Aurea (Salzburg, 1482).

Written some years before 1320, the anonymous and comprehensive encyclopaedia *Compendium philosophiae: compilacio de libris naturalibus Aristotilis, et aliarum quorumdam philosophorum de rerum natura* has a special importance in the history of the period. The work has been attributed to the Dominican friar preacher Hugh of Strasbourg (Hugues Ripelin)[1] the author of the well-known treatise *Compendium theologiae*. The contents of the *Compendium philosophiae*, which are divided into eight books, are arranged in the following manner:

Prologue
Book

I	Theology
II	Heavenly bodies; mineralogy
III	Flora
IV	Fauna
V	Man—physiology; the soul; faculties; death
VI	Metaphysics; and physics
VII	Philosophy
VIII	Ethics (a commentary on the Nicomachaen Ethics).

Of these, it is thought that the last book was added by another author.

The manuscripts now extant (of which the earliest is the Bibliothèque Nationale MS. lat. 15,879) are all copies of a revised version of the *Compendium philosophiae*: no text is known of the

---

[1] Michel de Boüard. *Une nouvelle encyclopédie médiévale: le* Compendium philosophiae. Paris, E. de Boccard, 1936, pages 116–17.

original edition, and consequently hope of confirming its author-ship and date is possibly lost for ever. The work is principally based on the writings of Aristotle, which the unknown author probably read in Latin translations, some of which had been made from Arabic translations! He also drew freely on the works of Averroes, al-Fergani, Avicenna, Plato, Chalcidius, Anaxagoras, Pythagoras, Cicero, Ovid, Virgil, St Augustine, Boethius, and from the Bible. He also copied whole passages from Isidore of Seville (largely with-out acknowledgement of his source). It is clear that he was greatly influenced by Albertus Magnus, particularly in the classification of his material on fauna, which is superior to that of any encyclo-paedia up to this time, and he pays special attention to the char-acteristics of each of the species.

With the writing of the *Compendium philosophiae*, the concept of the modern scientific encyclopaedia is at last reached. The influ-ence of Aristotle and Greek thought had gradually been penetrat-ing the philosophy and ideas of the Western world throughout the thirteenth century—mainly by way of direct translation into Latin, or into Latin from Arabic translations. The author of the *Compendium* was however the first encyclopaedist to adopt the impartial and enquiring attitude of the Greek philosophers in making his compilation, and the old wives' tales that still filled the bestiaries of the period find no place in his work, while he made every effort to place before his readers the latest scientific discoveries.

This encyclopaedia has never been published, though Michel de Boüard (*op. cit.*) gives extensive extracts in his study. In addition to the manuscript in the Bibliothèque Nationale, there are others at Cambrai (no. 1,008), Troyes (no. 1,488), Poitiers (no. 152), the University of Pavia (nos. 239 and 108), Balliol (no. 246), the Vatican (Rossianus 175 and lat. 3,009), and at the Laurentian Library in Florence (Ashburnham 1,251).

Another anonymous volume, the *Multifarium*, was compiled at Bologna in 1326, and is largely indebted to Vincent of Beauvais's *Speculum maius*. It was divided into ten books, and deals with the planets, anatomy, diseases, birds, animals, herbs and plants, stones, the poets, philosophers' dicta, and history.

The Prior of the Benedictine Abbey of St Eloy in Paris, Pierre Bercheure—known also as Bersuire or Berchorius—was born in 1290 and was a friend of Petrarch. About 1340 he compiled an encyclopaedia based on Bartholomaeus Anglicus's *De proprietatibus rerum*. His work, the *Reductorium, repertorium et dictionarium morale utriusque testamenti*, was divided into three parts, comprising:

I *Reductorium morale super totam Bibliam, 428 moralitates*. A commentary on the Bible.

II *Reductorium morale de proprietatibus rerum*. Dealing with natural history.

III *Dictionarius*. An alphabetical glossary of more than three thousand words in the Bible, with moral expositions.

An interesting feature of this work is its inclusion of a series of moralizations on Ovid's *Metamorphoses*, based on Petrarch's *Africa*. This section has been translated into French as *Ovide moralisé* (Bruges, Colart Mansion, 1484). Bercheure died in 1362.

The first part of Bercheure's encyclopaedia was printed at Strasbourg in 1474, and was reprinted twelve times by 1526 (including Anton Koberger's three-volume editions at Nuremberg in 1489 and 1499, G. B. Rembolt's at Paris in 1521–22 and 1526). The complete work, incorrectly entitled *Petri Berchorii opera omnia*, was published in three volumes by J. Keerberg at Antwerp in 1609; and was again issued at Cologne in 1631 and 1730–31.

Guglielmo di Iacopo da Pastrengo or Gulielmus Pastregicus— frequently referred to as William da Pastrengo, a friend of Petrarch, was born at Verona about 1290 and died in 1362. He was a lawyer who became ambassador successively at the courts of Venice and Avignon. His encyclopaedic work *De originibus rerum libellus . . . in quo agitur de scripturis virorum illustrium, de fundatoribus urbium, de primis rerum nominibus, de inventoribus rerum, de primis dignitatibus, deque magnificis institutionibus* was compiled about 1350. It is of no great significance, its main feature being an alphabetical bibliography of past writers, chiefly classical, but its great attention to the biographical aspect of encyclopaedias indicates a new trend reflecting the changing taste of the times. It was edited by and printed for Michel Angelo (Venice, 1547).

At the beginning of the fifteenth century the Chinese encyclopaedia *Yung lo ta tien*, comprising 22,937 chapters, was prepared, but only part of this has survived.

The *Imago mundi* of Cardinal Pierre d'Ailly—or Petrus de Aliaco (1350–*c.* 1420)—was written in 1410 and is often mentioned mistakenly as an encyclopaedia. It is in fact an astronomical compendium of great importance which was used (and annotated) by Christopher Columbus during his voyages. A photostatic reproduction of the copy (*c.* 1474–96) in the Biblioteca Columbina, bearing Columbus's annotations, has been issued by the Massachusetts Historical Society (Boston, 1927), and there is also a critical edition by Edmond J. P. Buron in three volumes (Paris, Gembloux, 1930), with the original Latin text, and a French translation.

A friend of Petrarch's, the humanist Domenico Bandini (*c.* 1335–1418) was born at Arezzo, and spent his life teaching at Florence, Bologna, and in his native city. He came into close contact with the new humanism during his years in Florence, and was in touch with Coluccio Salutati, the leader of the movement. His gigantic encyclopaedia, the *Fons memorabilium universi*, filled most of his leisure time until he died. It was divided into five parts in honour of Christ's wounds:

Part I. *Theology*

Book
1 God
2 The angels
3 The soul
4 Hell, the Devil, and his demons (includes an added treatise on the art of magic)

Part II. *The Universe and Astronomy*

Book
1 The world
2 The heavens
3 The stars and constellations (alphabetically arranged)
4 The planets (alphabetically arranged)
5 The seasons, and chronology

Part III. *The Elements*

Book
1 The elements in general
2 Fire
3 Air
4 Weather
5 Birds; animal husbandry
6 Seas and oceans
7 Lakes, rivers, marshes, streams and fountains
8 Fish

Part IV. *The Earth and its Geography*

Book
1 Provinces and regions, including the theory of politics and government
2 Islands
3 Cities and towns, ancient and modern
4 Notable buildings, and miscellaneous items
5 People and customs
6 Mountains
7 Trees and vines; wine-making
8 Herbs, vegetables, etc.
9 Quadrupeds
10 A tractate on the eating of flesh, fish and fowl
11 Reptiles and worms
12 Gems and precious stones
13 Metals (and an added treatise—in some copies—on alchemy)

(N.B. Books 1 to 9 of the Part are alphabetically arranged.)

Part V. *Man and his Conduct*

Book
1 Famous and illustrious men
2 Philosophical sects—and a world chronicle to 1315
3 Theological and moral virtues and vices
4 Some medical remedies
5 Heresies and heretical sects
6 Famous women.

Bandini's encyclopaedia is remarkable for its numerous cross-references, particularly in the sections devoted to history and geography. It is possible that some of the work may have been written by his son and literary executor, Lorenzo Bandini. This huge encyclopaedia of secular learning was designed to provide educated men who lacked books with accurate information on any subject, and with edifying lessons to guide them in their lives. It was widely read in his own country until the middle of the fifteenth century, but then fell into neglect for about three hundred years.

The outstanding feature of the *Fons* is Book 1 of Part V, the *De viris claris virtute aut vitio*, which is especially strong in information on Latin authors. The majority of people mentioned are in fact classical figures and their lives are based on classical sources, but there is some original material and much of interest in the selection and treatment of the subjects. It has been suggested that the *De viris* was intended to be an epitome of the *Fons*. The *Fons* has never been published—apart from brief extracts—but many manu-scripts have survived.

Al-Kalkashandī—Ahmad ibn 'Abd Allāh al-Kalkashandī also called Ibn Abi Ghuddah, died in the same year as Bandini. He wrote a well-organized and comprehensive encyclopaedia entitled the *Ṣubḥ al-Ashʾā fi Ṣināʾat al-Inshā* which is especially valuable for Middle East history and geography. It was printed in fourteen volumes in Cairo (Khed. Lby. 1913–19). Otto Spies's translation of the chapters on India in *An Arab account of India in the 14th century* (Stuttgart, Kohlhammer, 1936) describes al-Kalkashandī's sources, and further information is available in Heinrich Ferdinand Wustenfeld's *Die Geographie und Verwaltung von Aegypten nach dem Arabischen des Abul-'Abbas Ahmed ben 'Ali el-Calcaschandi (Abhand-lungen der Königlichen Gesellschaft der Wissenschaften zu Göttingen*, Band XXV, Dieterich, 1879).

Alfonso de la Torre, known as 'the great philosopher', was born near Burgos. For the Prince Carlos of Viana, son of the King Don Juan of Navarre and Queen Blanca, he compiled his *Visión delect-able de la philosophía y artes liberales, metaphísica y philosophía moral* about 1435. It was published in Burgos in 1485 and again about 1487, in Zamora in 1480, in Tolosa in 1489, in Zaragoza in 1496, in Valladolid in 1497, and in Seville in 1526. It was translated into Catalan and published in Barcelona in 1484. The *Visión* was plagiarized—without detection—by the Italian Domenico Delfino (1490–1560) as the *Sommario di tutte le scientie*: edited by Nicolò Croce, it was published in 1556 (Vinegia, Gabriel Giolito da Ferrari), while a revision by Lodovico Dolce was issued by the same publisher in 1565. Further editions were issued in Venice (S. Sansovino, 1568; and M. Ginami, 1621). But the remarkable publishing history of this work was by no means over. A translator, in ignorance of the original, issued a Spanish translation of Delfino's work as the *Libro intitulado Visión deleytable y sumario de todas las sciencias. Traducido . . . por Francisco de Caceres* (Amsterdam, David de Crasto Tartaz, 1663). And thus, in the hands of soldiers and politicians returning to their native country from service in the Netherlands, Alfonso de la Torre's work at last returned home after nearly a quarter of a millenium of bibliographical adventure, but in a form which he himself might have had some difficulty in recognizing.

La Torre's work was not an original piece of scholarship: he was heavily influenced by Isidore for grammar, rhetoric, arithmetic and music; by al-Ghazzāli (1058–1111) for logic, and by Martianus Capella for the very form of his book which adopts a rather heavy-handed allegorical approach. In his vision, La Torre sees the world in a chaotic state menaced by ignorance and wrong thinking. He is approached by the maiden Grammar, who is accompanied by her foster-child Understanding. On the first day she teaches the child the elements of grammar. On the second day La Torre and the maiden visit her sisters Logic, Rhetoric, Arithmetic, Geometry, Music, and Astrology, and are instructed in the secrets of their arts. With Astrology live Truth, Reason, Nature, and Prudence. Stripping himself of the 'sordid, shapeless and worn-out garments of vain opinions' La Torre approaches Truth who leads him to the palace of Prudence. There he is taught the contemporary attitude to the more difficult scientific problems, and proceeds to the palace of Reason, which is protected by the Cardinal Virtues. Here he is trained to deal with abstruse problems of scholastic philosophy and theology, and is catechized by Prudence, Justice, Strength, and Moderation (the Cardinal Virtues) on politics and the responsibilities of a ruler. The purpose of the book has been to give a brief account of the seven liberal arts, and philosophy and theology; and the last six chapters comprise a discussion of the *trivium* and the *quadrivium*. It is interesting that the Capella form of allegory could prove so popular in La Torre's time, and that a brand of thought which had recognized nothing more modern than Isidore should wield so much influence over the next two hundred years and more. A very good account of La Torre's treatment of his subjects is given in J. P. Wickersham Crawford's 'The seven liberal arts in the *Visión Delectable* of Alfonso de la Torre' (*Romanic review*, volume IV, 1913, pages 58–75).

A kind of encyclopaedia, comprising questions and answers on a very wide range of subjects, was compiled in the fifteenth century by the Persian lawyer and scholar Galāladdīn Muhammad ibn As'ad ad Dauwānī (1427–1501) under the title *Unmūdag al 'ulūm*. It included a list of sources. Shortly after its appearance a refutation was published, entitled *Maqālatar radd 'alā unmūdag al 'ulūm al Galālíja*, written by Gijāṭaddīn ibn Man ṣur ibn Muhammad al Ḥusainī as Sīrazī (died 1542).

The fifteenth-century German scholar Wenceslaus Brack compiled a brief encyclopaedic work, the *Vocabularius rerum*, of which about a third is devoted to Hugh of St Victor's *Didascalicon* (see page 47). A number of editions were printed in the last quarter of the century, notably by Peter Kollicker (Basle, 1483), and by Anton Sorg (Augsburg, 1487).

Gregor Reisch (died 1525), prior of the Carthusian monastery of Freiburg near the Black Forest, and confessor to the Emperor Maximilian, addressed his little *Margarita philosophica* to 'Ingenuous Youth (for it is to you in the first place that this Pearl is dedicated)'. In little more than two hundred pages he contrived to cover in a very pleasing style the whole university course of the day—both the Trivium and the Quadrivium:

Books
1–3   Grammar, dialectic, rhetoric
4–7   Arithmetic, music, geometry, astronomy

8–9   The principles and origin of natural things
10–11 The soul, psychology, logic
12   Ethics.

The work was an instant success on its first publication in Heidelberg in 1496, and was followed by a second edition issued under the title of *Aepitomae omnis philosophiae, alius Margarita philosophica* by Johann Scott at Strasbourg in 1504—preceded by an unauthorized reprint of the first edition by J. Grüninger in Strasbourg in the same year (reprinted 1515). The third edition was issued by Michael Furter and Johann Scott at Basle in 1508, and further editions were issued in that city in 1535 and 1583. An Italian translation, by Giovanni Paolo Gallucci, was published in 1600 (Venice, I. A. Somascho).

The Flemish grammarian, Hermann Torrentius—known also as Hermannus Torrentinus, and as Herman van der Boeke—was born at Zwolle and taught both there and at Groningen. He edited the *Eclogues* and the *Georgics* (1502), and revised and corrected the mediaeval grammar of Alexander de Villa Dei. His *Elucidarium carminum et historiarum, vel Vocabularius poeticus; continens fabulas, historias, provincias, urbes, insulas, fluvios et montes illustres . . .* was encyclopaedic in character and included place names, fables, and mythology, as well as classical allusions. It was published by Ricardus Pafraet in Delft in 1498, and also at Strasbourg about 1510. Torrentius died in 1520.

Although the Italian scholar Giorgio Valla (*c.* 1430–1500)—known as Placentinus from his birthplace, Piancenza—wrote his encyclopaedia in Latin, his plan confirms the revolution in outlook begun so many years before by Brunetto Latini. His work, *De expetendis, et fugiendis rebus opus*, was arranged thus:

Volume I

Books
  1–3   Arithmetic
  4–8   Music
  9–14   Geometry
  15–18 Astrology
  19–22 Physiology

Volume II

Books

1–7	Medicine
8	Problems
9–12	Grammar
13–15	Dialectic
16	Poetics
17–18	Rhetoric
19	Moral philosophy
20–22	Domestic economy
23	Politics
24–26	The body and the soul
27	Outward things (glory, grandeur, etc.).

The encyclopaedia, edited by his son Giovanni Valla, was published posthumously under the title *Georgii Vallae Placentini viri class. De expetendis, et fugiendis rebus opus* . . . (2 volumes; Venice, 1501).

The *Summa de exemplis et similitudinibus rerum* of the Italian scholar Giovanni Goro da San Gimignano—also known as Joannes de Sancto Geminiano—was published in Venice by Joannes Gregorius de Gregoriis de Forlivio in 1499. It is much shorter than but very similar in approach to Pierre Bercheure's *Reductorium* (see page 69), the first part of which, it will be remembered, had been enjoying great success in printed form during the past quarter of a century.

Domenico Nani Mirabelli—also known as Dominicus Nanni-Mirbelli, and as Dominicus Nannus Mirabellius—was active at the beginning of the sixteenth century. His *Polyanthea nova: hic est, opus suavissimis floribus celebriorum sententiarum exornatum* was first published at Savona by F. de Silva in 1503. It was popular, being reprinted as late as 1572 in Venice, and earning a new lease of life in Joseph Lang's *Polyanthea nova* (Frankfurt, 1607), and its later editions (see page 84). In some ways it may be said to have been the prototype of the Conversationslexikon: it is arranged alphabetically by subjects, and it is furnished with etymological derivations, complete with numerous illustrative quotations. From 1517 onwards, separate sequences of quotations from Dante and

Petrarch were added. Attention must also be drawn to the *Florilegium* or *Compendium moralium notabilium* of Geremia da Montagnone (*c.* 1255–*c.* 1321), lawyer and man of letters, which was published in Venice by Aldus in 1505, and which is sometimes referred to as an encyclopaedia, though it is really an anthology of the more memorable sayings of famous people of the past.

Raffaele Maffei (1451–1522) was born at Volterra, and is sometimes referred to as Raffaele Volaterranus. His encyclopaedic work *Commentariorum urbanorum libri XXXVIII*, first published in Rome by Johann Besick in 1506, made another step towards the complete secularization of encyclopaedias by giving much more attention to geography and biography. The thirty-eight books are divided as follows:

Volume I	Chapters I–XII	Geography	
II	XIII–XXIV	Anthropology	(*i.e.,*
		Biography)	
III	XXV–XXXVIII	Philology	

The encyclopaedia was a success and was frequently revised and reprinted for more than a hundred years.

The Arab scholar Muḥammad as-Ṣarīf ibn as-Saijid al Muwaqqi' Jā'u al Qādirī al Ḥasanī al Ḥanafī wrote an encyclopaedic survey and description of the various branches of knowledge in 1524, under the title of *Magma' multaqat az zuhūr birauḍa min al manzūm wal mantur*. An appendix comprised an alphabetical list of the names of God.

The author of the important *De veritate fidei Christianae* (Basle, J. Oporinus, 1544), the great Spanish humanist Juan Luis Vives (1492–1540), studied at Paris and Louvain, and was a friend and disciple of Erasmus. A pedagogue, he is chiefly remembered for his works on St Augustine, and on the education of women. During his residence in England (1522–25) under the aegis of Cardinal Wolsey, he lectured at Oxford where he was made a Doctor of Laws, and he also acted as tutor to the Princess Mary. In disgrace, owing to his protest against the king's divorce from Catherine of Aragon, he retreated to Bruges in the Spanish Netherlands, where he wrote his encyclopaedic work *De disciplinis* (1531), comprising the three treatises *De causis corruptarum artium, De tradendis disciplinis,* and *De artibus,* for the use of his pupil, the future Archbishop of Toledo.

In writing this group of works, he set out to convey his thoughts plainly, clearly, and adequately, but in a polished and attractive style. He emphasizes the importance of both Latin and Greek to the student, and asserts that they are still the best vehicles for contemporary books of standing. Though cleansing his classical studies of paganism, he grounds all his arguments on nature and makes no appeal to religious authority, being scrupulous not to confuse rational enquiry with theology. 'Truth', he wrote, 'is a virgin prairie: it is common property; it is not all in private preserve yet nor colonized. There is much left for future generations to discover.' In part I of *De disciplinis* he discusses modern methods of study and critically examines all the arts of the Trivium and the Quadrivium. The second part is concerned with the organization of schools and teaching staff, and their routine and training. *De disciplinis* was also published in Cologne in 1536, and in Lyons in 1551. The following works are especially important in studying Vives's contribution to the scholarship of his times:

Adolfo Bonilla y San Martín. *Luis Vives y la filosofía del Renacimiento.* Madrid, L. Rubio, 1929.
José Ontañon. *Vives: tratado de la enseñanza.* Madrid.
Foster Watson. *Vives: on education.* Cambridge University Press, 1913 (a translation of *De tradendis disciplinis*).

Humanism had indeed arrived and its influence is clear in the work of the Flemish scholar and pedagogue Joachim Sterck van Ringelbergh—also known as Joachimus Fortius Ringelbergius—who was born about 1499 and died about 1536. He wrote several small textbooks for his students, such as his *Libellus de usu vocum quae non flectuntur* (Paris, Chr. Wechel, 1530), and his *Dialectica, et Rhetorica* (Paris, Fr. Gryphius, 1540), but his chief claim to present-day notice is his posthumous *Lucubrationes, vel potius absolutissima Κυκλοπαιδεία, nempe liber de ratione studii* . . . (Basle, Westhemer, 1541), which was the first approach to the modern conception of an encyclopaedia.

The Chinese encyclopaedia *T'ien chung chi,* compiled by Ch'ên

Yao-wên, was completed in 60 chapters in 1550. This was followed by the *T'u shuh pien* of Chang Huang (1527–1608), which was completed in 127 chapters in 1577, and by P'êng Ta-i's *Shan t'ang ssŭ k'ao* of 1595.

Charles Estienne (1504–64)—also known as Carolus Stephanus— a member of the famous Parisian publishing firm and himself responsible for the *editio princeps* of Appian in 1551, showed early evidence of his interest in encyclopaedic dictionary-making with his *Dictionarium propriorum nominum* (Paris, 1544)—earlier anonymous works of the same title[1] had been appearing for at least the past forty years—followed by his Greek/Latin/French vocabulary *De re vestiaria, vascularia et navali* (Paris, Car. Stephanus, 1553). Again in 1553, he issued his *Dictionarium historicum, geographicum et poeticum*, which was the first indigenous French encyclopaedia and justly remained popular for over one hundred years. It was later revised and translated by D. de Juigné Broissinière under the title *Dictionnaire théologique, historique, poétique, cosmographique et chronologique* (see page 87). But for encyclopaedias in their own language, the French were still relying—in Estienne's time—on translations of the encyclopaedias of other nations, such as *Les diverses leçons de Pierre Messie, contenans de variables histoires et autres choses mémorables, mises en françoys par Cl. Gruget* (Paris, 1550; 2nd edition, 1554), the work of Pedro Mexia (1496–1552), a Spanish historian, whose mediocre work enjoyed enormous popularity in the sixteenth and seventeenth centuries. It was in fact no more than an encyclopaedic compilation dealing with a number of subjects such as the earth, the sun, philology, medicine, the invention of paper and printing, and so on.

It was at this mid-century period that Domenico Delfino's plagiarism of Alfonso de la Torre's *Visión deleitable . . . (c. 1435)* appeared under the title of *Sommario di tutte le scientie* (Venice, 1556). The plagiarism went unnoticed, and was followed by a remarkable sequel just over one hundred years later (see page 88).

Paul Scalich—also known as Paul Skalich, Paul Scaliger,

---

[1] Such as the *Dictionarium nomirum propriorum virorum, mulierum, populorum, idolorum, urbium, fluviorum, montium caeterumque locorum, quae passim in libris prophanis leguntur* which was issued frequently in Cologne at this period.

Paulus Scalichius de Lika, and as Count Scalitzius—had a life that in its adventures and intrigue closely resembled that of Cellini and Casanova. His *Encyclopaedia, seu Orbis disciplinarum, tum sacrarum quam prophanum Epitome* . . . (Basle, J. Oporinus, 1559) was a poor piece of compilation and is chiefly important nowadays for its successful introduction of the word Encyclopaedia—the nearest approach so far had been Ringelbergh's use of *Cyclopaedia* (see page 78), though Quintilian had long ago written 'Orbis ille doctrinae quam Graeci ἐνκύκλιον παιδείαν vocant' in his *Institutio oratoria* (volume I, X, 1); and in chapter 20 of his *Pantagruel* Rabelais had written that Thaumast had declared Panurge to have opened to him 'le vray puys et abysme de encyclopédie'. Within the next hundred years the word 'encyclopaedia' came to be very generally accepted throughout Western Europe, though for a long time it seemed as though the rival 'dictionary' would eventually triumph and, indeed, it has never been completely abandoned for encyclopaedic works.

BIBLIOGRAPHY

Philotheus Böhner and Etienne Gilson. *Christliche Philosophie von ihren Anfängen bis Nikolaus von Cues.* 3rd edition. Paderborn, Schöningh, 1954
L. M. Cappelli. *Primi studi sulle enciclopedie medioevali.* Modena, 1897
Frederick Coplestone. *A history of philosophy: volume II–Mediaeval philosophy, Augustine to Scotus.* London, Burns Oates & Washbourne, 1950 (reprinted 1954) (The Bellarmine Series, XII)
Bernhard Geyer. *Die patristische und scholastische Philosophie.* 11th edition. Berlin, Mittler, 1928 (Friedrich Überwegs Grundriss der Geschichte der Philosophie, II)
Etienne Gilson. *History of Christian philosophy in the Middle Ages.* London, Sheed & Ward, 1955 (originally published as: *La philosophie au moyen âge, des origines patristiques à la fin du XIVe siècle.* 2nd edition. Paris, Payot, 1944)
Martin Grabmann. *Die Geschichte der scholastischen Methode.* 2 volumes. Freiburg-im-Breisgau, Herder, 1909–11 (reprinted, Graz, Akademische Druck- und Verlagsanstalt, 1957)
—— *Mittelalterliches Geistesleben.* 3 volumes. Munich, M. Hueber, 1926-56
H. A. Mason. *Humanism and poetry in the early Tudor period: an essay.* London, Routledge & Kegan Paul, 1959
Josef Pieper. *Scholasticism: personalities and problems of mediaeval philosophy.* Translated by Richard and Clare Winston. London, Faber & Faber, 1961 (originally published as *Scholastik*; Munich, Koesel Verlag, 1960.)

Sir John Edwin Sandys. *A history of classical scholarship: volume I—From the sixth century B.C. to the end of the Middle Ages.* Cambridge University Press, 1903 (reprinted, London and New York, Hafner Publishing Company, 1958)

Erwin Panofsky. *Gothic architecture and scholasticism.* New York, Meridian Books; London, Thames & Hudson, 1957

George Sarton. *Introduction to the history of science.* 3 volumes in 5. Baltimore, Williams & Wilkins, for the Carnegie Institution of Washington, 1927-48 (Carnegie Institution of Washington, publication no. 376) (volumes 1 and 2 reprinted 1946)

Fernand van Steenberghen. *Philosophie des Mittelalters.* Bern, Franke, 1950

Lynn Thorndike. *A history of magic and experimental science.* 8 volumes. New York, Columbia University Press, 1923-58

Maurice de Wulf. *Histoire de la philosophie médiévale.* 6th edition. 3 volumes. Louvain, Vrin, 1934-47

Michel de Boüard. 'Encyclopédies médiévales sur la connaissance de la nature et du monde au moyen âge. *Revue des questions historiques*, volume 112, 1930: pages 258-304

Chapter III

**BACON TO THE
ENCYCLOPÉDISTES**

A lever to move the world.
BENJAMIN FARRINGTON:
Francis Bacon

The influence of Francis Bacon (1561–1626), Lord Verulam and
Viscount St Albans, on the future of encyclopaedia-making is of
the greatest importance. The outlines of the encyclopaedias so far
described demonstrate how curious and limited were the conceptions of the extent and ordering of human knowledge held by the
theologians, philosophers and scholars who were their compilers,
and how poor up till now had been their attempts to show the
relationships of individual subjects to each other. In his plan for
The great instauration—of which only a small part was ever completed—Bacon included an Encyclopaedia of Nature and Art
under the heading *The Phenomena of the Universe, or a Natural and
Experimental History for the Foundation of Philosophy*, which he also
suggested calling The Primary History or The Mother History.
His approach was revolutionary, though he was clearly influenced
by Pliny's example: he proposed to eschew the age-old controversies and academic disputes in favour of practical matters on
a universal scale. Bacon outlined 130 sections, divided into three
main divisions:

I   (Sections 1–40) *External Nature*
     Astronomy. Meteorology. Geography. The Greater
     Masses—Fire, Air, Water, and Earth. Species—mineral,
     vegetable, and animal.
II   (Sections 41–58) *Man*
     Anatomy. Physiology. Structure and Powers. Actions—
     voluntary and involuntary.
III (Sections 59–130) *Man's Action on Nature*
     Medicine. Surgery. Chemistry. Vision, and the Visual

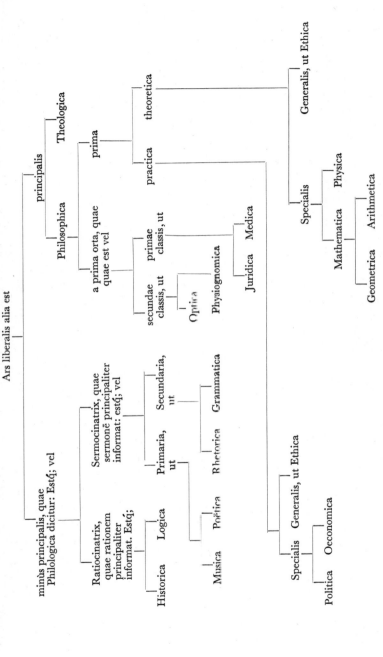

Matthias Martini's classification of knowledge from his *Idea methodica* . . . Herborn, 1606

In this Martini (1572–1630) discussed the classification and contents of a good encyclopaedia. Bacon was apparently unaware of this work

Arts. Hearing, Sound, and Music. Smell, and Smells.
Taste, and Tastes. Touch, and the Objects of Touch
(including physical love). Pleasure and Pain. The Emo-
tions. The Intellectual Faculties. Food, Drink, etc. The
Care of the Person. Clothing. Architecture. Transport.
Printing, Books, and Writing. Agriculture. Navigation.
Other arts of peace. The Arts of War. The History of
Machines. Arithmetic. Geometry. The Miscellaneous
History of Common Experiments which have not grown
into an art.

Bacon's plan was published in 1620. Of the actual work only two
(monthly) instalments—*The history of the winds* (November 1622),
and *The history of life and death* (January 1623)—were actually
published. His public disgrace, his other literary tasks, and finally
his untimely death all prevented his continuing a work which was
very dear to his heart. The mass of material that Bacon had collected for his encyclopaedia was posthumously published as the
Sylva sylvarum. But the influence of Bacon's plan was permanent:
Diderot frankly and generously acknowledged his debt to him in
the preface to his *Encyclopédie* and, from that time on, all encyclopaedists took good care that their own efforts should be equally
comprehensive and well-planned.

Reference is sometimes made to the *Florilegium* of Joseph Lang
or Langius (*c.* 1570–1615) as an encyclopaedia. This work, which
appeared under such varied titles as the *Polyanthea nova*, the
Anthologia sive Florilegium et materiarum selectarum, the *Loci communes
sive Florilegium*, the *Florilegium magnum*, or the *Florilegii magni seu
Polyantheae floribus novissimis sparsae*, in such cities as Frankfurt-am-
Main (1607), Strasbourg (1631), and Lyons (2 volumes; 1659),
was in fact a collection of quotations, arranged alphabetically by
subject, and culled from Dominicus Nanni-Mirbelli's *Polyanthea* of
1503 (see page 76).

The *Anatomia ingeniorum et scientiarum* (Venice, 1614) was the
work of the Bishop of Petina, Antonio Zara, who was born in 1574.
It is divided into four sections:

Section

I   *Man*
     Body, soul, and character
II   *Imagination*
     Writing; magic; poetry; oratory; courtiership; theoretical
     and mystical artithmetic; geometry; architecture; optics;
     cosmography; astrology; practical medicine; the arts of
     war; government
III *Intellect*
     Logic; physics; metaphysics; theoretical medicine; ethics;
     practical jurisprudence; the judicature; theoretical
     theology
IV   *Memory*
     Grammar; practical arithmetic; human history; the sacred
     canons; practical theology; sacred history; the creation;
     the apocalypse

a particular feature of this work being that it was completed with
an index—inadequate, but a welcome innovation.

Johann Heinrich Alsted (1588–1638) was born at Herborn in
Nassau. He was the son of a minister of the Reformed Church,
from whom he received his early education. By the time he had
returned to Herborn as a school-teacher, Alsted had toured the
universities of Germany and Switzerland and was already a man
of immense learning. In 1610 he had already achieved professorial
rank and his lectures were eagerly attended—among his students
was Johann Amos Comenius (1592–1670). A professor of theology
at the age of 31, Alsted spent the last ten years of his life in charge
of the new academy at Stuhl-Weiszenburg. His literary output was
enormous, the most notable of his publications being his encyclopaedia. This was preceded in 1608 by his *Cursus philosophici* (Herborn, Corvinus), which developed in its second edition into the
Cursus philosophici encyclopaedic (Herborn, Corvinus, 1620). From
this came the *Encyclopaedia, septem tomis distincta* (2 volumes; Herborn, G. Corvini, 1630).

Volume	Books	
I	1–4	Plan
II	1–6	Philology; including glossaries
III	1–10	Natural philosophy
IV	1–4	Practical philosophy, including economics, politics, and pedagogy
V	1–3	Theology; jurisprudence; medicine
VI	1–3	Mechanical arts
VII	1–5	Miscellaneous
Index		

This is the last of the great Latin works arranged in systematic order which developed into the *Scientiarum omnium encyclopaediae* (4 volumes in 2; Lyons, Huguetan & Ravaud, 1649).

In the seventeenth century, Yü An-ch'i's encyclopaedia *T'ang lei han* (in 200 chapters), and the *Ch'ien ch'io chü lei shu* or *Ch'ien ch'io lei shu* (120 chapters) of Ch'ên Jên-hsi (1581–1636) were compiled, in addition to the profusely illustrated *San ts'ai t'u hui* (*c.* 1609) in 106 chapters of Wang Ch'i and his son Wang Ssŭ-i, and Shên Tzŭ-nan's *I lin hui k'ao* (*c.* 1663).

Jean Macé (1600–71), known as Father Léon de Saint-Jean, compiled *Fr. Leonis, . . . Enciclopaediae praemessum, seu Delineatio sapientiae universalis . . .* (Paris, J. Guillemot, 1635). There were many such works, written by clerics for clerics, at that time, and this is chiefly important owing to the publication, by the author, of an extract from it in French, entitled *Le portrait de la sagesse universelle* (Paris, G. Bénard & A. Pasdeloup, 1655). This is a clear demonstration of the growing need for reference works in the vernacular. Thus, an encyclopaedia in Latin while having the advantage of being accessible to every considerable scholar throughout the Western world, had simultaneously the growing disadvantage of being incomprehensible to most of the compiler's own countrymen, so that its influence was to a great extent lost at a period when men's horizons—through the development of crafts and inventions, the discovery of new lands, and the growth of education—were steadily extending.

In 1643, D. de Juigné Broissinière—sometimes written as

Ivigné Broissinière—Sieur de Mollières, published his translation and revision of Charles Estienne's *Dictionarium historicum, geographicum et poeticum* (1553) under the title of *Dictionnaire théologique, historique, poétique, cosmographique et chronologique* (Paris, G. le Bé). This single-volume quarto book of reference enjoyed great popularity immediately and for a considerable period afterwards, some eight editions being published in both Paris and Lyons during the next 36 years.

Abraham Calovius *the elder* (1612–86), also known as Abraham Calan, Kalan, Calov, or Kalau—was a Lutheran divine from East Prussia who became Professor of Theology at Wittenberg. His *D. Encyclopaedias disciplinarum realium ideae, philosophiam universam, facultates superiores, ut et organon ὄργανων logicam facie sua genuina repraesentantes* (Lübeck, G. Venator, 1652) is a folio volume with 26 plates. Bibliographically it is a curious production for so late a period in European publishing, being printed on one side only of each leaf.

The first Hungarian encyclopaedia was published remarkably early in the history of encyclopaedia-making. It was the work of János Apáczai Cseri—also known as Johannes Apacius, and as János Apacai Cseri or Csere or Cserei—who, as his name shows, was born in 1625 at the village of Apáca in Transylvania. A brilliant scholar, he was sent to the Netherlands to complete his studies. There he studied at Leyden and Utrecht, and obtained a doctorate in theology at Harderwijk in 1651. He returned to Transylvania as a reformer in education, but met with so much opposition that he ended his days (1659) as a teacher in the primary school at Kolozsvár. His encyclopaedia, *Magyar encyclopaedia: az az, minden igaz és hasznos boltseségnek szép rendbe foglalása, és Magyar nyelven világra botsátása* (Utrecht, Officinâ Joannis à Waesberge, 1653–55), was a duodecimo volume whose contents were mostly based on foreign sources. Its eleven chapters cover the basic ideas and the principal aims of the abstract sciences. A new edition appeared (Györött) in 1803.

The Sieur Saunier, of whom nothing else is known, compiled the *Encyclopédie des beaux esprits, contenant les moyens de parvenir à la connaissance des belles sciences* (Paris, P. Lamy, 1657), a typical example of the kind of small handbook that was becoming popular in Court circles. It was reprinted in 1659.

The French Court was in fact at this time partial to informative compilations, if presented in palatable form: Louis XIV's historiographer, Jean de Magnon, even attempted the task of writing an encyclopaedia in French in 200,000 lines of heroic verse. Due to his murder in 1662, only one volume of his *La science universelle* (Paris, S. Martin, 1663) was ever published. It comprises some 11,000 lines on the subjects of divinity and original sin. The loss of the remainder of the work—judging from what has survived—has caused the world no hardship. It was in this same year that the final act in the extraordinary history of Alfonso de la Torre's *Visión delectable de la philosophía* was played (see page 72). Francisco de Cáceres, ignorant of Dominico Delfino's perfidy in passing off his translation of the *Visión* as his own original work, set himself to translate Delfino's Italian translation into Spanish! Thus the *Visión* reappeared in Spanish more than 200 years later as the *Libro intitulado Visión deleytable y sumario de todas las sciencias* (Amsterdam, David de Crasto Tartaz, 1663). It is unfortunate that La Torre's work was quite unworthy of so much attention over so long a period.

Attention must briefly be drawn to Michael Pexenfelder's curious *Apparatus eruditionis tam rerum quam verborum per omnes artes et scientias* . . . (Nuremberg, Endter, 1670; 3rd edition, Sulzbach, Endter, 1687), which systematically surveys the whole field of human knowledge in one volume by means of a series of conversations between a teacher and his pupil.

An unparalleled position in European society was achieved by *Le grand dictionnaire historique, ou le mélange curieux de l'histoire sainte et profane* (Lyons, J. Girin & B. Rivière, 1674), a one-volume folio work which was compiled by Louis Moréri (1643–80). The title fails to do justice to an encyclopaedia so strong in geographical and biographical material. Its immediate success caused a second edition—in which the word 'sainte' was changed to 'sacrée' in the title—to follow in 1681, and third, fourth, fifth and sixth editions in 1683, 1687, 1688 and 1691, respectively. And by 1759, when the twentieth and last edition was issued (Paris, Les libraires associés), the work had grown to ten folio volumes. New material, particularly contemporary events and biographical information, was immediately incorporated in each succeeding edition, which thus became an accurate mirror of the times. Thus each edition even now is worthy of preservation and provides valuable material for the research worker. The influence of Moréri's work in other countries was quite remarkable. The German encyclopaedias that were published from 1709 onwards, under the editorship of the Lutheran divine Johann Franz Buddeus (1667–1729), and that in Basle under the editorship of Jacob Christoph Iselin (1681–1737), were based partly on Moréri. A Spanish edition was published in 1753 (Paris and Leon, Hermanos de Tournes). And an English edition was issued in 1694 (London, printed for H. Rhodes), with a second edition in 1701, and a Supplement in 1705, in addition to numerous other English encyclopaedias which acknowledged their debt to 'Mr Moreri'. The French philosopher Pierre Bayle himself recognized Moréri's influence on his own *Dictionnaire*.

The *Lexicon universale, historiam, chronologiam, geographiam, genealogiam, mythologiam, omnemque antiquitatem . . .* (2 volumes; Basle, 1677) of Johann Jacob Hoffmann, had all the faults of a vast endeavour carried out by one man. Hoffmann (1635–1706) was a Professor of Greek at Basle. The main volumes of his encyclopaedia dealt mainly with history, biography and geography, but a two-volume supplement (Basle, 1683) continued the subjects in his previous work, and treated more briefly most of the remainder of the knowledge of his times—but only with passing reference to theology. Entries were arranged alphabetically, and there was also an index. A second edition, in four volumes, was published at Leyden in 1698.

The *Dictionarium historicum* (Oxford, 1670; reprinted 1671) of the philologist Nicholas Lloyd (1630–80), rector of St Mary, Newington Butts, was a one-volume folio work based chiefly on the dictionaries of Charles Estienne and Philip Ferrarius. But this Lloyd greatly enlarged and remodelled in encyclopaedia form as: *Dictionarium historicum, geographicum, poeticum . . . Opus admodum utile et apprime necessarium; à Carlo Stephano inchoatum; ad incudem vero revocatum, innumerisque pene locis auctum et emaculatum, per Nicolaum*

Lloydium . . . Editio novissima (London, 1686). Lloyd was clearly unaware of Moréri's recent work, although its fame must have reached England well before his death.

Daniel George Morhof (1639–90), professor first at Rostock and subsequently at the new university at Kiel, compiled an encyclo- paedia, the *Polyhistor literarius, philosophicus, et practicus*, which had a protracted publication timetable. The *Polyhistor literarius* section was issued in Morhof's lifetime at Lübeck in 1688. The com- plete encyclopaedia was edited by Johannes Moller (1661–1725) and was published in 1708:

> *Danielis Georgi Morhofi Polyhistor, in tres tomos, literarium, (cujus soli tres libri priores hactenus prodiere, nunc autem quatuor reliqui . . . et mss. accedunt) philosophicum et practicum divisus. Opus posthumum, ut multorum votis satisfieret accurate revisum, emendatum, ex autoris annota- tionibus αυτογαφοις* [sic] *et mss. aliis, suppletum passim atque auctum . . . à Johanne Mollero . . . Accedunt indices necessarii.* 3 volumes in 1. Lübeck, Peter Böckmann, 1708.

A second edition was issued by Böckmann in 1714, and this was again edited by Johann Albert Fabricius (1688–1736) of Hamburg and Johann Frick (1670–1739) and issued as the third edition (3 volumes in 2) by Böckmann in 1732. Still another edition appeared in 1747.

The plan of the encyclopaedia—perhaps owing to Morhof's untimely death—is very unequal. Though he devoted well over one thousand pages to literature, he gave less than half that to philosophy and history, and only 124 pages to the remainder of his subjects. The outline of the three volumes is:

Volume I. Literarius

Book
1   History of literature. Bibliography. Libraries
2   The study of Greek and Latin
3   Literary criticism
4   Language and literature
5   Writers on criticism and antiquities
6   Rhetoric and oratory
7   Poetics

Volume II. *Philosophicus*

Book

1 The history of philosophy
2 Physics
3 Divination and magic
4 Mathematics
5 Logic and metaphysics

Volume III. *Practicus*

Book

1 Ethics
2 Politics
3 Economics
4 History
5 Theology
6 Law
7 Medicine

to which were added very detailed indexes of both authors and subjects.

In spite of Morhof's very unequal treatment, which resulted in a very poor encyclopaedia, his work will always have a special attraction for librarians owing to the interest he took in their work, as the headings of the last fifteen chapters of Book 1 of the *Literarius* show:

Chapter

11 De libris physicis secretioribus praecipué chemicis
12 De eo, quod in disciplinis divinum est, excursus
13 De collegiis secretis
14 De aliis eruditorum societatibus
15 De conversatione erudita
16 De scriptoribus ad rem librariam et historiam literariam pertinentibus
17 De scriptoribus bibliothecariis
18 De catalogorum scriptoribus
19 De vitarum scriptoribus

20   De fructu omnis historiae bibliothecariae
21   De locorum communium scriptoribus
22   De eodem argumento et de polygraphis
23   De epistolarum scriptoribus
24   Continuatio prioris argumenti
25   De epistolis ineditis eruditorum.

To the importance of the Netherlands as a safe refuge at these times for scholars, politicians and free thinkers, is linked a special eminence as a cross-roads in the exchange of ideas throughout Europe. The brilliant Restoration circle of scientists and philosophers in England found here their easiest means of contact with their counterparts from France and the rest of the Continent. While Switzerland and several Courts in Germany provided shelter, it is true, for those who had spoken too openly in the land of Louis XIV, The Hague and Amsterdam and Rotterdam offered the advantage of freedom from patronage and ready access to England. It is therefore not surprising that the encyclopaedia of the Abbot of Chalivoy, Antoine Furetière, was first published (unfortunately after his death) in The Hague and Rotterdam.

Furetière, the eldest son of a secretary to the Chambre du roi, was born in 1619. A man of letters, he was the author of the realistic and satirical *Roman bourgeois* (1666), and the *Nouvelle allégorique, ou Histoire des derniers troubles arrivés au royaume d'Eloquence* (1658). The election of so keen a critic of humbug and affectation to the Académie Française in 1662 was therefore an act of faith from which the more timid members might well have shrunk. One of the tasks that had been assigned to the Académie in 1635 by Cardinal Richelieu was the preparation of a dictionary of the French language, but the work had proceeded extremely slowly. There was no lack of attendance at the committee meetings where the draft entries for the dictionary were examined and discussed in detail, for on punctual attendance depended the payment of the members' pensions; but the work was tedious, and few of the members were temperamentally suited to so gigantic, exacting and meticulous an undertaking. Furetière, whose energies were enormous, at first threw himself into the task with boundless enthusiasm, but he was soon fretting at the lack of progress and, even more, at the dearth of relevant knowledge possessed by most of his colleagues.

If Furetière is to be believed, he had already some years earlier started collecting his own information on the French language, and—in desperation—he eventually decided to go ahead and complete his own dictionary, a work which he felt would prove to be more in keeping with the times in which they lived and more useful in its practical applications. Unfortunately for him, the Académie had in 1674 secured the right to prevent all other dictionaries of the French language from being published for a period of twenty-five years after the date of publication of the first issue of their own compilation. In 1684 Furetière obtained from the French Chancellor permission to publish his own dictionary, this privilege being contradictory to but not cancelling that issued to the Académie. But this was not the first time such a position had arisen, for both Richelet and Rochefort had previously gained similar permissions for their own dictionaries, and in their cases the Académie had made no protest. In Furetière's case, however, the Académie were faced with rather a different problem: Furetière was collaborating in their own dictionary and his own work might conceivably have profited from the deliberations and decisions of their committees. Eventually the Académie even made this accusation publicly, and thus caused their members to divide into two factions. Most of the liberally minded men—such as Racine, Bossuet, and Despréaux—supported Furetière, but the opposition was very strong and, surprisingly, included La Fontaine.

This was the golden age of the French pamphleteers, and the whole of the seventeenth century in France is filled with similar wordy battles in which abuse, epigrams, popular songs, and political intrigue and influence were freely used on both sides even in very minor literary squabbles. Furetière, knowing his dictionary to be very different in approach from that of the Académie—even the order was different, for Furetière had adopted alphabetical order for his words, while the Académie's first edition was arranged by the *roots* of words—published some specimen sheets in 1684 under the title *Essais d'un Dictionnaire universel* (Paris, 1675, quarto; and Amsterdam, Desbordes, 1685, duodecimo). The Académie, infuriated, asked for Furetière's privilege to be cancelled, on the grounds of his unscrupulous plagiarism, and Furetière—undeterred by the pacifying efforts of well-wishers among his colleagues —replied with lampoons and personal insults on various members of the Académie and on their dictionary, to which they replied individually and collectively with vigour. As Furetière might have foreseen, the Académie, being an official institution, was bound to win in the end, and in 1685 his publishing permission was revoked and he was also expelled from the Académie. The rest of his life was spent in carrying on a useless battle of pamphlets and epigrams in which the lowest levels were reached by both sides. Furetière died unhonoured in 1688, his dictionary still unpublished.

Whatever the excesses of his accusations, Furetière was right concerning the nature and quality of his dictionary: his work and the Académie's had little in common. Furetière had in fact compiled one of the pioneer examples of the modern encyclopaedic dictionary, and he had tackled his task in a comprehensive fashion. Terms from both the arts and the sciences were included, whereas the Académie had decided to exclude the latter. His work was in truth the first to imitate the approach of Suidas in detail, and it is a landmark in the history of encyclopaedias, for on it are based many later works. Furetière claimed that his dictionary was the result of some forty years' intensive work; it may well have benefited from some of the Académie's deliberations, but there is no doubt that the vast majority of the entries were of his own devising and showed every evidence of research over a considerable period. Furetière had paid special attention to trade and popular terms, to etymology, and to current usage, and his dictionary quite put the Académie's (at last published in its first edition in 1694) in the shade.

In 1690 Furetière's *Dictionnaire universel des arts et sciences* was published posthumously in three volumes at The Hague and Rotterdam by A. and R. Leers. The great philosopher Pierre Bayle had himself contributed a Preface. This was followed in the next year by a second edition in two volumes, issued by the same

publishers: this edition was enriched by a large number of illustrative quotations. A third edition was edited by another exile, the
Protestant historian and jurist Henri Basnage, Sieur de Beauval
(1656–1710), and was issued in four volumes at The Hague in
1707. The fourth and last edition was revised by Brutel de la
Rivière and issued in four volumes at The Hague in 1727.

Under another name, however, and with alterations and additions of which Furetière would never have approved, his dictionary
was to have another half-century of life, for the Jesuits used his
work as a basis for their own *Dictionnaire de Trévoux* (see page 98),
but failed to make any acknowledgments to its forerunner!

In accounts of the history of encyclopaedias, reference is sometimes made to the *Lexicon rationale, sive Thesaurus philosophicus ordine
alphabetico digestus, in quo vocabula omnia philosophica explicare, et
universe quae lumine naturali sciri possunt, non tam concludere, quam
recludere* . . . (Rotterdam, P. van der Slaart, 1692), whose second
edition was issued under the title of *Lexicon philosophicum secundis
curis* (Leuwardden, F. Halma, 1713). This was the work of the
refugee Protestant divine and Cartesian philosopher Etienne
Chauvin (1640–1725) but, being in the main restricted to the field
of philosophy, requires only mention here for its influence on more
general works of reference during the next century.

The dramatist and Academician Thomas Corneille (1625–
1709), younger brother of the more famous Pierre Corneille (1606–
1684), was in the fortunate position of receiving a pension of one
thousand livres per annum from Louis XIV. In addition to collaborating with Donneau de Visé in the editorship of the influential journal *Mercure galant*, Thomas Corneille produced at the
request of the Académie Française *Le dictionnaire des arts et des
sciences* (2 volumes; Paris, J.-B. Coignard, 1694). This was published as a supplement to the first edition of the Académie's great
Dictionnaire of 1694, and was intended to fill the gap which has
already been mentioned in connection with Furetière's dictionary
(see page 94). As a rival to the latter it had some considerable
success, for Corneille was thorough in his approach and consulted
original works for his authority wherever possible. A reprint in two
volumes was issued in Amsterdam in 1696, and another in Paris

in 1720. The 1731 edition (2 volumes; Paris, J.-B. Coignard) was revised by Corneille's nephew, the illustrious writer Bernard le Bouvier de Fontenelle (1657–1757), author of the *Entretiens sur la pluralité des mondes* (1686). Corneille also compiled a three-volume *Dictionnaire universel géographique et historique* (Paris, J.-B. Coignard, 1708), but his influence during the next century—which was very great—undoubtedly derived principally from his supplement to the Académie's dictionary.

It was during this period that possibly the first of the encyclo-paedic compilations specially designed for children was issued. This was the *Pera librorum juvenilium* (Altdorf, 1695), the work of Johann Christoph Wagenseil (1633–1705). Similarly, the eccentric English bookseller John Dunton (1659–1733) issued in 1694 his *Ladies' dictionary* which, apart from its being addressed to a section of the public that had been overlooked since the days of the Abbess Herrad, had no other merit.

Inspired by the desire to correct and amplify Moréri's encyclo-paedia, the French rationalist philosopher Pierre Bayle (1647–1706) compiled an outstanding work, the *Dictionnaire historique et critique* (2 volumes; Rotterdam, R. Leers, 1697), whose influence for well over one hundred years was felt throughout Europe. Bayle soon proceeded far beyond his original intention and over-whelmed his entries with annotations and with illustrative quota-tions from other writers. To every point he applied a mercilessly scientific and enquiring mind that challenged the assumptions and the blind reverence for authority which had characterized almost all his predecessors in this field. A second edition in three volumes was issued in 1702 (Rotterdam, R. Leers); and a third in three volumes in 1715, which was revised in 1720 (4 volumes; Rotter-dam, M. Bohm). A supplement to the editions of 1702 and 1715 was issued in 1722 (Geneva, Frabri & Barrillot). The fourth edition (4 volumes; Amsterdam, P. Brunel, 1730) was 'much en-larged from his manuscripts' and edited by Prosper Marchand (died 1756) and Pierre Desmaizeaux (1666–1745). The latter, also known as Des Maizeaux or Des Maiseaux, was a French critic and historian who went into exile after the Edict of Nantes. He was a friend of Bayle and St Evremond and an international figure well known in London, where he became secretary to the Royal Society. Such men as Locke and Shaftesbury esteemed him highly. Desmaizeaux contributed a life of Bayle to this edition.

The fifth edition was issued by La Compagnie des Libraires in five volumes in Amsterdam in 1734 and was reprinted in the same city by P. Brunel in 1740, revisions being published in four volumes in both Basle (Brandmüller, 1738) and Amsterdam (Brunel, 1740). The final complete edition was the eleventh, edited by Adrien Jean Quentin Beuchot (1777–1851), which was published in sixteen volumes as late as 1820–24 (Paris, Desoer), and the first two volumes (no more issued) of the twelfth edition (Aaron-Alting) were published in Paris in 1830. A number of English translations of various editions were issued during the period 1709 to 1741; and the German poet and critic Johann Christoph Gottsched (1700–66), Professor of Poetry at Leipzig, translated the fourth edition into German under the title *Historisches und Critisches Wörterbuch, nach der neuesten Auflage von 1740 ins Deutsche übersetzt, auch mit einer Vorrede und verschiedenen Anmerkungen sonderlich bey anstössigen Stellen versehen* . . . (4 volumes; Leipzig, 1741–44).[1] And in 1758–59 Prosper Marchand was to publish a form of supplement of his own to Bayle's encyclopaedia (see page 106).

The non-juror Jeremy Collier (1650–1726) made no secret of the fact that his *The great historical, geographical, genealogical and poetical dictionary* (2 volumes; London, Henry Rhodes, Thomas Newborough, 1701–05) was 'collected from the best historians, more especially out of Lewis Morery his eighth edition'. In 1705 a supplement 'together with a continuation from the year 1688 to this time, by another hand' was issued, and this was reprinted in 1727. An appendix was published in 1721. The encyclopaedia was not a success: Collier had worked diligently, but his additions were not up to the standard of the original work and, moreover, he was unfortunate in that the publication of John Harris's *Lexicon technicum* in 1704 provided an unbeatable competitor (see page 99).

The official Cosmographer to the Venetian Republic, a

---

[1] See Erich Lichtenstein's *Gottscheds Ausgabe von Bayles Dictionnaire: ein Beitrag zur Geschichte der Aufklärung* (Beiträge zur neueren Literaturgeschichte. Neue Folge, 8. Heidelberg, 1915).

Franciscan friar called Vincenzo Maria Coronelli (*c.* 1650–1718), spent some thirty years compiling his *Biblioteca universale sacro-profano* (7 volumes; Venice, Antonio Tivani—volumes 6 and 7 issued by G. B. Tramontin—1701–06). These volumes comprised only the section A–Caque of an encyclopaedia which was planned to fill at least forty-five volumes, with some three hundred thousand entries. This would have made it easily the largest alphabetically-arranged encyclopaedia in existence at that time. But the work is important only for its plan: even additions, corrections and amendments were allowed for in the fortieth to forty-second volumes, while the last three volumes were reserved for various indexes. In addition, each volume was to have had an analytical subject index of its own, reference being facilitated by *numbering* each article. Another interesting feature of Coronelli's typically business-like approach[1] to the problems of encyclopaedia-making is his practice of italicizing the titles of books cited in the text, a system that has since become almost universal.

In 1704 the Jesuit Fathers of Trévoux issued their *Dictionnaire universel françois et latin* which, it will be remembered (see page 95), was based—without acknowledgment—on Furetière's encyclo-paedia, as revised by Basnage de Beauval. From its place of publication, Trévoux in Ain, it soon became known as the *Dictionnaire de Trévoux*. The theological and philosophical outlook of the Huguenot source was of course completely revised by eminent scholars such as Tournemine and Claude Buffier (1661–1737), and the encyclopaedia quickly became a favourite among the orthodox, while each edition grew in size:

Edition	Date	Number of Volumes
1st	1704	3
2nd	1721	5
3rd	1732	5
4th	1743	6
5th	1752	7 (the 7th vol. is a Latin–French dictionary)
6th	1771	8

[1] See Ermanno Armao's *Vincenzo Coronelli*. Florence, 'Bibliopolis', 1944 (Biblioteca di bibliografia italiana, XVII).

the work coming to an end with the misfortunes of the Jesuits in France in the eighth decade.

The *Lexicon technicum; or, An universal English dictionary of the arts and sciences, explaining not only the terms of arts, but the arts themselves* (London, 1704), the first purely English general encyclopaedia, was undertaken by John Harris (*c.* 1666–1719). Harris, who was an improvident divine and scientist, gave emphasis to practical and scientific subjects at the expense of the humanities. As a Fellow of the Royal Society (and its acting Vice-President for a time), he had ready access to many of the greatest scholars of the day, and his use of the works of such scientists as Ray and Newton is probably the first example of an encyclopaedia-maker drawing directly on the advice and help of experts and, as such, is the original precursor of the modern system of inviting contributions from specialists. A reprint of the *Lexicon* was issued in 1708, and a second volume was added in 1710 (this constituting, with the reprinted first volume, the second edition). The last edition was the fifth (2 volumes; London, J. Walthoe, 1736), but a 'Society of Gentlemen' prepared and issued in 1744 a folio *Supplement to Dr Harris's Dictionary of Arts and Sciences*. Harris's encyclopaedia was distinguished not only for its excellent plates, but also for its text line-drawings and diagrams, and for its provision of bibliographies for some of the more important scientific subjects. So far, England had been translating French encyclopaedias for domestic use: within a few years the leading French encyclopaedia was to be based on the English works of Harris and his successors.

Philipp Balthasar Sinold von Schütz, of whose personal life very little is known beyond the fact that he also wrote under the name of 'Amadeus Creutzberg', was the compiler of the first truly German encyclopaedia:

Reales Staats- und Zeitungs-Lexikon. Worinnen sowohl die Religionen und Orden, die Reiche und Staaten, Meere, Seen, Flüsse, Städte, Vestungen, Schlösser, Häfen, Berge, Vorgebürge, Pässe, Wälder und Unterschiede der Meilen . . . als auch Andere in Zeitungen und täglicher Conversation aus allerhand Sprachen bestehende Termini Artis, denen Gelehrten und Ungelehrten zu sonderbarem Nutzen klar und deutlich

*beschrieben werden, Nebst einem zweyfachen Register und Vorrede Herrn
Johann Hübner* . . . Leipzig, Johann Friedrich Gleditsch, 1704

which is usually referred to by the name of the writer of its Preface, Johann Hübner (1668–1731), Rector of the Johanneum at Hamburg. This encyclopaedia was designed to appeal to the educated classes rather than to scholars. This is recognized and emphasized in the title of the fourth edition (1709) which was enlarged to *Reales-, Staats-, Zeitungs- und Conversations-Lexikon*. In this amended title appears the first use of the term 'Conversations-Lexikon', an approach to encyclopaedia-making that was essentially German and which has set the style for German encyclopaedias right up to the present day. The encyclopaedia was a great success and ran into thirty-one editions, the last, edited by F. A. Rüder, being published as late as 1824–28. An Hungarian edition, translated by the university librarian at Pest, György Fejér (1766–1851), was published in that city in five volumes in 1816.

A supplement, the *Curieuses Natur-, Kunst-, Berg-, Gewerk- und Handlungslexikon* (Leipzig, Gleditsch, 1712) was compiled by Paul Jakob Marperger (1656–1730), and was also provided with a Preface by Johann Hübner. While Sinold von Schütz's original work dealt with geography, theology, and politics (being especially valuable for contemporary history), Marperger's supplement covered the sciences, art, and commerce. This work also was frequently revised and reissued, a new edition of 1746 being reprinted from time to time until as late as 1792.

A popular little French encyclopaedia was published in Paris: this was the Sieur de Chevigny's *La science des personnes de la cour, de l'épée et de la robe, par demandes et par réponses* . . . (2 volumes; J. de Nully, 1706). This was subsequently republished in Amsterdam (4 volumes; Chatelain, 1717). A sequel, written by H. P. de Limiers, the *Idée générale des études, choix qu'on en doit faire, but où on doit tendre . . . Avec un état des Bibliothèques . . . Pour servir de suite à la Science de la Cour*, was a small duodecimo volume of 209 pages. Limiers appears to have assumed responsibility for both works, later editions—the sixth (4 volumes; Amsterdam, L'Honoré & Chatelain, 1723), seventh (4 volumes; Amsterdam, Z. Chatelain,

1729), and last (18 volumes; Amsterdam, Z. Chatelain, 1752)—
appearing under his name. A four-volume edition was also
published in Rouen (Lottin, 1725), while a four-volume translation into Italian was issued in Venice (Baglioni, 1720). Even the
Russians published a translation of the 'Chronology' from the
original work (2 volumes; Moscow, N. I. Novikov, 1782).

The *Allgemeines historisches Lexikon* (3 volumes; Leipzig, 1709) is
more usually known as the *Leipziger Lexikon*. A supplementary
volume was published in 1714. It was probably the first of a long
series of German publishers' imitations of the best items in the
compilations of Bayle, Moréri, and their contemporaries. The
Foreword, and perhaps some of the editing, were the work of the
German Lutheran scholar and theologian, Johann Franz Buddeus
(1666–1729), by whose name the encyclopaedia is sometimes
referred to. A second edition was published in four volumes in
1722; and a third in 1730–32, with a two-volume supplement in
1740. On this encyclopaedia was based in turn the *Neu vermehretes
historisch- und geographisches allgemeines Lexikon* of 1726–27 (see
page 102).

Although Johann Christian Nehring died in 1682, his encyclopaedia did not appear for nearly a quarter of a century afterwards:

*Historisch-politisch-juristisches Lexicon; in welchem über die Erklärung
der juristischen und bey der Kauffmannschafft gebräuchlichen, auch ander
in denen Zeitungen vorkommende Redens-Arten, verschiedens die Religion,
den Staat, die vier Haupt-Fakultäten . . . bürgerliche und Kriegsbau-
Kunst angehende und dieselbe erläuternde Kunstwörter; nechst dem auch
viele biblische, jüdische, christliche, heydnische, griechische, römische und
alte teutsche . . . Antiquitäten und Gewohheiten, nicht weniger allerhand
ausländische Müntzen . . . in richtiger Alphabets-Ordnung dargestellet
und erkläret werden; nach des Autoris ableben an unziehlichen Orthen
vermehrt und verbessert . . . Gotha, J. Mevius, 1706*

a single volume of 1,263 pages. Like its later editions, it originally
appeared in parts. The encyclopaedia was very popular, frequent
editions appearing up to 1736. On the borderland of the world
of encyclopaedias is the single-volume *Teutsch-orthographisches*

Schreib-Conversation-Zeitungs- und Sprüch-Wörter-Lexicon (Leipzig, 1720) of Hermann Justus Spanutius.

Johann Theodor Jablonski (1654–1731)—possibly a brother of the eminent theologian Daniel Ernst Jablonski (1660–1741)—was the first secretary of the Prussian Academy (founded 1700). He compiled:

> *Allgemeines Lexicon der Künste und Wissenschaften; oder, Deutliche Beschreibung des Reichs der Natur, der Himmel und himmlische Cörper, der Luft, der Erde, sammt den bekannten Gewächsen, der Thiere, Steine und Erzte, des Meers und der darinne lebenden Geschöpfe; In gleichen Aller menschlichen Handlunge, Staats-Rechts-Kriegs-Policey-Haushaltungs- und Gelehrten Geschäfte, Hanthierungen und Gewerbe . . .* Königsberg and Leipzig, Johann Heinrich Hartung, 1721.

This was a two-volume quarto illustrated work which was in the new tradition of the Conversationslexicon. Though too short to be sufficiently comprehensive, it had an immediate success in Germany and a revised and enlarged edition was issued in 1748. A third edition was thoroughly revised by the scholar Johann Joachim Schwabe in 1767 (2 volumes in 4; Königsberg and Leipzig, bey Zeisens Witwe und Hartungs Erben).

Kung Mêng-jên's encyclopaedia *Tu shu chi shu lüeh* was compiled in 54 chapters by 1707, and reprinted in 1708 and again in 1880. The Chinese literary encyclopaedia *P'ei wên yün fu* was compiled by order of the Emperor K'ang Hsi in 1704–11, and was supplemented by the *Yün fu shih I* (1720). Other and similar works ordered by the Emperor included the *Pien tzŭ lei pien* (1726), and the *Tzŭ shih ching hua* (1727)—the latter being arranged under 280 sections.

The *Neu vermehrtes historisch- und geographisches allgemeines Lexicon* (Basle, J. Brandmüller, 1726–27) was published in four volumes. It is usually referred to as the *Basler Lexikon*, after the place of publication of this and subsequent editions, or by the name of Jacob Christoph Iselin (1681–1737) who was the writer of the Foreword and was probably responsible for some of the editing. It was based on the *Allgemeines historisches Lexicon* (see page 101). A second edition was published soon after, and a third in 1742–44 in six volumes (Basle, J. Brandmüller), the last two volumes also being published (1742–44) separately as a supplement to the second edition. The supplementary volumes were the work of Jacob Christoff Beck and August Johann Buxtorff. Attention is also briefly drawn to the single-volume popular *Bequemes Corre-spondenz- und Conversations-Lexikon* (Nuremberg, 1727) edited by Antonio Moratori.

Ephraim Chambers was born in the Lake District about 1680 and was trained as a map-maker. Inspired by the example of John Harris's *Lexicon technicum* (see page 99), he set out to compile a more comprehensive work. Though to Harris must go the honours of compiling the first true English encyclopaedia, Chambers is clearly the father of the modern encyclopaedia throughout the world. His *Cyclopaedia: or, An universal dictionary of arts and sciences, containing an explication of the terms and an account of the things signified thereby in the several arts, liberal and mechanical, and the several sciences, human and divine, compiled from the best authors* (London, James and John Knapton, 1728) was published, with engraved plates, in two folio volumes at the price of four guineas. It is dedicated to King George II, and the encyclopaedia's worth was immediately recognized by Chambers's being elected a member of the Royal Society in 1729. Among the contributors to later editions of Chambers's work was the Dr John Hill (*c.* 1716–75) whom Oliver Goldsmith satirized in his 'Reverie' paper in *The Bee* of 3rd November 1759.

Chambers's *Cyclopaedia* is particularly remarkable for its elabor-ate system of cross-references and for the broadening of Harris's coverage to include more of the humanities. Owing to legal difficulties, Chambers was unable to remodel his encyclopaedia in the form he had planned, but a second edition was issued in 1738 (2 volumes; London, D. Midwinter); a third in 1739 by the same publisher; a fourth in 1741, and a fifth in 1746—in addition to which a 'fifth edition' was also issued in Dublin (2 volumes; R. Gunne, 1742). In 1748–49, a nine-volume translation was pub-lished in Venice under the title *Dizionario universale delle arti e delle scienze*, which was revised and issued in six volumes in 1762–65. A seventh edition was published in 1751–52 (London, W. Innys) in two volumes; to this edition a two-volume supplement was added in 1753. This was the work of the mathematician George Lewis Scott (1708–80), who had been a pupil of De Moivre, and was a friend of James Thomson, Gibbon, Dr Charles Burney, and Dr Johnson, and was a sub-preceptor to Prince George (afterwards George III) and his younger brothers. Nevertheless, many people —including Goldsmith—condemned the supplement as worthless. It was re-edited by Abraham Rees (see page 109) in 1778, and again in 1781–86 (reprinted 1788–91). The influence of Chambers's encyclopaedia has been incalculable: Diderot's *Encyclopédie* would undoubtedly have taken a very different shape had it not been for Chambers's example. Abraham Rees's own encyclopaedia was modelled on Chambers's. The publication of the *Encyclopaedia Britannica* was stimulated by the appearance of the *Encyclopédie* . . . and almost every subsequent move in the world of encyclopaedia-making is thus directly traceable to the pioneer example of Chambers's work.

There has always been a tendency for encyclopaedias to exceed the size originally planned for them. Johann Heinrich Zedler (1706–60), a Leipzig bookseller and publisher, originally intended to publish a twelve-volume encyclopaedia: the result was a sixty-four folio volume work, printed in double columns, entitled the *Grosses vollständiges Universal-Lexicon aller Wissenschaften und Künste welche bishero durch menschlichen Verstand und Witz erfunden und verbessert worden* (Halle and Leipzig, 1731–50), to which four supplementary volumes (A–Caq only) were added during the years 1751–54. It is one of the largest encyclopaedias ever completed, and also one of the best. As in so many cases, the encyclopaedia had a chequered career. In spite of good financial support at the beginning, Zedler soon ran into difficulties, and his encyclopaedia only reached eventual completion by way of a lottery and through final co-operation by the whole of the Leipzig book trade. Quite apart from this, Zedler had to face tremendous prejudice among the publishers and booksellers of Leipzig. There were genuine fears that his encyclopaedia would be so comprehensive and up-to-date that no other books would be sold! In fact, the opposition of such powerful publishers as Gleditsch who was responsible for

Conversationslexikon

mit

vorzüglicher Rücksicht

auf

die gegenwärtigen Zeiten.

Erster Theil.

Leipzig,

bei Friedrich August Leupold.

1796.

מי כאלהים בורא כל עולמים
כי הוא נראשה עולם עליון
שם אור נטו שם עוה חביון
נט מלאכים ...וח על כל רמיס

לא יכור־שבט
מיהוד ומחוקק גני

אל רם הכן שמים כורת
הנקראים עולם הגלגלים
שמש עם ירק יורדים עולים
כהס נם ככבו טור שם תפלרת

חלק ראשון
מספר
העולמות או
מעשה טוביה
כולל דארבעה עולמות : ונחלק לחמשה
חלקים : רחלק הראשון מדבר בעולם
העליון שדוא עולם ררוחני : השני בעולם
דאמצעי שדוא עולם הגלגלים : השלישי
בעולם השפל שדוא דעולם שלנו : הרביעי
בעולם הקטן שדוא דאדם : דחמישי בימורי
העולם : ודנו כולל בסר אלפים ידיעות
חקרנ נם וכינ׳ו צעיר הרכבים ותוך
דרופאים טוביה מקק מיץ שנארץ
צרפת יע״א :
נדפס · **בויניציא**
בשנת מעשה טוביה כ״ז לפק

NELLA STAMPARIA
BRAGADINA
Con Licenza de' Superiori.

ונכתב
באנדרינופולי

תחתם סמונות אל ארבע יסודות
עהם מרכב העולם השפל
כי העניון עיקר אך זך תפל
כי כנפלות סות נכפסות

עולם קטן צר אל חד הלס
מרכב מסודות עונים לכ
מזגו שכו קר לח חם נם יבש
סוס נקמד כי דוף כשד ודם

Courtesy Messrs. H. K. Elliott, Ltd.

issuing such encyclopaedic works as those of Hübner and Marperger (see pages 99 and 100 respectively) was such that Zedler thought it wise to issue at least his first volume at Halle, and it was from the university of that city that Zedler obtained the Preface, written by the Chancellor, Johann Peter von Ludewig. The general editorship of the encyclopaedia was undertaken by Johann Christoph Gottsched (the translator of Bayle), and Johann Heinrich Rother, aided by nine specialist editors whose names have unfortunately not survived. From volume 19 onwards, the general editorship was taken over by Karl Günther Ludovici (editor of the *Kaufmanns-Lexikon*, 1753–56).

Zedler's work is still of great importance: for the first time biographies of living people were included; bibliographical citations were given in great detail, and the genealogical information is of exceptional quality. In general there is a high standard of accuracy. What is more is that, in spite of its size, the encyclopaedia was completed and, moreover, finished within a remarkably short time. It is one of the ironies of encyclopaedia history that, owing to his financial difficulties, Zedler never had a complete copy of his own encyclopaedia and, during the compilation of his later volumes, always lacked volumes 13 and 14.

Thomas Birch (1705–66), rector of Ulting in Essex, and a historian, was also secretary of the Royal Society (1752–65). He left a sum of some five hundred pounds to increase the salaries of some of the assistant librarians at the British Museum. His *A general dictionary, historical and critical; in which a new and accurate translation of that of ... M*r* Bayle ... is included, and interspersed with several thousand lives never before published* (10 volumes; London, G. Strahan, 1734–41), was followed by a second edition (5 volumes; London, J. J. & P. Knapton, 1734–38). Most of the 'several thousand lives' were written by Birch himself. At this time John Barrow, an historian of exploration and voyages of discovery, issued his *Dictionarium polygraphicum; or, the whole body of arts regularly digested* (2 volumes; London, 1735), of which a second edition was issued (London, C. Hitch & L. Hawes, 1758). The vogue for lengthy titles was not confined to England: 'Melissantes' [*i.e.*, Johann Gottfried Gregorii, 1685–1770] compiled a one-volume octavo encyclopaedia entitled *Gemüths vergnügendes historisches Handbuch für Bürger und Bauern in Form eines kurtz gefassten historischen Lexici von allerley Ständen, Künsten, Handwercken und Wissenschaften, deren Urhebern und Erfindungen kurtze Nachricht ertheilet wird* (Frankfurt and Leipzig, Johann Jacob Beumelburg, 1744), and Johann Georg Sulzer (1720–79) wrote a *Kurzer Begriff aller Wissenschaften und andern Theile der Gelehrsamkeit, worin jeder nach seinem Innhalt, Nuzen und Vollkomenheit kürzlich beschrieben wird* in 240 pages in 1759, which reached a third edition in 1772.

The naturalized Chevalier Dennis de Coetlogon, M.D., a knight of St Lazare, of whom very little is known, compiled a curious encyclopaedic work *An universal history of arts and sciences* (2 volumes; London, 1745), of which the only remarkable feature is his treatment of knowledge under main headings arranged alphabetically. There are advantages in doing so—in fact, the *Britannica* followed this method to a certain extent in its nineteenth-century editions to great effect—but the Chevalier perhaps overdid it, for no second edition appeared.

The first serious encyclopaedia in Italian was the richly illustrated *Nuovo dizionario, scientifico e curioso, sacro e profano* (12 volumes; Venice, 1746–51), written by Gianfrancisco Pivati (1689–1764), secretary to the Academy of Sciences at Venice. This encyclopaedia avoided the subject of history, unlike that of Jacques Georges de Chauffepié (1702–86)—written Jaques George de Chaufepié on the title-page—which he introduced with: 'L'Accueil qu'on avoit fait au *Dictionnaire Historique et Critique* de Mr Bayle, engagea le Libraire qui l'avoit imprimé, à former le Projet de faire travailler sur le même Plan, peu de tems après la mort du Savant de Rotterdam, afin de former un Supplément. Divers Savans se chargèrent de faire un certain nombre d'Articles, mais ce Projet n'eut pas de suite'. Accordingly Chauffepié issued his *Nouveau dictionnaire historique et critique, pour servir de Supplément ou de continuation au 'Dictionnaire historique'* de Mr Pierre Bayle (4 volumes; Amsterdam, Z. Chatelain, etc.; The Hague, Pierre de Hondt, 1750–56). This was followed by another supplement to the later editions of Bayle by Prosper Marchand (died 1756). It will be remembered that Marchand had himself prepared and much amended the fourth edition of Bayle, issued in 1730 (see page 96). Marchand's *Dictionnaire historique; ou, Mémoires critiques et littéraires, concernant la vie et les ouvrages de divers personnages distingués, particulièrement dans la république des lettres* . . . was issued posthumously in two volumes (The Hague, Pierre de Hondt, 1758–59), the final editorial work being done by Jean Nicolas Sébastien Allamand (died 1787). This supplementary work is chiefly important for its biographical and bibliographical details, particularly—as its title suggests—of literary personalities.

In France, the vogue set sixty years earlier by the Chevalier de Chevigny for pocket-size encyclopaedias and compendia continued unabated with the publication of works such as the duodecimo *Encyclopédie de pensées, de maximes et de réflexions, sur toutes sortes de sujets* . . . *par ordre alphabétique* (Paris, 1761), and by such people as Pons-Augustin Alletz (1703–85) and Augustin Roux (1726–76). Alletz, who had earlier written *L'Agronome; ou, Dictionnaire portatif du cultivateur* (2 volumes; Liège, Bassompierre, 1761), published in 1766 a duodecimo *Petite encyclopédie; ou, les Elémens des connoissances humaines, contenant les notions générales de toutes les sciences et de tous les arts utiles, et des matières qui ont rapport à la société* . . . (Paris, Nyon). Similarly, Roux had compiled a *Dictionnaire domestique portatif* (3 volumes; Paris, Vincent, 1762–64); he now issued a rival two-volume duodecimo *Nouvelle Encyclopédie portatif; ou, Tableau général des connoissances humaines* (Paris, Vincent, 1766). Such works as these, and Jean Baptiste Ladvocat's *Dictionnaire historique-portatif* (Paris, 1752)[1] have of course no importance beyond the fact that the ready market they found demonstrates the demand for easily assimilated knowledge in a handy form, which the publication of *L'Encyclopédie* had served to stimulate.

So far the English provinces had played no part in the publishing of encyclopaedias. There was however a very flourishing publishing business in Coventry in the mid-eighteenth century, and to this is due *The complete dictionary of arts and sciences. In which the whole*

---

[1] Which was translated into German and Spanish editions almost immediately, and—in spite of its being based chiefly on Moréri's work (see page 88)—was reissued as late as 1822!

circle of human learning is explained, and the difficulties attending the acquisition of every art, whether liberal or mechanical, are removed, in the most easy and familiar manner. The theological, philological, and critical branches, by the Rev. Temple Henry Croker . . . The medicinal, anatomical, and chemical, by Thomas Williams . . . The mathematical, by Samuel Clark . . . and the other parts by several gentlemen particularly conversant in the arts or sciences they have undertaken to explain. This curious work was published by John Jones—who reprinted the first edition of Dugdale's *Warwickshire* in 1765—in 150 parts of three sheets each from April 1765. The whole made one large folio volume, dated, on the title-page, 1764–66. Croker (*c.* 1730–*c.* 1790) had a strange career: he was Chaplain to the Earl of Hillsborough, and later engaged in commerce. A bankrupt, he sailed for the West Indies, where he died in obscurity. Croker, in his Preface, wrote: 'It is not, however, our intention to depreciate the works of others in order to recommend our own; but we will venture to promise, that everything valuable in Mr Chambers' Cyclopaedia, and the other works of that kind, particularly the Encyclopédie published at Paris, shall be contained in this dictionary, augmented with the discoveries and improvements made since these works were compiled.' Perhaps the best feature of this book is its 150 copper-plate illustrations; the text is mostly a plagiarization of Ephraim Chambers's.

Johann Georg Krünitz was born in 1728. His encyclopaedia, originally planned as a dictionary of economics and technology, became more and more general and, under his hands and those of his collaborators and successors, one of the largest works of its kind ever issued. The title of the encyclopaedia varies slightly: *Oekonomisch-technologische Enzyklopädie, oder allgemeines System der Staats-, Stadt, Haus- und Landwirtschaft* . . . (242 volumes; Berlin, J. Pauli, 1773–1858), volumes 9 to 12, and 14 to 242, having *technologisch*. Volumes 188–242 were published by E. Litfass. Krünitz was responsible for volumes 1–72. On his death in 1796 he was succeeded by Friedrich Jakob Flörke (1758–99) who saw the next five volumes through the press. His brother Heinrich Gustav Flörke (1764–1835) supervised the preparation of volumes 78–123, and then Johann Wilhelm David Korth took over the editorship until the completion of volume 188. With Carl Otto Hoffmann (1812–60), Korth edited volumes 189–196, 206–220, and 223–225. In addition, with Ludwig Kossarski (1810–73), Korth edited volumes 197–205 and 221–222. But the final volumes 226–242 were edited by Hoffmann. The short articles and the handy size of the octavo volumes made them of use for leisure reading in a way few encyclopaedias ever achieve. The encyclopaedia was reissued at Brünn from 1787 onwards. An abridged edition in 32 volumes, edited by M. C. von Schütz, was issued in Berlin during the years 1786–1809.

Among the posthumous papers of Oliver Goldsmith was discovered the draft prospectus of an encyclopaedia. This was to have been called a *Universal dictionary of arts and sciences*, which Goldsmith intended to publish with the aid of literary friends. Goldsmith planned to include comprehensive specialist articles by Dr Johnson, Burke, Sir Joshua Reynolds, Gibbon, Fox, Adam Smith, Sir William Jones, and Dr Burney. Unfortunately Goldsmith's death in 1774 prevented his implementing a project that was clearly designed to present the public with the British equivalent of the *Encyclopédie*.

Abraham Rees was born in 1743. He was the son of a Welsh independent minister, and himself became a doctor of divinity and a leading Presbyterian minister. In 1778 he re-edited George Lewis Scott's 1753 edition of Ephraim Chambers's *Cyclopaedia* in four volumes of text, and one of plates (London, W. Strahan). He later introduced much new material in a further edition in four folio volumes of text and one of addenda, index and plates (London, J. F. & C. Rivington, 1786–88), which was reissued in 1788–1791. This scholarly work brought him the honour of election as a Fellow to both the Royal Society and the Linnean Society. The need however for a completely new work led him to plan the issue in parts (published regularly) of his *The new cyclopaedia; or, Universal dictionary of arts and sciences . . . biography, geography and history . . .* (London, Longman, Hurst). The first part was issued on 2 January 1802, and the whole undertaking was completed in 44 quarto volumes (each comprising two parts), including four volumes of plates (arranged by subject, alphabetically) and one atlas volume, in August 1820. The encyclopaedia was largely Rees's own work, and was especially strong in new and well-written biographical articles, but the articles on music were written by Dr Charles Burney, and those on botany were mostly written by the founder of the Linnean Society, Sir James Edward Smith (1759–1828). The plates were well engraved, and were practical. Rees died in 1825.

The first German encyclopaedia to be modelled on Diderot's *Encyclopédie* was the *Deutsche Encyklopädie; oder, Allgemeines Real-Wörterbuch aller Künste und Wissenschaften, von einer Gesellschaft Gelehrten* (volumes 1–23, and one volume of plates). This was the work of Heinrich Martin Gottfried Köster and, from volume 18 onwards, Johann Friedrich Roos. It was published by Varrentrapp Sohn & Wenner in Frankfurt-am-Main from 1778 to 1807. Unfortunately it was never completed, reaching only the letter K. Georg Simon Klügel's *Encyklopädie, oder zusammenhängender Vortrag der gemeinnützigsten, insbesondere aus der Betrachtung der Natur und des Menschen gesammelten Kenntnisse* (3 volumes; Berlin, 1782–84), reached a third edition in seven volumes (Berlin and Stettin, F. Nicolai, 1806–17). It is of interest as an example of arrangement on systematic lines:

Volume
1   Natural history
2   Mathematics; chemistry; mineralogy
3   Astronomy; navigation; chronology; physical geography; mechanics; building
4   Navigation; the arts of war; philosophy
5   German language and literature
6, 7   Geography.

Here the emphasis is all on the more practical subjects, and notable omissions are religion, history, and biography.

A vast rearrangement of the contents of Diderot's *Encyclopédie* as a series of separate dictionaries was undertaken by the publishers Panckoucke and Agasse as the *Encyclopédie methodique, ou par ordre de matières, par une Societe de Gens de Lettres, de Savans, et d'Artistes* in

196 quarto volumes (Paris, 1782–1832). It was never completed. The contents are:

	Volumes of text	Volumes of plates
Agriculture	7	
Amusemens des sciences mathématiques et physiques	1	
Antiquités, mythologie, &c.	5	1
Architecture	3	†
Art aratoire et du jardinage	1	1
Art militaire	4	1
Artillerie	1	
Arts académiques: équitation, escrime, danse, &c.	1	1
Arts et métiers mécaniques	8	8
Assemblée nationale	3*	
Beaux-arts	2	1
Botanique	13	4
Tableau encyclopédique et méthodique des trois règnes de la nature. Botanique	3	
Chasse	1	1
Chirurgie	2	1
Chymie, pharmacie et métallurgie	6	1
Commerce	3	
Economie politique et diplomatique	4	
Encyclopédiana	1	
Finances	3	
Forêts et bois	1	
Géographie ancienne	3	
Géographie moderne	3	
Géographie physique	5	
Atlas		1
Atlas: géographie ancienne; géographie du moyen âge; géographie moderne		2
Grammaire et littérature	3	
Histoire	6	1
Histoire naturelle	10	
Tableau encyclopédique et méthodique des trois règnes de la nature	10	
Histoire naturelle des vers	4	3
Jeux mathématiques	1	
Jurisprudence	10	
Logique et métaphysique	4	
Manufactures: arts et métiers	4	1
Marine	3	1

* Of these, only volume 2 was published.
† A volume of plates was planned but not issued.

Mathématiques	3	1
Médecine	13	
Musique	2	
Pêches	1	1
Philosophie ancienne et moderne	3	
Physique	4	1
Système anatomique	4	1
Théologie	3	

Panckoucke's conception was remarkable, but he had much trouble to face: editors were dilatory, the Revolution robbed him of many of his subscribers, and he was heavily committed financially. Nevertheless, the work constitutes a kind of revision of the *Encyclopédie*, and there was even a Spanish translation (10 volumes, and one volume of plates; Madrid, 1806) of some of the volumes.

The new Royal cyclopaedia, and encyclopaedia; or, Complete, modern and universal dictionary of arts and sciences. On an entire new and improved plan . . . The mathematical, nautical, astronomical, and geographical parts, etc., revised by John Bettesworth . . . The historical, chronological, heraldic and antique departments, inspected by Henry Boswell . . . The philosophical, critical . . . and other scientific subjects, revised and corrected by Felix Stonehouse . . . and others (London, Alex. Hogg, 1788) was issued in three folio volumes. It was edited by George Selby Howard, but its bombastic title poorly concealed its extensive plagiarization of Chambers's encyclopaedia.

The literary historian and art critic Johann Joachim Eschenburg (1743–1820), who was a friend of Lessing and had translated the works of Shakespeare into German, wrote a small *Lehrbuch der Wissenschaftskunde: ein Grundriss encyclopädischer Vorlesungen* in 1892. It was systematically arranged on principles proposed by Immanuel Kant, and proved successful. A third edition appeared in 1809 (Berlin and Stettin, F. Nicolai).

The first real Russian encyclopaedia was attempted by the historian V. N. Tatischev. His *Leksikon rossiiskoi istoricheskoi, geographicheskoi, politicheskoi i grazhdanskoi* was planned in six volumes, but only the first three (A–Klyuchnik) were published in St Petersburg in 1793 and then the work was discontinued.

At the turn of the century there were a number of Chinese encyclopaedias. In 1796 Wang Chi compiled his *Shih wu yüan hui* in 40 books, covering well over two thousand topics which were roughly classified. Lu Fêng-tsao's *Hsiao chih lu* (12 volumes) was completed by 1804, and is particularly valuable for its coverage of terms relating to practical matters not hitherto defined in other encyclopaedias. In the same year appeared the *Ching Chuan I I*, compiled by Ch'en Wei in 50 volumes, which concentrates on historical matters and the great classics of the past. The *Ch'i ming chi shu* of Wang Ch'êng-lieh, issued in 1806 in 12 volumes, is stronger in biographical material.

BIBLIOGRAPHY

F. W. Bateson, editor. *The Cambridge bibliography of English literature.* 5 volumes. Cambridge University Press, 1940–1963

D. C. Cabeen, general editor. *A critical bibliography of literature.* Syracuse University Press, 1947 to date

R. S. Crane, and others. *English literature, 1660–1800: a bibliography of modern studies.* Princeton University Press, Oxford University Press, 1950 to date

K. Goedeke. *Grundriss zur Geschichte der deutschen Dichtung aus den Quellen.* 2nd edition. Düsseldorf, Ehlermann, 1884 to date

Georges Grente, editor. *Dictionnaire des lettres françaises.* Paris, Fayard, 1951 to date

J. Körner. *Bibliographisches Handbuch des deutschen Schrifttums.* 3rd edition. Berne, Francke, 1949

O. Klapp, editor. *Bibliographie der französischen Literaturwissenschaft/Bibliographie d'histoire littéraire française.* Frankfurt am Main, Klostermann, 1960 to date

Sir John Edwin Sandys. *A history of classical scholarship.* Volumes II & III. Cambridge University Press, 1908 (reprinted, London & New York, Hafner Publishing Company, 1958)

J. Simón-Diaz. *Bibliografía de la literatura hispánica.* Madrid, Consejo superior de Investigaciones Científicas, Instituto 'Miguel de Cervantes' de Filología Hispánica, 1950 to date

Storia letteraria d'Italia. 3rd edition. Milan, Vallardi, 1942 to date

Chapter IV

DIDEROT AND THE ENCYCLOPÉDISTES

> *Cet ouvrage immense et immortal semble accuser la brièveté de la vie des hommes.*
>
> VOLTAIRE

The Académie des Sciences (now the Institut de France) was founded by the great French statesman Jean Baptiste Colbert. Among the many aspects of French life to which Colbert applied his reforms were the industries and commerce of the country, and it is therefore not surprising that, with his eye for detail of the minutest form, Colbert should direct the Académie[1] in 1675 to compile a 'Traité de méchanique' in which were to be described 'toutes les machines en usage dans la pratique des Arts'. By 1694, some eleven years after Colbert's death, work on the project, under the title *Description et perfection des arts et métiers*, had begun with the preparation of an illustrated book on the art of printing. Although the first volume of the collection did not appear until 1761, the influence of the great undertaking was to have considerable impact on the progress of encyclopaedia-making throughout the eighteenth century, particularly in the field of illustrations, though the early recommendation of the need to pay attention to practical matters was of almost equal importance.

It was Colbert's secretary, the author Charles Perrault (1628– 1703) who, through his poem on the *Siècle de Louis le Grand* (1687) and his *Parallèle des anciens et des modernes* (4 volumes; 1688–96), gave rise to the famous controversy of the ancients and the moderns which raged throughout France and Britain, and inevitably to the idea of progress which dominated the end of the seventeenth century and found its finest expression in Condorcet's

---

[1] Just as Cardinal Richelieu had founded the Académie Française in 1635, and had seen to it that the newly formed body should include in its first tasks the duty of preparing a dictionary of the French language.

Esquisse d'un tableau historique des progrès de l'esprit humain, published posthumously nearly one hundred years later.

Thus, while the anglomania in France which had eagerly welcomed the works of Bacon, Hobbes, Locke and Newton, and had admired the pioneer efforts in encyclopaedia-making of Ephraim Chambers and John Harris, undoubtedly prompted the founders of the *Encyclopédie* to undertake their great task, their true inspiration was nevertheless essentially French. Corneille had published his *Dictionnaire des arts et des sciences* in 1694, Bayle's *Dictionnaire historique et critique* had appeared in 1697, and Chomel's *Dictionnaire oeconomique* in 1709, while behind them stood the early attempts of Jean Macé and of Saunier. Not one of these predecessors had exceeded two volumes for their works, so that the Encyclopédistes' eventual achievement of a 35-volume encyclopaedia is phenomenal and remains one of the most important advances in the history of recording the state of knowledge at any one time.

By 1704 the Académie des Sciences had made some progress with the preparation of the first volume of their encyclopaedic work, the *Description et perfection des arts et métiers*. This was Jaugeon's *Des arts de construire les caractères, de graver les poinçons des lettres, de fondre les lettres, d'imprimer les lettres et de relier les livres*, but even so it remained incomplete and unpublished for more than another fifty years. It was in this year that the Jesuits first issued their:

> *Dictionnaire universel françois et latin contenant la signification et la définition tant des mots de l'une et de l'autre langue . . . que des termes propres de chaque état et de chaque profession . . . l'explication de tout ce que renferment les sciences et les arts.* Trévoux (Ain), 1704

which, from its place of publication, soon became known as the *Dictionnaire de Trévoux*. Among the principal contributors were the Fathers Buffier, Bougeant, Castel, Ducerceau and Tournemine. The authority and scholarship of the work was thus evident, and further editions followed in 1721, 1732, 1740, 1743, 1752, and the seventh and last in 1771 (the Jesuits were expelled from France in 1767). This was the encyclopaedia that the Jesuits, not without justification, accused the Encyclopédistes of pillaging without acknowledgment, though they themselves had of course drawn heavily on Antoine Furetière's *Dictionnaire universel*.

About 1708, the famous scientist René Antoine Ferchault de Réaumur (1683–1757), who had been elected to the Académie des Sciences in that year, was made responsible for supervising work on the Académie's *Description et perfection des arts et métiers*, a task to which he was to devote some of his time over a very long period, and which in the end was to bring him into conflict with the Encyclopédistes.

In 1709 Noël Chomel (1632–1712) published the first edition of his *Dictionnaire oeconomique, contenant divers moïens d'augmenter son bien et de conserver sa santé* (Lyons, 1709) in two volumes, from which the Encyclopédistes were also accused of borrowing. The truth is that new encyclopaedias are always built on the structure of their fore-runners, and thus reflect the process of the accretion of knowledge itself.

Denis Diderot was born at Langres on 5th October 1713, son of the cutler Didier Diderot. In November 1717, Jean le Rond, known as d'Alembert, son of Louis Camus, Chevalier des Touches, Lieutenant-General of Artillery, and of Madame de Tencin, was born. His name was acquired through his abandonment on 16th November 1717 on the steps of the church of St Jean-le-Rond in Paris. These two Frenchmen were to have a profound effect on the subsequent history of encyclopaedias throughout the world.

John Harris's *Lexicon technologicum* had first been published in London in 1704. In 1728 it was followed by the issue of Ephraim Chambers's *Cyclopaedia*, and in 1731 by Fontenelle's revision of Corneille's *Le dictionnaire des arts et des sciences* (Paris, J.-B. Coignard, 1731). On 21st March 1737, Andrew Michael Ramsay, known as the Chevalier de Ramsay (1686–1743), proposed to his brother Freemasons a project for requesting suitable Freemasons in France to compile a 'dictionnaire universel des arts libéraux et de toutes les sciences utiles, la théologie et la politique seules exceptées', and on 24th June 1740 Louis, duc d'Antin (1707–43), Grand Master of the Freemasons in France, put forward the same suggestion in almost the same words. This early interest of the Freemasons in the idea of a great encyclopaedia is particularly significant since it may have been the spark which set off the whole scheme initiated by Le Breton.

André-François Le Breton (1708–79), a Parisian printer, had been Venerable Master since 1729 (at the age of 21!) of the first Orangist Lodge of France. As Le Breton continued to hold this post for at least thirty-six years, it may safely be assumed that he was fully aware of the Freemasons' wish for the preparation of a comprehensive encyclopaedia, though his own product failed to take account of the Scottish Ramsay's wise exceptions, an omission that brought him both much trouble and much profit.

Le Breton's early wealth and position came principally from the *Almanach* or *Calendrier* which had been founded in 1684 by his maternal grandfather Louis d'Houry. In 1700 this publication became the *Almanach royal* and continued to be published by d'Houry until his death in 1725 and was carried on by his widow until 1746, when Le Breton's name appears with hers on the title-page. Le Breton's name appeared there alone from 1751 until his death in 1779. Le Breton was officially recognized as a bookseller in 1733, and was appointed Printer to the King in 1740 but did not perform this function until 1746, a post which he held—throughout many difficulties with the law—until his death.

The year 1740 was also significant for the publication of one of the early ingredients of the *Encyclopédie*, the third edition of Thomas Dyche's *A new general English dictionary . . . begun by the late Rev. Mr Thomas Dyche, and now finished by William Pardon* (London, R. Ware, 1740). By 1742 Diderot was 30 and had just undertaken his first effort in translation from the English, a rendering of Temple Stanyan's revised edition of his *History of Greece* (London, 1739), which Briasson published in three volumes in Paris in 1743. On 6th November of that year Diderot clandestinely married Anne-Antoinette Champion at the church of St Pierre-aux-Boeufs in Paris.

The fifth revision of Chambers's *Cyclopaedia* had been published in London in the previous year, and in March 1745 Le Breton, having obtained the necessary licence (without which no publication could legitimately, or safely be undertaken) completed a contract with the English bank clerk John Mills for a French translation of Chambers's *Cyclopaedia*—a project which soon proved abortive. John Mills was to be associated in this work with a German professional translator, Godefroy Sellius, and their task was to provide four volumes of text and one of plates. In May 1745, Le Breton issued a prospectus for this work:

> *Encyclopédie, ou Dictionnaire universal des arts et des sciences, contenant l'explication des termes et des matières comprises sous ce titre, soit dans les sciences divines et humaines, soit dans les arts libéraux et méchaniques. La description des formes, des espèces, des propriétés, des productions, des préparations, & des usages des choses naturelles et artificielles; l'origine, le progrés, et l'état actuel des affaires ecclésiastiques, civiles, militaires, et du commerce; les différens systèmes, sectes, opinions, &c. des théologiens, philosophes, mathématiciens, médecins, antiquaires, critiques, &c. Ouvrage propre à servir d'un cours d'étude des anciens & des modernes; extrait des meilleurs auteurs, dictionnaires, journaux, mémoires, transactions, ephémérides, & autres Oeuvres publiées en différentes langues: traduit de l'anglois d'Ephraïm Chambers, membre de la Société royale de Londres. Cinq vol. in-fol. avec fig. en taille-douce, proposés par souscription.* Paris, Le Breton, 1745.

In general this prospectus was received favourably by the public—even by the Jesuits who, at that time, saw no danger in this enterprise—but by the summer quarrels had broken out between Le Breton and Mills, and on 28th August Le Breton's licence was revoked, this being closely followed by the annulment of the contract with Mills. Le Breton now had to apply for a new licence, and in doing so he took the opportunity to include John Harris's dictionary among his sources, and he finally obtained the necessary permission on 31st January 1746.

In the meantime, on 18th October 1745, Le Breton had signed an agreement with three other Parisian booksellers—Claude Briasson (Diderot's first publisher), Michel-Antoine David l'aîné, and Laurent Durand—for the joint production of the new encyclopaedia, Le Breton retaining a fifty per cent interest in the project throughout his life. It was these three associates who were beginning the publication of the translation of Robert James's *Medical dictionary* (3 volumes; London, 1743–45), the translators of which included the young Diderot. But a more important indication of Diderot's true leanings was the publication in that year of his rather free translation of Shaftesbury's *Inquiry concerning virtue and merit* under the title of *Principes de la philosophie morale, ou Essai de M. S*** sur le mérite et la vertu avec réflexions* (Amsterdam, Z. Chatelain, 1745).

During the Easter week-end of 1746 Diderot wrote his *Pensées philosophiques* which was published anonymously in The Hague almost immediately afterwards and was officially condemned by the French parliament (on 7th July 1746) to be burnt as 'scandalous, and contrary to religion and good taste'. In this eventful year, on 27th June, the associates appointed not Diderot but the Abbé Jean-Paul de Gua de Malves (1713–88), member of the Académie des Sciences and Professor of Philosophy at the Collège de France and an expert on the philosophy of Descartes, to take charge of the general editing of the *Encyclopédie*. Both Diderot and d'Alembert signed as witnesses to the contract, and both were associated with the Abbé in this work either then or shortly after.

But again the wrong editor had been chosen: the learned Abbé had not the temperament for the work and on 3rd August 1747 he resigned. In spite of the fact that Diderot's parish priest, the Curé of St Médard, Hardy de Levaré, had denounced Diderot to the police on 22nd June of that year for his authorship of the *Pensées philosophiques*,[1] Diderot, with d'Alembert, was appointed to succeed the Abbé in the general editorship on 16th October. Diderot was, of course, already well known to the associates for his abilities in translation, and d'Alembert (now 30) was already a well-known mathematician and a member (since 1741) of the Académie des Sciences. Both, moreover, had already demonstrated something of their editorial abilities while working under the Abbé's direction.

In 1748 Le Breton secured another licence for his project in which he included not only Chambers's and Harris's works as

---

[1] Anonymity was only relative in those days: Durand, the bookseller, for instance, knew of Diderot's authorship of this and others of Diderot's work since Diderot brought him copies for sale as soon as they came off the press!

sources, but also Dyche's dictionary as well. This was the year of the publication of Montesquieu's *De l'esprit des loix* (2 volumes; Geneva, 1748), whose influence and that of its author were to be felt throughout the long years of the issue of the *Encyclopédie*.

In his denunciation, the Curé of St Médard had said that he understood Diderot was writing a still more dangerous work against religion. Although Diderot published his *Mémoires sur différens sujets de mathématiques* (Paris, Durand & Pissot, 1748) and a licentious romance *Les bijoux indiscrets* (2 volumes; 'Au Monomotapa', 1748), and had a hand in Madame de Puisieux' questionnable *Conseils à une amie* (Paris(?), 1749) which was denounced by the police, it is most probable that the Curé was referring to Diderot's *Lettre sur les aveugles à l'usage de ceux qui voyent*, which was published anonymously in London in 1749. Diderot had been inspired to write this work by the success of the first operations on people who had been born blind, and by the case of the blind Cambridge Professor of Mathematics, Nicholas Saunderson (1682–1739), who denied the existence of God even on his death-bed.

The French police acted quickly on the complaint of an influential woman in Court circles and Diderot's papers were seized, and he himself arrested, subjected to detailed questioning, and imprisoned in the dungeons of Vincennes on 24th July. There he remained until 3rd November, though the conditions of his incarceration were gradually relaxed so that by the 21st August he had the run of the entire prison, on his signing an undertaking not to attempt to escape. It was here that he wrote his observations on the first volume of Buffon and Daubenton's *Histoire naturelle* which had been published that year.

Diderot's imprisonment was a great setback to the associates, and they immediately wrote to the Chancellor, the Comte d'Argenson, requesting the release of Diderot, 'a man of letters, and of recognized merit and probity who alone possesses the key' to the whole enterprise of the *Encyclopédie* in which they had already invested some eighty thousand livres. They stated that unless he were freed immediately they would face ruin. This they followed up with a letter on 28th July to Nicolas René Berryer, Lieutenant-General of Police, asking him, through his love of learning, to use his influence to get Diderot out of custody. Accordingly, Berryer interrogated Diderot on 1st August, when Diderot denied having written the *Pensées philosophiques*, the *Lettre sur les aveugles*, and several licentious works whose authorship the police were investigating. Diderot's denial was foolish, for the next day Berryer went to see Durand who freely admitted Diderot's implication in the case of at least three of these works.

Diderot was stubborn, and in a long letter of 10th August to Berryer, he continued to deny everything and to protest his intellectual probity. On the same day he wrote to the Chancellor in similar terms. All this was to no avail, and three days later Diderot wrote to Berryer confessing his authorship of the *Pensées philosophiques*, the *Bijoux indiscrets*, and the *Lettre sur les aveugles*. To this he probably owed his greater freedom at Vincennes during his last few weeks there.

When Diderot was released he set to work on the *Encyclopédie* with enthusiasm and vigour and, with some hint of the impatience of modern publishers, issued in October 1750 a prospectus which he had dated 1751. This new prospectus announced a very different kind of work from the one which Le Breton had first envisaged and offered to his subscribers. Its title-page ran:

> *Encyclopédie, ou Dictionnaire raisonné des sciences, des arts et des métiers recueilli des meilleurs auteurs et particulièrement des dictionnaires anglois de Chambers, d'Harris, de Dyche, &c., par une société de gens de lettres. Mis en ordre et publié par M. Diderot, et quant à la partie mathématique, par M. d'Alembert, . . . Dix volumes in-folio, dont deux de planches en taille-douce, proposés par souscription.* Paris, Briasson, David l'aîné, Le Breton et Durand, 1751.

The nine-page folio prospectus was enthusiastic in tone and pointed out that all existing encyclopaedias were already out of date. The subscription list was to close on 1st May 1751. Subscribers were asked to send 60 livres with their application, and warned that a further 36 livres were to be paid on the receipt of the first volume. The cost of the whole work was set at 280 livres. The first volume was promised for June 1751, and the encyclopaedia was to be completed by December 1754.

A table, 'Système figuré des connoissances humaines', is referred to by d'Alembert in his 'Discours préliminaire' in the first volume of the *Encyclopédie*, in which he discusses the composition of human understanding, and this formed the basis of the planning of the encyclopaedia's contents. The whole concept of the *Encyclopédie* had changed under Diderot's hand. It was no longer to be a mere commercial translation of two or three English works, adapted in some haphazard fashion to French tastes. It was now a philosophical undertaking on a scale which had never before been attempted, and to which the best writers and thinkers in Europe were being invited to contribute. Mills's and Sellius's translations were retained and adapted, but the vast content of the encyclopaedia was new work of a high standard.

The first volume was in fact published on 1st July 1751, and d'Alembert's 'Discours préliminaire' was greeted with delight. It is convenient here to give a complete conspectus of the final publication:

Encyclopédie, ou Dictionnaire raisonné des sciences, des arts et des métiers, par une société de gens de lettres. Mis en ordre et publié par M. Diderot, de l'Académie royale des sciences et des belles-lettres de Prusse; et, quant à la partie mathématique, par M. d'Alembert, de l'Académie royale des sciences de Paris, de celle de Prusse, et de la Société royale de Londres. Paris, Briasson, David l'aîné, Le Breton, Durand, 1751–57.

N.B. This title-page was used for the first seven volumes, covering the letters A to G inclusive. The remaining volumes, which were printed and published (in one set) in Paris, bore the following title, with its misleading imprint:

Encyclopédie, ou Dictionnaeir raisonné des sciences, des arts et des métiers, par une société de gens de lettres. Mis en ordre et publié par Mr^{xxx} . . . Neufchastel, S. Faulche & Cie, 1765.

N.B. The last ten volumes (VIII–XVII) bore this title, and covered the letters H to Z, with a supplement of 'articles omis' at the end of the seventeenth volume.

Recueil de planches sur les sciences, les arts libéraux et les arts méchaniques, avec leur explication. Paris, Briasson, David, Le Breton, Durand, 1762–72.

N.B. This formed a set of eleven folio volumes, each comprising at least two hundred plates (with explanatory text), and in one case (the tenth volume) some 337—in all 2,885 plates!

Nouveau dictionnaire pour servir de supplément aux dictionnaires des sciences, des arts et des métiers, par une société de gens de lettres. Mis en ordre et publié par M.ˣˣˣ . . . Paris, Panckoucke, Stoupe, Brunet; Amsterdam, M. M. Rey, 1776–77.

N.B. This supplement comprised four folio volumes, the contents being arranged in alphabetical order as in the main work and the volumes of plates.

Suite de recueil de planches sur les sciences, les arts libéraux et les arts méchaniques, avec leur explication . . . Paris, Panckoucke, Stoupe, Brunet; Amsterdam, M. M. Rey, 1777.

N.B. A one-volume work, comprising 244 folio plates and explanatory text, arranged in alphabetical order of subject.

Table analytique et raisonnée des matières contenues dans les XXXIII volumes in-folio du Dictionnaire des sciences, des arts et des métiers et dans son supplément. Paris, Panckoucke; Amsterdam, M. M. Rey, 1780.

N.B. A two-volume index to the whole contents of the encyclopaedia and its supplements, including the volumes of plates (given at the end of the second volume).

Thus, the sum total of the *Encyclopédie* is:

Main work:	Text	17 volumes
	Plates	11 volumes
Supplement:	Text	4 volumes
	Plates	1 volume
Index		2 volumes

in all, 35 folio volumes, the largest encyclopaedia ever achieved at that time in Europe, and still one of the larger reference works in its own class.

Towards the end of the year, Voltaire hailed the publication of the first volume in the words which head this chapter, in his *Siècle de Louis XIV*. The volume, which covered the letter 'A', included a dedicatory letter to the Comte d'Argenson, then Minister for War, and an allegorical frontispiece designed by C.-N. Cochin *le fils* and engraved by B.-L. Prévost, as well as a commentary on Bacon's classification of the sciences—Diderot had paid a handsome tribute to Bacon's conception of the divisions of human knowledge in the text of his prospectus. By the time the first volume was issued, two thousand people had entered their names as subscribers, and this number had doubled by the time the final ten volumes were published.

On 18th November 1751, the Abbé Jean-Martin de Prades, a priest at Montauban and one of Diderot's contributors, submitted his thesis for a doctorate in theology at the Sorbonne, where he vigorously and successfully defended his ideas. Nevertheless, the following year the same Faculty condemned his thesis, and this action was supported on 29th January 1752 by Christophe de Beaumont, Archbishop of Paris, and on 23rd February by Michel Verthamon de Chavagnac, Bishop of Montauban. This was the beginning of a long and bitter theological controversy which did much to compromise the *Encyclopédie* and partly contributed to the order of the Council of State of 7th February 1752 suppressing the first two volumes (volume 2, which had been dated 1751, actually appeared early in 1752), and unsuccessfully ordering all manuscript material to be seized.

But de Prades was not the only cause of the withdrawal of the first volumes of the *Encyclopédie* from the bookshops. Father Guillaume-François Berthier (1704–82), a Jesuit and editor of the *Mémoires de Trévoux* from 1745 to 1762, began the attack on the *Encyclopédie* as soon as the second prospectus appeared by severely criticizing Diderot's scheme of classification for the arts and sciences. Diderot took up the cudgels without delay, and the controversy continued in the *Mémoires*, the publication of the first volume of the *Encyclopédie* increasing the weight of the attacks, since the additional charge of plagiarism was now added. The Encyclopédistes were particularly accused of pillaging the *Diction-*

naire de Trévoux; the latter was in any case bound to suffer in its sales from the appearance cf this new and revolutionary encyclopaedia which was so much more in keeping with the sceptical tastes and the more scientific outlook of the age.

Powerful though the Church was, it did not carry the full sympathy of the Court and, by early May, some of the Ministers and Madame de Pompadour (who had her own private war to wage with the Jesuits) were begging Diderot and d'Alembert to renew their work on the *Encyclopédie*, an encouragement which was so effective that the third volume appeared in November 1753, just after the birth (2nd September) of Diderot's daughter Marie-Angélique (the two previous children having died at an early age). The next four volumes were issued without difficulty at the rate of one a year and reached the end of the letter 'G'. The independent attitude of the Court is reflected in La Tour's portrait of Madame de Pompadour, exhibited at the Salon of 1755, in which she is depicted with both Montesquieu's *Esprit des loix* and volume IV of the *Encyclopédie* plainly shown in the background. This in spite of the new and powerful attacks of Elie-Catherine Fréron who, from the publication of the first issue of his *L'Année littéraire* in 1754 until his death on 10th March 1776, remained an inveterate enemy of the Encyclopédistes and condemned their work constantly in his journal. In this he did not secure full clerical support, and it is evident that free-thinking was not entirely confined to the laity. But official censorship continued, not always to Diderot's detriment: Malesherbes, Director of Publications, suppressed the Jesuit Abbé Mallet's ten-page tendentious article 'Constitution' contributed to volume IV (1754) and substituted Voltaire's relatively unbiased account of the controversy over the Papal bull *Unigenitus* of 1713.

Montesquieu died on 10th February 1755, and in September the fifth volume included an 'Eloge' of the great philosopher by d'Alembert. The encyclopaedia was held in general esteem and was selling well, but in the following year an attack came from a new quarter. The great scientist Réaumur had, it will be remembered, been entrusted many years previously by his colleagues in the Académie des Sciences with the supervision of the preparation and publication of the plates for the Académie's long-promised *Descriptions des arts et métiers*. Just before his death, Réaumur wrote on 23rd February 1756 to Johann Heinrich Samuel Formey (1711–1797), Perpetual Secretary of the Prussian Academy at Berlin, complaining that he had already had some 150 plates engraved and that some of the engravers had betrayed him, with the result that the plates in the *Encyclopédie* would benefit greatly. The scandal which gradually developed over this unfortunate affair throughout the world of learning grew with the years, and even the Académie's eventual exoneration of the Encyclopédistes failed to heal the scars completely.

The attempt of Robert-François Damiens (1715–57) on the life of the king, Louis XV, on 5th January 1757, gave the Encyclopédistes their chance of some slight revenge on their attackers: although Damiens had performed only menial duties as a young man in the Jesuits' College at Paris, and had been dismissed by them at that time, the Encyclopédistes accused the Jesuits in their eighth volume almost of collusion in the conspiracy.

The official tolerance earned by the high quality of the early volumes of the *Encyclopédie* came suddenly to an end with the issue of the seventh volume in November 1757. In this volume d'Alembert had contributed the article on Geneva, and in this he ironically described the ministers of that city as Socinians and praised them for their beliefs. This naturally aroused the anger of Geneva's Calvinist clergy, and they protested strongly. The learned world took sides in what soon became an international dispute of the greatest feeling; Jean-Jacques Rousseau (who had written the articles[1] on various aspects of music) withdrew his support and broke with the Encyclopédistes. Nor did the publication of Claude-Adrian Helvétius's (1715–71) controversial *De l'esprit* in 1758 help the cause of the *Encyclopédie*. Although Helvétius was not one of its contributors, the general public believed that he was by the very nature and tone of his writings and identified him with the Encyclopédistes who thus shared in

---

[1] They were hastily written and earned scathing criticism from such people as Rameau. Eventually they were revised and incorporated in Rousseau's *Dictionnaire de Musique* (1768).

the storm which his book had aroused. Helvétius's book was suppressed by the Council of State on 10th August 1758, condemned by the Archbishop of Paris on 22nd November, and by the Pope, Clement XIII, on 31st January 1759. On 23rd January 1759 it was certainly no coincidence that the *Encyclopédie* was condemned by Parliament, but a further edict prescribed that it should be allowed to survive, owing to the considerable sums of money involved and its evident usefulness, with the proviso that the seven volumes already published should be thoroughly revised by a body of theologians, lawyers, and other learned people. This tolerance was not extended to Diderot's *Etrennes des esprits forts* (a revision of his *Pensées philosophiques*) or to Helvétius's *De l'esprit*, both of which were condemned by the same edict to be torn up and burnt by the public executioner. It is possible that the leniency towards the *Encyclopédie* may have been secured by the 'Mémoire' submitted by the associates in 1758 pointing out the losses everyone would suffer by the suppression of the great work. Nevertheless, on 21st July 1759, the Council of State ordered them to return a balance of 72 livres to each of the subscribers, a clear warning that no further volumes were to be issued.

In spite of the setback the *Encyclopédie* was experiencing in France, a second edition began publication in Italy:

> *Encyclopédie, ou Dictionnaire raisonné des sciences, des arts et des métiers . . . publié par M. Diderot, . . . et . . . par M. d'Alembert . . ., 2e édition . . . par M. Octavien Diodati, . . .* Lucca, Imprimerie de V. Giunti, 1758–71

a 28 folio-volume edition which was followed by a third edition, to which many notes had been added, and which was published at Livorno (Leghorn) in 33 volumes from 1770 to 1779.

Diderot's father died in 1759, and there was some difficulty over the distribution of his father's possessions between the three children which interfered with his work to a certain extent. On 7th March the Council of State put an interdict on further volumes of the *Encyclopédie*, and on 3rd September Pope Clement XIII condemned the *Encyclopédie* as a whole probably, as Diderot believed, because of the publication of the second edition in

Tuscany. Nevertheless, Le Breton on 8th September had been granted a licence to publish four folio volumes of plates to illustrate the volumes of the *Encyclopédie* already published. And Madame Marie-Thérèse Geoffrin (1699–1777) gave one hundred thousand écus towards the (secret) printing of the *Encyclopédie* as well as encouraging Diderot, and refurnishing his house—even though she would not receive him in her salon owing to his vulgarity and ignorance of good manners.

But probably the greatest stroke of good fortune for the Encyclopédistes was the retirement of Berryer and his succession on 1st December 1759 by Antoine-Raymond de Sartine (1729–1801) as Lieutenant-General of Police. Sartine was a friend of Diderot's and gave him the protection he needed to complete the printing of the *Encyclopédie* in secret in Paris itself. And on 19th December the Académie des Sciences published their report on the question of the plates, which Réaumur had raised, in which they cleared the editors of any personal wrong-dealing in this matter. There was, however, no doubt that the *Encyclopédie*'s engravers had seen and profited from many of the plates prepared for the Académie's *Descriptions des arts et métiers*. The first volume of the *Descriptions des arts et métiers faites ou approvées par MM. de l'Académie royale des sciences* was published by Desaint & Saillant of Paris in 1761, and comprised a description by Duhamel du Monceau of 'L'Art du charbonnier', a work which had been in preparation for over eighty-five years, while the plate which illustrated it had been engraved in 1717!

One of the most prolific contributors to the *Encyclopédie* was the Chevalier Louis de Jaucourt (1704–79), sometimes known by his pseudonym of 'Louis de Neufville'. Recruited to Diderot's team about 1751, Jaucourt, aided by about half-a-dozen secretaries, contributed according to Voltaire about three-quarters of the articles in the *Encyclopédie*. Indeed, Jaucourt spent so much of his own money on the task to which he had devoted his life that in 1761 he was forced to sell his house in Paris. Ironically enough, it was bought for 18,000 livres by Le Breton who, by this time, had amassed a fortune from the sales of the *Almanach royal* and the *Encyclopédie*.

In 1762 the first volume of the plates (with accompanying text) of the *Encyclopédie* was published:

Recueil de planches sur les sciences, les arts libéraux et les arts méch-aniques, avec leur explication. Paris, Briasson, David, Le Breton, Durand, 1762–72.

The contents of the eleven folio volumes were arranged in alphabetical order of subject: 'Agriculteur; Aguillier; Amidon-nier'; etc., and were of great beauty and clarity. It had been Diderot's habit to familiarize himself with every technical process of the industries he described, even to the extent of being able to perform the techniques himself, and as a result the plates and the text provided practical detail in a form and approach that had never before been achieved. In all the engravings comprised almost three thousand plates, the last volume being supplementary to the rest.

In the same year Frederick II invited the Encyclopédistes to Prussia to complete their work in peace and freedom, and about the same time Catherine II gave them a similar invitation to find their home in Russia. But in September printing of the *Encyclopédie* was secretly resumed in Paris—though how secretly, in view of the fact that some fifty workmen were employed on the task, is some-what doubtful—under the encouragement of Diderot's sym-pathizers, and he decided to stay on in France and complete the work. In any case, Diderot's most formidable enemies, the Jesuits, had been condemned by Parliament on 6th August, and their ability to harm him had vanished in a fashion which both astonished and delighted him until he realized that the same ignorance and prejudice that had banished the Jesuits could also destroy him and his undertaking.

Madame de Pompadour who, by the advice of the Abbé de Bernis, had done so much to encourage the Encyclopédistes, died on 15th April 1764, and in November Diderot received a second and more devastating blow—the discovery that Le Breton had for years been secretly censoring his copy. The procedure with regard to the manuscript of the *Encyclopédie* made this very easy. When Diderot had passed the text it was sent to the printer (in the case

K

of outside contributors, they very often sent their manuscript direct to the printers and Diderot's first glimpse of what they had written was in the galley-proofs). The printer set the text up in type and sent the galley-proofs to Diderot who corrected them meticulously. When the galleys were returned to the printer the chief proof-reader, under secret instructions from Le Breton, read through the text and marked 'doubtful' passages for Le Breton's attention. These passages were any which in the proof-reader's opinion laid the publisher open to action on the score of libel, blasphemy, treason, etc., a risk which no printer or publisher of those sensitive days would willingly undergo. As Diderot never saw his manuscript again, nor the final text until it was printed, this process had been going on for some time before he noticed it, although in fact there were very few articles apart from his own and Jaucourt's which were subjected to this unofficial but no less efficient censorship. In fact, it was only when Diderot inspected his favourite article on the 'Sarrasins' in volume XIV that he realized that the vague suspicions he had had some time previously were fully justified, and that some of the passages by which he set particular store had vanished. Diderot's fury and despair were such that he decided to abandon the work on which he had spent so much of his life; as the manuscript had been destroyed he was unable to check the degree of censorship, imagined that it had been imposed to the same extent on everyone's contributions, and that when the contributors came to recognize the mutilation of their articles the reputation of the *Encyclopédie* would be ruined. In fact the damage was neither as extensive nor as harmful as he had thought, though the truth had to wait for discovery for nearly two hundred years, when it was at last made plain in Douglas H. Gordon and Norman L. Torrey's *The censoring of Diderot's Encyclopédie and the re-established text* (New York, Columbia University Press, 1947). Readers are referred to that fascinating volume for a full account of the discovery and identification in 1933 of the original proof-sheets (which had always been thought to have been destroyed by Le Breton), with Diderot's markings, the proof-reader's warning signs, and Le Breton's elisions, carefully bound up and secreted by Le Breton himself against the time when he might have publicly to justify his actions. At the time, Le Breton produced no evidence, withstood the storm and Diderot's reproaches, and kept his own counsel. It is significant that even at the time of Luneau de Boisjermain's complaint years later, Le Breton still did not produce these conclusive pieces of evidence that he was on the side of law and order. Although Le Breton has always been reviled for his perfidy in this matter from that day to this, an examination of the proof-sheets leads the reader to a kindlier opinion of the publisher. Diderot was incorrigible in his attacks on the established order of things in France, and one is reminded of the extreme care with which Beardsley's publishers examined all his drawings before having them printed, knowing full well that that unscrupulous genius would slip in some indecency if there were the slightest let-up in their surveillance.

Eventually Briasson managed to persuade Diderot to complete his work on the *Encyclopédie*, for there remained only three more volumes to be seen through the press. When Le Breton first embarked on the enterprise, his original idea had been to issue the whole encyclopaedia complete at one time. Though this had been found to be impracticable, the last ten volumes were—to avoid endless acts of oppression and suppression—issued, with a false imprint, in 1765:

> *Encyclopédie, ou Dictionnaire raisonné des sciences, des arts et des métiers, par une société de gens de lettres. Mis en ordre et publie par Mr^xxx* . . . Neufchastel, S. Faulche & Cie, 1765

and comprised the letters H to Z, and a supplementary section in the last volume. The whole work had been completed on 12th December 1765, and Diderot had achieved the final success of a project on which he had been engaged for nearly twenty years. He had finished one of the greatest literary enterprises in the whole history of mankind, he had revolutionized the concept of the encyclopaedia in the world of learning and, though he may not have intended it, he had contributed very substantially by his work to the French Revolution itself.

Earlier in the year Diderot had sold his library (to be sent after his death) to Catherine II of Russia, and many years later (1773–1774) he made a journey to Russia to thank her for her generosity —which had enabled him to provide for his family—and to spend a winter at her Court. Though Diderot never forgave Le Breton for his censorship, he consented to undertake the supervision through the press of the remainder of the volumes of the plates, which continued to appear until 1772. The Académie's *Descriptions des arts et métiers*, though its publication started a little earlier, was not completed until 1788.

Le Breton's caution was not unfounded: on 23rd April 1766 Le Breton was sent to the Bastille for having sold sets of the last ten volumes of the *Encyclopédie* in France and even for sending a set to the Court at Versailles! The government's inspector of publishing said in a postscript to a letter to Sartine that this was essential if the clergy were to be mollified at their next meeting (and therefore vote their valued annual financial contribution to the State). On 30th April Le Breton was released. Nevertheless, the danger was still great, and Voltaire persuaded Frederick II to invite the Encyclopédistes to Clèves, but Diderot stayed quietly on in Paris supervising the publication of the volumes of plates, while d'Alembert had long since retired from active work on the *Encyclopédie*. The part played by the remainder of the 160-odd contributors was certainly not apparent, since articles in the last ten volumes were mostly unsigned. (In 1767 Panckoucke published a 30-volume *Grand Vocabulaire français* which was really a digest from the *Encyclopédie*.)

A most curious affair began in 1768: a certain Pierre-Joseph-François Luneau de Boisjermain brought an action against Briasson and Le Breton for failing to keep faith with their subscribers—to wit, that they had produced a 26-volume encyclopaedia instead of the promised 10-volume work, and that they had charged 850 livres for the complete work instead of the original subscription price of 280 livres. In 1771 the associates had to send to the Procurer-General all the relevant documents, and these were kept by him until 1778 when the case was finally settled in the associates' favour.

The year of the commencement of the action an anthology from

the *Encyclopédie* was made by the Abbé Joseph de La Porte
(1713-79):

> *L'Esprit de l'Encyclopédie, ou Choix des articles les plus curieux, les plus*
> *agréables, les plus piquans, les plus philosophiques de ce grand diction-*
> *naire.* Geneva and Paris, Vincent, 1768.

This was a popular little collection in five duodecimo volumes
which continued to be revised and republished until 1822.
Similarly, in London appeared a *Histoire générale des dogmes et*
opinions philosophiques, depuis les plus anciens temps jusqu'à nos jours;
tirée du Dictionnaire encyclopédique des arts et des sciences in 1769, a
three-volume octavo collection, mostly comprising articles written
by Diderot in the *Encyclopédie*.

The third edition of the *Encyclopédie*, with the addition of some
material, was published at Leghorn in 33 folio volumes from 1770
to 1779; and at Yverdon another edition started publication:

> *Encyclopédie, ou Dictionnaire universal raisonné des connoissances*
> *humaines, mis en ordre par M. de Felice.* Yverdon, 1770-80

a 58-volume edition (the last ten volumes comprising plates) in
quarto, the editor being Fortunato Bartholomeo de Felice, an
Italian monk, who had made an unauthorized revision of the text
(and who was also editor of the *Dictionnaire géographique, historique*
et politique de la Suisse (2 volumes; Neufchâtel, 1775)).

The next year Briasson applied for and obtained permission to
print the plates in the last three volumes (volumes IX–XI) of the
Recueil de planches, and the set was completed in 1772, the year of
the marriage of Diderot's daughter Marie-Angélique to Abel-
François-Nicolas Caroillon de Vandeul. By this time, Diderot, free
of the duties of supervising the printing and publication of the
plates, and knowing that his wife would be well looked after by
her daughter and her husband, undertook his long-promised trip
to Russia to thank the Empress for her timely purchase of his
library. Accordingly he set out for St Petersburg by way of The
Hague in June 1773, and returned to France fifteen months later.
And just before Diderot set out, Le Breton sold his printing

business to Jean-Georges-Antoine Stoupe, though he retained his title of Royal Printer until his death.

In 1769 the publisher Charles-Joseph Panckoucke had suggested to Diderot that he should undertake the supervision of the preparation of the supplement to the *Encyclopédie*, but this was done in such a graceless way that Diderot indignantly refused. In 1775 Panckoucke secured a licence to print and publish this supplement and, in 1776, a similar licence to cover an accompanying volume of plates. Thus, the four supplementary volumes appeared, without either the help of Diderot or of Le Breton, in the years 1776–77:

Nouveau dictionnaire pour servir de supplément aux Dictionnaires des sciences, des arts et des métiers, par une société de gens de lettres. Mis en ordre et publié par M.^{xxx} *...* Paris, Panckoucke, Stoupe, Brunet; Amsterdam, M. M. Rey, 1776–77

the arrangement of the contents of the four folio volumes being alphabetical as in the original work. Stoupe was responsible for the printing, and it will be noted that another name famous in bibliography, that of Brunet, is listed here in the imprint. There were 244 plates in the folio volume which appeared in 1777:

Suite de Recueil de planches sur les sciences, les arts libéraux et les arts méchaniques, avec leur explication ... Paris, Panckoucke, Stoupe, Brunet; Amsterdam, M. M. Rey, 1777

and, in this year, publication began of the Geneva edition:

Encyclopédie, ou Dictionnaire raisonné des sciences, des arts et des métiers ... publié par M. Diderot et ... par M. d'Alembert ... nouvelle édition. Geneva, Pellet, 1777–79

comprising 45 quarto volumes, to which six index volumes were added (Lyons, A le Roy, 1780–81). Another, smaller issue of this edition was published in 36 octavo volumes, with three quarto volumes of plates (Lausanne and Berne, chez les sociétés typographiques, 1778–81), to which a two-volume supplement was eventually added (Bern, Walthard, 1791–93).

In 1779, Panckoucke obtained a further licence for the issue of the last part of the *Encyclopédie*, the index volumes:

Table analytique et raisonnée des matières contenues dans les XXXIII volumes in-folio du Dictionnaire des sciences, des arts et des métiers et dans son Supplément. Paris, Panckoucke; Amsterdam, M. M. Rey, 1780

comprising two folio volumes which were prepared by Pierre Mouchon, and which covered the plates as well as the text.

Panckoucke secured another licence in 1780, this time for the production of a new encyclopaedia, based on the work of Diderot and d'Alembert, but rearranged in large subject-fields, an idea which the Abbé Fromageot had proposed to Le Breton as early as 1768, and which the latter had rejected. This was in fact a return to the ideas of former ages, and one to which the French have always been partial, a similar arrangement being adopted for a major French encyclopaedia as late as the middle of the twentieth century. There is much to be said for abandoning the strictly alphabetical arrangement of specific subjects, in favour of their grouping under major subject-fields, but experience has shown that the public invariably prefers the former.

Panckoucke, in his first prospectus of 1782, offered two editions of his *Encyclopédie méthodique, ou par ordre de matières*, the first in 42 quarto volumes (with three columns of text), the second in 84 octavo volumes (with two columns of text), each to be accompanied by seven volumes of plates. But the smaller edition did not attract many subscribers, so Panckoucke issued a new prospectus offering a single edition of 53 quarto volumes, printed in two columns, with seven volumes of plates. The new encyclopaedia was issued in fascicles for many years after, subscribers receiving parts belonging to many different volumes as they were completed. The first volume:

Encyclopédie méthodique. Grammaire et littérature . . . Tome Ier. Paris, Panckoucke, 1782

was edited by Marmontel. The edition was finally completed in 166 quarto volumes in 1832 by Panckoucke's daughter Thérèse-Charlotte, widow of his associate Henri Agasse.

The immortal story of the *Encyclopédie* is almost finished:[1] d'Alembert, haunted by the fear of being buried alive, and refusing to undergo an operation for the stone, died in great pain in Paris on 29th October 1783; Diderot survived him by only a few months, dying (also of the stone) in the same city on 31st July 1784. And yet there was a remarkable sequel: on 17th March 1794, Diderot's son-in-law Nicolas Caroillon de Vandeul was consigned to the St Lazare prison. On 7th April his wife, Marie-Angélique, 'Citizen Diderot', wrote a letter to the members of the Committee for Public Safety, asking for the liberation of her husband who, she claimed, was an ardent Republican and a friend of liberty, while she herself, as Diderot's daughter, gloried in having had philosophy for a cradle and in having been a Republican long before the Revolution. As a result her husband was released on 26th August. No doubt the Republicans were able to recognize as clearly as the refugee aristocrats in England the part which the *Encyclopédie* and its editor-in-chief had played in the early days of the revolutionary movement.

With all its faults—and the *Encyclopédie* had many for it was often tendentious, prejudiced, diffuse, and ill-proportioned—it was a wonderful achievement. Full justice had at last been done not only to science but also to technology, and the opinions of some of the greatest in Europe of that age were enshrined in its columns—Rousseau on music, Daubenton (Buffon's collaborator) on natural history, Holbach and Voltaire, Condorcet, Turgot, Montesquieu and Necker, Boulanger and Marmontel, to name only the more memorable of the 160-odd contributors—and there is no doubt that many more leaders of thought who did not actually contribute articles lent their advice, influence, and support to the completion of this unique achievement in publishing history.

---

[1] Andre de Chénier, the French poet (1762–94), when he commenced his *Hermès* in 1783, had the ambition to condense Diderot's *Encyclopédie* into a poem somewhat after the manner of Lucretius!

BIBLIOGRAPHY

Andre Billy. *Diderot.* Revised edition. Paris, Flammarion, 1943

Diderot et l'Encyclopédie: exposition commémorative du deuxième centenaire de l'Encyclopédie. Paris, Bibliothèque Nationale, 1951

Herbert Dieckmann. 'Bibliographical data on Diderot', in *Studies in honor of Frederick W. Shipley.* St Louis, Washington University Studies, 1942

Pierre Grosclaude. 'Bibliographical data on Diderot', in *Nouvelles éditions latines,* 1951

Joseph Legras. *Diderot et l'Encyclopédie.* Amiens, Edgar Malfère, 1928 (Les Grands événements littéraires)

John Morley. *Diderot and the Encyclopaedists.* 2 volumes. London, Macmillan, 1923 (1st edition, 1878)

Chapter V

THE ENCYCLOPAEDIA BRITANNICA

According to the best of dictionaries
Which encyclopedise both flesh and fish
BYRON: Don Juan

The remarkable history of the *Encyclopaedia Britannica* had its beginnings in the collaboration of three Scots who were inspired by the stormy triumph of the *Encyclopédie* of Diderot, and by their desire to improve on its shortcomings. Andrew Bell (1726–1809) was an engraver, Colin Macfarquhar (*c.* 1745–93) a printer, and William Smellie (1740–95) a printer and a scholar. All three lived in Edinburgh. The new encyclopaedia was to be compiled on a completely new plan: the principal subjects—some forty-five, all distinguished by titles printed across the whole page—were to be supported by another thirty lengthy articles, the whole being contained within one alphabetical sequence interspersed with numerous brief entries, supported by references where appropriate to the principal subjects. Some of the articles, notably those on medical subjects, extended to well over one hundred pages each. Thus, the editor attempted to have the best of both worlds: easy reference to individual items, terms and minor topics, combined with major treatment of important sciences and arts.

The hard-drinking William Smellie was only twenty-eight years of age when he undertook the editorship of this great endeavour, but his colleagues' confidence in him was fully justified by the result and by the speed with which the encyclopaedia was produced. In all, one hundred parts were issued: the first two appeared in December 1768, at a cost of 6*d.* each on plain paper or 8*d.* on finer quality paper. By 1769 the first volume had been completed and bound; the second by 1770; and the third by 1771—a total of 2,670 quarto pages, with 160 copperplate engravings by Andrew Bell, costing in all £12:

Encyclopaedia Britannica: or, a dictionary of arts and sciences, compiled upon a new plan. In which the different sciences and arts are digested into distinct treatises or systems; and the various technical terms, &c. are explained as they occur in the order of the alphabet. Illustrated with one hundred and sixty copperplates. By a society of gentlemen in Scotland. In three volumes. Edinburgh, printed for A. Bell and C. Macfarquhar; and sold by Colin Macfarquhar, at his printing-office, Nicolson-Street, 1771.

Thus reads the title-page of one of the milestones in the history of encyclopaedia-making. The volumes were reprinted, probably piratically, and issued by Edward and Charles Dilly in London in 1773, the names of the collaborators being prudently omitted from the title.

Although the first edition of the *Britannica* was a moderate success, there was much to criticize in its mixture of fact and old-wives' tales. Clinical and exact though its articles on surgery might be, there was too much superstition, prejudice and unequal treatment in many of its articles for the first issue to be called a true fore-runner of the magnificent scholarship of the ninth and eleventh editions. With Smellie unwilling to undertake the preparation of a new edition, Bell and Macfarquhar turned to a strange hack-worker, James Tytler (1747?–1805), who had a miscellaneous background of theology, practical aeronautics, medicine, pharmacy, and unsuccessful writing. Only about one year older than William Smellie had been when he started editing the first edition, Tytler began in 1776 the compilation of the second: the first part was issued in June 1777, the whole being completed in 181 parts in September 1784:

Encyclopaedia Britannica; or, A dictionary of arts, sciences, &c., on a plan entirely new: by which, the different sciences and arts are digested into the form of distinct treatises or systems, comprehending the history, theory and practice, of each, according to the latest discoveries and improvements; and full explanations given of the various detached parts of knowledge, whether relating to natural and artificial objects, or to matters ecclesiastical, civil, military, commercial, &c., together with a description of all countries, cities . . . a general history, ancient and modern, of the different empires, kingdoms and states, and an account of the lives of the most eminent persons in every nation, from the earliest ages down to the present times . . . 2nd edition, greatly improved and enlarged. Illustrated with above two hundred copper plates. . . . Edinburgh, printed for J. Balfour & Co., 1778–1784. 10 volumes.

This 'greatly improved and enlarged' edition, mostly written by Tytler himself, comprised 8,595 pages (the pagination, which was continuous, ended with page 9200, but 295 pages were inserted in various places, and page 7099 was followed by page 8000!), with 340 copperplates, the whole forming ten quarto volumes. The number of principal and major articles had been tripled, and the longest supplied with indexes of their own. An important improvement was the addition of historical and biographical articles, and another was the grouping of all the maps together in the entry for 'Geography'. In the last volume was a 200-page appendix, including botanical tables complete with a substantial bibliography. This edition marked a turning point in the planning of encyclopaedias; no later encyclopaedia of any merit dared to ignore the wider world outside the confines of the exact arts and sciences, and it was this edition that set the style for the inclusion of biographies of living people. It is notable that the American Revolution was completely ignored: the more remarkable since Tytler himself eventually died an outlaw in exile in Salem, Massachusetts, in 1805.

The third edition was announced in 1787: it was to be completed in 300 parts, comprising 15 volumes with 360 plates. The first number was published early in 1788, and the first volume was completed in October 1788. When the edition was finally completed in 1797 it was found to comprise 18 quarto volumes, with nearly fifteen thousand pages and 542 plates. Some excellent maps were grouped together in a special section. Of this edition some thirteen thousand sets were sold.

Though many articles were repeated from previous editions, there were some improvements, notably the development of the articles devoted to the history of individual countries. The title-page read:

Encyclopaedia Britannica; or, A dictionary of arts, sciences, and miscellaneous literature . . . 3rd edition . . . greatly improved. Illustrated with five hundred and forty-two copperplates . . . Edinburgh, A. Bell & C. Macfarquhar, 1788–97. 18 volumes.
—— *Supplement to the third edition of the Encyclopaedia Britannica; or, A dictionary of arts, sciences, and miscellaneous literature. In two volumes, illustrated with fifty copperplates. By George Gleig.* Edinburgh, printed for Thomson Bonar, 1801. 2 volumes (reprinted 1803).

Begun in 1800 or 1801, the fourth edition was completed in 1810 in 20 quarto volumes, comprising 16,033 pages with 581 plates engraved by Andrew Bell, for whom it was printed. In 1809 it was dedicated to the king.[1] As Bell did not possess the copyright, no articles were reprinted from the supplement to the third edition. Four thousand copies were sold at £36 per set. Bell had died at the age of 83 in 1809. Most of the volumes were little more than reprints of the contents of the main volumes of the third edition, but Professor Wallace contributed some notable articles on mathematics, and there was a very full account of Dr Edward Jenner's successful introduction of vaccination for cowpox in 1796.

Hardly had the completion of the fourth edition been achieved when a reprint was undertaken to meet the steadily growing demand: this was begun in 1810, but complications of ownership and publishing rights intervened, and what had been intended merely as a reprint became a new edition and took another seven years to reach its final volume. The negotiations between the young upstart Edinburgh bookseller and publisher, Archibald Constable (1774–1827) and Andrew Bell and his heirs, make fascinating if not particularly edifying reading. The purchase was

[1] 'The French *Encyclopédie* has been accused, and justly accused, of having disseminated far and wide the seeds of anarchy and atheism. If the *Encyclopaedia Britannica* shall in any degree combat the tendency of that pestifarous work, even these two volumes will not be wholly unworthy of your Majesty's attention.'

completed by 1814 and Dr James Millar, a physician and scholar, was appointed to correct and revise the last 15 volumes. The fifth edition finally comprised 20 volumes, with a total of over sixteen thousand pages, 582 plates, and sold for £36.

Even before the edition was completed Constable embarked on the publication of a six-volume supplement, issued in half-volume parts, the first of which was published in December 1816. In 1824, when the last volume of the supplement was published, the whole comprised nearly another five thousand pages, 125 plates, and nine maps. Of the 669 articles, about one-quarter were devoted to biographies of people who had mostly died during the preceding thirty years. This supplement is distinguished by several other innovations, notably the inclusion of no less than three preliminary dissertations, and by the invitation for the first time extended to foreign scholars to contribute. But the feature which was perhaps Constable's outstanding improvement on existing encyclopaedia publishing was his system of printing the initials of the contributors at the end of important articles, and of giving a key to these initials in each volume. The editor of this notable supplement was Macvey Napier (1776–1847), a brilliant and energetic young Scottish librarian and scholar, who was untiring in his efforts to obtain the services of the chief writers of the day.

Macvey Napier was later appointed editor of the famous *Edinburgh Review* (from 1829).

As early as 1820, Constable had already begun the issue of a sixth edition, but this was mostly a reprint of the fifth, with corrections of errors and a handful of new articles:

> *Encyclopaedia Britannica; or, A dictionary of arts, sciences, and miscellaneous literature; enlarged and improved. 6th edition.* Edinburgh, printed for Archibald Constable, 1820–1823. 20 volumes.

It was edited by Charles Maclaren (1782–1866), owner and editor of *The Scotsman*, his revision being chiefly confined to the historical and geographical articles. The new edition was issued in half-volume parts, the whole comprising 20 volumes, at 32s. per volume, and being completed in 1823.

Each successive edition of the *Encyclopaedia Britannica* marked a definite advance over its predecessors, and the seventh—begun in 1827—had several notable features. Edited by Macvey Napier, the first half-volume was published in March 1830, and it was finally completed in 21 quarto volumes in 1842, a set costing £24. The number of volumes was less than the promised twenty-five, but the pages were larger and there were more of them per volume, the whole comprising 17,101 pages and 506 plates. The edition was reset throughout and stereotyped. An assistant editor, James Browne (1793–1841), a Scottish journalist and author, was appointed to handle the burden of the editorial work, thereby setting a pattern for future editions. And the first volume was entirely devoted to the text of preliminary dissertations. Constable had died in 1827, and this edition was issued under the imprint of Adam Black:

> The Encyclopaedia Britannica; or, Dictionary of arts, sciences, and miscellaneous literature. 7th edition, greatly improved, with the supplements to the former editions incorporated, a general index, and numerous illustrative engravings. Edinburgh, A. & C. Black, 1827–1842. 21 volumes, and an index volume [the first volume comprised four dissertations].

Adam Black (1784–1874), an Edinburgh publisher, was the founder of the present firm of Adam and Charles Black, of Edinburgh and London. Mathematical diagrams were printed in the text from line blocks. But the chief feature of the new edition was the introduction of a supplementary volume of 187 pages, devoted entirely to an index to the whole work, and compiled by Robert Cox. Imperfect though the index was, even by the standards of those times, its introduction was a great success, and the devotion of the last volume to this purpose has remained a feature of the Britannica to this day, and has been adopted by many other encyclopaedias throughout the world.

While the seventh edition had cost more than one hundred thousand pounds to publish, the introduction of more efficient editorial methods resulted in the cost of the eighth edition being reduced to just over seventy-five thousand pounds. But this was also responsible for some detriment to the text: some articles were drastically reduced, and others suffered from inadequate revision. The title-page ran:

> *The Encyclopaedia Britannica; or, Dictionary of arts, sciences and general literature. 8th edition, with extensive improvements and additions; and numerous engravings.* Edinburgh, A. & C. Black, 1853–1861. 21 volumes, and an index volume [the first volume comprised *five* dissertations].

The editor—and himself a substantial contributor—was the Professor of Medical Jurisprudence at Edinburgh University, Dr Thomas Stewart Traill (1781–1862). While the articles devoted to scientific subjects were inclined to unequal treatment under Dr Traill's ministrations, the humanities gained and such authors as Lord Macaulay and Charles Kingsley contributed much to the success of the new edition.

Publication of the eighth edition began in 1853 and when it was completed in 1860 it comprised nearly eighteen thousand pages and 402 plates, in 21 quarto volumes. In 1861 an index volume of 239 pages was addded. The encyclopaedia was not wholly reset, and many of the long articles were retained almost or entirely intact. In addition to the plates many illustrations from line blocks were inserted in the text.

The ninth edition is deservedly famous. Publication began in 1875 under Professor Thomas Spencer Baynes of the University of St Andrews, the *Britannica*'s first English-born editor. Baynes, a philosopher and journalist, was born in 1823, but by 1881 was suffering so much from ill-health that he had to relinquish the editorship. One of his contributors, William Robertson Smith (1846–94), a Scottish scholar whose theological articles in the early volumes had aroused stormy controversy and who had thereby incurred the disfavour of the Free Church of Scotland, had been approached early in 1880 and joined him as co-editor and saw the work through to the end, Baynes dying in 1887. Baynes had been an outstanding editor and, although himself a considerable writer of merit, restricted his own contribution to one—but, at that, very important—article on Shakespeare. The title-page reads:

The Encyclopaedia Britannica: a dictionary of arts, sciences and general literature. 9th edition. Edinburgh, A. & C. Black, 1875–1888. 24 volumes, and an index volume

When the encyclopaedia was completed in 1888, it comprised 24 volumes of text, and while 9,000 sets were sold in Britain, five times that number were sold in the United States of America, in addition to many American pirated editions. The ninth edition retained a certain amount of material from the eighth, and over some of these articles a certain amount of criticism raged on the score that they were out-of-date. Nevertheless, the edition was substantially a new work and widely hailed as a masterpiece of scholarship. There were some sixteen thousand articles in its 20,000 pages, many superb line illustrations, some coloured plates, and special coloured maps of five major cities. An innovation which other encyclopaedias immediately copied was the addition of exact birth and death dates in the biographical articles. All the major articles had individual indexes and substantial bibliographies, and the index volume—added in 1889—was a complete guide to the contents. A definite attempt was made in this edition to relate the contents to everyday life: practical articles were inserted on such topics as building a refrigerator, making snowshoes, etc. Perhaps the most important complaint was one that the publishers could not remedy: publication volume by volume, each paying for the one that followed, was imperative owing to the limited finances available, and this problem was not to be solved for many years hence. It was this edition which was reprinted and issued at half the price by *The Times* in 1898, many copies being sold on the instalment system through advertisements in *The Times* and the *Daily Mail*.

This amazing development was due to the intervention of two remarkable Americans, James Clarke and Horace Everett Hooper (1859–1922) who took London by storm in that year and eventually very nearly succeeded in gaining control of *The Times* itself. Trained in the hard business of selling subscription sets in the Middle West of the late nineteenth century, these two pioneers in large-scale bookselling in Britain took advantage of *The Times*'s going just then through a very difficult period financially, to

L

engineer a scheme that sold an out-of-date encyclopaedia at the same time that it put Britain's most influential newspaper on its feet. The proposition was a revolutionary one: that Clarke and Hooper should sell 5,000 sets of the ninth edition of the *Britannica* through advertisements at fourteen guineas, *The Times* retaining one guinea from each hire-purchase order: probably the first time hire-purchase had been used in Britain to sell books. The guinea fees, in addition to the advertisement revenue, earned for *The Times* at least £12,000, and the profit from the sales fully justified the hopes of Hooper and his chief subsequent partner, Walter Montgomery Jackson, another American with a flair for advertisement.

It is not the purpose of this book to chronicle the fascinating adventures of Hooper and Jackson in the book world of Britain at the beginning of this century—for a full and absorbing account the reader will never regret the hours he may spend on Herman Kogan's well-written and astonishing work *The great EB: the story of the Encyclopaedia Britannica* (The University of Chicago Press, 1958). It is sufficient to say here that the world probably owes the continuance and present stature of the *Britannica* today to these two self-made men who made practical vision and energy a substitute for the scholarship that would have been needed in any others who had attempted the task of revivifying a work so large and of adjusting it to the needs of a very different age.

It was the manager of *The Times*, Charles Frederic Moberly Bell (1847–1911) who insisted that a tenth edition must be prepared, and this was announced in 1899. The tenth edition was not however to be a new edition, but the original (ninth) edition of 24 volumes, with a supplement of 11 new volumes. These were issued in 1902 under the joint editorship of Sir Donald Mackenzie Wallace (1841–1919), *The Times*'s foreign editor, Arthur Twining Hadley (1856–1930), President of Yale University, and Hugh Chisholm (1866–1924), editor-in-chief of the influential *St James's Gazette*. And for the first time an American editor, Franklin Henry Hooper (1862–1940) (Horace's brother), with a New York office, was appointed. The encyclopaedia was issued volume by volume, a set of the 11-volume supplement costing £20. The supplement included a volume of maps and the index volume

(volume 35) was elaborate and covered the contents of the entire work, comprising some six hundred thousand entries. The main editorial work had been brilliantly done by Chisholm.

It was obvious however that the public would not long remain content with a major encyclopaedia, much of whose text had been written some twenty-five to thirty years previously. This consideration, to which the handsome profits deriving from the reprint of the ninth and the issue of the tenth editions added a powerful motive, determined the partners on starting the preparation of the eleventh edition as soon as possible. By 1903 work had commenced, and it was clear that most of the text would have to be rewritten. Hugh Chisholm was chosen as editor-in-chief, with the historian Walter Alison Phillips (1864–1950) as his chief assistant editor (many of the more important historical articles in this edition were contributed by him), and a staff of assistant editors, and for the next six years the editorial work was carried out at *The Times*'s ancient office in Printing House Square. The firm of Adam and Charles Black had printed the tenth edition, and at one time it appeared as though *The Times* itself would publish the eleventh, but the daring take-over bid which Hooper and Jackson made for control of *The Times* itself was defeated by Lord Northcliffe and, after protracted negotiations, the copyright and control of the *Britannica* passed to the Syndics of the University of Cambridge in 1910. Most of the editorial work was done in London, but the American office under Franklin H. Hooper was maintained, and Hooper took a notable part in ensuring that the contents of the new edition were kept within the mental range of the average man.

The eleventh edition was probably the finest edition of the *Britannica* ever issued, and it ranks with the *Italiana* and the *Espasa* as one of the three greatest encyclopaedias in the world. It was the last edition to be produced almost in its entirety in Britain, and its position in time as a summary of the world's knowledge just before the outbreak of World War I is particularly valuable.

The Encyclopaedia Britannica: a dictionary of arts, sciences, literature and general information. 11th edition. New York, Encyclopaedia Britannica, Inc., 1910–11. 29 volumes bears the imprint of the New York office, but the recto of its half-title leaf bears the legend 'Copyright in all countries subscribing to the Bern Convention by the Chancellor, Masters and Scholars of the University of Cambridge'—a unique piece of collaboration across the Atlantic, at least for the period of its issue. The appeal to both New and Old Worlds is further emphasized in its dedication to both King George V and to the President of the United States of America, President William Howard Taft. And for the first time the familiar coarse paper of all previous editions gave place to a tough opaque India paper.

This was the first edition of the *Britannica* to be issued complete at one time: as the Preface states, 'The editors early decided that the new edition should be planned and written as a whole, and refused to content themselves with the old-fashioned plan of regarding each volume as a separate unit, to be compiled and published by itself. They were thus able to arrange their material so as to give an organic unity to the whole work and to place all the various subjects under their natural headings, in the form which experience has shown to be the most convenient for a work of universal reference.' The eleventh edition was, in fact, much more than a revision of the ninth: owing to the long period over which the ninth was issued, its arrangement was not properly encyclopaedic—it became rather a collection of detached monographs, many of which were of great scholarship and value, but which together failed to achieve the total conspectus of knowledge which it is the aim of any modern encyclopaedist to compass, and thus the organic unity of the whole work was largely lost.

As the editors pointed out in their Introduction: 'in an encyclopaedia it is only the alphabetization of the headings which causes them to fall into distinct volumes, and the accident of position separates the treatment of the same or closely related subjects in such a way that, if they are discussed from the point of view of widely different dates, the organic unity of the work is entirely lost'.

Thus, under the new system of issuing the whole work at one time, advantage was taken to redistribute the seventeen thousand articles of the ninth under some forty thousand more specific headings in the eleventh edition. As none of the work was printed or published until the whole of the edition was ready, new headings could always be introduced under their correct terminology and with their appropriate matter (a circumstance which some present-day editors might well envy!), according as the examination of what was written under another heading revealed omissions which showed that some related subject needed explanation on its own account, or according as the progress of time up to the year of publication involved the emergence of new issues, to which previously no separate reference would have been expected. The editorial system thus admitted of continual improvement in detail, irrespective of the distribution of matter under this or that letter of the alphabet, and could proceed in all its parts *pari passu*, the various articles being kept open for revision or rewriting, so as to present and represent the collective knowledge and the contemporary standpoint at that date when the whole work was issued.

The editorial control and planning was obviously of a much higher standard than previous editors had found possible to obtain or exert, and there is no doubt that individual contributions earned a much closer scrutiny and were very much more subject to editorial criticism and suggestion than in any previous edition. Such a clean sweep was made that the terminology of headings was closely examined and new headings, more in keeping with the times, introduced. This particularly applied to personal names, titled people now being entered under their titles and not under their family names (though references were provided in the index), and well-known authors (such as George Eliot, George Sand, and Mark Twain) being entered under their pseudonyms where those were better known than their real names, the work of referring the reader from one heading to another being again left largely to the Index volume (which constituted the twenty-ninth volume). Particular attention was paid to improving the coverage of recent biography, more especially in the British and American fields, including many contemporary figures; and a consistent spelling policy was worked out and maintained. The total sales of this edition amounted to more than 75,000 sets.

It is perhaps not generally realized that the *Britannica book of the year*, issued in 1938, might have had a quarter-of-a-century of predecessors, had it not been for World War I. Under the editorship of Hugh Chisholm, the first of what was planned to be a series of biennial supplements to the *Britannica* was issued in 1913:

> *Britannica year book: a survey of the world's progress since the completion in 1910 of the Encyclopaedia Britannica, eleventh edition, comprising a register of current events and additions to knowledge in politics, economics, engineering, industry, sport, law, science, art, literature, and other forms of human activity, national and international, up to the end of 1912.* New York, Encyclopaedia Britannica, Inc., 1913.

Prepared mostly by the contributors to the eleventh edition, this eleven-hundred-page volume, with its emphasis on British and American matters of the moment, was a very fair attempt—probably the first—at what is now a regular feature of modern encyclopaedia publishing. Unfortunately, the outbreak of the war made the first issue also the last, and it also put paid for many years to a proposal to publish a *Junior Britannica*.

'If it had not been for the World War, there would not have been any occasion, so early as 1922, for a Supplement to the Eleventh Edition of the *Encyclopaedia Britannica*, as published in 1911. But for the exceptional situation so created, the original intention not to take in hand anything equivalent to a Twelfth Edition until a much later date would undoubtedly have been maintained.' So wrote Hugh Chisholm—who had resumed his work with the *Britannica*—rather curiously, if present-day customs of issuing frequent editions are kept in mind, in the Preface to:

> *The Encyclopaedia Britannica: the new volumes, constituting, in combination with the twenty-nine volumes of the eleventh edition, the twelfth edition of that work, and also supplying a new, distinctive, and independent library of reference dealing with events and developments of the period 1910 to 1921 inclusive.* New York, Encyclopaedia Britannica, Inc.; London, The Encyclopaedia Britannica Company, Ltd., 1922. 3 volumes.

This was to be Hooper's last effort, and he took a very close interest in its preparation and publication right up to the moment of his

death in 1922. Successful though it was in stimulating sales of
the eleventh edition—within four years 65,000 sets of the twelfth
edition were sold—the structure of the supplement was not as
comprehensive or as well-planned as that of the eleventh edition.
The unhappy proximity of World War I tended to throw editorial
perspective out of balance, and many pages of the three-volume
supplement were devoted to blow-by-blow accounts of individual
battles and to step-by-step narratives of specific campaigns. Thus,
while the historical articles bring the encyclopaedia up-to-date in
that respect, and while due attention is paid to many branches of
science and technology and to the developments in those spheres
imposed by war needs, little more than lip-service is paid to the
advances in the humanities. Thus, over sixteen pages are devoted
to Artillery, and another sixteen (and two very detailed plates of
maps) to Battles in Artois, as against six for Drama (treated on a
world-wide basis), and four for an overall discussion of Music. A
detailed index to the supplement was included in the third volume.
Contributors included many from former enemy countries, and
also many names of the highest rank from all over the world—thus
Lindemann (later Lord Cherwell) wrote on Einstein, Pirenne on
Belgium, Marie Stopes on Botany, Vinogradoff on Denikin, Palme
Dutt on Communism, St John Ervine on Drama, Masaryk on
Czechoslovakia, and Danilov on the Russian Army.

Parallel with the main edition of the eleventh edition, Franklin
H. Hooper had produced a smaller edition, photographically
reduced ($6\frac{1}{2}$ by $8\frac{1}{2}$ inches as against the original $8\frac{3}{4}$ by $11\frac{3}{4}$ inches)
to be sold at less than half the price of the larger issue. Sales were
mostly by hire-purchase in America, and the sets were on sale from
1915 onwards. This edition was withdrawn from sale in 1923(?)—
by which time nearly 200,000 sets had been sold!—and a 'New
Form' edition in the larger format, but bound two volumes in one,
with narrower page margins, sold some 25,000 sets in the English-
speaking world in the following two years. In 1924 a two-volume
collection of articles was issued:

*These eventful years: the twentieth century in the making as told by many
of its makers.*

This consisted of contributions by outstanding personalities such as Shaw, Nitti, Garvin, Wellington Koo, Tirpitz, Ludendorff, Freud, Bertrand Russell, Jellicoe, Scheer, Dulles, Baruch, H. G. Wells, Madame Curie, and Lady Rhondda.

Work on the thirteenth edition began in 1925; the editor of *The Observer*, James Louis Garvin (1868–1947), was chosen as editor-in-chief, and the new edition was ready in 1926. From the short period allocated to preparation of the edition, it was apparent that this was only a stop-gap issue, and work began very quickly on the preparation of the fourteenth edition, again with Garvin as editor, and Franklin H. Hooper retaining his post as American editor. By this time, the system for selecting assistant editors, each responsible for a subject-field, had become firmly established, and in each case the *Britannica* chose an expert of international repute, such as (Sir) Julian Huxley for Biology and Zoology, John Dewey for Philosophy, etc. In this edition, for the first time the American contribution reached half the total contents. The fourteenth edition was issued in 1929, and its sales in the United States were severely affected by the economic depression.

The fourteenth edition was the last numbered edition of the *Britannica*: subsequent issues were subject to the process of continuous revision. This revolutionary change was introduced to cope with the besetting weakness of all encyclopaedias at that time: each edition of an encyclopaedia was attended with booms and slumps which made the undertaking precarious. There was usually a long interval between editions, and the task of reassembling a competent editorial staff and preparing a new edition took several years. In the interval the editorial and sales organizations had almost invariably been disbanded, and their reassembly was difficult and costly. Even more important was the effect of this periodicity on sales. As soon as it was known that a new edition was in preparation, sales of the current edition dried up, and the publishers had to finance editorial services on the new edition out of a steeply diminishing income. The *Britannica* editorial and sales staff made a study of the problem and came to the conclusion that much of the material in any one edition required only periodical correction, but that the remainder needed continually to be

Encyclopædia Britannica;

OR, A

DICTIONARY

OF

ARTS and SCIENCES,

COMPILED UPON A NEW PLAN.

IN WHICH

The different SCIENCES and ARTS are digested into
distinct Treatises or Systems;

AND

The various TECHNICAL TERMS, &c. are explained as they occur
in the order of the Alphabet.

ILLUSTRATED WITH ONE HUNDRED AND SIXTY COPPERPLATES.

By a SOCIETY of GENTLEMEN in SCOTLAND.

IN THREE VOLUMES.

VOL. I.

EDINBURGH:
Printed for A. BELL and C. MACFARQUHAR;
And sold by COLIN MACFARQUHAR, at his Printing-office, Nicolson-street.
M.DCC.LXXI.

Caricature by John Kay, the eighteenth-century Scottish painter and etcher, of two of the men responsible for the first edition of the ENCYCLOPAEDIA BRITANNICA: Andrew Bell (*left*), its engraver and one of its publishers, and William Smellie, the Edinburgh scholar who was its editor brought up-to-date. Thus, it was clear that more attention would always, for example, need to be devoted to scientific and technical subjects than to developments in the humanities. For the older method of issuing separate editions the *Britannica* therefore substituted the system of continuous editing and printing, corrections being made by a body of contributors constantly available, to the order of a permanent editorial board. Experience has shown that features requiring correction are completely rewritten every ten years, and that they receive an average revision of ten per cent annually. Some of the revisions, corrections and additions, particularly on current history and topics, are incorporated in the *Britannica year book* and then incorporated in the next printing of the encyclopaedia. Though the theory of this method has undoubtedly good sense on its side, the practice has led to numerous and powerful criticisms from time to time, and the volume of this has in turn affected the editorial policy, with the result that very recent issues of the *Britannica* have shown a much higher standard in scholarship and regard for modern discoveries and contemporary opinion.

In 1934(?) an edition for children under twelve was issued in the United States:

Britannica junior: an encyclopaedia for boys and girls, prepared under the supervision of the editors of the *Encyclopaedia Britannica*. Chicago, Ill., Encyclopaedia Britannica Inc., 1934. 12 volumes. based partly on the twelve-volume *Weedon's Modern encyclopaedia* which the *Britannica* had purchased. In 1938 the old idea of issuing a supplementary year-book was revived, and the first issue was made of:

Britannica book of the year: a record of the march of events of 1937; edited by Franklin H. Hooper. Chicago, Ill., Encyclopaedia Britannica Inc., 1938.

This recorded the events of 1937, and was illustrated with some two hundred photographs from *Life*. The *Britannica book of the year* has been issued annually ever since and has proved useful in many different ways—such as its section on New Words which was particularly valuable in the war years when so many new terms were suddenly introduced into the English language—and particularly through its detailed and thorough indexing.

Between the two World Wars a company was formed in London to market the *Britannica* in the Commonwealth and Europe. Sets were printed in the United States and shipped to England for distribution, but these ceased during World War II and the British staff was reduced to a minimum. After the war the managing director of the British company, Mr A. E. Dolphin, conceived the idea of having the *Britannica* reprinted in Britain for this market and, despite the difficulties of the immediate post-war years, he succeeded not only in having a British edition published in England, but also in gradually restoring the British share in editorial work on the encyclopaedia. A committee formed jointly from members of the universities of Oxford, Cambridge and London, under the general direction of the British editor, is responsible for the handling of certain categories of subjects in their entirety. Though the head office in Chicago still retains overriding editorial authority, these British contributions are in practice accepted without question. The British contributors now number more than seven hundred.

There is no point in attempting to list the various printings of the *Britannica* since 1929, since the differences between them are textually internal and impossible of analysis except by careful page-by-page comparison. Readers who are interested in making such a thorough examination will however find themselves helped considerably by the *Britannica*'s practice of inserting pages bearing lower-case letters of the alphabet in addition to the page numbers themselves. These indicate considerable revision and addition and can guide the reader to topics where the editorial staff have devoted much thought to bringing the material up-to-date. The basic pattern for many years has been a 24-volume set, of which the last volume is devoted to a detailed index of the contents of the other volumes, together with a comprehensive atlas and a gazetteer index. The contents of the encyclopaedia comprise somewhat over forty thousand articles of very varying length, of which about five per cent are new articles. In addition, about seven and a half per cent of the articles are subject to major revision each year, and another seventeen per cent to minor correction and alteration. Treatment of the scientific and technical fields is somewhat better than that of the humanities, but bibliographies and illustrations are usually of good quality. The *Britannica* has the longest history of any current encyclopaedia, and certainly the strangest in the history of all such works. It is greatly to the credit of all the many and diverse people who have had a hand in its making during the past 190 years that it should have survived in so satisfactory a form. It is by no means an ideal encyclopaedia, but it has for long approached more nearly this target than most of the works described in this book, moreover it continues to explore new fields. The British *Children's Britannica* was first published in 1960 and is subject to the same process of revision as the parent encyclopaedia. Since 1961 it has been supplemented by the *Children's Britannica Yearbook*. And in 1957, under the direction of Manuel Hinojosa Flores, the 15-volume *Enciclopedia Barsa* was issued by the Britannica. This work was prepared directly in Spanish for the Latin American public, and generally for all readers of the Spanish language.

BIBLIOGRAPHY

Herman Kogan. *The great EB: the story of the Encyclopaedia Britannica*. The University of Chicago Press, 1958 (the major work on the subject)

Lydia Marian Gooding. *The Encyclopaedia Britannica: a critical and historical study*. Columbia University, 1929 (an unpublished Master's thesis)

'The *Britannica* comes home . . .'. *Scope*, Dec. 1951, pages 57–9, 112

Julius R. Chitwood. 'Encyclopaedia Britannica'. *Library journal*, volume 86, no. 8, 15th April 1961, pages 1549–51 (a review of the 1961 printing of the *Britannica*)

Indexing manual. Chicago, Encyclopaedia Britannica, Inc , 1959 (staff manual for indexers of the encyclopaedia)

Chapter *VI* BROCKHAUS

No work of reference has been more useful and successful, or more frequently copied, imitated and translated . . .

Encyclopaedia Britannica, 11th edition

David Arnold Friederich Brockhaus (1772–1823), who preferred to be known as Friedrich Arnold Brockhaus, was the son of a Dortmund merchant. By the time he started his publishing career in Amsterdam in 1805, he had already had considerable experience in general trading. Energetic, imaginative, and encouraged by some of the best writers in Western Europe, by the time Friedrich Arnold set out to participate in the Leipzig Book Fair for the first time, in 1808, he had acquired also considerable experience in the publishing of both periodicals and books and, in spite of the troubled times, his books had had great success. From the first Friedrich Arnold had adopted an international viewpoint, and he was able to organize such a remarkable achievement as a journal (unhappily short-lived) which was edited in Paris, published in Amsterdam, printed in Leipzig, and aimed at the German market. Another of his journals was in French; he was also in favour of the import of literature, commissioning translations of various Danish writings and of Joanna Baillie's plays. His Leipzig visit had historic consequences: in that city he bought the first volumes of an incomplete encyclopaedia, a *Conversationslexikon*.

The Leipzig scholar Dr Renatus Gotthelf Löbel (1767–99) had set himself the task in 1796 of satisfying the need for a modern encyclopaedia. With his friend, the lawyer Christian Wilhelm Franke (died 1831), he began the collecting and editing of a work which even in its beginnings and title tended to large proportions: it was originally to comprise four modest quarto volumes entitled *Conversationslexikon mit vorzüglicher Rücksicht auf die gegenwärtigen Zeiten* and, at the same time, also a *Frauenzimmer-Lexikon zur Erleichterung der Conversation und Lektüre,* and to include the most im-

portant subjects of theoretical knowledge and the fine arts. Löbel
hoped, in fact, that his work would supersede Hübner's. Three
years later, after the completion of the third volume, Löbel died;
Franke, it is true, continued to edit the work, but sold the publishing concern which the two friends had created for this purpose.
The Leipzig publisher, F. A. Leupold, who bought it up, carried
on the enterprise without much skill: the fourth volume appeared
under his imprint in 1800, but this did not complete the work as
planned, bringing it only to the letter 'R'. In the next few years
the ownership of the unfortunate encyclopaedia changed hands
three times. In 1806 the fifth volume was issued, but still another
was needed to complete it. The first half of the sixth volume was
printed and published in 1808 when the new publisher became in-
solvent and the whole work landed without suitable means or
prospects of a market in the hands of the printer. It was this
apparently hopeless undertaking that Brockhaus discovered on his
visit to Leipzig and bought.

So that there should be no further delay in the delivery of the
second half of the sixth volume, Brockhaus came to a speedy
agreement with Franke, the editor, on the preparation not only
of this but also of the long-planned two supplementary volumes.
The editor worked on under the old conditions: he received eight
Thalers for each sheet, which meant that he must deliver his
manuscript word perfect for printing, and must himself compensate his contributors. From 1809 Brockhaus issued all the remaining copies of the original volumes, and all new volumes, under the
title:

*Conversations-Lexikon oder kurzgefasstes Handwörterbuch für die in der
gesellschaftlichen Unterhaltung aus den Wissenschaften und Künsten
vorkommenden Gegenstände, mit beständiger Rücksicht auf die Ereignisse
der älteren und neueren Zeit.*

The two supplementary volumes appeared in 1809 and 1811
respectively; they were very necessary, for the world had altered
profoundly since Löbel's first volume of 1796, which made no
mention of such people as Napoleon or of the beginnings of unrest
in Latin America.

The death of Brockhaus's young wife in 1809 in childbirth left the publisher with seven small children and he determined to return to Germany. Abandoning the idea of Leipzig as a suitable place for his business, he went on to Altenburg, but transferred to Leipzig finally in 1817. In the meantime, the whole of the encyclopaedia was sold out in the first months of 1811: it had been an edition of 2,000 copies, an impressive number for those days, though it will be remembered that Diderot had achieved some four thousand subscribers for the *Encyclopédie* by the time he was ready to issue the last ten volumes. But the young publisher had scored a distinct and unexpected success in the face of the misgivings of his more senior colleagues. The necessity for a revision had been apparent to him even when he bought up the encyclopaedia, and Brockhaus himself set about the work of bringing the whole of the material up-to-date. The energy with which he approached this task is apparent from the fact that the first volume of the second edition was ready by Easter 1812, the second by Michaelmas, and the third and fourth in 1813—a remarkable achievement for the printing conditions of those times, and one which was only possible as long as the edition was kept to fairly small numbers. Even so, with the issue of the third volume the demand was so great that the original print order for 1,500 copies had to be doubled. But the first four volumes of this second edition, which was planned to comprise ten volumes in all, had an additional success which in those troubled times was quite unexpected—they were already completely sold out in the autumn of 1813! Brockhaus was now faced with a dilemma: he held that an encyclopaedia should never be out of print, and also that it should be up-to-date. Characteristically he solved the problem by commencing the issue of a third edition. Thus from 1814 to 1816 he let the next volumes of the second and third editions appear concurrently: the encyclopaedia was now enjoying an unparalleled circulation. And after the publication of the seventh volume (volumes 5 to 10 were the same in each edition) a new event took place which had considerable effect on the publishing policy of the house of Brockhaus: the Württemberg publisher, A. F. Marklot, had begun a completely unauthorized reprint of the encyclopaedia. Angered by this open piracy, Brockhaus determined on publishing a thoroughly revised fourth edition immediately, in order to secure copyright for himself in Württemberg. By this time he had re-established his firm on a sound footing—thanks to his own genius and aptitude for work and to the steadfastness of his friends—so that he felt himself able to return to Leipzig, where he set up his own printing works as well. Thus, in 1817 and 1818, volumes of the second, third, and fourth editions were appearing concurrently —a curiosity in bibliography, in the history of the encyclopaedia, and in publishing history in general. Five printers in Altenburg, Leipzig, and Brunswick, and a few small provincial printers, were all employed on the production of the various editions of the encyclopaedia, and even their combined efforts were hardly sufficient: in itself a record, when it is remembered that at the peak of the printing of Diderot's encyclopaedia, only about fifty workmen were employed at any one time.

The encyclopaedia underwent several changes of title at this time, so that it may prove convenient to give here complete details of the first four editions:

Edition

Löbel   *Conversationslexikon mit vorzüglicher Rücksicht auf die gegenwärtigen Zeiten.* 6 volumes. Leipzig, [various publishers], 1796–1808.

1st   *Conversations-Lexikon oder kurzgefasstes Handwörterbuch für die in der gesellschaftlichen Unterhaltung aus den Wissenschaften und Künsten vorkommenden Gegenstände, mit beständiger Rücksicht auf die Ereignisse der älteren und neueren Zeit.* 6 volumes, and 2 supplementary volumes. Amsterdam and Leipzig, F. A. Brockhaus, 1809–11. (This comprises the 6 Löbel volumes, plus the 2 supplementary volumes commissioned by Brockhaus.)

2nd   *Conversations-Lexicon oder Hand-Wörterbuch für die gebildeten Stände über die in der gesellschaftlichen Unterhaltung und bei der Lecture vorkommenden Gegenstände, Namen und Begriffe, in Beziehung auf Völker- und Menschengeschichte; Politik und Diplomatik; Mythologie und Archäologie; Erd-, Natur-,*

Gewerb- und Handlungskunde; die schönen Künste und Wissen-
schaften: mit Einschluss der in die Umgangssprache übergegan-
genen ausländischen Wörter und mit besonderer Rücksicht auf
älteren und neuesten merkwürdigen Zeitereignisse. 10 volumes.
Altenburg and Leipzig, F. A. Brockhaus, 1812–19.

3rd   *Conversations-Lexikon oder encyclopädisches Handwörterbuch für*
gebildete Stände. 10 volumes. Altenburg and Leipzig, F. A.
Brockhaus, 1814–19. (Volumes 5 to 10 of this edition are
identical with volumes 5 to 10 of the 2nd edition.)

4th   *Allgemeine Hand-Encyclopädie für die gebildeten Stände In*
alphabetischer Ordnung. 10 volumes. Leipzig, Brockhaus,
1817–19.

The somewhat bewildering changes in title were due to the changing circumstances in Germany at that time. As Dr S. H. Steinberg
has pointed out, Brockhaus's original retention of the title *Con-*
versations-Lexicon had been wise: the implication of the right or
necessary knowledge for good society that was inherent in the
word 'Conversation' at that time, had the correct approach to the
rapidly growing middle-class that was arising in Germany at the
beginning of the nineteenth century. Nevertheless, throughout the
history of the German lexicography there has been a noticeable
tendency to cleanse the language of alien words and phrases,
powerfully aided in the eighteenth century by the dramatist and
literary critic Johann Christoph Gottsched, by the lexicographer
Johann Siegmund Valentin Popowitsch, and by the Director-
General of Schools in Bavaria, Heinrich Braun, followed in the
early nineteenth century by the philosopher and educationalist
Joachim Heinrich Campe. Thus, by the issue of the fourth edition,
the word 'Conversation' was no longer acceptable in some circles,
but Brockhaus also issued some sets of the fourth edition with the
title of the third followed by the words '4: Original Auflage', so that
purchasers could have whichever title they preferred!

With the issue of the fourth edition, the complete work was
published for the first time in the latest uniform edition. The
trouble that Brockhaus had devoted to the undertaking, the
accuracy on which he insisted so that the encyclopaedia should be

completely up-to-date, and the principle he maintained to ensure that all volumes were newly printed, were richly rewarded. It is to the credit of Brockhaus's farsightedness, that soon after the beginning of preparations for the second edition, he had already perceived what excessive demands on everyone's time the high standards he had set would inexorably make. And in order to lose no time, he realized that above all he would have always to depend at every stage on himself. A few friends of his in Altenburg helped him with the revision of the first volume of the second edition. However he realized that he would have to gather round him a circle of subject specialists. Very soon he secured the help of a number of prominent collaborators: his friend F. C. Hasse, the historians Pölitz and Hormayr, the philosophers Krause and Krug, the literary experts Ersch and Gruber (who were themselves to become famous as encyclopaedia-makers), and the theologian Koethe. Brockhaus also perceived that, in view of his many other duties as a publisher, it would be impossible to continue without a permanent sub-editor: from 1812 Dr Ludwig Hain (1781–1836), the great bibliographer, was at his side, though this association was to come to an unhappy end later. If the good fortune of the first edition, which Brockhaus had completed so quickly, was due to his skill in organizing its marketing and to his reliability in delivering the last volumes and the supplementary volumes, the surprising success of the second edition was undoubtedly due to the complete coverage of contemporary events and to the fact that the small defects which the first volume of this second edition still showed, disappeared with the growth of experience in later volumes.

The encyclopaedia's new policy met with very general approval: by the issue of the third volume of the second edition, the encyclopaedia had already so far outstripped the execution of Löbel and Franke's original work that the editor could say with complete sincerity that the new edition and the old had only the title of the encyclopaedia in common—and of that title, only the catchword 'Conversations-Lexikon' was left!

Even before the issue of the last volume of the fourth edition, the first volumes were already out of print. A new edition was therefore needed immediately and that, for Brockhaus, meant a complete revision once again. This he reckoned would cost him 50,000 Thalers. At this point, Brockhaus arranged the transfer of the supervision of his printing-house to his son Friedrich Brockhaus (1800–65). This was essential, since Brockhaus had many other publishing enterprises in hand, apart from the encyclopaedia, and notably the issue of French and German editions of the Memoirs of Casanova. In preparation for the fifth edition, Brockhaus now arranged that each of the more important subject-fields had its own editor whose duty was to supervise the preparation of the relevant articles. By summer of 1818 the manuscript of the first five volumes of the new edition had been delivered to five different printers, and Brockhaus's own printing-house was now working for the encyclopaedia. The edition ran to 12,000 copies—within a year it had sold out: within the next three years it was followed by two reprints of 10,000 copies each, and for the first time complete sets of the encyclopaedia could be bought:

Allgemeine deutsche Real-Encyclopädie für die gebildeten Stände. 10 volumes. Leipzig, Brockhaus, 1819–20

which also provided the alternative title of 'Conversations-Lexikon' for those who preferred it. In addition, supplementary volumes had been issued for the possessors of previous editions, so that they could have as much information at their disposal as the purchasers of the new set—an example, long forgotten, that present-day encyclopaedia-publishers might well take to heart!

Such success earned envy, and a number of competitive enterprises were called into being, and plagiarisms and unauthorized reprints were attempted—even in Austria, where the encyclopaedia had been condemned by the Censor. And fault-finders were not slow in voicing their complaints, such as those few original critics who sent in lists of missing topics—to one of whom the exasperated publishers proposed, after the completion of the original 10-volume octavo edition, to issue another in 100 folio volumes!

In 1822, preparations for the sixth edition were begun. It bore the same title as the previous edition:

Allgemeine deutsche Real-Encyclopädie für die gebildeten Stände (Conversationslexikon). 10 volumes. Leipzig, Brockhaus, 1824

and, as in all later editions, the expression 'Conversations-Lexicon'
was restored to the main title. This edition was Brockhaus's last
effort: though the revision was completed within a year, a method
which he had always regarded as the ideal way of achieving a
homogeneous work, he did not survive to see it in print. The publication of the first volumes was made in 1823, and the tenth was
issued in March 1824, but the whole of the edition bore the date
1824. Brockhaus, in collaboration with his friend Hasse, and later
with the famous historian Loebell, had borne the full burden of
editing the work. Brockhaus had also begun the preparation of a
supplementary work:

Neue Folge des Konversations-Lexicons. 2 volumes, each in 2 parts.
Leipzig, Brockhaus, 1824–26

which, in the eleventh and twelfth volumes of the main work (5th
and 6th editions) were to reflect all new events and personalities
except those of transitory interest. Heinrich Brockhaus, in his
reminiscences, says that this undertaking had a very important part
to play. But, he adds, 'the plan of the project fluctuated widely'.

Hardly had the last volume of the *Neue Folge* appeared than the
need for a new edition of the main work became pressing. Heinrich Brockhaus (1804–74), Brockhaus's second son, who had taken
over command of the publishing house, took over the general
editorship of the encyclopaedia, which he retained until 1863.
Heinrich had learnt much during the preparation of the *Neue Folge*
and, with Professor Hasse as his aide, brought the encyclopaedia
up-to-date, incorporating the contents of the *Neue Folge* in the
process. The encyclopaedia was now given a new format: up to
this time it had been printed on a rather greyish paper in small
octavo volumes. Now it was produced on a white paper in twelve
larger and more impressive volumes, and the type-size was
changed from Petit to Borgis. The cost of the improved edition was
fully repaid by sales: even before the publication of the last
volume of the seventh edition:

*Allgemeine deutsche Real-Encyclopädie für die gebildeten Stände (Con-
versations-Lexikon).* 12 volumes. Leipzig, Brockhaus, 1827–29

——2. durchgesehener Druck. Leipzig, Brockhaus, 1830

the whole work was sold out, and it was necessary to hurry through the press a second corrected reprint which was completely published between October 1829 and September 1830. In the same year a supplementary volume was issued for purchasers of the earlier edition.

By such remarkably quick and accurate work it was hoped to defeat the aims of the numerous imitations and unauthorized reprints that sprang up on every side. Marklot had, it is true, abandoned his reprints. But now there was the great *Rheinische Konversations-Lexikon* (12 volumes; Cologne and Bonn, 1824–33) which the bookseller Spitz had produced, which was composed almost entirely of articles filched from Brockhaus. The *Allgemeines deutsches Conversations-Lexikon für die Gebildeten eines jeden Ständes*, of the brothers Reichenbach in Leipzig (10 volumes; 1833–37; second edition, 1839–40), which purported to be compiled by a society of scholars, resembled the Brockhaus encyclopaedia even in appearance. Similar works were issued in Vienna, Augsburg, and Quedlinburg. But Brockhaus's methods and ideals proved triumphant, and his son Heinrich found, for example, that in Naples the Austrian officers were buying sets of Brockhaus whose sale was strictly forbidden in their homeland!

The revolution of 1830 changed in many respects the viewpoint of the man in the street, and there was a desire in ever-widening circles for knowledge and culture. Friedrich and Heinrich Brockhaus therefore decided to publish a supplement which, as the *Neue Folge* had attempted for the sixth, would now complement the seventh edition—and more especially its second corrected printing—with a full survey of contemporary events. Thus appeared in fascicles the:

Conversations-Lexikon der neuesten Zeit und Literatur. Leipzig, Brockhaus, 1832–34

for which a special editor, Wilhelm Adolf Lindau, was appointed. Publication in parts caught on, and nearly every great project in Germany from that time on appeared in this form, for which it was particularly suitable.

Parallel with the issue of the supplementary fascicles, preparation of the eighth edition began. Professor Hasse had left to become editor of the royal *Leipziger Zeitung*, and his place was taken by Dr Karl August Espe (1804–50) who remained with the firm till his death. The eighth edition:

> *Allgemeine deutsche Real-Encyclopädie für die gebildeten Stände (Conversations-Lexikon)*. 12 volumes. Leipzig, Brockhaus, 1833–37
>
> —— Universal-Register. 1839

was completed and complemented by a supplementary work, also edited by Dr Espe:

> *Conversations-Lexikon der Gegenwart*. 4 volumes. Leipzig, Brockhaus, 1838–41

which could also be used as a reference work on its own. About this time each edition of the encyclopaedia was amounting to some thirty thousand sets, an astonishing figure for those times, especially when it is remembered that more worthy rivals were now beginning to appear.

About this time, a brother-in-law of Friedrich Brockhaus, Dr Oswald Marbach, suggested there was a need for a popular illustrated encyclopaedia. Together with Dr August Kaiser, he therefore compiled:

> *Bilder-Conversations-Lexikon für das deutsche Volk, ein Handbuch zur Verbreitung gemeinnütziger Kenntnisse und zur Unterhaltung*. 4 volumes. Leipzig, Brockhaus, 1837–41

printed on thin paper, with 1,200 woodcuts in the text and 45 copper-engraved maps. But the appearance of this new venture, surprisingly enough, was practically ignored as a development in encyclopaedia publishing.

Six years after the completion of the publication of the eighth edition, appeared the ninth:

> *Allgemeine deutsche Real-Encyclopädie für die gebildeten Stände (Conversationslexikon)*. 15 volumes. Leipzig, Brockhaus, 1843–48

part of the delay being due to the planning of a larger encyclopaedia, the first great expansion for a quarter of a century. And at this time the firm set up a Geographisch-Artistische Anstalt (later known as the Kartographie) to prepare a suitable atlas for use with the encyclopaedia:

> *Bilder-Atlas zum Conversationslexikon, entworfen und nach den vorzüglichsten Quellen bearbeitet von Joh. Georg Heck, in 10 Abtheilungen, 500 in Stahl gestochenen Tafeln in Quart mit Text von über 100 Bogen in Octav.* Leipzig, Brockhaus, 1844–49

which was issued in 120 fascicles, each of four or five leaves. This was a highly successful enterprise: the Atlas continued to appear throughout the encyclopaedia's long history, and the services of the map house were greatly used by publishing houses abroad.

The ninth edition was to be accompanied by a supplement. Preparation for this began in 1847—then came the fateful events of March 1848 when the future of the whole of Central Europe was in the balance. The firm did not wait for quieter times but, convinced that the public's interest in current events and personalities was even more intense, set about the immediate publication of the supplement in fascicles:

> *Die Gegenwart.* Leipzig, Brockhaus, 1848–56.

This was edited by Dr August Kurtzel (1808–71) after Dr Espe's death in 1850. It began with an exact description of the February revolution in Paris, cast its net wider, and had a very successful run for a number of years. And in 1847 the firm issued a small atlas:

> *Vollständiger Handatlas über alle Theile der Erde.* Leipzig, Brockhaus, 1847

which had a modest success.

The events of the mid-century had made the issue of a new edition of the encyclopaedia most urgent. Accordingly the tenth edition was issued in the year of Britain's Great Exhibition:

> *Allgemeine deutsche Real-Encyclopädie für die gebildeten Stände (Conversationslexikon).* 15 volumes. Leipzig, Brockhaus, 1851–55

but its issue caused some difficulty: more room was needed for the immense advances in knowledge that were then taking place. The space was provided without any increase in price, a move which added much to the encyclopaedia's popularity. Even Pierer's *Universal-Lexikon*, which described itself as the newest of all encyclopaedic dictionaries, commented favourably—if somewhat enviously—on this generous action. When the tenth edition was completed, some three hundred thousand sets of the encyclopaedia proper had been sold since its inception, plus many more thousand volumes of the various supplements.

Shortly after the firm made another bid for the popular market by issuing in fascicles a new illustrated encyclopaedia:

Illustriertes Haus- und Familien-Lexikon, ein Handbuch für das praktische Leben. 7 volumes. Leipzig, Brockhaus, 1860–65

which was illustrated with more than two thousand woodcuts in the text. The editor, Dr Rudolf Arendt, had given his work almost without charge, but his careful efforts met with little response. It is true that a cheap edition was issued in 1867, but there was no demand for a second edition. The public taste is nearly always unpredictable: two illustrated works lacked success—a third, unillustrated, was a success from the start and has remained a bestseller up to the present day:

Kleines Brockhaus'sche Conversations-Lexikon für den Handgebrauch. 4 volumes. Leipzig, Brockhaus, 1854–56.

was prepared because the firm was convinced there was a demand for a smaller work for the practical man. It was edited by Wilhelm Cranmer. Edition followed edition: the second in 1861–64. The third, in two volumes (1879–80) was especially popular. The fourth (1888) included plates but not text illustrations. The fifth edition (1905) included both.

The road to the completion of the eleventh edition:

Allgemeine deutsche Real-Encylopädie für gebildeten Stände (Conversations-Lexicon). 15 volumes. Leipzig, Brockhaus, 1864–68

—— Supplementary volume. 1872

was long and troublesome: it was an unusual story in the history of the encyclopaedia. The main work showed some weaknesses, although an effort was made to cover many of the lacunae, and especially the political alterations of the 1870–71 war in a supplementary volume, *Encyklopädische Darstellung der neuesten Zeit nebst Ergänzungen früherer Artikel* (1872). Dr Kurtzel edited this edition but died before he could undertake the supplement and was replaced by Oskar Piltz. Kurtzel had also undertaken yet another enterprise. In the years between the tenth and eleventh editions it was thought essential to issue a supplementary work covering contemporary events in the fashion of *Die Gegenwart*. In monthly parts the firm therefore issued:

> *Jahrbuch zum Conversations-Lexikon: Unsere Zeit.* Leipzig, Brockhaus, 1857–64.

When the eleventh edition began to appear, a change was made: the editorship of the *Jahrbuch* was given to Dr Rudolf von Gottschall (1823–1909). The parts now appeared twice a month, and the title was changed to:

> *Unsere Zeit: Deutsche Revue der Gegenwart. Monatschrift zum Conversations-Lexikon. Neue Folge.* Leipzig, Brockhaus, 1865–74.

After the completion of the eleventh edition the connection implied in the title with the encyclopaedia was dropped: from 1873 it was altered into a journal of contemporary political and historical comment, the *Deutsche Revue der Gegenwart*, and was edited until 1887 by Dr Rudolf von Gottschall, and then by Dr Friedrich Bienemann (1838–1903). When the firm relinquished its publication towards the end of the century, the journal ceased publication.

A new atlas was begun about this period:

> *Bilder-Atlas. Ikonographische Encyklopädie der Wissenschaften und Künste, ein Ergänzungswerk zu jedem Conversations-Lexikon.* Leipzig, Brockhaus, 1869–74

which was issued in fascicles, and included specialist as well as general maps, and utilized all the resources of modern map-making at that time to achieve a satisfactory product. The second edition of 1878–79 was even more successful than the first, and there was also a cheap popular edition, issued in 1886 under the title of *Bilder-Atlas der Wissenschaften, Künste und Gewerbe*.

Allgemeine

Hand-Encyclopädie

für

die gebildeten Stände.

In alphabetischer Ordnung

und

in zehn Bänden.

Erster Band.

A bis Boy.

Vierte Original-Auflage.

Mit Königl. Würtembergischen Privilegien.

Altenburg und Leipzig:

F. A. Brockhaus.

1817.

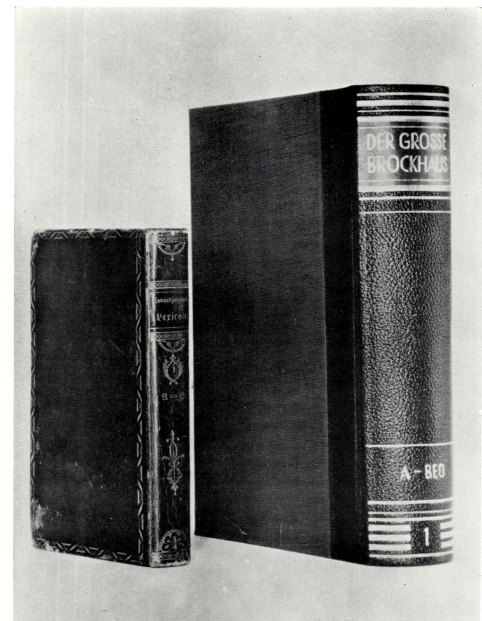

The twelfth edition was issued in 180 fascicles:

Allgemeine deutsche Real-Encyclopädie (Conversations-Lexikon). 15 volumes. Leipzig, 1875–79.

Dr Piltz had died and his place had been taken by Dr Gustave Stockmann, who was assisted by two sub-editors Dr Moritz Brasch and Max Holtzmann. But times were changing and there was a demand for illustrated reference works. So a thirteenth edition, heavily illustrated, was published under Stockmann's leadership. For the first time, double-column setting was introduced and has been retained ever since:

Brockhaus-Conversations-Lexikon. Allgemeine deutsche Real-Encyclopädie. 16 volumes. Leipzig, 1882–87

and in 1887 a supplementary volume was also issued, complete with many indexes.

The new German orthography was fully reflected in the title of the fourteenth edition—had not Daniel Sanders himself been called to Berlin as late as 1875 to help the Ministry of Education in its work of eliminating all foreign terms and expressions from the German language! Thus ran the title:

Brockhaus-Konversationslexikon. 16 volumes. Leipzig, Brockhaus, 1892–95.

The first volume, bearing the date 1892, was issued in November 1891. Its success was immediate: annual reprints of every volume were called for up to the appearance of the supplementary volume in 1897, which brought everything (including statistics) up-to-date. The great collected edition of seventeen volumes of the fourteenth edition which was issued in 1898 was called the revised Jubilee edition (revidierte Jubiläumsausgabe), referring to Löbel's first effort in 1796. A revision of this revised Jubilee edition was issued in seventeen volumes in 1901–04, and a fourth revised edition of the fourteenth edition was issued in 1908, this for the first time having over four thousand text illustrations, about one thousand plates, and hundreds of maps and plans. To this was added a supplementary volume in 1907.

In 1890, in the time of Heinrich's grandson, Albert Eduard Brockhaus (1855–1921), a branch of the firm of Brockhaus was set up in St Petersburg under the name of Brockhaus & Efron. It was this branch that was responsible for the issue of a 43-volume edition in Russian of Brockhaus's encyclopaedia during the years 1890–1906, the last eight volumes (1903–06) being supplementary to the main work. The branch did not of course survive World War I, but the memory of the great encyclopaedia lingered on in Russian minds with surprising results some forty years later.

The fifteenth edition was planned for publication in 1912, and for the preparation of this edition the typewriter was used for the first time! But the war intervened and work on the revision was laid aside. To meet the post-war demand a revision of the fourteenth edition was issued in 1920. The first post-war edition was a small version entitled:

> Brockhaus: Handbuch des Wissens. 4 volumes. Leipzig, Brockhaus, 1921–23

and known to the trade as the *Neue Brockhaus*. A single-volume *Kleine Brockhaus* was issued (1929) with such improvements as stress indications, pronunciation, and quick-reference signs. It was an immediate success, and a second edition was issued in 1930.

Over one thousand authors wrote the two hundred thousand articles in the fifteenth edition:

> Der Grosse Brockhaus. 21 volumes. Leipzig, Brockhaus, 1928–35.

This was produced by Albert Eduard's brother Dr Fritz Brockhaus (1874–1952) and his son Hans Brockhaus (born 1888). The increasing attention paid to scientific and technological matters in the later editions is particularly noticeable in this edition, and in this edition the practice of printing half-tone illustrations in the text was introduced. This edition was also notable for the considerable number of small colour plates mounted in their correct position in the text: a most useful but expensive method of illustration which was not repeated in later editions. Autographs of distinguished people were given for the first time. All the plates and maps were new. In all there were some sixteen thousand text illustrations. The first volume, issued in 1928, had to be reprinted twice to satisfy demand, and the size of the issue of subsequent volumes was accordingly stepped up. Every year three volumes were issued, and this can rightly be termed the finest of all the many editions of the encyclopaedia: it represented the highest standard of encyclopaedia-making ever attempted, and remains a valuable work of reference today.

This edition was issued under the general editorship of Dr Hermann Michel (born 1877) and, when he retired in 1933, his place was taken by Dr Karl Pfannkuch who has retained that post to the present day. In spite of the many political difficulties which the house of Brockhaus faced in its determination to maintain an objective standpoint at all costs and thus preserve the agelong reputation of the firm for integrity and scholarship, Dr Pfannkuch completed the issue of the fifteenth edition in 1935. In 1934 a *Volks-Brockhaus* was issued in one volume: this was an immediate success, being reprinted many times, and having gone into some dozen new editions since that date. And in 1935 appeared the *Sprach-Brockhaus*, the first illustrated dictionary of the German language, inspired by the example of the world-famous one-volume illustrated dictionary of Larousse.

The *Neue Brockhaus*, the *Allbuch* (1936–38), was issued in four volumes plus an atlas, and replaced the four-volume *Brockhaus: Handbuch des Wissens* of fifteen years earlier. It comprised the whole of the *Sprach-Brockhaus*, plus subject and biographical articles. It included 10,000 text illustrations and 266 plates and maps. The Atlas volume included historical maps and hundreds of illustrations. A second edition was published in 1941–42, but no atlas was issued. In 1940 a supplementary volume to the main work, the *Taschen-Brockhaus zum Zeitgeschehen*, was published, a second edition following in 1942.

The Brockhaus headquarters for a century-and-a-quarter were destroyed in 1943—only the key-word list for the next edition of the encyclopaedia survived—but in 1944 sufficient machinery was reconditioned to run off a fifth edition of the *Sprach-Brockhaus*. In the same year a tenth edition of the *Volks-Brockhaus* was printed in Prague. The Russians took over Leipzig in 1945 and, moved by memories of the great encyclopaedia published by Brockhaus & Efron in Russia at the beginning of the century, treated Brockhaus rather more leniently than most of the publishing houses in that city. Nevertheless, Brockhaus had an unhappy time in which very little publishing was achieved: the eleventh edition of the *Volks-Brockhaus*, of which the first half-volume was issued in 1950, was immediately branded as reactionary and banned.

An improved edition of *Der Sprach-Brockhaus: Deutsches Bilder-wörterbuch für Jedermann* was issued in Wiesbaden in 1949—for the first time the text was printed in a roman face, Antiqua, even though the firm is still convinced that Fraktur is easier (for Germans) to read. A sixth edition of the *Sprach-Brockhaus* was issued in 1951, and this was reprinted several times.

During the war five publishers had united in Switzerland as the Encyclios-Verlag to publish the seven-volume *Schweizer-Lexikon*—at the end of 1949 a two-volume work with the same title was issued, and a second edition was issued as *Die Kleine Enzyklopädie* in 1952.

In 1949, Brockhaus resumed their publication of encyclopaedias in their new headquarters by the issue of:

Der Kleine Brockhaus. 2 volumes. Wiesbaden, Brockhaus, 1949–1950

which in spite of its size (less than 1,500 pages) included nearly six thousand illustrations at the top and bottom of the pages, and a number of maps in the text. And in 1952 preparation began for the issue of the sixteenth edition of the encyclopaedia:

Der Grosse Brockhaus. 12 volumes. Wiesbaden, Brockhaus, 1952–1957.

This was of course smaller than the fifteenth edition and not so elaborate in plan or execution. In all there are well over nine thousand pages, nearly thirty thousand text illustrations (many of them excellent half-tones) and some eight hundred plates, as well as 124 maps. The text is in roman, and the bibliographies, though brief, are up-to-date. A supplementary volume and an atlas volume were issued in 1958.

In 1955 a Jubilee-edition (celebrating the 150th anniversary of the founding by Friedrich Arnold Brockhaus of his publishing house in 1805) of *Der Volks-Brockhaus* was issued: this was a triumph of good publishing in difficult conditions—some forty thousand entries, 3,500 illustrations and about twenty coloured maps. After the completion of the *Grosse Brockhaus* work began on the third edition of:

Der Neue Brockhaus. 5 volumes, plus an Atlas volume. Wiesbaden, Brockhaus, 1958–60

which has been completely revised. And, of course, preparations for the seventeenth edition of the main encyclopaedia are well under way.

BIBLIOGRAPHY

Heinrich Eduard Brockhaus. *Die Firma F. A. Brockhaus von der Begründung bis zum hundertjährigen Jubiläum 1805–1905.* Leipzig, Brockhaus, 1905

Arthur Hübscher. *Hundertfünfzig Jahr F. A. Brockhaus, 1805 bis 1955.* Wiesbaden, Brockhaus, 1955

Ernst Herbert Lehmann. *Geschichte des Konversationslexikons.* Leipzig, Brockhaus, 1934

This exaggerated laudation of Encyclopedism.

THOMAS CARLYLE

The beginning of the nineteenth century brought with it a boom in encyclopaedia publishing: the example of the *Encyclopédie* and the *Encyclopaedia Britannica* had proved that encyclopaedias were needed, and that good profits could be expected from sales to the rapidly increasing middle-class section of the population in Western Europe. What was overlooked by many of the speculative booksellers and publishers who ventured into this market was that, to be lasting, an encyclopaedia must be thorough, well written and informative, and that it must be neither too small nor too large. A large encyclopaedia was too costly (both to publisher and reader) and took too long to complete: a small encyclopaedia failed to impress, inevitably scamped some subjects and ignored others, and usually indicated some inadequacies in planning. There was, in fact, a philosophical background to every good encyclopaedia: this, however, did not guarantee its success—for this a good business-man was needed. The combination of the man of business and the scholar had become essential by the time Diderot began his work, and lack of one or other partner proved the ruin of many a good nineteenth-century encyclopaedia-publishing venture. In particular, the problem of financing the publication of encyclopaedias had increasingly hampered new projects, and even now this has not been completely solved.

The century began with the issue of a new edition of Abraham Rees's *Encyclopaedia* (see page 109), a scholarly work which was well received. It has also to be remembered that throughout the century re-impressions and new editions of both *Brockhaus* and the *Britannica* were appearing at frequent intervals and were gaining in sales and prestige. Thus new encyclopaedias had substantial competition to meet, and there was a great tendency to copy at least the features—if not the exact text—of these giants, and to under-cut the market by offering rather smaller encyclopaedias at a lower cost. Thus, a host of hack-workers were busy throughout the period industriously plagiarizing, translating and abbreviating the articles in other contemporary encyclopaedias, while bolder publishers were not averse to pirating whole editions with considerable success.

The *Handwörterbuch der Wissenschaften und Künste* was the work of Karl Heinrich Poelitz. The first part (A–H) was published at Regensburg in 1805, but it failed to get popular support and was not continued. A curious situation arose in England in the next four years: the Prebendary of St Paul's, Dr George Gregory (1754–1808) was named as the editor of *A dictionary of arts and sciences* (2 volumes; London, 1806–07). In opposition to this some London booksellers commissioned the compilation of *The British encyclo-paedia; or, Dictionary of arts and sciences. Comprising an accurate and popular view of the present improved state of human knowledge* (6 volumes; London, Longman, Hurst, Rees & Orme, 1809), of which the scientist and inventor William Nicholson (1753–1815) was named as editor. But Gregory was much involved in cathedral duties, and Nicholson (who had once been Josiah Wedgwood's agent at Am-sterdam!) was fully occupied in the scientific field. The result was that neither played much part in the compilation of their respec-tive encyclopaedias, and both works—though rivals—were in fact compiled by the same anonymous (but see page 176) scholar turned hack-worker for this purpose! The *British encyclopaedia* was the more successful of the two, and three editions were sub-sequently issued in Philadelphia by Mitchell & Ames (1816–17, 7 volumes; 1818, 12 volumes; 1819–21, 12 volumes).

An important event of 1808 was the issue of the first volume of *The Edinburgh encyclopaedia* (18 volumes; Edinburgh, William Blackwood, 1808–30), which was edited by the great scientist Sir David Brewster (1781–1868). Originally planned in twelve vol-umes, with more than 150 contributors, the encyclopaedia was particularly notable for its scientific articles, many of which were written by Brewster himself. As he proudly pointed out, two sub-jects—the polarization of light, and electromagnetism—were fully treated (the latter by its founder, Oersted) in the later volumes, though they had not even been known by these names when the work was commenced. Similarly, contemporary events—such as Hansteen's scientific exploration of Siberia in 1829—were fully discussed. Brewster's aim was in fact to distinguish his encyclopaedia 'by two features that had not been exhibited in any similar work published in England [sic], namely, by the Originality and the Selectiveness of its articles'. Scotland had in truth produced a worthy complement to the *Britannica*. By its side *The imperial encyclopaedia: or, Dictionary of the Sciences and Arts; comprehending also the whole circle of miscellaneous literature* (4 volumes; London, 1809–14), compiled by the mathematician Thomas Exley (1775–1855) and the Reverend William Moore Johnson, curate at Henbury, Gloucestershire, made a poor showing. The type of amateur effort that Croker (see page 108) had issued in the eighteenth century was continuing to be published, but the more scholarly productions were already winning the day.

Midway between the two extremes were however such works as the *Pantologia* (12 volumes; London, 1802–13). This, as the theologian and mathematician Olinthus Gilbert Gregory (1774–1841) said, 'was commenced by Mr Bosworth [i.e., Newton Bosworth] in 1802. On my removal to Woolwich in January 1803, another gentleman was associated with us, who, however, in consequence of an unexpected accession of property, retired from the labour in about twelve months. Shortly afterwards a speculating bookseller, who had ascertained that this Universal Dictionary was in preparation, with a view to anticipate us both in object and name, commenced the publication of a new Cyclopaedia, of which Dr George Gregory [see page 175] was announced as the editor, while, in fact, the late Mr Jeremiah Joyce was the principal, if not the only, person engaged upon the work. This manœuvre suggested the expediency of new arrangements, as well as of a new title, for our Encyclopaedia; and Mr Good [i.e., the physician John Mason Good (1764–1827)] having recently published his 'Song of songs' at Mr Kearsley's the bookseller, who was the chief proprietor of the new undertaking, his high reputation for erudition, and for punctuality in the execution of his engagements, induced us to look to

him as an admirably qualified individual to co-operate with us in
our important enterprise. Some time elapsed before we could
overcome his objections to the placing his name *first* on the title-
page of a work, of which he was not to take the general super-
intendence; but at length the scruple was removed; and from 1805,
when our joint preparations commenced, to the spring of 1813,
when the task was completed, he continued with the utmost
promptness, regularity, and versatility of talent, to supply the
various articles and treatises that were comprehended in the extensive portion of the Dictionary which he undertook to compose.'
(Olinthus Gregory, *Memoirs of the life, writings and character, literary,*
professional, and religious, of the late John Mason Good, M.D., . . .
London, Henry Fisher, 1828; pages 88–89.)

This extract has been quoted at length, not only because it
throws light on the origins of the *Pantologia*, but also for its information on the contemporary competitive practices in the field of
encyclopaedia-making. The allusion to the name of Jeremiah Joyce
(1763–1816) is of great interest. Joyce was a journeyman glazier
who inherited a small copyhold property on the death of his father
in 1778. He studied for the Unitarian ministry, and became tutor
to the sons of Earl Stanhope, Pitt's brother-in-law. Owing to his
advanced political views and opinions, he became a member of
both the Society for Constitutional Information, and of the London Corresponding Society. At Stanhope's house he was arrested
on 4th May 1794, being charged with 'treasonable practices'. He
was in fact the victim of Pitt's annoyance with Stanhope. The
Privy Council examined Joyce, but as he had been refused the aid
of counsel, he would not answer their questions, and was eventually committed to the Tower of London on a charge of high
treason. At first found guilty, he was subsequently acquitted and
released. He was a very well informed man who wrote a number of
popular works on scientific subjects, and it may therefore be too
harsh to describe his editing of Gregory's and Nicholson's encyclopaedias (see page 176) as hack-work.

The *Encyclopaedia Perthensis, or Universal dictionary of knowledge,*
collected from every source, and intended to supersede the use of all other
English books of reference. Illustrated with plates and maps (23 volumes;

Perth, C. Mitchell, 1806) was first issued in weekly parts from 1796 to 1806. It was edited by Alexander Aitchison, and his bold claim that this work was to supersede the use of all other English books of reference is repeated in the preface where, moreover, the reader is assured that 'there is not a word in the English language; a technical term in any Art of Science; an event of any importance in the history of mankind; a city, town, kingdom, republic, or empire in the Known World; an opinion in Religion; an article in Mythology; a system of Philosophy; or a great or learned character in the annals of Biography, that is not mentioned or described in the Encyclopaedia Perthensis'. Despite these words, only a second edition was issued—first in parts, 1807 to 1816, and then as a set (24 volumes; Edinburgh, J. Brown, 1816), the last volume being supplementary to the main work. In this edition, the sub-title was altered to 'or, Universal dictionary of the arts, sciences, literature, etc., . . .'

James Millar (1762–1827), who edited the fourth and part of the fifth editions of the *Encyclopaedia Britannica* (and contributed extensively to both), also planned and edited a more popular work, the *Encyclopaedia Edinensis; or, Dictionary of arts, sciences and literature* (6 volumes; Edinburgh, J. Anderson, 1827). It is interesting to see how widely publishers' ideas varied concerning the suitable format for encyclopaedias at this time: the *Encyclopaedia Perthensis*, for example, was octavo, whereas the *Edinensis* was—like the *Britannica*—a quarto. Just as the Court circles in France had influenced the production of duodecimo reference works in the preceding centuries, so there was undoubtedly public demand in the nineteenth century for the issue of encyclopaedias in a form that could easily be handled, and even in this century the *Britannica* found it worth while to publish a miniature edition (see page 151).

What should have been the greatest encyclopaedia of the century was, unfortunately, a comparative failure. The reasons why the *Encyclopaedia metropolitana* did not secure lasting public support can perhaps be summarized as follows:

1. Abandoning the current fashion, it substituted systematic for alphabetical order of contents, based on an evolutionary

system envisaged by the poet Samuel Taylor Coleridge (1772–1834).

2. The long period over which it was produced (1817–45) not only involved a change of editorship on three occasions, but also the danger that what appealed to the country's tastes in 1817, may well have gone out of fashion by the time the work was completed nearly thirty years later.

3. The rivalry of such established favourites as the *Britannica* must have hampered sales considerably.

Certainly, the *Metropolitana's* misfortunes could not be ascribed to defects of quality, for its contributors included most of the leading scholars of the day.

The *Encyclopaedia metropolitana; or, Universal dictionary of knowledge, on an original plan: comprising the three-fold advantage of a philosophical and an alphabetical arrangement, with . . . engravings. Edited by the Rev. Edward Smedley . . . the Rev. Hugh James Rose . . . and the Rev. Henry John Rose . . .* was published in 28 quarto volumes during the period 1817 to 1845 (London, B. Fellowes, F. & J. Rivington; etc.). The original editor was Thomas Curtis (see page 182), but after six parts had been issued—in all, fifty-nine parts were published—the publishing arrangements were changed, and Edward Smedley (1788–1836), who was a frequent contributor to the *Penny cyclopaedia* (see page 185), took over the editorship in 1822. Smedley continued to work with the *Metropolitana* until his death. Editorial responsibility was then assumed in 1836 by Hugh James Rose (1795–1838) who was also Principal of King's College, London, for a brief period. On Hugh's death, he was succeeded by his younger brother Henry John Rose (1800–73), who had already become a contributor and joint-editor. During the years 1848–58 a revised edition of the *Metropolitana* was published in 40 *octavo* volumes (London, J. J. Griffin). Both editions were heavily illustrated, and copies of the *Metropolitana* are well worth preserving both for their plates and for their many authoritative articles.

Another and greater failure was the gigantic encyclopaedia of Johann Samuel Ersch (1766–1826) and Johann Gottfried Gruber (*c.* 1774–1851): the *Allgemeine Encyclopädie der Wissenschaften und*

PLAN OF THE ENCYCLOPAEDIA METROPOLITANA

N.B. This **was** modified from Coleridge's original conception.

FIRST DIVISION.

PURE SCIENCES.
— 2 Vols.

FORMAL. {
Universal Grammar.
Logic:—Rhetoric.
Mathematics.
Metaphysics.
}

REAL. {
Morals.
Law.
Theology.
}

SECOND DIVISION.

MIXED AND APPLIED SCIENCES.
— 6 Vols.

MIXED. {
Mechanics.
Hydrostatics.
Pneumatics.
Optics.
Astronomy.
}

I. EXPERIMENTAL PHILOSOPHY. {
Magnetism:—Electro-Magnetism.
Electricity, Galvanism.
Heat.
Light.
Chemistry.
Sound.
Meteorology.
Figure of the Earth.
Tides and Waves.
}

II. THE FINE ARTS. {
Architecture.
Sculpture.
Painting.
Heraldry.
Numismatics.
Poetry.
}

III.
THE USEFUL ARTS. { Political Economy. Carpentry. Fortification. Naval Architecture. Manufactures. }

IV.
NATURAL HISTORY { Inanimate:—Crystallography, Geology, Mineralogy. Insentient:—Phytonomy, Botany. Animate:—Zoology. }

V.
APPLICATION OF NATURAL HISTORY. { Anatomy, Materia Medica. Medicine. Surgery. }

THIRD DIVISION.

BIOGRAPHICAL AND HISTORICAL.

—

5 VOLS.

Biography CHRONOLOGICALLY arranged, interspersed with introductory Chapters of National History, Political Geography, and Chronology, and accompanied with correspondent Maps and Charts. The far larger portion of HISTORY being thus conveyed, not only in its most interesting, but in its most philosophical, because most natural and real form; while the remaining and connecting facts are interwoven in the several preliminary chapters.

FOURTH DIVISION.

MISCELLANEOUS AND LEXICOGRAPHICAL.

—

12 VOLS.

Alphabetical, Miscellaneous, and Supplementary:—containing a GAZETTEER, or complete Vocabulary of Geography: and a Philosophical and Etymological LEXICON of the English Language, or the History of English Words;—the citations arranged according to the Age of the Works from which they are selected, yet with every attention to the independent beauty or value of the sentences chosen, which is consistent with the higher ends of a clear insight into the original and acquired meaning of every word.

INDEX.—Being a digested and complete Body of Reference to the whole Work.

Künste, von genannten Schriftstellern bearb. (Leipzig, Brockhaus, 1818–1889), which stopped publication, still incomplete, when 167 volumes had been issued. To accelerate its issue the editors divided the alphabet into three sections: A–G; H–N; and, O–Z, issuing volumes in each of these sections as soon as they were completed. Of the three, only the first was completed, in 99 volumes, in 1882; the second stopped at Ligature, volume 43, in 1889; and the third stopped at Phyxios, volume 25, in 1850. Many of the entries were enormous: Britain covered 700 pages, India 356, Jewish literature 414, and Greece 3,668! Ersch & Gruber is the greatest Western encyclopaedia ever attempted, and though its very size and consequent delays defeated its conclusion, it remains a vast storehouse of information for future research workers. By its side, the octavo volumes of the *Encyklopädisches Wörterbuch der Wissenschaften, Künste und Gewerbe* (26 volumes; Altenburg, 1822–1836), subsequently re-issued as the *Universal-Lexikon, oder vollständiges encyklopädisches Wörterbuch* (35 volumes; Altenburg, 1835), appears negligible. But its editors, A. Binzer and Heinrich August Pierer, were accurate and able workers: they issued a very good encyclopaedia which, moreover, included definitions and foreign equivalents of words. The encyclopaedia became known as 'Pierer', and supplements were published in the form of a year-book, *Pierers Jahrbuch*, from 1865 onwards. The last edition of the encyclopaedia, edited by Joseph Kürschner, was published in 12 volumes at Altenburg, 1888–1894.

The *London encyclopaedia; or, Universal dictionary of science, art, literature, and practical mechanics* (London, T. Tegg, 1829), was issued in 22 octavo volumes, and is chiefly remarkable for being edited by T. Curtis 'the original Editor of the *Encyclopaedia Metropolitana*'. At this time, quite a number of unimportant encyclopaedias were appearing in Western Europe to meet the growing demand for reasonably priced reference works; it is unnecessary to give them all space here, but they are listed in an Appendix (see 231). One, however, merits more extensive treatment: *The cabinet cyclopaedia* (London, 1829–49) was completed in no less than 133 octavo volumes. Its editor was Dionysius Lardner (1793–1859) who had contributed articles on scientific subjects to both the *Encyclopaedia*

Edinensis and the *Metropolitana*. In 1827 he was elected to the Chair of Natural Philosophy and Astronomy at what is now University College, London. Satirized by Thackeray, lampooned by Maclise, he nevertheless did excellent editorial work, and his encyclopaedia is filled with good articles by the leading experts of the day.

Noah Webster was born at West Hartford, Connecticut, in 1758. A teacher and journalist by profession, he published his pioneer *A grammatical institute of the English language* in 1783–85. Its great success—sales had reached more than a million copies annually by 1850—enabled him to undertake the compilation of *A compendious dictionary of the English language*, published in 1806, from which developed his great two-volume *American dictionary of the English language*, whose first edition appeared in two quarto volumes in 1828. This was in fact an encyclopaedic dictionary, for Webster's work was noted for its clear and comprehensive definitions. A two-volume and larger second edition was published by George and Charles Merriam in 1841. Webster died in 1843, and the one-volume third edition of 1847 was edited by his son-in-law Professor Chauncey A. Goodrich of Yale, a pictorial supplement being issued in 1859. Dr Noah Porter, later President of Yale, edited the fourth edition—popularly known as the 'Unabridged'—of 1864, and a supplement was added in 1879. In 1890 the fifth edition appeared under the title of *Webster's International dictionary of the English language*, again edited by Noah Porter; a supplement was issued in 1900. Under the title of *Webster's New International dictionary of the English language*, a sixth edition was published in 1909 under the editorship of William Torrey Harris, who had edited the 1900 supplement. A seventh edition, with the title *Webster's New international dictionary, second edition*, was edited by Dr William Allan Neilson, President of Smith College, and was issued in two volumes in 1934. The present edition is the eighth: *Webster's Third new international dictionary of the English language, unabridged* (2 volumes; Springfield, Mass., G. & C. Merriam Company; London, G. Bell, 1961). It has been edited by Dr Philip Babcock Gove who has boldly abandoned some of the encyclopaedic features that bring the past editions within the scope of this book. Former editions are therefore well worth preserving for their contribution to the state of knowledge at the periods they were issued.

The *Encyclopaedia Americana: a popular dictionary* (13 volumes; Philadelphia, Carey, Lea & Carey, 1829–33) was edited by a recently arrived German exile Francis Lieber (1800–72). It was based on the seventh edition of *Brockhaus*, and was an immediate success. Reprints and revisions appeared in 1835, 1836, 1847–48, 1849, and 1858, and a supplementary volume was issued from 1848 onwards. *The Encyclopaedia Americana: a supplementary dictionary of arts, sciences, and general literature* (4 volumes; New York and Philadelphia, J. M. Stoddart, 1883–89), often referred to as 'Stoddart', had no connection with the preceding works of the same title, being described in some issues as a 'Supplement to *Encyclopaedia Britannica*, ninth edition'. At the end of the century arrangements were made to revive the original work by Lieber and his associates, in collaboration with the publishers of the journal *Scientific American*. Frederick Converse Beach, editor of the *Scientific American*, was appointed editor of the new edition of the *Encyclopaedia Americana*, which at length appeared in 20 volumes in 1911, a two-volume supplement being published in the following year. This edition was therefore strong in scientific and technical subjects, a feature which—although the connection with the *Scientific American* was broken in 1911—has continued ever since. A revised edition in 30 volumes was issued in 1918–20 under the editorship of George Edward Rines. In 1923 publication began of an annual supplement, the *Americana annual*, edited by Alexander H. McDannald, who also edited the encyclopaedia itself from 1920 to 1948. The *Americana*, one of the most popular of North American encyclopaedias today, is subject to continuous revision, new issues being made annually. A special feature is its histories of individual centuries. It also devotes much space to American people and topics. It also includes—like Larousse—reviews and summaries of outstanding works of literature and music, entered under their titles.

The famous Parisian publisher Ambroise Firmin Didot (1790–1876), perhaps inspired by the success of *Brockhaus*, issued in 1833–39 his *Dictionnaire de la conversation et de la lecture: répertoire des connaissances usuelles*, in 52 octavo volumes. This was edited by the

United Irishman, William Duckett (1768–1841) who, in exile, became a professor at Sainte-Barbe. Duckett was also responsible for the initiation of the 15 supplementary volumes that were issued up to 1858. A further five-volume supplement 'offrant le résumé des faits et des idées de notre temps (. . . en réalité, une Encyclopédie des hommes et des choses des quinze dernières années)' was published from 1864 to 1882. Didot also issued an *Encyclopédie de famille: répertoire générale des connaissances usuelles* in 13 volumes in 1868–69.

The *penny cyclopaedia of The Society for the Diffusion of Useful Knowledge* (London, Charles Knight, 1833–43) was issued in 27 small volumes, and two supplementary volumes were issued 1851–1856. It 'is not an attempt [as most other encyclopaedias] to form systems of knowledge, but to give pretty fully, under each separate head, as much information as can be conveyed within reasonable limits. But while it endeavours to present in detail the explanation of those terms of Art and Science, the right understanding of which is independent of any system, it also attempts to give such general views of all great branches of knowledge, as may help to the formation of just ideas on their extent and relative importance, and to point out the best sources of complete information.' This encyclopaedia, which was illustrated with line cuts, was—in spite of its name—issued at 9*d*. per part, or '7*s*. 6*d*. per volume, bound in cloth'. But the publisher, Charles Knight (1791–1873), found no profit in it, for the venture cost him £40,000 in all, owing to the heavy excise duty on paper at that time. The editor, Edward George Long (1800–79), who was the first Professor of Ancient Languages at the newly formed University of Virginia (1824–28), was a prominent member of the Society for the Diffusion of Useful Knowledge, and he also helped to found the Royal Geographical Society. A full index to the encyclopaedia was promised but not issued. Knight later published the *English encyclopaedia: a new dictionary of useful knowledge* (22 volumes; London, 1854–62), with a four-volume supplement (1869–73); and the *National cyclopaedia of useful knowledge* (12 volumes; London, 1847–51; 14 volumes, 1881).

The *Penny cyclopaedia* is not to be confused with the *Pfennig-Encyklopädie; oder, Neues elegantes Conversations-Lexicon für Gebildete aus allen Ständen* (4 volumes; Leipzig, 1834–37), which was edited by Oscar Ludwig Bernhard Wolff; a supplementary volume was issued 1839–41.

The scientist Charles Frederick Partington (died 1857) did a great deal to teach and popularize scientific and technical subjects among the working classes. In addition, he edited and wrote much of *The British cyclopaedia of arts and sciences, manufactures, commerce, literature, history, geography, politics, biography, natural history, Biblical criticism and theology, on the basis of the German conversations-lexicon, with such additions as will adapt it to the present state of science* (2 volumes; London, Orr & Smith; Philadelphia, T. Wardle, 1833–35). The wording of the title-page of the second volume varies very much in detail from that of the first. It was at this time that the Russians started issuing the *Entsiklopedicheskogo leksikona* (St Petersburg, 1835–41); this was to have been a very large work, but it remained uncompleted at volume 17 (Da–Dyat).

A powerful rival to *Brockhaus* arose in the 1840's in *Der grosse Conversations-Lexikon für die gebildeten Stände,* issued by the firm of Josef Meyer (1796–1856) at Hildburghausen. The first edition comprised 46 octavo volumes, with six supplementary volumes issued over the period 1840 to 1855. From the first 'Meyer'—as it was always called—was of a high standard, and paid particular attention to scientific and technical subjects. It was deservedly popular and had reached its sixth edition (24 volumes; Leipzig, Bibliographisches Institut) in 1902–12 (the last three volumes being supplementary), to which a three-volume war and post-war supplement was added during the years 1916 to 1920. The seventh edition was published in 12 volumes, 1924–30 (with three supplementary volumes, and an atlas and gazetteer, 1931–33); but the eighth edition was never completed—the editors and publishers fell under the influence of National Socialism and the firm was eventually liquidated in 1945, so that only volumes 1–9 and volume 12 were issued (Leipzig, Bibliographisches Institut, 1936–1942). The older editions are well worth preserving for their admirable articles and excellent illustrations and maps. Many small and condensed 'Handlexikons', etc., were also issued by Meyer throughout the century of its existence.

In 1847–55 a Russian journalist, A. Starchevskii, completed and published at St Petersburg a 12-volume encyclopaedia, the *Spravochnii entsiklopedicheskii slovar'*, which owed much to the example of *Brockhaus* and other similar encyclopaedias of that time. Similarly, Dr Spencer Fullerton Baird (1823–87), the American naturalist, translated and edited Brockhaus's picture atlas (see page 66) as the *Iconographic encyclopaedia of science, literature and art, systematically arranged. By G. Heck* (4 volumes, and 2 volumes of plates; New York, Rudolph Garrigue, 1849–51).

The *Konversations-Lexikon*, issued by the firm of Herder at Freiburg-im-Breisgau (1st edition; 5 volumes; 1853–57) provided a definite Catholic viewpoint, but its general impartiality, scholarship, accuracy and thoroughness earned it a wider audience. A third edition (9 volumes; Freiburg-im-Breisgau, and St Louis, Mo., Herder, 1902–07) was brought up-to-date by the issue of a supplement (2 volumes in 3; 1910–21); a fourth edition was issued 1931–35, and a fifth —published 1953–56—is in ten volumes, of which the last is a general survey entitled 'Der Mensch in seiner Welt'. Various smaller versions, 'Volkslexikons', etc., have been issued throughout the period.

Charles Anderson Dana (1819–97), American journalist and friend of Abraham Lincoln, was second Secretary of War (1864–1865) and editor of the New York *Sun* (1868–97). With George Ripley (1802–80) he edited *The new American cyclopaedia: a popular dictionary of general knowledge* (New York, Appleton, 1858–63), which was issued in 16 volumes. This encyclopaedia was a praiseworthy effort: well over three hundred contributors collaborated in its compilation, and it quickly gained authority in North America. A second edition, under the title of *The American cyclopaedia*—with the same editorship and publishers—was issued in 1873–83 in 16 volumes, a supplement being appended to the contents of each volume. This was in turn supplemented by *Appleton's annual cyclopaedia and register of important events . . .*, which was issued by Appleton's of New York during the years 1862 to 1903, covering the years 1861 to 1902 (the first 14 volumes being issued under the title of *The American annual cyclopaedia and register of important events*, 1861–74). Cumulative indexes to the annual volumes cover the whole period and make the set invaluable for its detailed chronicle of administrative and social events—particularly during the Civil War and Reconstruction periods—and for its biographical material relating to countless minor American personalities.

The Polish *Encyklopedja powszechna* (Warsaw, S. Orgelbrand, 1858–68), often referred to by the name of its publisher, was issued in 28 volumes. It was similar to *Brockhaus* in its policy of using brief informative articles and proved very popular, especially for its wealth of biographical material. A new edition in 18 volumes (the last part of volume 16, and the whole of volumes 17 and 18 being supplementary) was published in 1898–1912.

Chambers's Encyclopaedia: a dictionary of universal knowledge . . . (on the basis of the latest edition of the German Conversations Lexicon) . . . (10 volumes; London, W. & R. Chambers, 1860–68) had no connection with Ephraim Chambers's pioneer work. The new encyclopaedia took its name from the Scottish publishers William and Robert Chambers. William Chambers (1800–83) began as a bookseller, founded *Chambers's Edinburgh journal* in 1832, and joined with his brother Robert (1802–71) in founding a publishing business. The firm published a large number of standard and reference works—Robert himself compiled the famous *Book of days* (2 volumes; 1863)—but their most important publication was the encyclopaedia, which was edited by Dr Andrew Findlater (1810–1885), assisted by John Merry Ross, who later edited *The Globe encyclopaedia* (see page 193). Findlater, who had been headmaster of Gordon's Hospital at Aberdeen, had already gained some experience by editing the 1857 edition of Chambers's *Information for the people*. In compiling the encyclopaedia, the Chambers brothers took an active part, Robert being especially interested since he had been influenced at an early age by access in his home to a set of the *Encyclopaedia Britannica*. A revised edition of *Chambers's Encyclopaedia*, with a supplement and an index, was published in ten volumes in 1874, and another in 1888–92 (10 volumes; London and Edinburgh, W. & R. Chambers). Further editions, each in ten volumes, appeared in 1895, 1901, 1908 (with a preface by David Patrick), 1922–27 (edited by David Patrick and William Geddie), and

1935. A special issue of the last was given the title of the *British universities encyclopaedia*. In 1944 the encyclopaedia was taken over by another publisher, completely revised under the editorship of Margaret D. Law (who had at one time been on the staff of the *Encyclopaedia Britannica*), and issued as *Chambers's Encyclopaedia. New edition* (15 volumes; London, George Newnes, 1950). This was followed by supplements, *Chambers's Encyclopaedia world survey*, issued at intervals from 1952 onwards, and by a new edition in 15 volumes in 1955. Unlike the 'continuous revision' system of the *Britannica*, the *Americana*, and many other encyclopaedias of today, *Chambers's* have instead adopted a system of complete revision at intervals of approximately every five years. The latest edition of *Chambers's* appeared in 1960, and another is planned for 1965. Throughout its long history, *Chambers's* has achieved a special place in the world of reference books by its great reputation for reliability and scholarship, and it has continued to reject the temptation to imitate some of the sales features of its rivals in favour of an individual line that has earned general respect and confidence.[1]

Eastern Europe was by now becoming increasingly encyclopaedia-conscious. The Hungarian *Egyetemes magyar encyclopaediá* (13 volumes; Pest, Szent-István-Társulat, 1860–76) was edited by Janos Török. It had been preceded by the Bohemian *Slovník naučný* (10 volumes, and 2 supplementary volumes; Prague, Kober, 1859–87), edited by František Vladislav Rieger and J. Malý), which was often referred to as 'Kober'. These were followed by the Russian *Nastol'nyi slovar' dlya spravok po vsem otraslyam znaniya: spravochnyi entsiklopedicheskii leksikon* (3 volumes, and 1 supplementary volume; St Petersburg, 1863–66), which was edited by Feliks G. Toll and V. R. Zotov, and which was strong in biographical material.

Pierre Athanase Larousse was born at Toucy (Yonne) on 23rd October 1817, the son of the village blacksmith. At sixteen he was admitted to the Ecole Normale at Versailles, and by the age of twenty he was already in charge of the primary school in his

[1] See *Announcing the new Chambers Encyclopaedia* (London, George Newnes, 1950. 51 pages).

native village. Three years later he left for Paris, where he spent eight years attending lectures and studying assiduously at the Sorbonne and other learned institutions. In 1851 he met Augustin Boyer (1821–96) who had been brought up in a neighbouring village and had succeeded to the headmastership of the local school there. Larousse had already published his *Lexicologie des écoles*, but he was anxious to become his own publisher. In 1852 the two young associates founded the Librairie Larousse & Boyer, and in 1858 a periodical, *L'Ecole normale*, designed for teachers, was started, while in 1860, *L'Emulation*, a journal for students, followed. From 1849 to 1871 Larousse also wrote more than twenty textbooks, including the *Encyclopédie du jeune âge* in 1853, the *Dictionnaire de la langue française* in 1856, and the *Dictionnaire complet de la langue française* in 1869. In 1865 he commenced publication of the famous encyclopaedia *Grand dictionnaire universel du XIXᵉ siècle*, which was anti-clerical in policy and combined the features of both dictionary and encyclopaedia. This was completed in 15 volumes in 1876, and supplementary volumes were issued in 1878 and 1888. Larousse, inspired by the work of Diderot and d'Alembert, had set himself to produce 'un livre où l'on trouvera, chacune à son ordre alphabétique, toutes les connaissances qui enrichissent aujourd'hui l'esprit humain. La richesse que j'ai acquise, je ne l'emploierai pas pour mon usage personnel, et je n'y perdrai pas grand'chose, car les jouissances exclusivement personnelles laissent le cœur vide et ne sont que vanité au point de vue du bonheur réal.' Eventually Larousse and Boyer parted company and Larousse set up his own printing works, but in 1875 he died, leaving behind him a gigantic publishing enterprise that had already become world famous in his own lifetime.

The *Grand dictionnaire* was revised by Claude Augé (Jean Claude Augé, 1854–1924) and published as the *Nouveau Larousse illustré* in seven volumes in 1897–1904. Augé had set himself to produce a new work in keeping with the times, and his success is measured by sales of more than a quarter-of-a-million copies. A supplement was published three years later. In addition, in 1907 the *Larousse mensuel illustré: revue mensuel encyclopédique* was started. This too was edited by Claude Augé; it fully reflected contemporary events and affairs, and was copiously illustrated. In 1906 the first edition of the *Petit Larousse illustré* was published, followed by the two-volume *Larousse pour tous: Dictionnaire encyclopédique* in 1908, both edited by Claude Augé. The *Petit Larousse illustré* was in fact the direct successor to Larousse's *Dictionnaire* of 1856; it was divided into three parts—French language; foreign quotations (including Latin); history and geography. In 1922 *Larousse pour tous* was superseded by the *Larousse universel: dictionnaire encyclopédique* in two volumes. This was edited by Claude Augé, and was more comprehensive and better illustrated than its predecessor. The *Nouveau petit Larousse* was issued in 1924.

The *Larousse ou XXᵉ siècle* (1927–33, 6 volumes), which was edited by Paul Augé, paid particular attention to World War I history. A supplement to the revised edition (1948–50) was published in 1953. The *Grand mémento encyclopédique*, whose contents were arranged systematically, was issued in 1937 in two volumes. Publication of the *Nouveau Larousse universal* was interrupted by the beginning of World War II, and the work did not appear until 1948. It was edited by Paul Augé. The *Nouveau petit Larousse illustré: dictionnaire encyclopédique* was re-issued in 1948, 1952 and 1959. The 1959 edition was a centenary number, issued to mark the founding of the Librairie Larousse: it is probably unique in offering its users 'une brochure contenant la liste des mots supprimés depuis l'édition de 1948 . . . à la disposition des amateurs de mots croisés'! Its contents comprise: French language; grammar; Latin and foreign expressions; fine arts, literature, science- and, a universal chronology. In 1960 publication commenced of the *Grand Larousse encyclopédique*, a ten-volume work, still combining the functions of a dictionary and encyclopaedia. Derivations of words and examples of their use—Larousse had once written 'Un dictionnaire sans exemples est un squelette'—and quotations from classical and modern writers are included. It is profusely illustrated and bibliographies are appended to each volume. Larousse is one of the few encyclopaedias that has proved successful in another language: the *Petit Larousse illustré* was adapted in Spanish by Miguel de Toro y Gisbert under the title of *Pequeño Larousse ilustrado* in 1912; more recent issues bear the title *Nuevo pequeño Larousse ilustrado*. And in 1957 Larousse issued a children's encyclopaedia entitled *Encyclopédie Larousse des enfants*.

Two Dutch encyclopaedias made their appearance at this time. *De algemeene nederlandsche encyclopedie voor den beschaafden stand. Woordenboek van kunst, wetenschap, nijverheid, landbouw en handel. Naar de laatste, omgewerkte, verbeterde en vermeerderde drukken van Brockhaus' Conversations-lexicon, Nieuwenhuis' Woordenboek van kunsten en wetenschappen, en naar de beste andere bronnen voor Nederland bewerkt* . . . (15 volumes in 8; Zütphen, P. B. Plantegna, 1865–68) derives, as the title says, not only from *Brockhaus* but also from *Nieuwenhuis' Woordenboek van kunsten en wetenschappen* (Leiden, 1851–68). This was followed by the *Geïllustreerde encyclopaedie* (16 volumes; Amsterdam, 1868–82), edited by Anthonij Winkler Prins. This proved very successful, and by 1914 it was in its fourth edition, under the title *Winkler Prins' Geïllustreerde encyclopaedie*, edited by Henri Zondervan. A fifth edition was issued in 16 volumes in 1932–38; and the sixth edition, under the title *Winkler Prins encyclopaedie*, was issued in 19 volumes (the last being a supplement and including an index) in 1947–55 (Amsterdam, Elsevier). A seventh edition, under the title *Algemene Winkler Prins encyclopaedie*, was begun in 1956, to be completed in 1960 in 11 volumes. In 1951 a yearbook, *Winkler Prins boek van het jaar*, covering events of the previous year, was started. This is an excellent and thorough encyclopaedia, with very good illustrations and maps, and it has not slavishly followed the Brockhaus example, awarding instead very extensive treatment to important subjects in its more recent editions.

A curiosity in the encyclopaedia world appeared in the United States at a time when emigration from Central Europe was at a very high figure. For the benefit of German-speaking people living in the United States, Professor Alexander Jacob Schem (1826–81) compiled the *Deutsch-amerikanisches Conversations-Lexicon. Mit specialler Rücksicht auf das Bedürfnisz der in Amerika lebenden Deutschen, mit Benutzung aller deutschen, amerikanischen, englischen und unter Mitwirkung vieler hervorragender deutschen Schriftsteller Amerika's* . . . (11 volumes; New York, E. Steiger, 1869–74). This was originally issued in 110 parts. There is a 'Nachträge'—including 'Totenschau' in volume

11 (pages 690 to 806), but the 'Supplemente' mentioned in that volume were never published.

Alvin J. Johnson's *New universal encyclopaedia* was first published in four volumes (New York, 1874–78), and was re-issued in a new edition in eight volumes in 1893–95. This edition was edited by Charles Kendall Adams, who had been President of Cornell University (1885–92). It was then enlarged as the *Universal cyclopaedia* (New York, Appleton, 1900) in 12 volumes. The Swedish *Nordisk familjebok*, originally issued in 18 volumes (and two supplementary volumes) in Stockholm in 1875–94, developed in its second edition into the *Nordisk familjebok: konversationslexikon och realencyklopedi* (38 volumes; Stockholm, Nordisk Familjeboks Förlag, 1904–26), edited by B. Meijer. The second edition, owing to the war, had taken a very long time to complete, and in the meantime the third edition—under the editorship of E. Thyselius—had already begun (23 volumes; Stockholm, Familjebokens Förlag, 1923–27). The reduction in the number of volumes has continued in the fourth edition, edited by S.-E. S. Bergelin (22 volumes: Malmö, Förlagshuset Norden, 1951–56), so that it is wise to retain all editions of this encyclopaedia. In general, the *Nordisk familjebok* follows the Brockhaus pattern of short articles, many textual illustrations, and good maps.

Continuing the long list of Arabic encyclopaedias, a new item appeared in the Lebanon. This was the work of Butrus al-Bustani. The *Da'irat al-Maarif* was published in Beirut 1876–87 (volumes 1–9) and Cairo 1898–1900 (volumes 10 and 11). Volumes 1–6 were completed by Butrus al-Bustani, volumes 7–8 by his son Salim al-Bustani, and volumes 9–11 by Najib and Amin al-Bustani. No more volumes were published, but a new edition, edited by Fuad Afram al-Bustani, was begun in 1956 (Beirut, Catholic Press).

John Merry Ross (1833–83), the Scottish educationalist who had assisted Dr Andrew Findlater in the compilation of the first edition of *Chambers's Encyclopaedia* (see page 188), also edited *The globe encyclopaedia of universal information* (6 volumes; Edinburgh, T. C. Jack, 1876–81). A new edition was issued as *The illustrated globe encyclopaedia* (6 volumes; London, Virtue & Co., 1890–93). The original

o

encyclopaedia was also re-issued as *The student's encyclopaedia of universal knowledge* (London, Hodder & Stoughton, 1883) in six volumes.

The modern type of concise one-volume handbook began to make its appearance with the publication of *Cassell's Concise cyclopaedia* (London, Cassell, 1883), comprising 1,340 octavo pages edited by William Heaton. The demand for this kind of work is shown by the issue of a revised edition (1888), a 'popular edition' (1896), and a re-issue (1899). Nevertheless, the one-volume encyclopaedia has never had the success in the English-speaking world that Larousse achieved in France, though since World War II a succession of good handbooks of this type have found a new market in school libraries.

One of the most important encyclopaedias of modern times was published during the last quarter of the nineteenth century: *La grande encyclopédie: inventaire raisonné des sciences, des lettres et des arts, par une société de savants et de gens de lettres* ... (31 volumes; Paris, Lamirault, 1886–1902), was due to the inspiration of F. Camille Dreyfus who was the 'Secrétaire général' for the first 18 volumes. The remainder of the volumes were supervised by André Berthelot. There were twelve subject editors—including Dreyfus and Berthelot—and they included Hartwig Derenbourg (1844–1908), the orientalist and son of the orientalist Joseph Derenbourg (1811–1895). The result was an outstanding achievement: authoritative signed articles, thorough bibliographies, excellent biographical material. Much attention was paid to the definition of scientific and technical terms. Though much of the encyclopaedia is now out of date, it is still an important source for many subjects.

Another Bohemian encyclopaedia, the *Ottuv slovník naučný: illustrovaná encyklopaedie obecných vědomastí* (Prague, Otto, 1888–1909) was issued in 28 volumes, of which the last was supplementary. In Greece the *Enkuklopaideia de Politis* (6 volumes, and 1 supplementary volume; Athens, 1890–1902) was issued, and another 'Conversations Lexikon' was issued in 1890 in the form of the Russian (Brockhaus & Efron) translation of *Brockhaus* (see page 170). A short Hungarian encyclopaedia was issued in Budapest in 1891–93: I. Acsádi's *Az Athenaeum kezi lexikona: a tudomanyok encziklopédiája különös tekintettel Magyarországra* (2 octavo volumes). A larger encyclopaedia followed shortly after: Jozsef Bokor's *A Pallas nagy lexikona, az összes ismeretek enciklopédiája* (18 volumes; Budapest, Pallas irodalmi és nyomdai résvénytárság, 1893–1904), of which the last two volumes are supplementary. In the Netherlands, *Sijthoff's Woordenboek voor kennis en kunst* (Leiden, 1890–98) was issued in ten volumes. In Rumania Cornelius Diaconovich's *Enciclopedia Română* (3 volumes; Sibiu (Hermannstadt), 1898–1904) was published at the instigation and under the auspices of the Transylvanian Association for the Encouragement of Rumanian Literature and Culture. In Bulgaria L. Kasarov issued his *Enciklopedičeski rečnik* (Plovdiv, 1899–1907) in three octavo volumes. In Spain appeared the *Diccionario enciclopédico hispano-americano de literatura, ciencias y artes* (25 volumes; Barcelona, Montaner y Simón, 1887–1899), usually referred to as Montaner & Simón, of which the last two volumes were supplementary and were themselves supplemented by three further volumes by 1910. And in Russia there were the *Entsiklopedicheskii slovar'* (Moscow, Granat, 1895), first issued in eight volumes, which proved immensely popular and achieved its seventh edition 1910–48 in 59 volumes (volume 56 never published), which included an article on Materialism by Lenin; and Florentii Pavlenkov's little *Entsiklopedicheskii slovar'* (St Petersburg, 1899), which was last published (5th edition) in 1913.

It was, however, in Denmark that the most notable turn-of-the-century events in encyclopaedia publishing occurred. *Allers illustrerede Konversationsleksikon, redigeret af G. Lütken* . . . was issued in six octavo volumes in Copenhagen during the years 1892 to 1899. It coincided unfortunately with two powerful rivals. *Hagerups Illustrerede konversations leksikon* was first issued in Copenhagen in 1892–1900. A second edition, *Illustreret konversations leksikon*, edited by E. Rørdam, was published in nine volumes in 1907–13. The third edition, edited by E. Rørdam and P. Engelstoft, appeared in nine volumes in 1920–1925; and the fourth edition, edited by the latter, was issued in ten volumes (Copenhagen, Hagerup, 1948–53). This is a thorough-going encyclopaedia, profusely illustrated, and with good maps. *Salmonsens Store illustrerede konversationsleksikon* was first issued in Copenhagen in 19 volumes in 1893–1911. The second edition, *Salmonsens Konversations leksikon*, edited by Christian Blangstrup, was published in 26 volumes (Copenhagen, Schultz, 1915–30), and is still an outstanding reference work which has never been superseded. A more popular work, *Den lille Salmonsen* (12 volumes; Copenhagen, Schultz, 1937–40), has been supplemented by the monthly *Salmonsen Leksikontidsskrift*, issued since 1941, which is very well indexed. There is also the two-volume *Den nye Salmonsen: A–Å* (Copenhagen, Schultz, 1949).

In the later years of the nineteenth century demand for a type of work that was vaguely encyclopaedic developed, of which an outstanding example is *Whitaker's Almanack*. Joseph Whitaker (1820–1895) started as a bookseller, but soon became a publisher (he founded the *Bookseller*). During the period he spent editing *The Gentleman's magazine* (1856–58) he compiled for office use a Commonplace Book of notes, news cuttings, etc., complete with index. This eventually provided the raw material for his *Almanack*, the first issue of which was published in November 1868—orders for 36,000 copies had been received even before it was published. This annual publication soon became a household word and it is a tribute to the wise planning of Joseph Whitaker that, although the size of the *Almanack* has increased almost threefold, the contents and their arrangement have followed the same general pattern throughout the near-century of its existence. *The World almanack*, started by the New York *World*, was also founded in 1868. Discontinued during the years 1876 to 1885, it was revived by *The World*'s publisher, Joseph Pulitzer (1847–1911), in 1886, and has been published annually to date. *Information please almanack* was started in 1947.

A partner of Messrs. A. & F. Pears, soapmakers, Thomas J. Barratt, joined the firm in 1865. He will long be remembered for his daring use of Sir John Millais's painting 'Bubbles' as an advertisement for Pears' soap. But he was also responsible for founding *Pears Cyclopaedia* in 1897, a popular annual that has gained and kept a large public in this century. Another popular handbook, the *Daily Mail year book*, was started in 1901. But the oldest of all these compendia, *Enquire within upon everything* (founded 1856,) seems to have ceased publication with the 119th edition of 1952.

Towards the end of the century a number of Chinese encyclopaedias appeared. Tai Chao-ch'un had completed his *Ssu shu wu ching lei tien chi ch'êng*, in 34 volumes, by 1887. It is historical in character and was designed for the use of candidates for government service. Wei Sung's *I shih chi shih*, which had been compiled in 22 volumes (and 1 supplementary volume), in 1823, was issued in 1888. It comprises over 1,500 topics grouped in 22 sections, and concentrates on the history of practical things. In 1899 Liu K'o-i completed his *Chiu T'ung T'ung* in 248 volumes, which was printed in 1902. It is in large measure a reassembly of material in the older encyclopaedias in a more useful system of arrangement. Yang Ch'ên's *San kuo hui yao* was printed in 22 volumes in 1900. Material is grouped in 16 sections; the items are largely drawn from previous encyclopaedias. The most important work of this period is Huang Shu-lin's *Erh shih ssu shih chiu t'ung chêng tien lei yao ho pien*, printed in 320 volumes in 1902. The material, which is largely historical and biographical, is well classified, with sources quoted, and chapter contents lists.

Liu Chin Tsao's *Huang ch'ao hsü wên hsien t'ung k'ao*, known also as the *Ch'ing ch'ao hsü wên hsien t'ung k'ao*, was first published in 320 volumes in 1905. A revised and enlarged edition in 400 volumes was completed in 1921. It includes material on practical matters, including contemporary fiscal, administrative and industrial affairs.

BIBLIOGRAPHY

F. Baldensperger and W. P. Friederich. *Bibliography of comparative literature.* Chapel Hill, University of North Carolina Press, 1950

J. Blanck, compiler. *Bibliography of American literature.* Yale University Press; Oxford University Press, 1955 to date

G. Díaz-Plaja. *Historia general de las literaturas hispanicas: Volume 4—Siglos XVIII y XIX.* Barcelona, Barna, 1956

K. Goedeke. *Grundriss zur Geschichte der deutschen Dichtung aus den Quellen. Neue Folge* [1830–1880]. Düsseldorf, Ehlermann, 1955 to date

G. Lanson. *Manuel bibliographique de la littérature française moderne.* New edition. Paris, Hachette, 1931

H. Serís. *Manual de bibliografía de la literatura espanola.* Syracuse, N.Y., Centro de Estudios Hispánicos, Hall of Languages, 1948 to date

Larousse, 1852–1952. Paris, Larousse, 1952 (this mentions the issue in 1958 of the 3-volume Hispano-American edition of the *Nouveau Larousse Universel* under the title *Larousse universal*)

G. Mentz. *Hundert Jahre Meyers Lexicon.* Leipzig, Bibliographishes Institut, 1939

Storia letteraria d'Italia: Volume 10—Il novecento, by A. Galletti. Milan, Vallardi, 1945

H. P. Thieme. *Bibliographie de la littérature française de 1800 à 1930.* 3 volumes. Paris, Droz, 1933

W. D. Templeman, and others. *Bibliographies of studies in Victorian literature for the 13 years 1932–44.* Urbana, University of Illinois Press, 1945

A. Wright, editor. *Bibliographies of studies in Victorian literature for the ten years, 1956–54.* Urbana, University of Illinois Press, 1956.

> *It is presumed that Encyclopaedias are required by different classes of readers.*
>
> The Rev. HENRY JOHN ROSE

At the turn of the century a new stage in encyclopaedia-making had been reached. Most Western nations had at least one substantial and fairly recent encyclopaedia of their own. Some current encyclopaedias were of very long standing: the *Britannica* and *Brockhaus* had both completed a century of publication, while *Larousse*, *Meyer* and *Herder* were each within half a century of use. The general principles of the form which an encyclopaedia should take were almost universally accepted:

(*a*) written in the language of the country in which it was published;

(*b*) contents arranged in alphabetical order;

(*c*) articles of any substance written by specialists;

(*d*) subject specialists employed either wholly or part-time as sub-editors;

(*e*) inclusion of living people's biographies;

(*f*) inclusion of illustrations, maps, plans, etc.;

(*g*) provision of bibliographies appended to the longer articles;

(*h*) provision of an analytical index of people and places and minor subjects;

(*i*) provision for the publication of supplements to bring the main work up-to-date;

(*j*) provision of numerous and adequate cross references in the text.

Any variation from these principles can be seen now—if not at the time of publication—to be an indication that the encyclopaedia was not of lasting value and stood little chance of surviving the competition of its more thorough competitors. But however good the encyclopaedia, it was still in peril of lasting only one or two editions unless it had good business management and an energetic sales policy to support it. The great problem—how to keep the editorial staff together between editions—still had to be solved, for continuity was and is an essential ingredient of the first-class encyclopaedia. Further dangers included war and revolution. The French Revolution had robbed Panckoucke of a large number of the subscribers to his *Encyclopédie méthodique* (see page 110), and the Russian Revolution and the two world wars of the twentieth century were in turn to be responsible for the downfall of more than a few good encyclopaedias.

In 1900 four encyclopaedias commenced publication. S. N. Yushakov's *Bol'shaia entsiklopediia: slovar' obshchedostupnykh svedenyii po vsem otrasliam znaniia* (20 volumes; St Petersburg, 1900–05) was based on the system popularized by Meyer; two supplementary volumes were published by 1909. E. Dennert's *Volks-Universal-Lexikon* (Berlin, 1900) reached a second edition in two volumes in 1909. *Vivats geïllustreerde encyclopedie* was published in 11 volumes (Amsterdam, 1900–6). And the first comprehensive Estonian encyclopaedia, K. A. Herman's *Eesti üleüldise teaduse raamat ehk encyklopädia konversationilexikon* began publication in Tartu.

The first edition of the *New international encyclopaedia* (17 volumes; New York, 1902–04), was followed by a corrected and expanded re-issue in 20 volumes in 1907, and by another in 1912. The second edition (23 volumes; New York, Dodd, 1914–16) was the result of a thorough revision. This was re-issued in 24 volumes in 1922, with some changes including greater attention to World War I history. The editors, Frank Moore Colby and Talcott Williams, introduced some interesting features. The maps were mounted on inserts, with the intention of enabling subscribers to replace them as new maps were issued. In the bibliographies references were given to translations as well as to the original titles of foreign works. Much attention was paid to Latin American subjects. And there was a supplementary volume devoted to courses of study. Two supplementary volumes were issued in 1925, and another two in 1930. A revised re-issue of the main encyclopaedia was published in

1927. The *New international year book: a compendium of the world's progress*, edited by Frank Moore Colby, started publication in 1908 with the volume covering the events of 1907 (and, more briefly, those of 1903–06). This, like most yearly supplements to encyclopaedias, is especially valuable for its biographical material.

One of the outstanding encyclopaedias of the century began publication in 1905: the *Enciclopedia universal ilustrada europeoamericana* (70 volumes in 71; Barcelona, Espasa, 1905–30) has long been referred to generally as the 'Espasa'. A ten-volume appendix was published 1931–33; and since then a *Suplemento anual* has been published at frequent but irregular intervals. This work is remarkable for its detail: maps and plans of even remote and obscure places; reproductions and descriptions of works of art entered under their titles; lengthy bibliographies, international in scope; full dictionary treatment of individual words with, in many cases, foreign equivalents; and usually affording full scope to lengthy treatment of important subjects. One volume (no. 21) is devoted to Spain, and is revised and re-issued separately about every ten years. A miniature edition, the *Espasa-Calpe: diccionario enciclopédico abreviado* reached a sixth edition in 1955 (7 volumes; Madrid, Espasa).

The Harmsworth encyclopaedia: everybody's book of reference (London, Amalgamated Press, and Thomas Nelson), edited by George Sandeman, was published serially from 1905. It met a genuine popular need and sold half a million copies immediately.

Haakon Nyhuus's *Illustreret norsk konversations-leksikon* (6 volumes; Oslo, 1907–13) developed, in its second edition, into *Aschehougs konversations-leksikon; redaktor Anders Krogvig, redaktionssekretaer Trygve Aalheim* . . . (9 volumes, and 1 supplementary volume; Oslo, Aschehoug (W. Nygaard), 1920–32). The third edition, edited by Sem Saeland, Werner Werenskiold, and A. H. Winsnes, with Trygve Aalheim as Generalsekretaer, was issued in 15 volumes (and one supplementary volume) in 1939–52. The fourth, and current edition, to be completed in 18 volumes, began publication in 1954 under the editorship of Arthur Holmesland, Alf Sommerfelt, and Leif Størmer, with John Dahl as Redaksjonssekretaer. This encyclopaedia follows the Conversationslexikon policy of short well-illustrated articles and comprehensive biographical coverage.

Alfred Mézières edited the *Encyclopédie universelle du XXe siècle* (12 volumes; Paris, Librairie nationale, 1908–10), an encyclopaedia popular in approach with emphasis on current topics and personalities. The great Hungarian encyclopaedia, *Révai nagy lexikona: az ismeretek enciklopédiája* (21 volumes; Budapest, Révai Testvérék Irodalmi Intézet Részvénytarsaság, 1911–35), of which the last two volumes are supplementary, is a substantial work with good detailed articles and useful illustrations. The main articles are well documented, and the encyclopaedia has not so far been superseded by more recent works. A two-volume short version was issued 1947–48. The *Everyman encyclopaedia* first made its appearance in 12 volumes, edited by Andrew Boyle, in 1913 (London, Dent; New York, Dutton). Its small size, practical approach, and reasonable price made it a success in spite of the comparatively small number of illustrations. New editions, in 12 volumes, were issued in 1931, 1950 and 1958.

Little attempt—apart from Larousse's pioneer effort—had so far been made to provide encyclopaedias specifically for children. It is therefore of some importance that, after several years of planning and preparatory work, the *World book encyclopaedia* was first published just before the end of World War I:

> The World book: organized knowledge in story and picture. Editor-in-chief: M. V. O'Shea . . . Editor: Ellsworth D. Foster . . . Editor for Canada: George H. Locke . . . assisted by one hundred and fifty distinguished scientists, educators, artists and leaders of thought in the United States and Canada . . . Chicago, New York, etc., Hanson-Roach-Fowler Company, 1917–18. 8 volumes

The encyclopaedia was quickly re-issued in ten volumes in a second edition in 1918, and in a new issue in 1919 the publisher was changed to W. F. Quarrie of Chicago. The next issue was in 1921, followed by new editions in 1922 and 1923, and every year from 1925 to 1929 inclusive, each edition comprising ten volumes.

In 1929, the encyclopaedia was again expanded into 13 volumes, under the new title:

> The World book encyclopaedia: modern, pictorial, comprehensive . . . Editor-in-chief: M. V. O'Shea . . . managing editor: Ellsworth D. Foster; editor for Canada: George

H. Locke . . . art director: Gordon Saint Clair, assisted by two hundred and fifty out-standing leaders in their respective fields . . . Chicago, W. F. Quarrie & Co., 1929–1930. 13 volumes

Expansion had been the watchword from the first: for example, the first edition had originally been planned for five volumes with five thousand pages and five thousand illustrations, whereas by publication date the project had expanded into eight volumes with more than six thousand pages and well over six thousand illustrations. By 1925, revision had begun to be made annually, with new and re-written articles. And the present edition not only added two volumes of text, but also a volume devoted to 'Reading courses and study units'. The separate index was replaced by innumerable cross-references in the text. A new edition in 22 volumes was published in 1931, and the next issued in 1933 comprised 19 volumes with a total of nearly ten thousand pages. After that, annual editions were issued without interruption up to the present day.

In 1947, all 19 volumes were completely rebuilt and redesigned throughout. The entire subject content was reviewed and thousands of new articles added to keep abreast of the swiftly moving tide of events. All existing articles were newly written, completely rewritten or completely revised. The illustrations were expanded to more than nineteen thousand, and thousands of new diagrams, original art work, and photographs were introduced for the first time, many of them in colour. Typographical and layout improvements were also introduced. In 1948, the encyclopaedia was further improved by the introduction of bibliographies, divided into books for younger, and books for older readers.

In 1949, the second issue of that year was given a new title:

The World book encyclopaedia. Managing editor: J. Morris Jones. Chicago, Field Enterprises, 1949. 19 volumes

In 1952, a supplementary volume of *Official United States population figures, based on the 1950 census of the United States: a special supplement* was added to the issue for that year as a twentieth volume. Shortly after, the cartographic firm of Rand, McNally & Co. began preparing their Cosmo relief series of maps expressly for the encyclopaedia. The title of the encyclopaedia was again changed in 1957:

> *The World book encyclopaedia, and Reading and study guide*. Chicago, Field Enterprises Educational Corporation, 1957. 19 volumes

and in 1960, the encyclopaedia was again increased in size: this time to 20 volumes, of which the last continued to be a *Reading and study guide*. Publication began in 1922 of an annual supplement to the encyclopaedia:

> *The World book: organized knowledge in story and pictures: loose-leaf annual*. Chicago, Toronto, W. F. Quarrie, 1922

each issue reflecting the events of the year named. In 1941 the title of the supplement was changed to *The World book encyclopaedia annual: a version of the events of the year 1941*. No volume was issued in 1942, and in 1943 the title was changed to its present form:

> *The World book encyclopaedia . . . annual supplement, reviewing important events and developments*, 1942–   . Chicago, W. F. Quarrie & Co., 1943—

each issue reviewing the events of the previous year. The issues from 1936 to 1940 each included an index cumulating from 1931. From 1941 onwards, each issue has included an index covering the events of the previous ten years.

In 1960, the encyclopaedia comprised 20 volumes and more than 11,700 pages. Illustrations were improved and increased, and more use was made of colour, and both black-and-white and colour printing were done in a single process. The encyclopaedia is designed for family use, though its great attention to school needs—for example, simple pronunciations are included—finds it a ready sale for classroom use. The need for an index is eliminated by the use of a lavish system of cross-references in the main alphabetical order, and many articles have detailed references to many related articles. A policy of continuous revision enables two editions to be printed each year, and it is estimated that about three thousand pages are revised annually.

In 1961 the first Braille edition of the encyclopaedia was issued in 145 volumes, comprising nearly forty thousand pages. Most illustrations were eliminated from this edition, but many of the diagrams and graphs have been retained and, in many cases, captions for pictures that could not be included, have been incorporated in the text. In the same year, a British editorial and sales office was set up in London, with the object of preparing, under the editorship of Gilbert C. E. Smith, an international edition for the English-speaking world, the first issue of which is planned for 1966. In 1963 the same publishers issued the *World book encyclopaedia dictionary*, and in 1964 the first general encyclopaedia for the use of the partially blind—this is in a set of 30 volumes printed in a special large type.

Another children's encyclopaedia, the eight-volume *Compton's pictured encyclopedia*, was founded in 1922 by the educationalist Frank Compton, and edited by Guy Stanton Ford. Today, this 15-volume work, under the editorship of Charles Alfred Ford, is subjected to continuous revision and is issued at least once a year. At the end of each volume there is a 'Fact-index' covering related material—both text and illustrations—throughout the other volumes. Bibliographies are provided for both younger readers, and for advanced students and teachers. References are given at the end of all major articles to related articles. It is supplemented by *The Compton yearbook*.

The question of how to keep an encyclopaedia up-to-date has always troubled publishers and editors. One attempted solution was *Nelson's Perpetual loose-leaf encyclopaedia . . . editor-in-chief, John H. Finley* (12 volumes; London & New York, Nelson, 1920). Each page bore the date of publication, the principle being that the text could be kept up-to-date by replacing or adding to the information already received by new pages issued twice a year. In theory the idea was very good indeed, but the method was eventually abandoned. The idea was to be adopted again in a French encyclopaedia some years later (see page 209).

The first edition of *Bonniers Konversations lexikon* was issued in 13 volumes (of which one was supplementary) in Stockholm 1922–32. The second edition: *Bonniers Konversations lexikon . . . Huvudredaktör: A. Elvin* (14 volumes, and 1 supplementary volume; Stockholm, Bonnier, 1937–50) keeps mainly to a plan of small articles on specific subjects, with innumerable text and full-page illustrations. It serves also as a dictionary, definitions and pronunciations being included. A smaller edition, *Bonniers folklexikon: illustrerad uppslagsverk* was published in five volumes in 1951–53 (Stockholm, Ab Nordiska Uppslagsböcker).

A second edition of the *Da'irat al-Maarif–al-Qarn al-Rabi' 'ashar–al-'ishrin* (see page 193) was prepared by Muhammad Farid Wajdi and published in ten volumes (Cairo, Matbaat Da'irat maarif al-Qarn al'ishrin, 1923–25). To some extent this encyclopaedia is supplemented by the translation of the *Encyclopaedia of Islam* (Cairo, Matba'at al'itimad, 1933 to date) which is being made by Muhammad Thabet al-Fandi, Ahmad al-Shinshanari, Ibrahim Zaki Khorshid, and Abdul Hamid Yunis; Muhammad Jad al-Maula and Muhammad Mahdi 'Allam are responsible for revision of the text.

The first edition of the *Bol'shaia sovetskaia entsiklopediia* (65 volumes, and 1 supplementary volume; Moscow, 1926–47) was eventually discredited. The supplementary volume was devoted to the U.S.S.R., and of this an indexed German edition (2 volumes; Berlin, Verlag Kultur & Fortschritt, 1950) was made. The second edition (53 volumes; Moscow, 1950–58), of which the last two volumes are devoted to an index, has a Marxist-Leninist approach, but is less biased on non-political subjects. The editor, B. A. Vvedensky, drew on the intellectual resources of the whole of the Soviet Union, and approaching eight thousand scholars contributed. The bibliographies are international in scope—for example, the article on Encyclopaedias is remarkably well and thoroughly treated, and the appended bibliography shows that the writers were well acquainted with recent Western (and Eastern) thought on the subject. The encyclopaedia has been supplemented by a yearbook, the *Ezhegodnik Bol'shoi sovetskoi entsiklopedii*, from 1957 onwards, covering the events 1956 to date. The fiftieth volume of the main encyclopaedia was again devoted to the U.S.S.R. and was made available separately.

The *Malaia sovetskaia entsiklopediia* was first published in ten volumes in 1928–31, and was followed by a second edition in 11 volumes in 1933–47. The third edition (Moscow, 1958–60) is in 11 volumes (the last being supplementary), and is a well illustrated compact work with particular reference to the U.S.S.R.

The two modern Greek encyclopaedias appeared at this time. The *Megalē hellenikē enkyklopaideia* (24 volumes; Athens, 'Pyrsos', 1926–34) has lengthy articles, with illustrations and bibliographies. The *Eleutheroudakē enkyklopaidikon leksikon. Dieuthuntēs: Kostas Eleutheroudakēs* (12 volumes; Athens, 'Eleutheroudakis', 1927–31) follows the Conversationslexikon pattern of short illustrated articles, with bibliographical notes. Both encyclopaedias are strong in biographical material. The Czechs, at last freed from foreign domination, also published two encyclopaedias. The *Masarykuv slovník naučný: lidová encyklopedie všeobecných vědomostí* . . . (7 volumes; Prague, Nákladem 'Československého Kompasu', 1925–33) comprised mostly short illustrated articles, with brief bibliographies. A larger work, Antonín Dolenský's *Novy veliký ilustrovaný slovník naučný* (20 volumes; Prague, 1929–32)—of which the last three volumes were supplementary—was similarly strong in biographical material.

One of the most important encyclopaedias of the twentieth century began to appear in Italy in 1929; this was the *Enciclopedia italiana di scienze, lettere ed arti* (36 volumes; Rome, Istituto della Enciclopedia Italiana, 1929–39). The Institute had been founded by Giovanni Treccani and the editor-in-chief was the philosopher Giovanni Gentile. This is one of the finest examples of the national encyclopaedia ever produced and, although it was intended to mirror the wealth and stature of contemporary Italian knowledge, its contents are admirably international in their approach—a feature that is particularly shown in its bibliographies which cite works and periodical articles in many languages. The articles on all aspects of art are notable and the standard of reproduction of illustrations has never been surpassed in a work of similar nature. Every article is signed and the longer and more important articles are subdivided into aspects. Volume 36 comprises the index to the previous 35 volumes and also to the Appendix in volume 37. The second Appendix, covering the years 1938–48 was published in two volumes in 1948–49, and a further two-volume Appendix covers the following twelve years.

The *Svensk uppslagsbok* (30 volumes, and Supplement; Malmö, Förlagshuset Norden, 1929–37), the standard encyclopaedia of

Sweden, appeared in a second edition (32 volumes) in 1947–55. This is well illustrated and, like the *Enciclopedia italiana*, has many good detailed maps. The more important articles are signed and are provided with excellent bibliographies. The editors are G. Carlquist and J. Carlsson. In Denmark, the first edition of *Gyldendals leksikon: haandbog for skole og hjem* was edited by Jens Rosenkjaen (Copenhagen, 1931–32) in four volumes. This was followed in 1948 by *Gyldendals Etbinds leksikon* based partly on this and partly on *Norstedts Uppslagsbok* (1945). The present edition, *Gyldendals Nye konversasjonsleksikon*, edited by L. Amundsen, is published by Gyldendal in Oslo (3rd edition, 1954). At this time a six-volume Norwegian encyclopaedia was also issued: the *Norsk konversasjonsleksikon: Kringla heimsins*, (Oslo, Nasjonalforlaget, 1931–1934) which was followed by a second edition in eight volumes in 1948–54 and annual supplementary volumes.

So far the illustrations in an encyclopaedia had almost always been subordinate to the text. But in 1935 the Bibliographisches Institut at Leipzig produced the *Duden Pictorial encyclopaedia* whose avowed principle was 'to explain a conception by means of a picture. In order to get the precise meaning of a word, more specially of a technical expression, it should not be taken out of its context but should be treated as a member of a group of words referring to a special subject. The same holds true of an explanatory drawing which usually forms part of a complete picture, thus giving the precise meaning of a word.' The latest edition, the *Duden-Lexikon in drei Bänden; herausgegeben und bearbeitet von den Fachredaktionen des Bibliographischen Instituts in Gemeinschaft mit der Dudenredaktion*, was published in three volumes (Mannheim, Dudenverlag des Bibliographischen Instituts, 1961–63), and gives the equivalents of each term in five languages. It may be argued that these are really vocabularies, but they stem from Diderot's original illustrations for his *Encyclopédie* in that they convey a conception of the whole machine or object in providing a comprehensive illustration rather than unrelated details. Another example of this type of pictorial encyclopaedia is one in which half-tone illustrations depict people, places, events, etc., accompanied by a few words of text, as in *I see all*.

The Columbia encyclopædia in one volume, edited by Clarke F. Ansley was first issued by Columbia University Press in 1935. This is a very scholarly attempt to bridge the gap between the large learned encyclopaedias and the cheap popular works; though it is compact it is comprehensive for, by omitting definitions, more space has been made available for essentially encyclopaedic information. Cross-references are plentiful, thus eliminating the need for repeating information, and the encyclopaedia concentrates on providing 'first aid and essential facts' rather than technical treatises, the editor's aim being to compile an entirely new general encyclopaedia compact enough and simply enough written to serve as a guide to the 'young Abraham Lincoln'. Clarke Fisher Ansley died in 1939, and the second edition was edited by William Bridgwater and Elizabeth J. Sherwood (1950), with a small Supplement (issued in 1959). The third edition was issued in 1963. Illustrations and very good brief bibliographies are included.

The *Grande enciclopédia portuguesa e brasileira* was issued in 38 volumes in 1935–37 (Lisbon and Rio de Janeiro, Editorial Enciclopédia), with plans for supplementary volumes. It is heavily illustrated with well over fifteen thousand black-and-white and coloured illustrations, but the bibliographical equipment is rather sparse. A more elaborate and complex work was just commencing in France and was hailed by H. G. Wells in his *World brain* (Methuen, 1938, page 130) as a very admirably planned encyclopaedia. This was the *Encyclopédie française*, originally planned on the loose-leaf principle, its contents being arranged in systematic order. Founded by Anatole de Monzie, the editorship was undertaken by Lucien Febvre. The original publishers, the Comité de l'Encyclopédie Française, subsequently changed their name to the Société de Gestion de l'Encyclopédie Française, and, more recently, to the Société Nouvelle de l'Encyclopédie Française. The plan of the work is as follows:

Volume
  1 L'Outillage mental; pensée; langage; mathématique. 1937
     (Supplement: La sémantique, la mathématique, la
     cybernétique).

2   La physique. 1955.
3   Le ciel et la terre. 1956.
4   La vie. 1937.
5   Les êtres vivants. 1937.
6   L'être humain. 1936 (Supplement: La médecine depuis 1940).
7   L'espèce humaine. 1936.
8   La vie mentale. 1938.
9   Techniques et industrie.
10 L'état moderne; aménagement, crise, transformations. 1935.
11 La vie internationale. 1957.
12 L'univers économique.
13 L'univers social.
14 La civilisation quotidienne. 1954.
15 Education et instruction. 1939.
16⎫
   ⎬ Arts et littératures. 1935–36.
17⎭
18 La civilisation écrite. 1939.
19 Philosophie; religion. 1957.
20 L'histoire: du passé au présent.
21 Tables générales.

Each volume includes a bibliographical appendix, and its own index. Some of the volumes have already been replaced by revised issues or have been issued under different titles:

4   La vie: fondement, maintien, reproduction. 2 volumes, 1961.
9   L'Univers économique et social. 1961.
12 Chimie, science et industries. 1959.
20 Le monde en devenir. 1959.

This possibly indicates the future lines on which this remarkable encyclopaedia may develop.

This was not the only encyclopaedia to suffer difficulties owing to the outbreak of war in 1939. The Rumanian scholarly compilation, *Enciclopedia României*, was planned in six volumes, of which the first two were to be devoted to politics and government, the next two to economics, and the remainder to culture. Of these only the first four appear to have been published (Bucarest, Asociatia Stiintifica Pentru Enciclopedia României, 1938–43). And L. Savadjian's *Encyclopédie balkanique permanente* (Paris, Société générale d'imprimerie et d'édition, 1936– , volume 1–) was another casualty of invasion.

The next few years saw no developments in the field of encyclopaedias: even established works limited themselves to some reprinting, the issue of a few parts, and the preparation of post-war editions. But in 1945 the *Schweizer Lexikon* commenced publication, and its excellent paper, binding and illustrations were welcomed by a world that had been starved of all three for so long a period. It was finally completed in 1948 (Zürich, Encyclios-Verlag) in seven volumes, followed by a two-volume edition in 1949–50 which has been revised—under various titles—in 1954 and 1958 (*Universal-Lexikon*).

The official Turkish encyclopaedia was originally issued under the name *Inönü ansiklopedisi*, but from fascicle 34 it changed its title to *Türk ansiklopedisi* (Ankara, Millî Eğitim Basimevi, 1946 to date). This is a well-illustrated work and promises to be large (the first eight volumes have reached only the letter B).

The Netherlands produced the next systematically arranged encyclopaedia, the *Eerste nederlandse systematisch ingerichte encyclopaedie* (10 volumes; Amsterdam, ENSIE, 1946–52) which was edited by H. J. Pos. The arrangement is as follows:

Volume
1 Philosophy; religion; psychology. 1946.
2 Literature; painting; music; entertainment. 1947.
3 History; sociology; folklore and folk art; economics; law; government; politics. 1947.
4 Natural history. 1949.
5 Geodesy and cartography; meteorology. 1948.
6 Biology; anthropology; pharmacy. 1949.
7 Agriculture. 1950.
8 Technology. 1950.

9   Construction. 1950.
10 Dictionary; index. 1952 (latter includes a certain amount
    of additional information).

It is interesting to compare this conception of the field of knowledge with that of the *Oxford junior encyclopaedia* which was appearing at the same time (13 volumes; London, Oxford University
Press, 1948–56.) Under the editorship of L. E. Salt, R. Sinclair, and
G. Boumphrey, the arrangement of this work was as follows:

Volume
1   Mankind. 1948.
2   Natural history. 1949.
3   The Universe. 1949 (revised 1951).
4   Communications. 1951.
5   Great lives. 1953.
6   Farming and fisheries. 1952.
7   Industry and commerce. 1951.
8   Engineering. 1955.
9   Recreations. 1950.
10 Law and order. 1952.
11 The home. 1955.
12 The arts. 1954.
13 Index, and ready-reference volume. 1956.

Unlike the *Encyclopédie française*, the *Oxford junior* arranges the contents of each volume alphabetically. The work is well illustrated
and is cross-referenced.

Two more Scandinavian encyclopaedias made their appearance
at this time: the Danish *Raunkjaers Konversations leksikon* was published in 12 volumes (Copenhagen, Det Danske Forlag, 1948–57),
and was edited by P. Raunkjaer. This is well illustrated, and some
of the more important articles are signed and have bibliographies.
The *Norsk allkunnebok* was edited in ten volumes (plus an atlas) by
A. Sudmann (Oslo, Fonna, 1948–61). This is the first encyclopaedia to be written completely in the nynorsk (landsmål)
language.

An entirely new American encyclopaedia appeared under the

name of *Collier's Encyclopedia* in 20 volumes in 1950–51. The president of the P. F. Collier Company, Ralph Smith, took the unusual action in 1946 of asking the help of the American Library Association in the fashioning of this work. On their advice, Mr Smith appointed Dr Louis Shores as library adviser, and in the second edition (1962), Dr Shores became editor-in-chief, and the encyclopaedia was extended to 24 volumes. From the first, Dr Shores was able to put his ideas into operation, these comprising eight criteria: (*a*) authority, (*b*) scope, (*c*) treatment, (*d*) arrangement, (*e*) bibliography, (*f*) format, (*g*) maps, (*h*) updating. Dr Shores has treated these points in some detail in 'Our good encyclopaedias', an address before the California Library Association in November 1962, and this is recommended to readers as a thorough-going summary of the criteria which are observed by the editors of the more scholarly encyclopaedias today. As Dr Shores says in his concluding remarks: 'Like librarianship itself, I consider the encyclopedia one of the few generalizing influences in a world of over-specialization. It serves to recall that knowledge has unity.'

Collier's Encyclopedia's 18,864 pages are matched with almost as many illustrations and a large number of maps. There is a separate classified bibliography of over twelve thousand titles, and an index of 400,000 entries. The work is supplemented by *Collier's Encyclopedia yearbook* which, since 1960, has included a survey of research in progress.

Two countries now published encyclopaedias for the first time. The *Encyclopaedia Hebraica* was published in 18 volumes in 1949–59 (Tel Aviv, Encyclopaedia Publishing Company): it is in Hebrew, is sparsely illustrated but is scholarly and has good bibliographies. The Mexican *Diccionario enciclopédico U.T.E.H.A.* (Mexico City and Barcelona, Unión Tipográfica Editorial Hispano Americana, 1950–52, reprinted 1953) is in ten volumes. It is well illustrated and is particularly strong on Latin American subjects. There was also a small Russian encyclopaedia of the popular kind, the *Entsiklopedicheskii slovar'* edited, in three volumes, by Bors Alekseievich Vvedenskii, which was published in Moscow in 1953–55.

The *Ensiklopedia Indonesia* (Bandung and The Hague, W. van

Hoeve, 1954–) was a small compilation planned to be completed in three volumes. Written in Indonesian, its chief value is in its entries on Asian subjects. Another Asian encyclopaedia, the *Myanma Swezon Kyan: Sapay Beikman I Yokepya Bahuthu-ta Ban*, is also known as the *Encyclopaedia Burmanica* and is described as an 'illustrated book of general knowledge'. Its publication in Rangoon was started by the Burma Translation Society in 1954. Two Middle Eastern encyclopaedic compilations are also worthy of note: the *Da'irat al-Maarif* (Beirut, Catholic Press, 1956 to date), which is edited by Fuad Afram al-Bustani; and *al-Mawsou'at al-'arabiyyah*, a one-volume work edited by Albert Rihani (Beirut, Matba'at Dar Rihani, 1955).

The great Jugoslav encyclopaedia, the *Enciklopedija Jugoslavije*, edited by M. Krleža, is to be completed in eight volumes (Zagreb, Leksikografski Zavod FNRJ, 1955 to date). It is a prestige work, well illustrated and with good bibliographical references. A parallel work, from the same publishers, the *Enciklopedija leksikografskoy zavoda*, was commenced in 1955, and is to be completed in six volumes.

Not to be confused with ENSIE (see page 211), the *A.N.S.I.E.: Algemeine Nederlandse systematisch ingerichte encyclopedie* commenced publication in 1955 (Amsterdam, Amsterdamsche Boek- en Courant-Maatschappij). It is to be completed in three illustrated volumes. The Italian encyclopaedic dictionary, *Dizionario enciclopedico italiano*, is to be completed in 12 volumes (Rome, Istituto della Enciclopedia Italiana); it is well illustrated, but has few bibliographical references.

In 1956 La Pléiade in Paris announced the publication of the *Encyclopédie de la Pléiade*: this may be termed an encyclopaedic series since the works published to date have each been self-contained and are written in narrative form. They comprise:

Histoire des littératures. 3 volumes.
Histoire universelle. 3 volumes.
Histoire de la musique.
Histoire de la science.
La Terre.

Botanique.

Histoire de l'art: Le monde non-chrétien.

L'Histoire et ses méthodes.

It is clear that there are many more volumes to come. Treatment is comprehensive and the volumes are well equipped with bibliographies, maps, etc. No announcement has so far been made of any cumulative index, but presumably one will be issued in due course.

Systematic arrangement was also chosen for the *Enciclopedia Labor* (Barcelona, Madrid, Buenos Aires, etc., Editorial Labor, 1955), which commenced publication in 1955, and is planned for completion in nine volumes with (presumably) a final index volume. The arrangement is as follows:

Volume

I   *The Universe and the Earth:* Astronomy; meteorology; physical geography (external geodynamics); general geology (internal geodynamics); geognosy: (i) mineralogy, (ii) Petrography.

II   *Matter and Energy:* General physics; general chemistry; geochemistry; biochemistry; chemistry of crystals; atomic energy.

III   *Life:* Botany; botanic geography; zoology; human biology; history of the Earth and of life (Palaeontology).

IV   *Man and the Earth:* Cartography; human geography; economic geography; descriptive geography.

V   *Man through the Ages:* Primitive mankind; universal political and cultural history; the history of Spain; the history of the Latin American nations.

VI   *Language. Mathematics:* Linguistic theory in general; the substance of language; the techniques of language; the art of expression; appendix of practical grammar; Latin; French; Italian; Portuguese; English; German; arithmetic and algebra; geometry; goniometry; analytical geometry, and the infinitesimal calculus.

VII   *Literature. Music:* Literary techniques; the history of universal literature; the history of Spanish literature; the

history of Latin American literature; the general theory
of music; the origins of music; the history of music.

VIII   *Fine Arts. Sports. Entertainment:* The fundamental concepts of art; historical synthesis of art; the techniques of
art; the dance; the theatre; the cinema; sports; games.

IX   *Society. The Mind. God:* The law; economics; empirical
psychology; the fundamentals of philosophy; the history
of philosophy; the history of religions; Catholic theology;
the history of the Church.

The contents have been given in detail as they reveal both the
extent of the work and its drawbacks. It is clear that Spanish and
Latin American matters have been given pride of place, and that
—for example—Asian and Australian subjects may be treated in
much less detail. Nevertheless, this is a substantial compilation,
profusely illustrated with both colour and half-tone photographs
and drawings. Each volume has its own index and its own
specialist editors and contributors.

Another well-illustrated short encyclopaedia is the *Focus uppslagsbok: Almqvist & Wiksells stora illustrerade bildnings- och uppslagsverk* which was published in five volumes (of which the last is an
index) in 1959–60 (Stockholm, Almqvist & Wiksell). The *Új
magyar lexikon* (New Hungarian encyclopaedia) was edited by
Andor Berei; it was completed in six volumes, the last including a
few pages of supplementary material, in 1959–62 (Budapest,
Akadémiai Kiadó). It is well illustrated in both colour and black-
and-white, but there are no bibliographies—authors' writings are
however mentioned in the text.

Two new encyclopaedias were commenced in 1962. The *Příruční
slovník naučný* is issued by the Ceskoslovenska Akademie Věd
Encyklopedický Institut at Prague, and is to be completed in four
volumes. From the first volume (A–F) issued in 1962, it is evident
that it is constructed on the *Conversationslexikon* principle. It is well
illustrated. Bogdan Suchodolski edits the *Wielka encyklopedia
powszechna PWN* (Warsaw, Państwowe Wydawnictwo Naukowe,
1962 to date), another well-illustrated encyclopaedia which is to be
completed in 13 volumes. Most of the articles are short, but the

longer ones are provided with bibliographies. Two small popular encyclopaedias have also been issued by the same publisher, each in one volume of well over a thousand pages: the *Mała encyklopedia powszechna PWN* (1959–61), and the *A–Z encyklopedia popularno PWN* (1962).

In 1963 the first volume of the new *Sinhalese encyclopedia* appeared. This is edited by D. E. Hettiaratchi, and is issued by the Department of Cultural Affairs of the Government of Ceylon from their Colombo office. This work is completely in Sinhalese; it is well illustrated and produced, and the longer articles are signed.

The preface to the new *Oxford illustrated dictionary* (Oxford, Clarendon Press, 1962) includes the following explanation: 'According to the distinction used by H. W. Fowler in the preface to the *Concise Oxford dictionary*, a dictionary normally takes the use of words and phrases as such for its subject-matter and is concerned with giving information about the things for which these words and phrases stand only so far as correct use of the words depends upon knowledge of the things. In an encyclopaedia, on the other hand, the emphasis will be much more on the nature of the things for which the words and phrases stand. This book attempts to combine in a form that can be handled conveniently the essential features of dictionary and encyclopaedia. Where things are more easily explained by pictures or diagrams than by words, illustration has been used to help out definition. As the dictionary thus becomes the first Oxford English dictionary to make use of illustration (apart from the *Oxford dictionary of nursery rhymes* where illustration is used for a different purpose and in a different way), it has been given a title which distinguishes it from the rest of the family by its most conspicuous feature.' This is elaborated later in the preface: 'So far as possible the illustrations have been planned to support the function of the text and each of them is independent and self-explanatory: each is intended to show the meaning of a word or indicate the character of the thing for which the word stands. To avoid wasteful repetition many subjects have been grouped together, especially where the members of the group help to explain one another: the picture of a machine, for example, will not only illustrate the machine itself but will exhibit the nature of its parts, and their relation to one another and to the whole.'

Thus the tradition of the illustrated encyclopaedic dictionary is preserved and extended. This too is done in the *World book encyclopedia dictionary* (Chicago, Field Enterprises Educational Corporation, 1963), edited by Clarence L. Barnhart. Aided by an International Editorial Advisory Committee of 45 members—under the chairmanship of Professor W. Cabell Greet—and with the co-operation of 143 American and British special consultants, the Corporation has set out to produce the first dictionary specially designed to act as companion to an encyclopaedia.

The growth of specialist encyclopaedias has been particularly notable in the twentieth century. Not all the works that include the word 'encyclopaedia' in their title can be assumed to be encyclopaedias in the true sense of the term, and, on the other hand, there are a number of important specialist encyclopaedias that more modestly call themselves 'dictionary' or 'handbook', etc. By no means the whole field of knowledge is covered by such works: there are many subjects—especially in engineering, industry, the fine arts, etc—which are not suited to this form of reference compilation. Thus, a collection of specialist encyclopaedias can never supersede the general encyclopaedias: their rôle is to amplify the information in the latter and to address themselves to a more informed audience. The only kind of encyclopaedia which in fact replaces the printed works is the library itself whose contents act as one vast encyclopaedia embracing every form of source of information.

Several of the great encyclopaedias devoted to religion have so wide a scope that librarians often use them as supplementary sources in their search for material in the humanities. These include the *Catholic encyclopedia* (New York, Catholic Encyclopedia Press, 1907–22), a work in 17 volumes (the index is in the sixteenth volume, the seventeenth being a supplement), with a two-volume loose-leaf second Supplement (New York, Gilmary Society), which is rich in philosophical, literary, historical and fine arts material. A new edition is in preparation. Similarly the *Enciclo-*

pedia cattolica (12 volumes: Vatican City, Enciclopedia Cattolica, 1948–54) is, *inter alia*, valuable for its wealth of illustrations and reproductions.

Under the inclusive title of the *Encyclopédie des sciences ecclési-astiques*, a remarkable series of encyclopaedias have been appearing during the past fifty years:

Dictionnaire de la Bible. 1907 to date. Volume 1– ;
Dictionnaire de théologie catholique. 1909 to date. Volume 1– ;
Dictionnaire d'archéologie chrétienne et de liturgie. 1928–53.   15 volumes in 30;
Dictionnaire d'histoire et de géographie ecclésiastiques. 1929 to date. Volume 1– ;
Dictionnaire de droit canonique. 1935 to date. Volume 1– ;

all of which are published by Letouzey in Paris. These are comprehensive works of great scholarship, very wide in scope and well equipped with bibliographical references. Another important work in this field is the *Dictionnaire de la spiritualité* (Paris, Beauchesne, 1937 to date), which will take many years to complete. The three volume *Evangelisches Kirchenlexikon* (Göttingen, Vandenhoeck & Ruprecht, 1955–61) and the second edition of the *Lexikon für Theologie und Kirche* (Freiburg, Herder, 1957 to date) should also be noted.

James Hastings (1852–1922), the founder and first editor of *The Expository Times*, was responsible for a series of encyclopaedic compilations of great value:

Encyclopaedia of religion and ethics. 1908–26. 13 volumes;
A dictionary of the Bible. 1898–1904. 5 volumes;
A dictionary of Christ and the Gospels. 1906–08. 2 volumes;
Dictionary of the Apostolic Church. 1915–18. 2 volumes;

all of which were published by T. & T. Clark of Edinburgh, and which together have a far wider scope than their titles indicate. Mention must also be made of the *New Schaff-Herzog encyclopedia of religious knowledge* (13 volumes; New York, Funk, 1908–12) which was based on Johann Jakob Herzog's *Realencyklopädie für protestantische Theologie und Kirche* (3rd edition, 24 volumes; Leipzig, Hinrichs, 1896–1913). This is supplemented by *Twentieth century encyclopedia of religious knowledge: an extension of The New Schaff-Herzog encyclopedia of religious knowledge* (2 volumes; Grand Rapids, Michigan, Baker Book House, 1955)—this publisher also reprinted the original *New Schaff-Herzog encyclopedia* in 1949–50. Two further works in this field are important; the *Oxford dictionary of the Christian Church* (London, Oxford University Press, 1957), a one-volume compilation which has paid particular attention to the provision of adequate bibliographies; and the new *Die Religion in Geschichte und Gegenwart* (3rd edition, Tübingen, Mohr, 1957 to date) which is planned to be completed in seven volumes, of which the last will be devoted to an index.

Many of the works mentioned above pay much attention to philosophy and ethics. The basic work in this field is J. M. Baldwin's *Dictionary of philosophy and psychology* (3 volumes in 4; New York, Macmillan, 1901–05), which can be supplemented by Rudolph Eisler's *Wörterbuch der philosophischen Begriffe* (4th edition, 3 volumes; Berlin, Mittler, 1927–30), by André Lalande's excellent *Vocabulaire technique et critique de la philosophie* (8th edition, Paris, Presses Universitaires de France, 1960), and by the Centro di Studi Filosofici di Gallarate's *Enciclopedia filosofica* (4 volumes; Venice and Rome, Istituto per la Collaborazione Culturale, 1957).

There are three major Jewish encyclopaedias:

The Jewish encyclopedia. 12 volumes. New York, Funk & Wagnalls, 1901–06;
The universal Jewish encyclopedia. 11 volumes. New York, Universal Jewish Encyclopedia, 1939–44 (last volume comprises an index and reading guide);
Encyclopaedia Judaica; das Judentum in Geschichte und Gegenwart. Volumes 1–10 only (A–L). Berlin, Eschkol, 1928–34;

which between them cover a far wider field than Judaism, and are particularly useful for information on the areas of archaeology, classical times, biography, and folk customs. Similarly *The encyclopaedia of Islam* (4 volumes and Supplement; Leiden, Brill, 1911–1938), now slowly being superseded by the second edition (5 volumes; Leiden, Brill, 1954 to date) is an invaluable reference work for many aspects of the whole of the regions of the world through which Islam has spread.

Sir Robert Palgrave's *Dictionary of political economy; edited by Henry Higgs* (last edition, 3 volumes; London, Macmillan, 1923–1926) has never been effectively replaced and, though mostly out of date, is still to be found on the shelves of most reference libraries. The *Encyclopaedia of the social sciences* (15 volumes; New York and London, Macmillan, 1930–35), often referred to simply by the surname of its editor-in-chief, E. R. A. Seligman, was compiled under the auspices of some of America's leading learned societies in this field. Its range is vast, extending in some entries to medicine, art, biology and, particularly, biography. J. Conrad's *Handwörterbuch der Staatswissenschaften* was first published in six volumes in 1890–94 and, throughout its successive editions, maintained its international reputation for the leading reference work in its field. Its last appearance under this title was in 1923–29 (4th edition, 8 volumes and Supplement; Jena, Fischer), a post-war *Handwörterbuch der Sozialwissenschaften* (Tübingen, Mohr, 1951 to date), planned to be completed in 12 volumes (the last being devoted to a general index), having a far wider scope.

The *McGraw-Hill Encyclopedia of science and technology* (15 volumes; New York & London, McGraw-Hill, 1960) is supplemented by a yearbook. This is a lavishly illustrated work and is the only current attempt to cover this field on a comprehensive basis. An older work, Hutchinson's *Technical and scientific encyclopaedia* (4 volumes; London, Hutchinson, 1935–36), is still of value in many of its articles, and *Van Nostrand's Scientific encyclopedia* (3rd edition—new edition in preparation; Princeton, N.J., and London, Van Nostrand, 1958) also covers the technological field.

The *Encyclopédie des sciences mathématiques pures et appliquées* (volumes 1–7; Paris, Gauthier-Villars, 1904–14), though never completed, remains one of the most important sources in this subject, the German edition, *Encyklopädie der mathematischen Wissenschaften* (6 volumes in 23; Leipzig, Teubner, 1898–1935) was equally ill-fated in its second edition (Leipzig, Teubner, 1939), only part of volume 1 being published.

In physics, the *Encyclopaedic dictionary of physics* (Oxford, Pergamon Press, 1961–63) was completed in nine volumes and is being kept up-to-date by annual supplements. It is particularly strong in articles on the practical applications of the subject. Sir Richard Glazebrook's *Dictionary of applied physics* (5 volumes; London, Macmillan, 1922–23), for long the principal source in this field, is still important for the historical aspects of the subject. *Thorpe's Dictionary of applied chemistry* was first issued in four volumes in 1890–93; the present edition (12 volumes; London, Longmans, Green, 1937–56) maintains a standard encyclopaedic approach. The *Encyclopedia of chemical technology* (15 volumes; New York, Interscience, 1947–57) is being kept up-to-date by a series of substantial Supplements. It is often referred to as 'Kirk-Othmer', the surnames of the principal editors. Fritz Ullmann's standard *Enzyklopädie der technischen Chemie* was first published in 10 volumes in 1914–23; the third edition (Munich, Urban & Schwarzenberg, 1951 to date) is to be completed in 14 volumes. Medicine has its own encyclopaedia, *The British encyclopaedia of medical practice*, which was first published in 1936–39. The present edition, edited by Lord Horder (13 volumes; London, Butterworth, 1950–53) has cumulative supplements, and a series of annual reports of progress in medicine.

The Istituto per la Collaborazione Culturale sponsored the publication of the *Enciclopedia universale dell' arte* in 1958 and, almost immediately, an English-language version adjusted to suit the needs of the English-speaking countries started appearing (New York and London, McGraw-Hill, 1959 to date). This will comprise 15 volumes (the last, an index): it is entitled *Encyclopedia of world art*. Coverage of the fine arts is comprehensive, and the work is especially valuable both for its illustrations (both coloured and black-and-white) and for its biographical entries. Art, archaeology, history and religion are included in the *Reallexikon für Antike und Christentum* (Stuttgart, Hiersemann, 1950 to date) and the *Enciclopedia dell'arte antica, classica e orientale* (Rome, Istituto della Enciclopedia Italiana, 1958 to date), two large new scholarly works.

Classical times are also covered in Charles Daremberg and Edouard Saglio's long-established *Dictionnaire des antiquités grecques et romaines* (6 volumes; Paris, Hachette, 1873–1919), which includes most aspects of the life of those times, apart from biography and literature. August Friedrich von Pauly (1796–1845) began the compilation of his *Real-Encyclopädie der classischen Altertumswissenschaft* in 1839. It was continued by Wilhelm Sigismund Teuffel

(1820–78). The present edition was begun by George Wissowa—hence the familiar appellation 'Pauly-Wissowa' (Stuttgart, Metzler, 1893 to date)—and is particularly strong in the two subjects omitted by Daremberg. A vast series of monographs forming, in all, an encyclopaedic work, the *Handbuch der Altertumswissenschaft* (Munich, Beck, 1887 to date), covers language, history, philosophy, religion, archaeology, law, so far.

Music has a number of good encyclopaedias. Sir George Grove (1820–1900) first compiled his *Dictionary of music and musicians* in four volumes in 1878–1889. The present edition was edited by Eric Blom (1888–1959) in nine volumes (5th edition, London, Macmillan, 1954), to which a supplement was added in 1961. This remains the standard work, but another comprehensive encyclopaedia has begun publication: *Die Musik in Geschichte und Gegenwart* (Kassel, Bärenreiter, 1949 to date) edited by Friedrich Blume (b. 1893). One of the founders of the study of musicology, Hugo Riemann (1849–1919), found time in the midst of a remarkably busy life to compile a standard *Musiklexikon* in 1882 which has been revised many times. The present edition (12th edition, Mainz, Schott, 1959 to date), is to be completed in three volumes under the editorship of one of Riemann's pupils, Willibald Gurlitt.

But music has had its encyclopaedias for well over two hundred years. After a trial run with his *Alte und neue musikalische Bibliothek, oder musikalisches Lexikon,* a 64-page pamphlet published in 1728, Johann Gottfried Walther (1684–1748) published the first true encyclopaedia of music under the title *Musikalisches Lexikon, oder Musikalische Bibliothek* (1732). Its supplement, the *Historisch-biographisches Lexikon der Tonkünstler* (2 volumes; 1790–92) of Ernst Ludwig Gerber (1746–1819) was such a success that it was enlarged to four volumes and issued as the *Neues historisch-biographisches Lexikon der Tonkünstler* in 1812–14. In 1806, the future Director of the Brussels Conservatoire, François-Joseph Fétis (1784–1871), began the compilation of his *Biographie universelle des musiciens et bibliographie générale de la musique,* which was first published in eight volumes in 1833–44; a second edition following in 1860–65, with a two-volume supplement in 1878–80. Gustav Schilling (1803–81), subsequently an emigré to North America, compiled at Stuttgart his voluminous *Enzyklopädie der gesammten musikalisches Wissenschaften, oder Universal-Lexikon der Tonkunst* (6 volumes; 1835–38), which was revised in seven volumes (1840–42). Hermann Mendel (1834–76), a pupil of Mendelssohn, began the *Musikalisches Conversations-Lexikon* which was completed in 11 volumes in 1876 (Supplement, 1881) by August Reissmann (1825–1903). This should not be confused with Gathy's *Musikalisches Conversationslexikon* (1870) which Reissmann also edited.

Albert Lavignac (1846–1916), dean of the faculty at the Paris Conservatoire, began the *Encyclopédie de la musique et Dictionnaire du Conservatoire* which was planned to cover the history of music in the five volumes of Part I, and technique, instruction and aesthetics in the six volumes of Part II—edited by Lionel de La Laurencie (1861–1933) after Lavignac's death. The third part, a dictionary of the subjects and names covered in the first two parts, was never published. Delagrave of Paris issued the completed volumes (1913–31). Walter Willson Cobbett (1847–1937), a businessman and a patron of music, compiled the *Cyclopaedic survey of chamber music* (2 volumes; London, Oxford University Press, 1929–30; new edition, 3 volumes, 1963.)

On the theatre there is a new and lavish encyclopaedia: the *Enciclopedia dello spettacolo* (9 volumes; Rome, Maschere, 1954 to date) which has had the support of specialists and specialist librarians throughout the world. The result is an excellent scholarly work, with innumerable illustrations, and good bibliographical apparatus. Sport has had no large compilations for some years, but the Earl of Suffolk and Berkshire's *Encyclopaedia of sport and games* (new edition, 4 volumes; London, Heinemann, 1911) is still of importance for its historical material and for its illustrations. Gardening has its own reference work, the Royal Horticultural Society's *Dictionary of gardening* (first issued in 1951); the present edition is in four volumes, with a supplementary volume (Oxford, Clarendon Press, 1956).

Biographical material has always occupied a major part of general encyclopaedias, and to the specialist works mentioned above must therefore be added the long range of biographical reference works, particularly Michaud's *Biographie universelle* (first issued in 84 volumes in 1811–57 and subsequently revised and enlarged in 45 volumes; Paris, Desplaces, 1843–65); and its rival, Hoefer's *Nouvelle biographie générale* (46 volumes; Paris, Didot, 1853–66). Supplementing and amplifying these are the numerous national biographical dictionaries: the British *Dictionary of national biography* (London, Oxford University Press, 1885 to date); the American *Dictionary of American biography* (New York, Scribner, 1928 to date) and *National cyclopaedia of American biography* (New York, White, 1892 to date); the French *Dictionnaire de biographie française* (Paris, Letouzey, 1933 to date); the German *Allgemeine deutsche Biographie* (56 volumes; Leipzig, Duncker & Humblot, 1875–1912) and its successor the *Neue deutsche Biographie* (13 volumes; Berlin, Duncker & Humblot, 1953 to date); etc. Unfortunately not every country has its own retrospective biographical dictionary, but where there is one it can often be used as a general encyclopaedia of material on that country, by examining the lives of the people connected with the subject under investigation. Similarly, the various biographical works devoted to specific professions—*Baker's Biographical dictionary of musicians*, Baker's *Biographia dramatica*, Ancona's *Dictionnaire des miniaturistes du moyen âge et de la Renaissance*, the *Biographisches Lexikon der hervorragenden Ärtzte aller Zeiten und Völker*, etc.—supplement both general and national biographical reference sources.

The latest national encyclopaedia, the Bulgarian Academy of Sciences' *Concise Bulgarian encyclopaedia* (1963– . 5 volumes), has many predecessors. The *Encyclopédie belge* was puplished in 1934. Canada has at least two: *The encyclopedia of Canada* (6 volumes and Supplement; Toronto, University Associates of Canada, 1935–49), and the *Encyclopedia Canadiana* (10 volumes; Ottawa, Canadiana Company, 1957–58). *The Australian encyclopaedia* was first issued in two volumes in 1925–26; the new edition has been expanded to ten volumes (Sydney, Angua & Robertson, 1958). Edward Green Balfour (1813–89), surgeon-general of Madras, compiled a *Cyclopaedia of India and of eastern and southern Asia* in 1857 which reached a third edition (3 volumes; London, Quaritch, 1885).

Much of Africa is not yet the subject of specialist encyclopaedias, but Heinrich Schnee compiled a *Deutsches Kolonial-Lexikon* (3

Q

volumes; Leipzig, Quelle, 1920), the French compiled an *Encyclopédie coloniale et maritime* (Paris, Editions de L'Empire Français, 1941 to date), and the Belgians a *Grande encyclopédie de la Belgique et du Congo* (Brussels, Wauthoz-Legrand, 1938 to date).

In Latin America, coverage is rather patchy. A four-volume *Diccionario geográfico, estadístico, histórico, de la isla de Cuba*, by Jacobo de la Pezuela y Lobo, was published in 1863–66 (Madrid, Mellado). Antonio Garcia Cubas' *Diccionario geográfico, histórico y biográfico de los Estados Unidos Mexicanos*, in five volumes, was published in 1888–91 (Mexico City, Secretaría de Fomento), but there is also the recent *Enciclopedia yucatenense* (Mexico City, Yucatan Government Printing Office, 1944–47) in eight volumes. For Salvador there is Miguel Angel García's *Diccionario histórico-enciclopédico de la Republica de El Salvador* (San Salvador, 'La Luz', 1927 to date), and Venezuela has also made some tentative efforts in the first two volumes of Rafael Domingo Silva Uzcátegui's *Enciclopedia larense* (Caracas, Impresores Unidos, 1941).

A sad memorial of the changing times is the discontinued but excellent *Encyclopaedie van Nederlandsch-Indië* (The Hague, Nijhoff, 1917–40) whose supplements to the four basic volumes ceased at the beginning of World War II.

From the history of encyclopaedias throughout the ages some facts become clear. First, no encyclopaedia can escape serious criticism: not all the facts it records will be accurate, for research and discovery develop faster than the printing-press, and what is true today must often be modified tomorrow. This however will never prevent people from buying encyclopaedias, for the serious man will always read critically, and will tend to check his notes with other sources before retailing them elsewhere. Newspapers and magazines, broadcasting and films, all help to keep the modern man informed of changes in detail, so that no encyclopaedia remains his one authority. Moreover, there is a choice of many encyclopaedias today, and they are easily accessible so that there is always a tendency to compare the account of a subject given in one with that given in another.

Since encyclopaedias take so long to pass through the press, it may be argued that in many fields they are out of date before they reach their readers' hands. Is then this form of conveying information outpaced by modern standards? This may depend on the attitude of the user: a dentist looking up details of nucleic acid may be well aware of the latest developments, but grateful to the encyclopaedia for providing him with the history of the subject—it is the origins of things that are so often imperfectly understood.

And, finally, in spite of the best efforts of the editor-in-chief and his specialist editors, the ultimate responsibility for any encyclopaedia article must rest with its writer—to a certain extent it remains the viewpoint of one man, or may reflect the attitude of a group in the ascendancy of a particular subject-field. But to leave the matter there would be to fail to do justice to the philosophy of encyclopaedia-making. There is something in the very nature of an encyclopaedia that calls forth, on many occasions, something bigger than the man—be he writer or editor. The request to write an article for an encyclopaedia becomes a challenge for all but the worst hack-writers. There is something in the discipline imposed that confronts the specialist with an interesting problem. Is it possible to condense the salient points of his subject in readable fashion in only a few hundred words? The controversies so familiar to him—can they be explained in such a way that the 'man in the street' can appreciate them and their significance without paying more attention to the questions they raise than to the main outlines of the subject? And, what can be omitted?—the most trying of all issues, for there are so many candidates for the inadequate amount of space at the writer's disposal. In the end, the imperfections of his script are only too apparent to him, and yet is not this summary account better than the thousands of words and details he would have liked to include and which, had he done so, would most likely have frightened his reader away? Even casual reading of articles in encyclopaedias will often make one realize that here and there is a little masterpiece of style and content—so much so, that it is a matter of regret that one never sees a thorough-going review of an encyclopaedia in any journal apart from the American Library Association's admirable *Booklist and subscription books bulletin.*

The saving grace of all good encyclopaedias is of course the bibliographies attached to their articles. As editors of encyclopaedias progressed in their technique they gradually—along with their readers—came to realize the value of even a short bibliography in providing sources that could modify, correct and amplify the necessarily brief amount of information for which there was space. A glance at the three editions of the *Columbia encyclopedia* will be ample proof of this: in the second edition the bibliographies were greatly improved, and the third edition shows more improvement still, so that the reader has every chance of following up his subject with adequate references, even though he is using only a one-volume reference work. In future editions of encyclopaedias, one very welcome addition to their bibliographies would be the titles of the two or three leading periodicals in the subject-field, so that the reader would no longer be anchored to the year in which the article was written, or last revised, but would be able to proceed immediately to the latest reliable information available.

BIBLIOGRAPHY

The Booklist and subscription books bulletin: a guide to current books. Chicago, American Library Association. Semi-monthly from 1956 has included excellent reviews of encyclopaedias. Reviews of encyclopaedias prior to 1956 included in the quarterly *Subscription books bulletin*, 1930–56

Hart, Laurance H. *Comparison of encyclopaedias: the Hart chart.* Metuchen, N.J., Hart, issued twice a year

Smith, Reginald. *Towards a living encyclopaedia: a contribution to Mr. Wells's new encyclopaedism.* London, Andrew Dakers, 1948

Underbrink, Robert L. *About encyclopaedias: an annotated bibliography.* Jacksonville, Illinois, Underbrink, 1960

Walsh, James P. *General encyclopedias in print.* Newark, Delaware, Reference Books Research Service, 1964 (a comparative analysis)

Wells, H. G. *The work, wealth and happiness of mankind.* London, Heinemann, 1932. Pages 763–776: 'The rôle of an encyclopaedia in a progressive civilisation'

Wells, H. G. *World brain.* Methuen, 1938
     Particularly 'World encyclopaedia' (1936); 'The brain organization of the modern world' (1937); 'The idea of a permanent World Encyclopaedia' (1937); and, 'Passage from a speech to the Congrès Mondial de la Documentation Universelle' (Paris, 20 August 1937)

**THE ENCYCLOPAEDIA
METROPOLITANA**

> *What a strange abuse has been made of the
> word encyclopaedia!*
>
> SAMUEL TAYLOR COLERIDGE, in
> a letter to Robert Southey, July 1803

Information that has recently come to light concerning the financial background and business organization of the *Encyclopaedia
Metropolitana* enables one to understand more clearly the problems
that beset the publisher of any large encyclopaedia in the early
nineteenth century. The experience of Diderot and Le Breton in
the issue of the *Encyclopédie* had demonstrated the need for
thorough planning and a sound commercial technique if the
encyclopaedia was to be a success, and if it was ever to reach
completion. Brockhaus, warned by the example of Löbel, set
about his task in a businesslike way with success from the first,
and the *Britannica* was finally set on its feet by the skill and energy
of the young publisher Constable. But, by the time the *Metropolitana* came to be planned, it faced some powerful rivals, notably
Rees and the *Britannica*. Marketing research did not exist at that
time, but it was apparent that in a Britain of some twenty million
population there could be only a small proportion of possible
purchasers. These included the libraries of universities, clubs, and
subscription societies, and those members of the public who were
sufficiently well educated and able to afford the price of a large set
of volumes. When it is considered that a large number of these
were already committed to its rivals, the *Metropolitana* enterprise
needed to make a special appeal if it was to be carried through to a
successful and profitable conclusion.

When the *Metropolitana* was first discussed, the number of
volumes was to be 28 (altered in a few weeks to 29), and the
encyclopaedia was to be issued in parts over a period of eight years.
The cost of each part was to be 15*s*. 9*d*. for the ordinary (Demy)

edition, and 27s. for the Royal edition. Thus the total cost of some 56 to 58 parts projected would be in the region of £45 or £75 respectively. According to the various estimates of money values at that time, these figures should be multiplied by at least three and possibly four to gain an idea of the present equivalents. Thus, the purchase of an encyclopaedia was a considerable investment, the more so since the subscriber would have to face additional costs for binding the parts in a suitable style. There were further hazards: sales of initial parts are always higher in any subscription work than those for some time later, since some people are curious to know whether the work is of interest to them, others regret their undertaking so large an expenditure, while still others do not continue to subscribe for various reasons such as illness, loss of income, etc. Moreover, the publisher faces the problem of changing costs of living: if he has undertaken by contract to supply the complete work over a number of years at a certain price, any drop in currency purchasing power may reduce or nullify his profits. In this, the payments to editors and contributors are also involved. On the one hand, subscribers may insist on the contract being honoured, while on the other hand the employees of the encyclopaedia may demand a more realistic payment for their work.

Adequate capitalization of any encyclopaedia was just as important in the early nineteenth century as in the twentieth. Paper, printing, wages, advertisements, etc., all had to be paid for long before any real income from the subscriptions was forthcoming. It is true that the publishers of the *Metropolitana* were not the first to gamble on the idea that the proceeds of the first part would pay for the costs of the second, those from the second would finance the third, and so on, but this all depended on a resounding success from the first, and one that would last throughout the entire enterprise. Any delay, dropping off in appeal, or lack of reserve funds could ruin the project. And so it turned out in the initial operations of the issue of the *Metropolitana*, and it remained for an experienced consortium of publishers and booksellers to come to the rescue and to put the encyclopaedia on a proper business footing.

In 1817 a young publisher called Rest Fenner and his associates

Thomas and Samuel Curtis—Thomas Curtis had editorial experience, and his brother Samuel was a printer—believed that they had discovered the formula that could overcome all the difficulties facing any publisher of a new encyclopaedia. At a meeting on 7th April 1817 they invited Samuel Taylor Coleridge to discuss with them the form of the ideal encyclopaedia. Coleridge was at that time 45 years of age and had already established an impressive reputation as a scholar of the first order. His knowledge of German had enabled him to absorb the ideas of Kant and Schelling and Schmid, and he was known to have pronounced ideas on the function and form of the ideal encyclopaedia. In addition, he was acquainted with most of the leading scholars of the age and, for the most part, able to command their respect. Fenner had already published some of Coleridge's books, and could therefore make a special appeal to Coleridge whom he knew, moreover, to be in financial difficulties.

On that historic occasion Coleridge expounded his ideas on the perfect encyclopaedia which, as he saw it, should be classified. Alphabetical order he held in contempt: 'To call a huge unconnected miscellany of the *omne scibile*, in an arrangement determined by the accident of initial letters, an encyclopaedia, is the impudent ignorance of your Presbyterian bookmakers!' (his letter to Robert Southey, July 1803). As he understood it, an encyclopaedia should fulfil the promise of its name and provide the reader with an all-round education. It is not surprising, therefore, that Fenner and the Curtises offered Coleridge the general editorship of the *Metropolitana*, for they had in their grasp an apparently sure appeal to the general public—an encyclopaedia on a new plan, edited by an outstanding scholar. It is true that the contents of the *Encyclopédie méthodique* had been classified, but there was no equivalent in the English language, and it was unlikely that any rival would appear, for the problems of establishing the order of knowledge were too great unless undertaken by a man of Coleridge's stature. Coleridge, who had long talked and written of the difficulties of presenting the development of various branches of knowledge in systematic form, was naturally flattered by the invitation to put his ideas into practice. There was the additional and substantial attraction that the offer appeared to present him with a way out of his financial troubles, while the lure of being responsible for a very considerable enterprise was irresistible. Nevertheless, he foresaw that a great deal of drudgery would be involved, and that he might have little time left for the numerous literary projects he always had in mind to complete: 'at length I have been compelled to give up all thought & hope of doing anything of a permanent nature, either as a Poet or a Philosopher— and have (not without a sigh of anguish) hired myself as a Jobwriter and compiler to a great House who are now engaging in a work that will, if it succeed at all, consume all the years, I can expect to live' (his letter to the Rev. Francis Wrangham of 5th June 1817).

But Coleridge's health was a complicating factor. Since 1816 he had been living with his doctor, James Gillman, at the latter's home in Highgate Village. Fenner and the Curtises made it a condition of the agreement that Coleridge should remove to Camberwell (where Samuel Curtis had his printing works) and devote his whole time to the editorship. In this way Coleridge would be able to supervise the work through the press, and the partners would have instant access to their Editor. No doubt they also had in mind that this was the only way of keeping Coleridge to his side of the bargain, for he was always ready to be sidetracked into anything but the work in front of him. Coleridge, however, in spite of the offer of £500 per annum, could not accept this, and his refusal must have been heavily reinforced by his doctor who knew that only careful supervision could prevent Coleridge's return to the constant drug-taking that had ruined his health. It was in vain that Coleridge offered to go three or four days a week to Fleet Street and work there regular hours; the partners could not accept this, and Thomas Curtis was appointed General Editor, while Coleridge was to act as adviser and contributor.

Coleridge's plan for a classified order of contents was still regarded as the right one, and the partners asked him to outline his scheme in a prospectus which they proposed to issue to the public. This Coleridge did, and the Prospectus was issued with all the authority of Coleridge's name and writing. Nonetheless, modifications to Coleridge's classification had already been made by Sir John Stoddart: much to Coleridge's misgiving, his original eight main divisions had been reduced to four, and the main subject Fine Arts—on which he set such store—had been moved to a subdivision of the Mixed and Applied Sciences. The final blow came when he found that the Dictionary, originally planned for issue at the conclusion of the encyclopaedia, was to be issued as a section of each part, so that the eight years on which he had counted for its adequate preparation was no longer available.

It was at this point that Coleridge refused to continue as an adviser and contributor and cut himself off from what he thereafter constantly described as a fraud. In spite of this, the partners needed Coleridge's promised 'Treatise on Method', expounding the principles on which the encyclopaedia was to be constructed, for issue in their first part. This Coleridge supplied, and it appeared in what he always claimed was a severely mangled form in the *Metropolitana's* first issue. During the next year or so Coleridge and the partners did their best to blacken each other's names and reputation, and Coleridge condemned the *Metropolitana* to all his friends and acquaintances. Small wonder that Rest Fenner went bankrupt in March 1819 when only four parts of the encyclopaedia had been issued, and that he and Thomas Curtis eventually departed for America. It subsequently appeared that Fenner had cheated Coleridge of part of the royalties on his books, and that the partners had estranged his relations with other publishers. It was a sad episode in Coleridge's life and prevented the world from knowing how far Coleridge could have achieved his ideal of the perfect encyclopaedia.

The question remains whether the *Metropolitana* under Fenner's and Coleridge's management could ever have kept going. Unfortunately the accounts for the first five parts have not survived, but in 1821 the effects of the *Metropolitana* were auctioned at the Albion Tavern, London, on 3rd July and were sold for £890 to a consortium of publishers and booksellers under the leadership of Benjamin Fellowes. From that time on a strict accounting was kept of the sales and the costs incurred of each part, and there is in this way on record an unrivalled analysis of the financial transactions involved in the issue of a large encyclopaedia over a considerable number of years.

When the consortium took over the stock of Rest Fenner in 1821, they found that the following copies of each part had been disposed of by sale or in other ways. The remainder, plus a complete set of Part 5 (250 Royal and 2,500 Demy copies) fell to the new publishers. At full price the parts disposed of:

Part 1	*Royal*	36	*Demy*	1,810
2		32		1,101
3		28		1,033
4		31		1,398
		127		5,342

would have fetched £4,645, but the sum actually realized would have been less owing to parts distributed gratis, bad debts, discounts, despatch costs, etc. Thus, assuming that Rest Fenner had received an average of £1,000 for each part, he was incurring a loss—judging by the consortium's later experience of the costs of publishing the *Metropolitana*. Even if Fenner had pared his own costs to a minimum it is doubtful whether he was breaking even on the *Metropolitana*, and the bonanza on which he had counted had evidently not materialized. On the other hand, at £890 the consortium, if they organized the affair properly, were getting a knockdown bargain which would encourage them to make an energetic fresh start.

The issue of a single part under the new management cost approximately £1,500. Since Rest Fenner's enterprise was largely a family one (Samuel Curtis owning the Camberwell Printing Works where the encyclopaedia was produced), his costs were probably smaller, but there were items that would vary little no matter what the management. Thus the consortium's accounts show that of the £1,500, nearly one-third was taken up by 'Literary Expenses', nearly a fifth by printing, a sixth by paper, another sixth for plates and plate-printing, while advertisements and prospectuses cost £85, 'boarding' £69, and reference books £55. With regard to the last item, it is commendable that reference books seem to have been liberally provided—even Fenner had not neglected this item, and the consortium paid £245 for the works (including some of Coleridge's own writings) already amassed. The books were always carefully controlled: every transfer of a book is carefully recorded in the accounts.

The consortium paid their Editor (the Rev. W. R. Lyall for parts 6 and 7; then the Rev. Edward Smedley; Hugh James Rose, for a brief period after Smedley's death in 1836; and, on his death in 1838, his younger brother Henry, for the final volumes) one hundred guineas per part and this figure, like those for their contributors, remains constant throughout the years until the completion of the *Metropolitana*. Payments to contributors varied with their standing. Sir John Herschel was paid at the top rate of ten guineas per sheet. Writers of the standing of Professor Charles Babbage received seven guineas, and most of the remainder five guineas per sheet. Incidentally, Coleridge, in spite of his determination not to have anything more to do with the *Metropolitana*, must have relented, for there are entries in the accounts for parts 6 and 8 showing small payments to him at 5 guineas per sheet. Contributions were scrupulously measured down to page and column length, *e.g.:*

Mr Lardner	Contributions	1 page at 7.7.0	18s. 6d.
Mr Herschel		9 sheets at 10.10.0	94. 10s. 0d.
Mr Lush		2 pages & 1 Col. at	
		5.5.0	1. 12s. 11d.
Mr Bell		6 pages & 1 Col. at	
		5.5.0	4. 5s. 7d.

But contributors were also supplied with free paper: for 1822 the consortium paid one guinea for two reams of contributors' paper.

The *Metropolitana* is justly praised for it fine engraved plates. This work was commissioned from good artists and well paid, *e.g.:*

Plates

Engraving 11 Plates (Lowry) at 15.15.0		173. 5. 0
Drawings for 8 do. do. at 10.6		4. 4. 0
do. for 3 do. (Clement)		13. 2. 0
Engraving & Drawing on Plate (Griffiths)		9. 9. 0
		200. 0. 0

Copper Plate Printing

Printing 1750 No: each 12 plates at 4/– per 100	42.	0. 0
Printing 2 each 12 Plates India Proofs at 9*d.*		18. 0
	42.	18. 0

Advertising was highly organized and was by no means inexpensive. Between December 1821 and 30th April 1823, three hundred advertisements were inserted in 'various Town and Country Newspapers, Magazines, etc.' at a cost of £128 3*s.* 0*d.*, while another £41 13*s.* 0*d.* was paid for the 'insertion of 50,000 Prospectuses in various Reviews and Magazines'. And advertising did not stop here: there is an entry in the 1822 accounts for £4 17*s.* 0*d.*, representing 'Half expence of ½ Sheet Circular, of the Ency: and Lingard, to Lords and Comm[s]'. Free copies to the copyright deposit libraries and to contributors, etc., were carefully costed at full price, and it is clear that the consortium was presented at all times with a realistic statement of its financial position.

With such expenses to meet it is inconceivable that Rest Fenner and his partners could have survived for long. It does not appear possible that they could have continued to pay Coleridge at the rate of £500 per annum, or that they could have afforded to pay out such large sums regularly to their contributors. It would only in fact have been feasible had the *Metropolitana* proved an outstanding success from the start. As it was, the consortium, with all their experience of handling the marketing of publications, lost a total of at least £15,000 on the enterprise, which had cost approximately £44,000 for the 59 parts it eventually reached. This is revealed in a letter written by Messrs Griffin to the Archbishop of Dublin on 17th March 1849: 'Not a sixth part of the subscription continued regularly to the end.' And this probably took into account the purchase price of £4,465 which Messrs J. & J. Griffin paid when they took over the *Metropolitana* from the consortium in 1847.

But if Coleridge had failed to demonstrate in practice the form of the ideal encyclopaedia, he had at any rate left a very full account of his ideas on the subject in his 'Treatise on Method'.

This is unique in the English language and important for its adaptation of German philosophical ideas to English requirements. For the whole period since it was written, its original text has remained in some doubt since Coleridge asserted that the publishers of the *Metropolitana* altered it out of all recognition, and that he was unable to regain possession of the original manuscript so that he could re-establish the text as he had written it. Professor Earl Leslie Griggs, in his definitive edition of Coleridge's letters, has, however, proved recently that Coleridge did in fact ultimately recover the manuscript in a battered form, and more recently still some other evidence has come to light that puts the matter in a different perspective. This comprises copies of a brief correspondence between Messrs Griffin and Sara Coleridge (Mrs H. N. Coleridge), Coleridge's daughter and literary executor. It appears that in 1849 Messrs Griffin were proposing to re-issue the 'Treatise' and submitted the text as published in the *Metropolitana* to Mrs Coleridge for amendment. Mrs Coleridge spent considerable time on the matter before replying, and then her amendments were of the slightest. As Mrs Coleridge was fully familiar with the controversy and was at liberty to make any alterations she thought necessary, it seems that after all the text as originally printed is what Coleridge himself wrote. The version that follows in Appendix 2 is therefore that of the *Metropolitana*, and is reprinted here as one of the very few contributions to the philosophy that lies behind the compilation of encyclopaedias.

Appendix 2 SAMUEL TAYLOR COLERIDGE ON 'SCIENTIFIC METHOD'

GENERAL INTRODUCTION

OR

PRELIMINARY TREATISE ON METHOD

Non simpliciter nil sciri posse; sed nil nisi certo ordine certâ viâ sciri posse.—BACON

SECTION I: ON THE PHILOSOPHICAL PRINCIPLES OF METHOD

Nature of the work

The word ENCYCLOPAEDIA is too familiar to modern literature to require, in this place, any detailed explanation. It is current amongst us as the title of various Dictionaries of Science, whose professed object is to furnish a compendium of human knowledge, whatever may be their plan. But to *methodize* such a compendium has either never been attempted, or the attempt has failed, from the total disregard of those general connecting principles, on which Method essentially depends. In presenting, therefore, to the Public an entirely new work, intended to be methodically arranged, we are not insensible to the difficulties of our undertaking; but we trust that we have found a clue to the labyrinth in those considerations which we are now about to submit to the reader.

As METHOD is thus avowed to be the principal aim and distinguishing feature of our publication, it becomes us, at the commencement, clearly to explain what we mean in this Introduction by that word; to exhibit the principles on which alone a correct philosophical Method can be founded; to illustrate those principles by their application to distinct studies and to the history of the human mind; and lastly to apply them to the general concatenation of the several arts and sciences, and to the most perspicuous, elegant, and useful manner of developing each particular study. Such are the objects of this Essay, which we conceive must form a necessary Introduction to a work, that is designated in its title from the place whence it originates,—the ENCYCLOPAEDIA METROPOLITANA; but claims from its mode of execution to be also called '*a* METHODICAL *Compendium of Human Knowledge.*'

The word Method

The word METHOD (*μέθοδος*), being of Grecian origin, first formed and applied by that acute, ingenious, and accurate people, to the purposes of scientific arrangement; it is in the Greek language that we must seek for its primary and fundamental signification. Now, in Greek, it literally means *a way, or path, of transit.* Hence the first idea of Method is *a progressive transition* from one step in any course to another; and where the word Method is applied with reference to many such transitions in continuity, it necessarily implies a principle of UNITY WITH PROGRESSION. But that which unites, and makes many things *one* in the mind of man, must be an act of the mind itself, a manifestation of intellect, and not a spontaneous and uncertain production of circumstances. This act of the mind, then, this leading thought, this 'key note' of the harmony, this 'subtile, cementing, subterraneous' power, borrowing a phrase from the nomenclature of legislation, we may not inaptly call the INITIATIVE of all Method. It is manifest, that the wider the sphere of transition is, the more comprehensive and commanding must be the initiative: and if we would discover an *universal Method* by which every step in our progress through the whole circle of art and science should be directed, it is absolutely necessary that we should seek it in the very interior and central essence of the human intellect.

The Science of Method

To this point we are led by mere reflection on the meaning of the word Method. We discover that it cannot, otherwise than by abuse, be applied to a dead and arbitrary arrangement, containing in itself no principle of progression. We discover, that there is a *Science of Method;* and that *that* science, like all others, must necessarily have its *principles*; which it therefore becomes our duty to consider, in so far at least as they may be necessary to the arrangement of a Methodical Encyclopaedia.

Its objects, and relations

All things, in us, and about us, are a chaos, without Method: and so long as the mind is entirely passive, so long as there is an habitual submission of the understanding to mere events and images, as such, without any attempt to classify and arrange them, so long the chaos must continue. There may be transition, but there can never be progress; there may be sensation, but there cannot be thought: for the total absence of Method renders thinking impracticable; as we find that partial defects of Method proportionably render thinking a trouble and a fatigue. But as soon as the mind becomes accustomed to contemplate, not *things* only, but likewise *relations* of things, there is immediate need of some path or way of transit from one to the other of the things related;— there must be some law of agreement or of contrast between them; there must be some mode of comparison; in short, there must be Method. We may, therefore, assert that the *relations of things* form the prime objects, or so to speak, the *materials of Method*: and that the contemplation of those relations is the indispensable condition of thinking methodically.

Of these relations of things, we distinguish two principal kinds. One of them is the relation by which we understand that a thing *must be*: the other, that by which we merely perceive that it *is*. The one, we call the relation of LAW, using that word in its highest and original sense, namely, that of *laying down* a rule to which the subjects of the law must necessarily conform. The other, we call the relation of THEORY.

Relation of Law

The relation of LAW is in its absolute perfection conceivable only of God, that Supreme Light, and Living Law, 'in whom we live and move, and have our being;' who is ἐν παντί, and πρὸ τῶν πάντων. But yet the human mind is capable of viewing some relations of things as necessarily existent; that is to say, as predetermined by a truth in the mind itself, pregnant with the consequence of other truths in an indefinite progression. Of such truths, some continue always to exist in and for the mind alone, forming the *pure sciences*, moral or intellectual; whilst others, though originating in the mind, constitute what are commonly called the great laws of nature, and form the groundwork of the *mixed sciences*, such as those of Mechanics and Astronomy.

Relation of Theory

The second relation is that of THEORY, in which the existing forms and qualities of objects, discovered by observation, suggest a given arrangement of them to the mind, not merely for the purposes of more easy remembrance and communication; but for those of understanding, and sometimes of controlling them. The studies to which this class of relations is subservient, are more properly called *scientific arts* than sciences. Medicine, Chemistry, and Physiology, are examples of a Method founded on this second sort of relation, which, as well as the former, always supposes the necessary connection of cause and effect.

Fine Arts

The relations of law and theory have each their Methods. Between these two, lies the Method of the FINE ARTS, a Method in which certain great truths, composing, what are usually called the *laws of taste*, necessarily predominate; but in which there are also other laws, dependent on the external objects of sight and sound, which these arts embrace. To prove the comparative value and dignity of the first relation, it will be sufficient to observe that what is called 'tinkling' verse is disagreeable to the accomplished critic in poetry, and that a fine musical taste is soon dissatisfied with the Harmonica, or any similar instrument of glass or steel, because the *body* of the sound (as the Italians phrase it), or that effect which is derived from the materials, encroaches too far on

R

the effect derived from the proportions of the notes, which proportions are in fact laws of the mind, analogous to the laws of Arithmetic and Geometry.

Principle of union; Ideas

We have stated, that Method implies both an *uniting* and a *progressive* power. Now the relations of things are not united in human conception at random—*humano capiti—cervicem equinam*; but there is some rule, some mode of union, more or less strictly necessary. Where it is absolutely necessary, we have called it a relation of law; and as by law we mean the laying down the rule, so the rule laid down we call, in the ancient and proper sense of the word, an *Idea*: and consequently the words Idea and Law, are correlative terms, differing only as object and subject, as being and truth. It is extremely necessary to advert to this use of the word Idea; since, in modern philosophy, almost any and every exercise of any and every mental faculty, has been abusively called by this name, to the utter confusion and *unmethodizing* of the whole science of the human mind, and indeed of all other knowledge whatsoever.

Definite or instinctive

The idea may exist in a clear, distinct, definite form, as that of a circle in the mind of an accurate geometrician; or it may be a mere *instinct*, a vague appetency toward something which the mind incessantly hunts for but cannot find, like a name which has escaped our recollection, or the impulse which fills the young poet's eye with tears, he knows not why. In the infancy of the human mind, all our ideas are instincts; and language is happily contrived to lead us from the vague to the distinct, from the imperfect to the full and finished form: the boy knows that his hoop is round, and this, in after years, helps to teach him, that in a circle, all the lines drawn from the centre to the circumference, are equal. It will be seen, in the sequel, that this distinction between the instinctive approach toward an idea, and the idea itself, is of high importance in methodizing art and science.

Principle of progression

From the first, or initiative idea, as from a seed, successive ideas germinate. Thus, from the idea of a triangle, necessarily follows that of equality between the sum of its three angles, and two right angles. This is the *principle* of an indefinite, not to say infinite, *progression*; but this progression, which is truly Method, requires not only the proper choice of an initiative, but also the following it out through all its ramifications. It requires, in short, a constant wakefulness of mind; so that if we wander but in a single instance from our path, we cannot reach the goal, but by retracing our steps to the point of divergency, and thence beginning our progress anew. Thus, a ship beating off and on an unknown coast, often takes, in nautical phrase, 'a new departure;' and thus it is necessary often to recur to that regulating process, which the French language so happily expresses by the word *s'orienter*, i.e. to find out the east for ourselves, and so to put to rights our faulty reckoning.

State of mind adapted to

The habit of Method, should always be present and effective; but in order to render it so, a certain training, or education of the mind, is indispensably necessary. Events and images, the lively and spirit-stirring machinery of the external world, are like light, and air, and moisture, to the seed of the mind, which would else rot and perish. In all processes of mental evolution the objects of the senses must stimulate the mind; and the mind must in turn assimilate and digest the food which it thus receives from without. Method, therefore, must result from the due mean, or balance, between our passive impressions and the mind's re-action on them. So in the healthful state of the human body, waking and sleep, rest and labour, reciprocally succeed each other, and mutually contribute to liveliness, and activity, and strength. There are certain stores proper, and as it were, indigenous to the mind, such as the ideas of number and figure, and the logical forms and combinations of conception or thought. The mind that is rich and exuberant in this intellectual wealth, is apt, like a miser, to dwell upon the vain contemplation of its riches, is disposed to generalize and methodize to excess, ever philosophizing, and never descending to action;—spreading its wings high in the air above some beloved spot, but never flying far and wide over earth and sea, to seek food, or to enjoy the endless beauties of nature; the fresh morning, and the warm noon, and the dewy eve. On the other hand, still less is to be expected, toward the methodizing of science, from the man who flutters about in blindness, like the bat; or is carried hither and thither, like the turtle sleeping on the wave, and fancying, because he moves, that he is in progress.

Proper direction of; Gradation of ideas

The paths in which we may pursue a methodical course are manifold: at the head of each stands its peculiar and guiding idea; and those ideas are as regularly subordinate in dignity, as the paths to which they point are various and eccentric in direction. The world has suffered much, in modern times, from a subversion of the natural and necessary order of science; from elevating the terrestrial, as it has been called, above the celestial; and from summoning reason and faith to the bar of that limited physical experience, to which by the true laws of Method, they owe no obedience. The subordination, of which we here speak, is not that which depends on immediate practical utility; for the utility of human powers, in their practical application, depends on the circumstances of the moment; and at one time strength is essential to our very existence, at another time skill: and even Caesar in a fever could cry—

> ——Give me some drink Titinius,
> As a sick girl.——

In truth there is scarcely any one of the powers or faculties with which the Divine Goodness has endowed his creatures, which may not in its turn be a source of paramount benefit and usefulness; for every thing around us is full of blessings: nor is there any line of honest occupation in which we would dare to affirm, that by a proper exercise of the talent committed to his charge, an individual might not justly advance himself to highest praise. But we now allude to the subordination which necessarily arises among the different branches of knowledge, according to the difference of those ideas by which they are initiated and directed; for there is a gradation of ideas, as of ranks in a well ordered state, or of commands in a well regulated army; and thus above all partial forms, there is one universal form of GOOD and FAIR, the καλοκἀγαθόν of the Platonic philosophy. Hence the expressions of Lord Bacon, who in his great work the Novum Organum, speaks so much and so often of the *lumen siccum*, the pure light, which from a central focus, as it were, diffuses its rays all around, and forms a lucid sphere of knowledge and of truth.

Metaphysical and physical

We distinguish ideas into those of essential property, and those of natural existence; in other words, into metaphysical and physical ideas. Metaphysical ideas, or those which relate to the essence of things as possible, are of the highest class. Thus, in accurate language, we say, the *essence* of a circle, not its nature; because, in the conception of forms purely geometrical, there is no expression or implication of their actual existence: and our reasoning upon them is totally independent of the fact, whether any such forms ever existed in nature, or not. Physical ideas are those which we mean to express, when we speak of the *nature* of a thing actually existing and cognizable by our faculties, whether the thing be material or immaterial, bodily or mental. Thus, the laws of memory, the laws of vision, the laws of vegetation, the laws of crystallization, are all physical ideas, dependent for their accuracy, on the more or less careful observation of things actually existing.

Nature

In speaking of the word Nature, however, we must distinguish its two principal uses, viz. first, that to which we have adverted, and according to which it signifies whatever is requisite to the reality of a thing as existent, such as the nature of an animal or a tree, distinguished from the animal or tree itself: and secondly, the sum total of things, as far as they are objects of our senses. In the first of these two meanings the word Nature conveys a physical *idea*, in the other only a material or sensible *impression*.

Mere arrangement

Even natural substances, it is true, may be classed and arranged for various purposes, in a certain order. Such *mere* arrangement, however, is not properly methodical, but rather a preparation toward Method; as the compilation of a dictionary is a preparation for classical study.

The limits of our present Essay will not allow us to do more than briefly to touch the chief topics of a general dissertation on Method; but enough we trust has here been said, to render intelligible the principles on which our Methodical Encyclopaedia must be constructed. We have shewn that a Method, which is at all comprehensive, must be founded on the *relations of things*: that those relations are of two sorts, according as they present themselves to the human mind as *necessary*, or merely as the result of *observation*. The former we have called relations of law, the latter of theory. Where the former alone are in question, the Method is one of necessary connection throughout; where the latter alone, though the connection be considered as one of cause and effect, yet the necessity is less obvious, and the connection itself less close. We have observed, that in the Fine Arts there is a sort of middle Method, inasmuch as the first and higher relations are necessary, the lower only the results of observation. The great principles of all Method we have shown to be two, viz. *Union* and *Progression*. The relations of things cannot be united by accident: they are united by an *idea* either definite or instinctive. Their union, in proportion as it is clear, is also progressive. The state of mind adapted to such progress holds a due mean between a passiveness under external impression, and an excessive activity of mere reflection; and the progress itself follows the path of the idea from which it sets out; requiring, however, a constant wakefulness of mind, to keep it within the due limits of its course. Hence the orbits of thought, so to speak, must differ among themselves as the initiative ideas differ; and of these latter, the great distinctions are into *physical* and *metaphysical*. Such, briefly, are the views by which we have been guided, in our present attempt to methodize the great mass of human knowledge.

Section II: Illustration of the Preceding Principles

The principles which have been exhibited in the preceding section, and in respect to which we claim no other merit, than that of having drawn them from the purest sources of philosophy, ancient and modern, are, we trust, sufficiently plain and intelligible in themselves; but as the most satisfactory mode of proving their accuracy, we proceed to illustrate them by a consideration of some particular studies, pursuits and opinions; and by a reference to the general history of the human mind.

Domestic economy

And first, as to the general importance of Method;—what need have we to dilate on this fertile topic? For it is not solely in the formation of the human understanding, and in the constructions of science and literature, that the employment of Method is indispensably necessary; but its importance is equally felt, and equally acknowledged, in the whole business and economy of active and domestic life. From the cottager's hearth or the workshop of the artisan, to the palace or the arsenal, the first merit, that which admits neither substitute nor equivalent, is, that *every thing is in its place*. Where this charm is wanting, every other merit either loses its name, or becomes an additional ground of accusation and regret. Of one, by whom it is eminently possessed, we say proverbially, that he is like clock-work. The resemblance extends beyond the point of regularity, and yet falls short of the truth. Both do, indeed, at once divide and announce the silent and otherwise indistinguishable lapse of time: but the man of methodical industry and honourable pursuits, does more; he realizes its ideal divisions, and gives a character and individuality to its moments. If the idle are described as killing time, he may be justly said to call it into life and moral being, while he makes it the distinct object not only of the consciousness, but of the conscience.

He organizes the hours, and gives them a soul: and to that, the very essence of which is to fleet, and *to have been,* he communicates an imperishable and a spiritual nature. Of the good and faithful servant, whose energies, thus directed, are thus methodized, it is less truly affirmed, that he lives in time, than that time lives in him. His days, months, and years, as the stops and punctual marks in the records of duties performed, will survive the wreck of worlds, and remain extant when time itself shall be no more.

Conversation

Let us carry our views a step higher. What is it that first strikes us, and strikes us at once in a man of education, and which, among educated men, so instantly distinguishes the man of superior mind? Not always the weight or novelty of his remarks, nor always the interest of the facts which he communicates; for the subject of conversation may chance to be trivial, and its duration to be short. Still less can any just admiration arise from any peculiarity in his words and phrases; for every man of practical good sense will follow, as far as the matters under consideration will permit him, that golden rule of Caesar's—*Insolens verbum, tanquam scopulum, evitare.* The true cause of the impression made on us, is that his mind is *methodical.* We perceive this, in the unpremeditated and evidently habitual arrangement of his words, flowing spontaneously and necessarily from the clearness of the leading idea; from which distinctness of mental vision, when men are fully accustomed to it, they obtain a habit of foreseeing at the beginning of every sentence how it is to end, and how all its parts may be brought out in the best and most orderly succession. However irregular and desultory the conversation may happen to be, there is *Method* in the fragments.

Moral conduct

Let us once more take an example which must come 'home to every man's business and bosom.' Is there not a *Method* in the discharge of all our relative duties? And is not he the truly virtuous and truly happy man, who seizing first and laying hold most firmly of the great first Truth, is guided by that divine light through all the meandering and stormy courses of his existence? To him every relation of life affords a prolific *idea* of duty; by pursuing which into all its practical consequences, he becomes a good servant or a good master, a good subject or a good sovereign, a good son or a good father; a good friend, a good patriot, a good Christian, a good man!

Scientific discoveries

It cannot be deemed foreign from the purposes of our disquisition, if we are anxious, before we leave this part of the subject, to attract the attention of our readers to the importance of speculative meditation (which never will be fruitful unless it be methodical) even to the *worldly* interests of mankind. We can recall no incident of human history that impresses the imagination more deeply than the moment, when Columbus, on an unknown ocean, first perceived that startling fact, the change of the magnetic needle! How many such instances occur in history, where the *ideas* of nature (presented to chosen minds by a Higher Power than nature herself) suddenly unfold, as it were, in prophetic succession, systematic views destined to produce the most important revolutions in the state of man! The clear spirit of Columbus was doubtless eminently *methodical.* He saw distinctly that great leading idea, which authorized the poor pilot to become 'a promiser of kingdoms:' and he pursued the progressive development of the mighty truth with an unyielding firmness, which taught him 'to rejoice in lofty labours.' Our readers will perhaps excuse us for quoting, as illustrative of what we have here observed, some lines from an Ode of Chiabrera's, which in strength of thought and in lofty majesty of poetry, has but 'few peers in ancient or in modern song.'

COLUMBUS

Certo, dal cor, ch' alto Destin non scelse,
Son l'imprese magnanime neglette;
Ma le bell' alme alle bell' opre elette;
Sanno gioir nelle fatiche eccelse:
Ne biasmo popolar, frale catena,
Spirto d'onore il suo cammin raffrena.

Cosi lunga stagion per modi indegni
Europa disprezzó l'inclita speme:
Schernendo il vulgo (e seco i Regi insieme)
Nudo nocchier promettitor di Regni;
Ma per le sconosciute onde marine
L'invitta prora ei pur sospinse al fine.
Qual uom, che torni al gentil consorte,
Tal ei da sua magion spiegó l'antenne;
L' ocean corse, e i turbini sostenne
Vinse le crude imagini di morte;
Poscia, dell 'ampio mar spenta la guerra,
Scorse la dianzi favolosa Terra.
Allor dal cavo Pin scende veloce
E di grand' Orma il nuovo mondo imprime;
Nè men ratto per l' Aria erge sublime,
Segno del Ciel, insuperabil Croce;
E porse umile esempio, onde adorarla
Debba sua Gente.

Chiabrera, vol. i

Mathematics and physics

We do not mean to rest our argument on the general utility or importance of Method. Every science and every art attests the value of the particular principles on which we have above insisted. In mathematics they will, doubtless, be readily admitted; and certainly there are many marked differences between mathematical and physical studies: but in both a previous act and conception of the mind, or what we have called an *initiative*, is indispensably necessary, even to the mere semblance of Method. In mathematics, the definition *makes* the object, and pre-establishes the terms, which alone can occur in the after reasoning. If an existing circle, or what is supposed to be such, be found not to have the radii from the centre to the circumference perfectly equal: it will in no manner affect the mathematician's reasoning on the properties of circles; it will only prove that the figure in question is not a circle according to the previous definition. A mathematical idea, therefore, may be perfect. But the place of a perfect idea cannot be exactly supplied, in the sciences of experiment and observation, by any theory built on generalization. For what shall determine the mind to one point rather than another; within what

limits, and from what number of individuals, shall the generalization be made? The theory must still require a prior theory for its
own legitimate construction. The physical definition follows and
does not precede the reasoning. It is representative, not constitutive, and is indeed little more than an abbreviature of the
preceding observation, and the deductions therefrom. But as the
observation, though aided by experiment, is necessarily limited
and imperfect, the definition must be equally so. The history
of theories, and the frequency of their subversion by the discovery of a single new fact, supply the best illustrations of this
truth.

Electricity

But in experimental philosophy, it may be said, how much do
we not owe to accident? Doubtless: but let it not be forgotten, that
if the discoveries so made stop there; if they do not excite some
master IDEA; if they do not lead to some LAW (in whatever dress
of theory or hypothesis the fashions and prejudices of the time may
disguise or disfigure it); the discoveries may remain for ages
limited in their uses, insecure and unproductive. How many
centuries, we might have said millennia, have passed, since the
first accidental discovery of the attraction and repulsion of light
bodies by rubbed amber, &c. Compare the interval with the
progress made within less than a century, after the discovery of the
phaenomena that led immediately to a theory of ELECTRICITY.
That here, as in many other instances, the theory was supported by
insecure hypotheses; that by one theorist two heterogeneous fluids
were assumed, the vitreous and the resinous; by another, a plus
and minus of the same fluid; that a third considered it a mere
modification of light; while a fourth composed the electrical aura
of oxygen, hydrogen, and caloric: all this does but place the truth
we have been insisting on in a stronger and clearer light. For,
abstract from all these suppositions, or rather imaginations, that
which is common to, and involved in them all; and there will
remain neither notional fluid or fluids, nor chemical compounds,
nor elementary matter,—but the idea of *two—opposite—forces*, tend-
ing to rest by equilibrium. These are the sole factors of the calculus,

alike in all the theories: these give the *law* and with it the *Method* of arranging the phaenomena. For this reason it may not be rash to anticipate the nearest approaches to a correct system of electricity from those philosophers who since the year 1798 have presented the idea most distinctly as such, rejecting the hypothesis of any material substratum, and contemplating in all electrical phaenomena the operation of a law which reigns through all nature, viz: the law of *polarity*, or the manifestation of one power by opposite forces.

Magnetism

How great the contrast between electricity and MAGNETISM! From the remotest antiquity, the attraction of iron by the magnet was known, and noticed; but century after century it remained the undisturbed property of poets and orators. The fact of the magnet, and the fable of the Phoenix, stood on the same scale of utility, and by the generality of mankind, the latter was as much credited as the former, and considered far more interesting. In the thirteenth century, however, or perhaps earlier, the *polarity* of the magnet, and its communicability to iron, were discovered. We remain in doubt whether this discovery were accidental, or the result of theory; if the former, the purpose which it soon suggested was so grand and important, that it may well be deemed the proudest trophy ever yet raised by accident in the service of mankind. But still it furnished no genuine *idea*; it led to no *law*, and consequently, to no *Method*; though a variety of phaenomena, as startling as they are at present mysterious, have forced on us a presentiment of its intimate connection with other great agencies of nature. We would not be understood to assume the power of predicting to what extent, or in what directions, that connection may hereafter be traced; but amidst the most ingenious hypotheses, that have yet been formed on the subject, we may notice that which, combining the three primary laws of magnetism, electricity, and galvinism,[1] considers them all as the results of one common power, essential

---

[1] See the experiments of Coulomb, Brugmans, and Goethe. To which may be added, should they be confirmed, the curious observations on Chrystallization, first made in Corsica, and since pursued in France.

to all material construction in the works of nature. It is perhaps more an operation of the fancy than of the reason, which has suggested that these three material powers are analogous to the three dimensions of space. Hypothesis, be it observed, can never form the ground-work of a true scientific method, unless where the hypothesis is either a true *idea* proposed in an hypothetical form, or at least the symbol of an idea as yet unknown, of a law as yet undiscovered; and in this latter case the hypothesis merely performs the function of an unknown quantity in algebra, and is assumed for the purpose of submitting the phaenomena to a scientific calculus. But to recur to the contrast presented by electricity and magnetism, in the rapid progress of the former, and the stationary condition of the latter: What is the cause of this diversity? Fewer theories, fewer hypotheses have not been advanced in the one than in the other; but the theories and fictions of the electricians contained an *idea*, and all the same idea, which has necessarily led to METHOD; implicit indeed, and only regulative hitherto, but which requires little more than the dismission of the imagery to become constitutive, like the ideas of the geometrician. On the contrary, the assumptions of the magnetists (as for instance, the hypothesis that the earth itself is one vast magnet, or that an immense magnet is concealed within it; or that there is a concentric globe within the earth, revolving on its own independent axis) are but repetitions of the same fact or phaenomenon, looked at through a magnifying glass; the *reiteration* of the problem, not its solution. This leads to the important consideration, so often dwelt upon, so forcibly urged, so powerfully amplified and explained by our great countryman Bacon, that one fact is often worth a thousand. 'Satis scimus,' says he, '*axiomata recté inventu, tota agmina operum secum trahere.*' Hence his indignant reprobation of the '*vis experimentalis, caeca, stupida, vaga, praerupta*'! Hence his just and earnest exhortations to pursue the *experimenta lucifera*, and those alone; discarding for their sakes, even the *fructifera experimenta*. The natural philosopher, who cannot, or will not see, that it is the 'enlightening' fact, which really causes all the others to *be* facts, in any scientific sense—he who has not the head to comprehend, and the soul to reverence this parent experiment—he to whom the εὕρηκα is not an exclamation of joy and rapture, a rich reward for years of toil and patient suffering—to him no auspicious answer will ever be granted by the oracle of nature.

Zoology

We have said that improgressive arrangement is not Method: and in proof of this we appeal to the notorious fact, that ZOOLOGY, soon after the commencement of the latter half of the last century, was falling abroad, weighed down and crushed as it were by the inordinate number and multiplicity of facts and phaenomena apparently separate, without evincing the least promise of systematizing itself by any inward combination of its parts. JOHN HUNTER, who had appeared, at times, almost a stranger to the grand conception, which yet never ceased to work in him, as his genius and governing spirit, rose at length in the horizon of physiology and comparative anatomy. In his printed works, the finest elements of system seem evermore to flit before him, twice or thrice only to have been seized, and after a momentary detention, to have been again suffered to escape. At length, in the astonishing preparations for his museum, he constructed it, for the scientific apprehension, out of the unspoken alphabet of nature. Yet notwithstanding the imperfection in the annunciation of the idea, how exhilarating have been the results! It may, we believe, be affirmed with safety, that whatever is grandest, in the views of CUVIER, is either a reflection of this light, or a continuation of its rays, well and wisely directed, through fit media, to its appropriate object.

Botany

From Zoology, or the laws of animal life, to BOTANY, or those of vegetable life, the transition is easy and natural. In this pursuit, how striking is the necessity of a clear *idea*, as initiative of all Method! How obvious the importance of attention to the conduct of the mind in the exercise of Method itself! The lowest attempt at botanical arrangement consists in an artificial classification of plants, for the preparatory purpose of a nomenclature; but even in this, some *antecedent* must have been contributed by the mind itself; some *purpose* must be in view; or some question at least must have been proposed to nature, grounded, as all questions are, upon *some* idea of the answer. As for instance, the assumption,

'That two great sexes animate the world.'

For no man can confidently conceive a fact to be universally true who does not proportionally anticipate its necessity, and who does not believe that necessity to be demonstrable by an insight into its nature, whenever and wherever such insight can be obtained. We acknowledge, we reverence, the obligations of Botany to LIN-NAEUS, who adopting from Bartholinus and others the sexuality of plants, grounded thereon a scheme of classific and distinctive marks, by which one man's experience may be communicated to others, and the objects safely reasoned on while absent, and recognized as soon as and wherever they occur. He invented an universal character for the language of Botany, chargeable with no greater imperfections than are to be found in the alphabets of every particular language. The first requisites in investigating the works of nature, as in studying the classics, are a proper accidence and dictionary; and for both of these Botany is indebted to the illustrious Swede. But the inherent necessity, the true *idea* of sex, was never fully contemplated by Linnaeus, much less that of vegetation itself. Wanting these master-lights, he was not only unable to discern the collateral relations of the vegetable to the mineral and animal worlds, but even in respect to the doctrine which gives name and character to his system, he only avoided Scylla to fall upon Charybdis: and such must be the case of every one, who in this uncertain state of the initiative idea, ventures to expatiate among the subordinate notions. If we adhere to the general notion of sex, as abstracted from the more obvious modes in which the sexual relation manifests itself, we soon meet with whole classes of plants to which it is found inapplicable. If, arbitrarily, we give it indefinite extension, it is dissipated into the barren truism, that all specific products suppose specific *means* of production. Thus a growth and a birth are distinguished by the mere verbal definition, that the latter is a whole in itself, the former not: and when we would apply even this to nature, we are baffled by objects (the flower polypus, &c. &c.) in which each is the other. All that can be done by the most patient and active industry, by the widest and most continuous researches; all that the amplest survey of the vegetable realm, brought under immediate contemplation by the most stupendous collections of species and varieties, can suggest; all that minutest dissection and exactest chemical analysis, can unfold; all that varied experiment and the position of plants and their component parts in every conceivable relation to light, heat, and whatever else we distinguish as imponderable substances; to earth, air, water; to the supposed constituents of air and water, separate and in all proportions—in short all that chemical agents and re-agents can disclose or adduce;—all these have been brought, as conscripts, into the field, with the completest accoutrement, in the best discipline, under the ablest commanders. Yet after all that was effected by Linnaeus himself, not to mention the labours of Caesalpinus, Ray, Gesner, Tournefort, and the other heroes who preceded the general adoption of the sexual system, as the basis of artificial arrangement—after all the successive toils and enterprizes of HEDWIG, JUSSIEU, MIRBEL, SMITH, KNIGHT, ELLIS, &c. &c.—what is BOTANY at this present hour? Little more than an enormous nomenclature; a huge catalogue, *bien arrangé*, yearly and monthly augmented, in various editions, each with its own scheme of technical memory and its own conveniencies of reference! The innocent amusement, the healthful occupation, the ornamental accomplishment of *amateurs*; it has yet to expect the devotion and energies of the philosopher. Whether the *idea* which has glanced across some minds, that the harmony between the vegetable and animal world is not a harmony of resemblance, but of contrast, may not lead to a new and more accurate method in this engaging science, it becomes us not here to determine: but should its objective truth be hereafter demonstrated by induction of facts in an unbroken series of correspondences in nature, we shall then receive it as a *law* of organic existence; and shall thence obtain another splendid proof, that with the knowledge of Law alone dwell power and prophecy, decisive experiment, and scientific Method.

Chemistry

Such, too, is the case with the substances of the LABORATORY, which are assumed to be incapable of decomposition. They are mere exponents of some one law, which the chemical philosopher, whatever may be his theory, is incessantly labouring to discover. The law, indeed, has not yet assumed the form of an idea in his mind, it is what we have called an Instinct; it is a pursuit after unity of principle, through a diversity of forms. Thus as 'the lunatic, the lover, and the poet,' suggest each other to Shakespeare's Theseus, as soon as his thoughts present him the ONE FORM, of which they are but varieties; so water and flame, the diamond, the charcoal, and the mantling champagne, with its ebullient sparkles, are convoked and fraternized by the theory of the chemist. This is, in truth, the first charm of chemistry, and the secret of the almost universal interest excited by its discoveries. The serious complacency which is afforded by the sense of truth, utility, permanence, and progression, blends with and ennobles the exhilarating surprise and the pleasurable sting of curiosity, which accompany the propounding and the solving of an enigma. It is the sense of a principle of connection given by the mind, and sanctioned by the correspondency of nature. Hence the strong hold which in all ages chemistry has had on the imagination. If in the greatest poets we find nature idealized through the creative power of a profound yet observant meditation, so through the meditative observation of a DAVY, a WOLLASTON, a HATCHETT, or a MURRAY,

> —— 'By some connatural force,
> Powerful at greatest distance to unite
> With secret amity things of like kind,'

we find poetry, as it were, substantiated and realized.

Poetry

This consideration leads us from the paths of physical science into a region apparently very different. Those who tread the enchanted ground of POETRY, oftentimes do not even suspect that here is such a thing as *Method* to guide their steps. Yet even here we undertake to show that it not only has a necessary existence, but

s

the strictest philosophical application; and that it is founded on
the very philosophy which has furnished us with the principles
already laid down. It may surprise some of our readers, especially
those who have been brought up in schools of foreign taste, to find
that we rest our proof of these assertions on one single evidence,
and that that evidence is SHAKSPEARE, whose mind they have
probably been taught to consider as eminently *immethodical*. In the
first place, Shakspeare was not only endowed with great native
genius (which indeed he is commonly allowed to have been), but
what is less frequently conceded, he had much acquired knowledge. 'His information,' says Professor WILDE, 'was great and
extensive, and his reading as great as his knowledge of languages
could reach. Considering the bar which his education and circumstances placed in his way, he had done as much to acquire knowledge as even Milton. A thousand instances might be given, of the
intimate knowledge that Shakspeare had of facts. I shall mention
only one. I do not say, he gives a good account of the Salic law,
though a much worse has been given by many antiquaries. But he
who reads the archbishop of Canterbury's speech in Henry the
Fifth, and who shall afterwards say, that Shakspeare was not a man
of great reading and information, and who loved the thing itself, is
a person whose opinion I would not ask or trust upon any matter
of investigation.' Then, was all this reading, all this information,
all this knowledge of our great dramatist, a mere *rudis indigestaque
moles?* Very far from it. Method, we have seen, demands a knowledge of the relations which things bear to each other, or to the
observer, or to the state and apprehension of the hearers. In all and
each of these was Shakspeare so deeply versed, that in the person-
ages of a play, he seems 'to mould his mind as some incorporea-
material alternately into all their various forms.'[1] In every one of
his various characters we still feel ourselves communing with the
same human nature. Everywhere we find individuality: no where
mere portrait. The excellence of his productions consists in a happy
union of the universal with the particular. But the universal is an
idea. Shakspeare, therefore, studied mankind in the *idea* of the

[1] ὁ τὴν ἑαυτοῦ ψυχὴν ὥσει ὕλην τίνα ἀσώματον μορφαῖς ποικίλαις μορφώσας.
                                                      THEMISTIUS.

human race; and he followed out that idea into all its varieties, by a *Method* which never failed to guide his steps aright. Let us appeal to him, to illustrate by example, the difference between a sterile and an exuberant mind, in respect to what we have ventured to call the Science of Method. On the one hand observe Mrs Quickley's relation of the circumstances of Sir John Falstaff's debt:

FALSTAFF: What is the gross sum that I owe thee?

Mrs QUICKLEY: Marry, if thou wert an honest man, thyself and the money too. Thou didst swear to me upon a parcel-gilt goblet, sitting in my dolphin chamber, at the round table, by a sea-coal fire, on Wednesday in Whitsun week, when the prince broke thy head for likening his father to a singing man in Windsor—thou didst swear to me then, as I was washing thy wound, to marry me and make me my lady thy wife. Canst thou deny it? Did not goodwife Keech, the butcher's wife, come in then and call me gossip Quickley?—coming in to borrow a mess of vinegar: telling us she had a good dish of prawns—whereby thou didst desire to eat some— whereby I told thee they were ill for a green wound, &c. &c. &c.

(*Henry IV. P. I. Act II. Scene I.*)

On the other hand consider the narration given by Hamlet to Horatio, of the occurrences during his proposed transportation to England, and the events that interrupted his voyage. (*Act V. Scene II.*)

> HAM. Sir, in my heart there was a kind of fighting
> That would not let me sleep: methought I lay
> Worse than the mutines in the bilboes. Rashly,
> And prais'd be rashness for it—*Let us know,*
> *Our indiscretion sometimes serves us well,*
> *When our deep plots do fail; and that should teach us*
> *There's a divinity that shapes our ends,*
> *Rough-hew them how we will.*
>
> HOR. That is most certain.
>
> HAM.   Up from my cabin,
> My sea-gown scarf'd about me, in the dark
> Grop'd I to find out them; had my desire;
> Finger'd their pocket; and, in fine, withdrew
> To my own room again: making so bold,
> *My fears forgetting manners,* to unseal
> Their grand commission; where I found, Horatio,
> A royal knavery—an exact command,
> *Larded with many several sorts of reasons,*
> *Importing Denmark's health, and England's too,*

> With, ho! such bugs and goblins in *my* life,
> That on the supervize, no leisure bated,
> No, not to stay the grinding of the axe,
> My head should be struck off!

HOR.   Is't possible?

HAM.   Here's the commission.—Read it at more leisure.
>   I sat me down;
> Devis'd a new commission; wrote it fair.
> *I once did hold it, as our statists do,*
> *A baseness to write fair, and labour'd much*
> *How to forget that learning*; but, sir, now
> It did me yeoman's service. Wilt thou know
> The effect of what I wrote?

HOR.   Aye, good my lord.

HAM.   An earnest conjuration from the king,
> As England was his faithful tributary;
> *As love between them, like the palm, might flourish;*
> *As peace should still her wheaten garland wear,*
> *And many such like As's of great charge—*
> That on the view and knowing of these contents
> He should the bearers put to sudden death,
> No shriving time allowed.

HOR.   How was this sealed?

HAM.   Why, even in that was heaven ordinant.
> I had my father's signet in my purse,
> Which was the model of that Danish seal:
> Folded the writ up in the form of the other;
> Subscribed it; gave't the impression; plac'd it safely,
> The changeling never known. Now, the next day
> Was our sea-fight; and what to this was sequent,
> Thou knowest already.

If, overlooking the different value of the matter in these two narrations, we consider only the form, it must be confessed, that both are *immethodical*. We have asserted that Method results from a balance between the passive impression received from outward things, and the internal activity of the mind in reflecting and generalizing; but neither Hamlet nor the Hostess hold this balance accurately. In Mrs Quickley, the memory alone is called into action, the objects and events recur in the narration in the same order, and with the same accompaniments, however accidental or impertinent, as they had first occurred to the narrator. The necessity of taking breath, the efforts of recollection, and the abrupt rectification of its failures, produce all her pauses; and constitute most of her connections. But when we look to the Prince of Denmark's recital the case is widely different. Here the events, with the circumstances of time and place, are all stated with equal compression and rapidity; not one introduced which could have been omitted without injury to the intelligibility of the whole process. If any tendency is discoverable, as far as the mere facts are in question, it is to omission: and accordingly, the reader will observe, that the attention of the narrator is called back to one material circumstance, which he was hurrying by, by a direct question from the friend (HOW WAS THIS SEALED?) to whom the story is communicated. But by a trait which is indeed peculiarly characteristic of Hamlet's mind, ever disposed to generalize, and meditative to excess, all the digressions and enlargements consists of reflections, truths, and principles of general and permanent interest, either directly expressed or disguised in playful satire.

Instances of the want of generalization are of no rare occurrence: and the narration of Shakspeare's Hostess differs from those of the ignorant and unthinking in ordinary life, only by its superior humour, the poet's own gift and infusion, not by its want of Method, which is not greater than we often meet with in that class of minds of which she is the dramatic representative. Nor will the excess of generalization and reflection have escaped our observation in real life, though the great poet has more conveniently supplied the illustrations. In attending too exclusively to the relations which the past or passing events and objects bear to general truth, and the moods of his own mind, the most intelligent man is sometimes in danger of overlooking that other relation, in which they are likewise to be placed to the apprehension and sympathies of his hearers. His discourse appears like soliloquy intermixed with dialogue. But the uneducated and unreflecting talker overlooks *all* mental relations, and consequently precludes all Method, that is not purely accidental. Hence,—the nearer the things and incidents in time and place, the more distant, disjointed and impertinent to each other, and to any common purpose, will they appear in his narration: and this from the absence of any leading thought in the narrator's own mind. On the contrary, where the habit of

Method is present and effective, things the most remote and diverse in time, place, and outward circumstance, are brought into mental contiguity and succession, the more striking as the less expected. But while we would impress the necessity of this habit, the illustrations adduced give proof that in undue preponderance, and when the prerogative of the mind is stretched into despotism, the discourse may degenerate into the wayward, or the fantastical.

Shakspeare needed not to read Horace in order to give his characters that methodical *unity* which the wise Roman so strongly recommends:

> Si quid inexpertum scenae committis, et audes
> Personam formare novam; servetur ad imum
> Qualis ab incoepto processerit, et sibi constet.

But this was not the only way in which he followed an accurate philosophic Method: we quote the expressions of SCHLEGEL, a foreign critic of great and deserved reputation—'If Shakspeare deserves our admiration for his characters, he is equally deserving of it for his exhibition of *passion*, taking this word in its widest signification, as including every mental condition, every tone from indifference or familiar mirth, to the wildest rage and despair. He gives us the history of minds: *he lays open to us, in a single word, a whole series of preceding conditions.*' This last is a profound and exquisite remark: and it necessarily implies, that Shakspeare contemplated *ideas*, in which alone are involved conditions and consequences *ad infinitum*. Purblind critics, whose mental vision could not reach far enough to comprize the whole dimensions of our poetical Hercules, have busied themselves in measuring and spanning him muscle by muscle, till they fancied they had discovered some disproportion. There are two answers applicable to most of such remarks. First, that Shakspeare understood the true language and external workings of passion better than his critics. He had a higher, and a more ideal, and consequently a more methodical sense of harmony than they. A very slight knowledge of music will enable any one to detect discords in the exquisite harmonies of HAYDN or MOZART; and Bentley has found more false grammar in the PARADISE LOST than ever poor boy was whipped for through all the forms of Eton or Westminster: but to know why the minor note is introduced into the major key, or the nominative case left to seek for its verb, requires an acquaintance with some preliminary steps of the methodical scale, at the top of which sits the author, and at the bottom the critic. The second answer is, that Shakspeare was pursuing two Methods at once; and besides the psychological[1] Method, he had also to attend to the poetical. Now the poetical method requires above all things a preponderance of pleasurable feeling: and where the interest of the events and characters and passions is too strong to be continuous without becoming painful, there poetical method requires that there should be, what Schlegel calls 'a musical alleviation of our sympathy.' The Lydian mode must temper the Dorian. This we call Method.

We said that Shakspeare pursued two methods. Oh! he pursued many, many more—'both oar and sail'—and the guidance of the helm, and the heaving of the lead, and the watchful observation of the stars, and the thunder of his grand artillery. What shall we say of his moral conceptions? Not made up of miserable clap-traps, and the tag-ends of mawkish novels, and endless sermonizing;—but furnishing lessons of profound meditation to frail and fallible human nature. He shows us crime and want of principle clothed not with a spurious greatness of soul; but with a force of intellect which too often imposes but the more easily on the weak, misjudging multitude. He shows us the innocent mind of Othello plunged by its own unsuspecting and therefore unwatchful confidence, in guilt and misery not to be endured. Look at Lear, look at Richard, look in short at every moral picture of this mighty moralist! Whoso does not rise from their attentive perusal 'a sadder and a wiser man'—let him never dream that he knows any thing of philosophical Method.

Nay, even in his style, how methodical is our 'sweet Shakspeare.' Sweetness is indeed its predominant characteristic; and it has a few immethodical luxuriances of wit; and he may occasionally be convicted of words, which convey a volume of thought, when the

---

[1] We beg pardon for the use of this *insolens verbum*; but it is one of which our language stands in great need. We have no single term to express the philosophy of the human mind: and what is worse, the principles of that philosophy are commonly called *metaphysical,* a word of very different meaning.

business of the scene did not absolutely require such deep meditation. But pardoning him these *dulcia vitia*, who ever fashioned the
English language, or any language, ancient, or modern, into such
variety of appropriate apparel, from 'the gorgeous pall of scepter'd
tragedy,' to the easy dress of flowing pastoral.

> More musical than lark to shepherd's ear,
> When wheat is green and hawthorn buds appear.

Who, like him, could so methodically suit the very flow and tone of
discourse to characters lying so wide apart in rank, and habits,
and peculiarities, as Holofernes and Queen Catharine, Falstaff and
Lear? When we compare the pure English style of Shakspeare with
that of the very best writers of his day, we stand astonished at the
Method, by which he was directed in the choice of those words and
idioms, which are as fresh now as in their first bloom; nay, which
are at the present moment at once more energetic, more expres-
sive, more natural, and more elegant, than those of the happiest
and most admired living speakers or writers.

But Shakspeare was 'not methodical in the structure of his
fable.' Oh gentle critic! be advised. Do not trust too much to your
professional dexterity in the use of the scalping knife and toma-
hawk. Weapons of diviner mould are wielded by your adversary:
and you are meeting him here on his own peculiar ground, the
ground of *idea*, of thought, and of inspiration. The very point of
this dispute is ideal. The question is one of *unity*: and unity, as we
have shown, is wholly the subject of ideal law. There are said to be
three great unities which Shakspeare has violated; those of time,
place, and action. Now the unities of time and place we will not
dispute about. Be ours the poet,

> —— qui pectus inaniter angit
> Irritat, mulcet, falsis terroribus implet
> Ut magus, et *modo me Thebis, modo ponit Athenis.*

The dramatist who circumscribes himself within that unity of
time, which is regulated by a stop-watch, may be exact, but is not
methodical; or his method is of the least and lowest class. But

> Where is he living clipt in with the sea,
> That chides the banks of England, Wales, or Scotland?

who can transpose the scenes of Macbeth, and make the seated heart knock at the ribs with the same force as now it does, when the mysterious tale is conducted from the open heath, on which the weird sisters are ushered in with thunder and lightning, to the fated fight of Dunsinane, in which their victim expiates with life, his credulity and his ambition? To the disgrace of the English stage, such attempts have indeed been made on almost all the dramas of Shakspeare. Scarcely a season passes which does not produce some ὕστερον πρότερον of this kind in which the mangled limbs of our great poet are thrown together 'in most admired disorder.' There was once, a noble author, who by a refined species of murder, cut up the play of Julius Caesar into two good set tragedies. M. Voltaire, we believe, had the grace to make but one of it; but whether his Brutus be an improvement on the model from which it was taken, we trust, after what we have already said, we shall hardly be expected to discuss.

Thus we have seen, that Shakspeare's mind, rich in stores of acquired knowledge, commanded all these stores and rendered them disposable, by means of his intimate acquaintance with the great laws of thought, which form and regulate Method. We have seen him exemplifying the opposite faults of Method in two different characters; we have seen that he was himself methodical in the delineation of character, in the display of passion, in the conceptions of moral being, in the adaptations of language, in the connection and admirable intertexture of his ever-interesting fable. Let it not, after this, be said, that Poetry—and under the word Poetry we will now take leave to include all the works of the higher imagination, whether operating by measured sound, or by the harmonies of form and colour, or by words, the more immediate and universal representatives of thought—is not strictly methodical; nay, does not owe its whole charm, and all its beauty, and all its power, to the philosophical principles of Method.

Philosophy

But what of philosophy herself? Shall she be exempted from the laws, which she has imposed on all the rest of the known universe? *Longé absit!* To philosophy properly belongs the EDUCATION of the mind: and all that we have hitherto said may be regarded as an indication (we have room for no more) of the chief laws and regulative principles of that education. Philosophy, the 'parent of life,' according to the expression of the wise Roman orator; the 'mother of good deeds and of good sayings,' the 'medicine of the mind,' is herself wholly conversant with Method.

True it is, that the ancients, as well as the moderns, had their machinery for the extemporaneous coinage of intellect, by means of which the scholar was enabled *to make a figure* on any and all subjects, on any and all occasions. They too had their glittering vapours, which (as the comic poet tells us) fed a host of sophists—

> μεγάλαι θεαὶ ανδράσιν ἀργοῖς
> Αἵπερ γνώμην καὶ διάλεξιν καὶ νοῦν ἡμῖν παρέχουσιν,
> Καὶ τερατείαν καὶ περίλεξιν καὶ κροῦσιν καὶ κατάληψιν.
> > *ΑΡΙΣΤΟΦ. Νεφ. Σκ. δ΄.*

> Great goddesses are they to lazy folks,
> Who pour down on us gifts of fluent speech,
> Sense most sententious, wonderful fine *effect*,
> And how to talk about it and about it,
> Thoughts brisk as bees, and pathos soft and thawing.

But the philosophers held a course very different from that of the sophists. We shall not trouble our readers with a comparative view of many systems; but we shall present to their admiration one mighty ancient, and one illustrious modern, PLATO, and BACON. These two varieties will sufficiently exemplify the species.

Plato

Of PLATO's works, the larger and more valuable portion have all one common end, which comprehends and shines through the particular purpose of each several dialogue; and this is, to establish the sources, to evolve the principles, and to exemplify the art of METHOD. This is the clue, without which it would be difficult to exculpate the noblest productions of the 'divine' philosopher from the charge of being tortuous and labyrinthine in their progress, and unsatisfactory in their ostensible results. The latter indeed appear not seldom to have been drawn, for the purpose of starting a new problem, rather than of solving the one proposed as the subject of previous discussion. But with the clear insight, that the purpose of the writer is not so much to establish any particular truth, as to remove the obstacles, the continuance of which is preclusive of all truth, the whole scheme assumes a different aspect, and justifies itself in all its dimensions. We see, that the EDUCATION of the intellect, by awakening the *method* of self-development, was his proposed object, not any specific information that can be *conveyed into it* from without. He desired not to assist in storing the passive mind with the various sorts of knowledge most in request, as if the human soul were a mere repository, or banqueting room, but to place it in such relations of circumstance as should gradually excite its vegetating and germinating powers to produce new fruits of thought, new conceptions, and imaginations, and ideas. Plato was a poetic philosopher, as Shakspeare was a philosophic poet. In the poetry, as well as in the philosophy, of both, there was a necessary predominance of ideas; but this did not make them regardless of the actual existences around them. They were not visionaries, or mystics; but dwelt in 'the sober certainty' of waking knowledge. It is strange, yet characteristic of the spirit that was at work during the latter half of the last century, that the writings of PLATO should be accused of estranging the mind from plain experience and substantial *matter-of-fact*, and of debauching it by fictions and generalities. Plato, whose method is inductive throughout, who argues on all subjects not only *from*, but *in* and *by*, inductions of facts! Who warns us indeed against the usurpation of the senses, but far oftener, and with more unmitigated hostility, pursues the assumptions, abstractions, generalities, and verbal legerdemain of the sophists. Strange! but still more strange, that a notion, so groundless, should be entitled to plead in its behalf the authority of Lord BACON, whose scheme of logic, as applied to the contemplation of nature, is Platonic throughout. It is necessary that we should explain this circumstance at some length, in order to establish by the concurrence of authorities, vulgarly supposed to be contradictory, the truth of a system which we have already maintained on so many other grounds.

Bacon

What Lord Bacon was to England, Cicero was to Rome—the first and most eloquent advocate of philosophy. It is needless to remind the classical scholar of that almost religious veneration with which the accomplished Roman speaks of Plato, whom, indeed, he calls, in one instance, *'deus ille noster,'* and in other places, 'the Homer of philosophers;' their 'prince;' the 'most weighty of all who ever spoke, or ever wrote;' 'most wise, most holy, divine.' This last appellation, too, it is well known, long remained, even among Christians, as a distinguishing epithet of the great ornament of the Socratic school. Why Bacon should have spoken detractingly of such a man; why he should have stigmatized him with the name of 'sophist,' and described his philosophy (with the tyrant Diony-sius), as *'verba otiosorum senum ad imperitos juvenes,'* it is much easier to explain, than to justify, or even to palliate. He was, perhaps, influenced, in part, by the tone given to thinking minds by the Reformation, the founders and fathers of which saw in the Aris-totelians, or schoolmen, the antagonists of Protestantism, and in the Italian Platonists (as they conceived) the secret enemies of Christianity itself. In part, too, Bacon may have formed his notions of Plato's doctrines from the absurdities of his mis-interpreters, rather than from an unprejudiced and diligent study of his works. —Be it remembered, however, that this unfairness was not less manifested to his contemporaries; that his treatment of GILBERT was cold, invidious, and unjust; and that he seems to have dis-dained to learn either the existence or the name of Shakspeare. At this conduct no one can be surprised, who has studied the life of this

—— wisest, brightest, meanest of mankind.

But our present business is not with his weaknesses, or his failings, but with those philosophical principles, which, especially as dis-played in the Novum Organum, have deservedly obtained for him the veneration of succeeding ages.

Those who talk superficially about Bacon's philosophy, that is to say, nineteen-twentieths of those who talk about it at all, know little more than his induction, and the application which he makes of his own method, to particular classes of physical facts; applications, which are at least as crude, for the age of Gilbert, Galileo, and Kepler, as were those of Aristotle (whom he so superciliously reprehends) for the age of Philip and Alexander. Or they may perhaps have been struck with his recommendation of tabular collections of particulars; and hence have placed him at the head of a body of men, but too numerous in modern days—the minute philosophers. We need scarcely say, that this is venturing his reputation on a very tottering basis. Let any unprejudiced naturalist turn to Bacon's questions and proposals for the investigation of single problems; to his 'Discourse on the Winds;' or to what may almost be called a caricature of his scheme, in the 'Method of improving Natural Philosophy,' by ROBERT HOOKE[1] (the history of whose philosophical life is alone a sufficient answer to all such schemes)—and then let him fairly say whether any desirable end could reasonably be hoped for, from this process—whether by this mode of research any important discovery ever was made, or ever could be made? Bacon, indeed, always takes care to tell us, that the sole purpose and object of collecting together these particulars, is to concentrate them, by careful selection, into universals: but so immense is their number, and so various and almost endless the relations in which each is to be separately considered,

---

[1] We refer particularly to pp. 22 to 42 of the above-mentioned work; and we would, above all, notice the following admirable specimen of confused and disorderly minuteness:—'The history of potters, tobacco-pipe-makers, glaziers, glass-grinders, looking-glass-makers or foilers, spectacle-makers and optic-glass makers, makers of counterfeit pearl and precious stones, bugle-makers, lamp-blowers, colour-makers, colour-grinders, glass-painters, enamellers, varnishers, colour-sellers, *painters, limners, picture-drawers, makers of baby heads, of little bowling stones or marbles,* fustian-makers, (query whether *poets* are included in this trade?) music-masters, tinsey-makers, and taggers.— The history of schoolmasters, writing-masters, printers, book-binders, stage-players, dancing-masters, and vaulters, *apothecaries, chirurgeons, seamsters, butchers, barbers, laundresses, and cosmetics!* &c. &c. &c. &c. (the true nature of each of which being exactly determined) WILL HUGELY FACILITATE OUR INQUIRIES IN PHILOSOPHY'!!!

In parallel, or rather in contrast, with the advice of Mr Robert Hooke, may be fairly placed that of the celebrated Dr WATTS, which was thought, by Dr Knox, to be worthy of insertion in the *Elegant* Extracts, vol. ii. p. 456, under the head of

DIRECTIONS CONCERNING OUR IDEAS

Furnish yourselves with *a rich variety of Ideas*. Acquaint yourselves with *things* ancient and modern; *things* natural, civil, and religious; *things* of your native land, and of foreign countries; *things* domestic and national; *things* present, past, and future; and above all, be well acquainted with God and yourselves; with animal nature, and the workings of your own spirits. *Such a general acquaintance with things will be of very great advantage.*

that the life of an ante-diluvian patriarch would be expended, and his strength and spirits wasted, long before he could commence the process of simplification, or arrive in sight of the law, which was to reward the toils of the over-tasked PSYCHE.[1]

Had Bacon done no more, than propose these impracticable projects, we should have been far from sharing the sentiments of respect every where attached to his philosophical character. But he has performed a task of infinitely greater importance, by constructing that methodical system, which is so elegantly developed in the Novum Organum. It is this, which we propose to compare with the principles long before enunciated by Plato. In both cases, the inductions are frequently as crude and erroneous, as might readily be anticipated from the infant state of natural history, chemistry, and physiology, in their several ages. In both cases, the proposed applications are often impracticable; but setting aside these considerations, and extracting from each writer that which constitutes his true philosophy, we shall be convinced that it is identical, in regard to the science of Method, and to the grounds and conditions of that science. We do not see, therefore, how we can more appropriately conclude this section of our inquiry, than by a brief statement of our renowned countryman's own principles of Method, conveyed, for the greater part, in his own words: or in what more precise form, we can recapitulate the substance of the doctrines asserted and vindicated in the preceding pages. For we rest our strongest pretensions to approbation on the fact, that we have only re-proclaimed the coinciding precepts of the Athenian Verulam, and the British Plato.

Their common system

In the first instance, Lord Bacon equally with ourselves, demands, as the motive and guide of every philosophical experiment, what we have ventured to call the intellectual or mental *initiative*; namely, some well-grounded purpose, some distinct impression of the probable results, some self-consistent anticipation, the ground

---

[1] See the beautiful allegoric tale of Cupid and Psyche in the original of Apuleius. The tasks imposed on the hapless nymph, through the jealousy of her mother-in-law, and the agency by which they are at length self-performed, are noble instances of that hidden wisdom 'where more is meant than meets the ear!'

of the *'prudens quaestio'* (the forethoughtful enquiry), which he affirms to be the prior *half* of the knowledge sought, *dimidium scientiae.* With him, therefore, as with us, an *idea* is an experiment proposed, an experiment is an idea realized. For so he himself informs us:—
'neque scientiam molimur tam sensu, vel instrumentis, quam *experimentis*; etenim experimentorum longe major est subtilitas, quam sensûs ipsius, licet instrumentis exquisitis adjuti. *Nam de iis loquimur experimentis, quae, ad intentionem ejus quod quaeritur, perité, et secundum artem excogitata et apposita sunt.* Itaque perceptioni sensûs immediatae et propriae *non multûm tribuimus*: sed eò rem deducimus, ut *sensus tantûm de experimento, experimentum de re judicet.*' The meaning of this last sentence is intelligible enough; though involved in antithesis, merely because Bacon did not possess, like Shakspeare, a good method in his style. What he means to say is, that we can apprehend, through the organs of sense, only the sensible phaenomena produced by the experiment; but by the mental power, in virtue of which we shaped the experiment, we can determine the true *import* of the phaenomena.

Now, he had before said, that he was speaking only of those experiments, which were skilfully adapted to the intention, or purpose of him, who conducted the research. But what is it, that forms the intention, or purpose, and adapts thereto the experiment? What Bacon calls *lux intellectûs*; viz. the understanding of the individual man, who makes the experiment. This light, however, so he argues at great length, is obscured by *idols*, which are false and spurious notions. His peculiar use of the word idols, is again a proof of faulty method in his style; for it gives a sort of pedantic air to his reasonings; but in truth, he means no more by it, than what Plato means by *opinion*, ($\delta \delta \xi a$) which the latter calls 'a medium between knowledge and ignorance.' So, Bacon distinguishes the idols of the mind into various kinds (*idola specûs, tribûs, fori, theatri*), that is, opinions derived from the passions, prejudices, and peculiar habits of each man's understanding: and as these idols, or opinions, confessedly produce a sort of mental obscurity, or blindness; so, the ancient and the modern master of philosophy both agree in prescribing remedies and operations calculated to remove this disease; to couch the 'mind's eye;' and to restore it to the enjoyment of a purer vision. Bacon establishes an unerring criterion between the ideas and the idols of the mind; namely, that the latter are empty notions, but the former are the very seals and impresses of nature; that is to say, they always fit and cohere with those classes of things, to which they belong; as the idea of a circle fits and coheres with all true circles. His words are these: 'Non leve quiddam interest inter humanae mentis *idola*, et divinae mentis *ideas*, hoc est, inter placita quaedam inania, et veras signaturas atque impressiones factas in creaturis, prout Ratione sanâ et sicci luminis, quam, docendi causâ, interpretem naturae vocare consuevimus, inveniuntur.' NOVUM ORGANUM, XXIII. & XXVI.

Some idols, says Bacon, are adventitious to the mind; others innate. And here, we may observe, that he goes somewhat farther than the mere doctrine of innate ideas, by holding that of innate idols. However, we say not this in disparagement of his *system* which is clear and correct; nor, on the other hand, do we mean to espouse all its *parts*, which must be left to speak for themselves. What he means by innate idols, he thus illustrates:—not only do the rays of truth, from without, fall obliquely on the mirror of the mind, but that mirror itself is not pure and plain; it discolours, it magnifies, it diminishes, it distorts. Hence, he uses the words *intellectus humanus, mens hominis,* &c. in a sense now peculiar but, in his day conformable to the language of the schools, to signify not intellect in general, or mind in its perfection, but the intellect or mind of man, weakened and corrupted, as it is, more or less, in every individual. A necessary consequence of this corruption, is the arrogance, which leads man to take the forms and mechanism of his own reflective faculty, as the measure of nature, and of the Deity. Of all idols, or of all opinions, this is the most difficult to remedy, or extirpate; and therefore, in this view, the intellect of man is more prone to error, than even his senses. Such is the sound and incontrovertible doctrine of Bacon; but herein he does no more, than repeat what both Plato and Heraclitus had long before urged, with most impressive argument. The forms of the reflective faculty are *subjective*; the truths to be embraced are *objective*: but according to Plato, as well as to Bacon, there can be no hope of any fruitful and secure *Method*, so long as forms, merely subjective, are arbitrarily assumed to be the moulds of objective truth, the seals and impresses of nature.

What then! Does Bacon abandon the hope of rectifying the obliquities of the human intellect; or does he suggest, that they will be remedied by the casual operation of external impressions? Neither of these. He considers, that its weaknesses and imperfections require to be strengthened and made perfect by a higher power; and that this is possible to be done. He supposes, that the intellect of the individual, or *homme particulier*, may be refined by the intellect of the ideal man, or *homme général*. He assumes, that as the evidence of the senses is corrected by the judgment, so the evidence of the judgment, beset with idols, may be corrected by the judgment, walking in the light of ideas. It is surely superfluous to urge, that this corrector and purifier of all reasoning, this inextinguishable pole star—

Which never in the ocean waves was wet;

whether it be called, as by Bacon, *lumen siccum*, or as by Plato, νοῦς, or φῶς νοερόν, is one and the same light of *Truth*, the indispensable condition of all pure science, contemplative, or experimental. Hence, it will not surprise us, that Plato so often denominates ideas living *laws*, in and by which the mind has its whole true being and permanence; or that Bacon, vicè versâ, names the laws of nature, *ideas*; and represents the great leading facts of science as signatures, impressions, and symbols of those ideas. A distinguishable power self-affirmed, and seen in its unity with the Eternal Essence, is, according to Plato, an I D E A: and the discipline by which the human mind is purified from its idols, and raised to the contemplation of Ideas, and thence to the secure and progressive, investigation of truth and reality, by scientific method, comprehends what the same philosopher so highly extols, under the title of *Dialectic*. According to Lord Bacon, as describing the same truth, applied to natural philosophy, an idea would be defined as— Intuitio, sive inventio, quae in perceptione sensûs non est (ut quae purae et sicci luminis Intellectioni sit propria) idearum divinae mentis, prout in creaturis, per signaturas suas, sese patefaciant. 'That (saith the judicious H o o k e r) which doth assign to each

T

thing the kind, that which determineth the force and power, that which doth appoint the form and measure of working, the same we term a LAW.'

From all that has been said, it seems clear, that the only difference between Plato and Bacon was, that, to speak in popular language, the one more especially cultivated natural philosophy, the other metaphysics. Plato treated principally of truth, as manifested in the world of intellect; Bacon of the same truth, as manifested in the world of sense; but far from disagreeing, as to the mode of attaining that truth, far from differing in their great views of the *education of the mind*, they both proceeded on the same principles of *unity* and *progression*; and consequently both cultivated alike the *Science of Method*, such as we have here described it. If we are correct in these statements, then may we boast to have solved the great problem of conciliating ancient and modern philosophy.

Historical view

That the *Method*, of which we have hitherto treated, is not arbitrarily assumed in any, or all of the pursuits, to which we have adverted; nor is peculiar to these in particular, but is founded in the laws and necessary conditions of human existence, is further to be inferred from a general view of the history of the human race. As in the individual, so in the whole community of mankind, our cogitations have an infancy of aimless activity; and a youth of education and advance towards order; and an opening manhood, of high hopes and expectations; and a settled, staid, and sober middle age, of ripened and deliberate judgment.

First period

'The antiquity of time was the youth of the world and of knowledge,' said Bacon. In that early age, the *obedience of the will* was first taught to man. He was required to look up, in submission, to that Spirit of Truth, which, after all, we find to be at the head of wisdom. This innocent age was happily prolonged, among those, whose first care was to cultivate the moral sense, and to seek in faith the evidence of things not seen. To them were propounded a Spiritual Creator, and a spiritual worship, and the assured hope of a future and spiritual existence; and therefore they were less curious to watch the motions of the stars, or to become 'artificers in brass and iron,' or to 'handle the harp and the organ.' They were less wise in their generation, than the 'mighty men of old, the men of renown;' but their ideas were plain, and distinct; they were 'just and perfect men;' and they 'walked with God;' whilst, of the others 'every imagination of the thoughts of the heart was only evil continually.' For the latter wilfully chose an opposite *method*: they determined to shape their convictions and deduce their knowledge from *without*, by exclusive observation of outward things, as the only realities. Hence they became rapidly *civilized*. They built cities, and refined on the means of sensual gratification, and the conveniencies of courtly intercourse. They became the great masters of the agreeable, which fraternized readily with cruelty and rapacity: these being, indeed, but alternate moods of the same sensual selfishness. Thus, both before and after the flood, the vicious of mankind receded from all true cultivation, as they hurried towards civilization. Finally, as it was not in their power to make themselves wholly beasts, and to remain without a semblance of religion, and yet, as they were faithful to their original maxim,—determined to receive nothing as true, but what they derived, or believed themselves to derive from their senses, or (in modern phrase) what they could prove *a posteriori*;—they became idolaters of the Heavens, and of the material elements; and finally, out of the idols of the mind, they formed material idols: and bowed down to stocks and stones, as to the unformed and incorporeal Divinity.

Second period

A new era next appeared, representative of the youth and approaching manhood of the human intellect: and again Providence, as it were, awakened men to the pursuit of an idealized Method, in the developement of their faculties. Orpheus, Linus, Musaeus, and the other mythological bards, or perhaps brotherhoods of bards impersonated under individual names, whether deriving their light, imperfectly and indirectly, from the inspired writings of the Hebrews, or graciously visited, for high and important purposes, by a dawning of truth in their own breasts, began to spiritualize Polytheism, and thereby to prevent it from producing all its natural, barbarizing effects. Hence the mysteries and mythological hymns; which, on the one hand, gradually shaped themselves into epic poetry and history, and, on the other, into tragedy and philosophy: whilst to the lifeless statuary of the Egyptians was superadded a Promethean animation; and the ideal in sculpture soon extending itself to painting, and to architecture, the Fine Arts at once shot up to perfection, by a Method founded wholly on a mental initiative, and conducted throughout its progress by the developement of ideas. This rapid advance, in all things which owe their existence and character to the mind's own acts, intellectual or imaginative, forms a singular contrast with the rude and imperfect manner, in which those acts were applied to the investigation of physical laws and phaenomena. While Phidias, Apelles, Homer, Demosthenes, Thucydides, and Plato, had, each in his individual sphere, attained almost the summit of conceivable excellence, the natural history and the natural philosophy of the whole world may be said to have lain dormant; especially if we compare them with the efforts which the moderns made in these directions, in the very morning of their strength.

Romans

Of the Roman era it is scarcely necessary to speak at large, inasmuch as the Romans were confessedly mere imitators of the Greeks in every thing relating to science and art. They sustained a very important part in the civil, and military, and ecclesiastical history of mankind; and their devotion to these objects was, in their own eyes, a sufficient apology for their want of originality in what they held to be far inferior pursuits.

> Excudent alii spirantia mollius aera:
> Credo equidem, vivos ducent de marmore vultus:
> Tu regere imperio populos, Romane, memento.

Still less will it be expected, that we should devote much space to the consideration of those dark ages, which brought the countless hordes of sensual barbarians from their northern forests to meet, in the southern and middle parts of Europe, the spiritualizing

influence of Christianity: but one remarkable effect of that influence we cannot suffer to pass unnoticed. We allude to the
gradual abolition of domestic slavery, in virtue of a principle
essential to Christianity, by which a *person* is eternally differenced
from a *thing*; so that the *idea* of a human being necessarily excludes
the idea of property, in that being.

Reformation

We come down, then, to the great period of the REFORMA-
TION, which, regarded as an epoch in the education of the human
mind, was second to none for its striking and durable effects. The
defenders of a simple and spiritual worship, against one which was
full of outward forms and ceremonies; the partisans of religious
liberty, against the dominion of a visible head over the whole
Christian church; and generally speaking, the advocates of the
ideal and internal, against the external, or imaginative; maintained a zealous, and in great part of Europe, a prosperous conflict. But the revolution of thought, and its effects on the science of
Method, were soon visible beyond the pale of the church or the
cloister: and the schoolmen were attacked as warmly in their philosophical, as they had before been in their ecclesiastical character.
It is needless to dwell on the various attempts toward introducing
into learning a totally new method. That of our illustrious countryman, BACON, was completely successful: and we have already
shown, that it was, in truth, the completion of the ideal system, by
applying the same method to external nature, which Plato had
before applied to intellectual existence.

Modern philosophy

It is only in the union of these two branches of one and the same
method, that a complete and genuine philosophy can be said to
exist. To this consideration the great mind of Bacon does not seem
to have been fully awake: and hence, not only is the general scope
of his work directed almost exclusively to the contemplation of
physical ideas; but there are occasional expressions, which seem
to have misled many of his followers into a belief, that he considered all wisdom and all science, both to begin and to end with

the object of the senses. In this gross error are laid the foundations of the modern French school, which has grown up into the monstrous puerilities of CONDILLAC, and CONDORCET; men whose names it would be absolutely ridiculous to mention, in a history of science, if their pupils did not unhappily compensate, in number, what their works want in common sense and intelligibility; and if upon such writers, the French nation did not mainly rest its pretensions to give the law to Europe, in matters of science and philosophy.

SECTION III: APPLICATION OF THE PRINCIPLES OF METHOD TO THE GENERAL CONCATENATION AND DEVELOPEMENT OF STUDIES

WE have already dwelt so much on the general importance of Method—we have recurred to it so frequently—we have placed it in so many various lights, that we ought perhaps to apologize for venturing on one more attempt to illustrate our meaning, partly in the way of simile, and partly of example. Let us, however, imagine an unlettered African, or rude, but musing Indian, poring over an illumined manuscript of the inspired volume; with the vague, yet deep impression, that his fates and fortunes are, in some unknown manner, connected with its contents. Every tint, every group of characters, has its several dream. Say, that after long and dissatisfying toils, he begins to sort, first, the paragraphs that appear to resemble each other; then the lines, the words; nay, that he has at length discovered, that the whole is formed by the recurrence and interchange of a limited number of cyphers, letters, marks and points, which, however, in the very height and utmost perfection of his attainment, he makes twenty-fold more numerous than they are, by classing every different form of the same character, intentional or accidental, as a separate element. And yet the whole is without soul or substance, a talisman of superstition, or a mockery of science; or is employed perhaps, at last, to feather the arrows of death, or to shine and flutter amid the plumes of savage vanity. The poor Indian too truly represents the state of learned and systematic ignorance—arrangement guided by the light of no leading idea; mere orderliness without METHOD!

But see, the friendly missionary arrives! He explains to him the nature of written words, translates them for him into his native sounds, and thence into the thoughts of his heart: how many of these thoughts are then first unfolded into consciousness, which yet the awakening disciple receives not as aliens! Henceforward the book is unsealed for him; the depth is opened; he communes with the *spirit* of the volume, as with a living oracle. The words become transparent: he sees them, as though he saw them not; whilst he mentally devours the meaning they contain. From that moment, his former chimerical and useless arrangement is discarded, and the results of method are to him life and truth.

If some particular studies are yet confessedly deficient in the vivifying power of Method, we much fear that the attempts to bind together the whole body of science have been, in certain instances, worse than immethodical. A slight glance at the particular department of literature which we have chosen, especially as it has been filled on the Continent; from the memorable combination of deistical talent in the *Dictionnaire Encyclopédique*, to a work, on the same principles, said to be now publishing in France, will demonstrate, that the best interests of mankind have suffered serious injury from this cause; that the fountains of education may be poisoned, where the stream appears to flow on with increasing power and smoothness; and that the *insinuation* of sceptical principles into works of Science, is fraught with the greatest danger to posterity.

To oppose an effectual barrier to the rage for desultory knowledge, on the one hand, and to support that body of independent attachment to the best principles of *all* knowledge, which happily distinguishes this country, on the other, the ENCYCLOPAEDIA METROPOLITANA has been projected.

We do not undertake, what the most gigantic efforts of man could not atchieve, *an universal Dictionary of Knowledge*, in the most absolute sense of the terms. But estimating the importance of our task rather by the principles of *unity* and *compression*, than by those of variety and extent, we have laboured to build upon what is essential, that which is obviously useful, and upon both whatever is elegant or agreeable in science; and this, we conceive, cannot be well and usefully effected, but by such a philosophical Method, as we have already indicated.

We have shown that this METHOD consists in placing one or more *particular* things or notions, in subordination, either to a pre-conceived *universal* idea, or to some lower form of the latter; some class, order, genus, or species, each of which derives its intellectual significancy, and scientific worth, from being an ascending step toward the universal; from being its representative, or temporary substitute. Without this master-thought, therefore, there can be no true Method: and according as the general conception more or less clearly manifests itself throughout all the particulars, as their connective and bond of unity; according as the light of the idea is freely diffused through, and completely illumines, the aggregate mass, the Method is more or less perfect.

The first pre-conception, or master-thought, on which *our* plan rests, is the *moral origin and tendency* of all true science; in other words, our great objects are to exhibit the Arts and Sciences in their philosophical harmony; to teach Philosophy in union with Morals; and to sustain Morality by Revealed Religion.

There are, as we have before noticed, two sorts of relation, on the due observation of which all Method depends. The first is that, which the ideas or laws of the mind bear to each other; the second, that which they bear to the external world: on the former are built the Pure Sciences; on the latter those which we call Mixed and Applied.

Pure sciences

The *Pure Sciences*, then, represent pure acts of the mind, and those only; whether employed in contemplating the *forms* under which things in their first elements are necessarily viewed and treated by the mind; or in contemplating the substantial *reality* of those things.

Formal and real

Hence, in the pure sciences, arises the known distinction of *formal* and *real*: and of the first, some teach the elementary forms, which the mind necessarily adopts in the processes of reasoning;

and others, those under which alone all particular objects can be grasped and considered by the mind; either as distinguishable in quantity and number, or as occupying parts of space. The *real* sciences, on the other hand, are conversant with the true nature and existence, either of the created universe around us; or of the guiding principles within us, in their various modifications and distinguishing movements; or, lastly, with the real nature and existence of the great Cause of all.

Grammar

We begin, then, with that class of pure sciences which we have called formal; and of these, the first two that present themselves to us, are *Grammar* and *Logic*. By Grammar we are taught the rules of that speech, which serves as the medium of mental intercourse between man and man; by *Logic*, the mental operations are themselves regulated and bound together, in a certain method or order. As the communication of knowledge is the more immediate object of our present discussion, so we begin with that science by which it is regulated in its forms. Grammar, then, apart from the mere material consideration of the sound of words, or shape of letters, and regarding speech only as a thing significant, teaches that there are certain laws regulating that signification; laws which are immutable in their very nature: for the relation which a noun bore to a verb, or a substantive to an adjective, was the same in the earliest days of μερόπων ἀνθρώπων, in the first intelligible conversations of men, as it is now; nor can it ever vary so long as the powers of thought remain the same in the human mind. This, then, is a pure science proceeding from a simple or elementary idea of the form necessary for the conveyance of a single thought, and thence spreading and diffusing itself over all the relations of significant language.

Logic

Grammar brings us, naturally, to the Science of *Logic*, or the knowledge of those forms which the conceptions of the mind assume in the processes of reasoning. And it is manifest, that this science is no less subject than the former, to fixed laws; for the reasoning power in man can only operate within those limits which Almighty Wisdom has thought fit to prescribe. It is a discursive faculty, moving in a given path, and by allotted means. There is no possibility of subverting or altering the elementary rules of Logic; for they are not hypothetical, or contingent, or conventional, but positive and necessary.

Mathematics

Under the general term *Mathematics*, are comprised the sciences of *Geometry*, which is conversant about the laws of figure, or limitations of space; and *Arithmetic*, which concerns the laws of number. Now these laws are purely ideal. It is not externally to us that the general notion of a square, or a triangle; of the number three, or the number five, exists; nor do we seek for external proof of the relations of those notions; but on the contrary, by contemplating them, as ideas in the mind, we discover truths which are applicable to external existence.

Metaphysics, Morals, and Theology

The sciences, which we have hitherto noticed, relate to the forms of our mental conceptions; but it is natural for man to seek to comprehend the principles and conditions of real existence, both with regard to the universe in general, with regard to his own internal mover, or conscience, and, above all, with regard to the cause, by which conscience and the whole universe were called into being, and continue to exist, namely, GOD. Hence, as we advance from form to reality, the sciences of *Metaphysics* and *Morals* first present themselves to view, and these lead us forward to the summit of human knowledge; for at the head of all pure science stands *Theology*, of which the great fountain is revelation. It is obvious, that both Metaphysics and Morals are conversant solely about those relations, which we have called relations of law; for it would be a contradiction to say, that a real existence could be, at the same time, a mere theory or hypothesis. These sciences have, therefore, all the purity and all the certainty, which belong to that which is positive and absolute; and as far as they are distinctly apprehended by the mind, they approach the nearest to that clear intellectual light, which, in the peculiar phraseology of Lord Bacon, is called *lumen siccum*. In the proper philosophical method, the reality of our speculative knowledge, exhibited in the science of Metaphysics, unites itself at last with the reality of our ethical sentiments displayed in that of Morals; and both together are at once lost and consummated in Theology, which rises above the light of reason to that of faith.

Mixed and Applied Sciences

These are all the sciences which embrace solely relations of law: and it is plain that in these, not only the initiative, but every subsequent step, must be an act of the mind alone. But when we descend to the second order of relations, namely those which we bear to the external world, Theory is immediately introduced; new sciences are formed, which in contradistinction from the pure, are called the *mixed* and *applied* Sciences; and in these new considerations relative to Method, necessarily find a place.

Every physical theory is in some measure imperfect, because it is of necessity progressive; and because we can never be assured that we have exhausted the terms, or that some new discovery may not affect the whole scheme of its relations. The discoveries of the ponderability of air, of its compound nature, of the increased weight of the calces, of the gasses in general, of electricity, and more recently the stupendous influences of Galvanism on the successive chemical theories; are all so many exemplifications of this truth. The doctrines of vortices, of an universal ether, of a two-fold magnetic fluid, &c. are *theories* of gravitation: but the science of Astronomy is founded on the *law* of gravitation, and remains unaffected by the rise and fall of the theories. In the lowest condition of Method, the initiative is supplied by *an hypothesis*; of which we may distinguish two degrees. In the former, a fact of actual experience is taken, and placed experimentally as the common support of certain other facts, as equally present in all: thus, that oxygen is *a* principle of acidification and combustion, is an experienced fact; and became an hypothesis, by the assumption that it is the *sole* principle of acidification and combustion. In the latter, a fact is imagined: as, for instance, an atom or physical point, praeternaturally hard, and therefore infrangible in the corpuscular philosophy; or a primitive unalterable figure, in some systems of crystalization.

In all this, we see, that knowledge is a matter not of necessary connection, but of a connection arising from observation, or supposition; that is, it consists not of law, but of theory, or hypothesis. True theory is always in the first and purest sense a *locum tenens* of law; when it is not, it degenerates into hypothesis, and hypothesis melts away into conjecture. Both in law and in theory, there must be a mental antecedent; but in the latter, it may be an image or conception received through the senses, and originating from without; yet even then there is an inspiring passion, or desire, or instinctive feeling of the truth, which is the immediate and proper offspring of the mind. Now, we may consider the facts which are to be reduced to theory, as arranged over the whole surface of a plane circle. If by carrying the power of theory to a near identity with law, we find the centre of the circle, then proceeding toward the circumference, our insight into the whole may be enlarged by new discoveries; it never can be wholly changed. A magnificent example of this has been realized in the science of Astronomy; a recent addition of facts has been effected by the discovery of other planets, and our views have been rendered more distinct by the solution of the apparent irregularities of the moon's motion, and their subsumption under the general law of gravitation. But the Newtonian was not less a system before, than since, the discovery of the Georgium Sidus; not by having ascertained its circumference, but by having found its centre; the living and salient point, from which the method of discovery diverges, the law in which endless discoveries are contained implicitly, and to which as they afterwards arise, they may be referred in endless succession.

These reasonings, it is hoped, will sufficiently explain the nature of the transition, from the *Pure Sciences* to the *Mixed and Applied Sciences*, and will serve to trace the inseparable connection of the latter with the constitution of the human mind. And as each of these great divisions of knowledge has its own department in the grand moral science of man, it is obvious that a scheme, which, like our own, not only contains each separately, but combines both as indivisible, the one from the other; must present, in the most advantageous point of view, whatever is useful and beautiful in either. In speaking of the mixed and applied sciences, we must be permitted, however, to remark that the word science, is evidently used in a looser and more popular form, than when we denominate mathematics, or metaphysics, a science; for we know not, for instance, the truth of any general result of observation in nosology, as we know that two and two make four, or that a human person cannot be identical with another human person. And in like manner, when the word law, is used with relation to the mixed and applied sciences; as when we speak of any supposed law of vegetation; we use a more popular language than when we speak of a law of the conscience, which is not to be prevaricated. The strictness of ancient philosophy, therefore, refused the name of science to these pursuits: and it might be at least convenient, if in speaking generally of the pure, the mixed, and the applied sciences, we gave them the common name of studies, inasmuch as we study them all alike, but we do not know them all with the same sort of knowledge.

Mixed

Of these, then (be they studies or sciences), we call those *mixed* in which certain ideas of the mind, are applied to the general properties of bodies, solid, fluid, and aerial; to the power of vision, and to the arrangement of the universe; whence we obtain the sciences of *Mechanics, Hydrostatics, Pneumatics, Optics,* and *Astronomy.* It is matter not of certain science, but of observation, that such properties do really exist in bodies, that vision is effected in such or such a manner, and that the universe is disposed in this or that relative position, and subjected to certain movements of its parts. Therefore these sciences may vary, and notoriously have varied; and though Kepler would demonstrate that Euclid *Copernicized,* or had some knowledge of the system afterwards adopted by Copernicus; yet of this there is little proof: and certainly for many ages after Euclid it was the universal opinion, that the earth was the fixed and immoveable centre of the universe. Nor have we here unadvisedly used the word *opinion*; since, as we before showed, it is the ancient expression, signifying a medium between knowledge and ignorance: and well did that acute Italian exclaim, *Opinione, regina del mondo!*—for as it is impossible that ignorance, which cannot govern itself, should govern any thing else; so to expect that all the world should be wise enough to submit to the government of wisdom, would be to show that we had followed very little Method in our study either of history, of living men, or even of ourselves.

Applied; Experimental philosophy

When certain ideas, or images representative of ideas, are applied still more particularly, not to the investigation of the general and permanent properties of all bodies, but of certain changes in those properties, or of properties existing in bodies partially, then we popularly call the studies relative to such matters by the name of *Applied Sciences*; such are *Magnetism, Electricity, Galvinism, Chemistry*, the laws of *Light* and *Heat*, &c. We have already so fully shown the uncertainty of the first principles in these studies, and have so distinctly traced the cause of that uncertainty, in every case, to a want of clearness in the first idea or mental initiative of the science, that it will be unnecessary here to do more than refer to our preceding observations.

Fine Arts

We come now to another class of applied sciences, namely, those which are applied to the purposes of pleasure, through the medium of the imagination; and which are commonly called the Fine Arts. These are *Poetry, Painting, Music, Sculpture, Architecture*. We have before said, that the Method to be observed in these, holds a sort of middle place between the method of law, or pure science, and the Method of theory. In regard to the mixed sciences, and to the first class of applied sciences, the mental initiative may have been received from without; but it has escaped some critics, that in the fine arts the mental initiative must necessarily proceed from within. Hence we find them giving, as it were, recipes to form a poet, by placing him in certain directions and positions; as if they thought that every deer-stealer might, if he pleased, become a Shakspeare, or that Shakspeare's mind was made up of the shreds and patches of the books of his day; which by good fortune he happened to read in such an order, that they successively fitted into the scenes of Macbeth, Othello, the Tempest, As you like it, &c. Certainly the fine arts belong to the outward world, for they all operate by the images of sight and sound, and other sensible impressions; and without a delicate tact for these, no man ever was, or could be either a musician, or a poet; nor could he attain to excellence in any one of these arts: but as certainly he must always be a poor and unsuccessful cultivator of the arts, if he is not impelled first by a mighty, inward power, a feeling, *quod nequeo monstrare, et sentio tantum*; nor can he make great advances in his art, if in the course of his progress, the obscure impulse does not gradually become a bright, and clear, and living idea!

Useful Arts

Pursuits of utility, we daily find, are capable of being reduced to Method. Thus *Political Economy*, and *Agriculture*, and *Commerce*, and *Manufactures*, are now considered scientifically; or as the more prevalent expression is, philosophically. It may, perhaps, be difficult, at first, to persuade the experimental agriculturist, that he also pursues, or ought to pursue, an ideal Method: nor do we mean by this that he must deal only in ideal sheep and oxen, and in the groves and meads of Fairy Land. But these studies, soberly considered, will be found wholly dependent on the sciences of which we have already treated. It is not, surely, in the country of ARKWRIGHT, that the philosophy of commerce can be thought independent of mechanics: and where DAVY has delivered lectures on agriculture, it would be folly to say that the most philosophic views of chemistry were not conducive to the making our vallies laugh with corn.

Natural history

We have already spoken of LINNAEUS, the illustrious Swede, to whom the three *kingdoms*, as they are aptly called, of *Natural History*, are so deeply indebted: and if, with all his great talents, he yet failed in establishing the united empire of those three mighty monarchies, on firm laws, and a fixed constitution; we have shewn, that it was only owing to a want of precision in the first ideas of his theory.

Applications of

Natural history itself becomes a rule for dependent pursuits, such as those of *Medicine* (under which are *Pharmacy*, and the *Materia Medica*), and *Surgery*, in which is included *Anatomy*. That in these and the other theoretical studies, so much still remains to be done, ought not to be a subject for regret; but on the contrary, for a laudable and generous ambition. Yet that ambition should be regulated and moderated by a due consideration of the place, which the particular pursuit in question, holds in the great circle of the sciences; and by observing the only proper *Method* which can be pursued for its improvement. If, in what we have here said, we have done any thing towards the excitement, the regulation, and the assistance of that ambition; if we have faintly sketched an outline of the great laws of Method, which bind together the various branches of human knowledge, we may not improperly indulge a hope that the ensuing work, in its progress, will be found conducive to the promotion of the best interests of mankind.

History and Biography

Our Plan would not completely meet the views of those to whom such works as the following are eminently useful and agreeable, if besides the philosophic Method already described, we did not present some view of the actual history of mankind. We have therefore devoted a large portion of our labours to the History of the Human Race, on a new, and we trust it will be found an improved system. Biography and history tend to the same points of general instruction, in two ways: the one exhibiting human principles and passions, acting upon a large scale; the other shewing them as they move in a smaller circle, but enabling us to trace the orbit which they describe with greater precision. The one brings man into contact with society, actuated by the interests which agitate and stimulate him in the various social combinations of his existence; and human nature presents itself in the varied shapes impressed upon it by the different ranks which it occupies. The other brings before us the individual, when he stands alone, his passions asleep, his native impulses under no external excitement; in the undress of one who has retired from the stage, on which he felt he had a part to sustain; and even the monarch, forgetting the pomp and circumstance of his royalty, remembers here only that he is a man. Assuredly the great use of History is to acquaint us with the Nature of Man. This end is best answered by the most faithful portrait; but Biography is a collection of portraits. At the same time there must be some mode of grouping and connecting the individuals, who are themselves the great landmarks in the map of human nature. It has therefore occurred to us, that the most effectual mode of attaining the chief objects of historical knowledge, will be to present History in the form of Biography, chronologically arranged. This will be preceded by a general Introduction on the Uses of History, and on the line which separates its early facts from fable; and it will, in the course of its progress, be interspersed with connecting chapters on the events of large and distinguishing periods of time, as well as on political Geography and Chronology. Thus will the far larger portion of History be conveyed, not only in its most interesting, but in its most philosophical and real form; while the remaining facts will be interwoven in the preliminary and connecting chapters. If in tracing thus the 'eventful history' of man, and particularly of our own country, we should perceive, as we must necessarily do in all that is human, evils and imperfections; these will not be without their uses, in leading us back to the importance of intellectual Method as their grand and sovereign remedy. Hence shall we learn its proper national application, namely, the *education of the mind*, first in the man and citizen, and then, inclusively, in the State itself.

Alphabetic arrangement

Such are our views in the philosophical and historical branches of our work. Of the Miscellaneous or Alphabetical Division we have little to add. But well aware that works of this nature are not

υ

solely useful to those who have leisure and inclination to study science in its comprehensiveness, and unity; but are also valuable for daily reference on particular points, suggested by the desires or business of the individual; we could not hold ourselves dispensed from consulting the convenience of a numerous and most respectable class of Readers; while the preceding remarks will go to prove that for many local and supplementary illustrations of science, no other depository could be furnished.

As the philosophical arrangement is, however, most conducive to the purposes of intellectual research and information, as it will most naturally interest men of science and literature; will present the circle of knowledge in its harmony; will give that unity of design and of elucidation, the want of which we have most deeply felt in other works of a similar kind, where the desired information is divided into innumerable fragments scattered over many volumes, like a mirror broken on the ground, presenting, instead of one, a thousand images, but none entire; this division must of necessity, have that prominence in the prosecution of our design, which our conviction of its importance to the due execution of the plan demands; and every other part of the arrangement must be considered as subordinate to this principal organization. With respect to the whole work, it should be observed, that in what concerns *references* we are guided by principle, not by caprice; nor do we ever recur to them as our only means of escape from an exigency. Throughout the ENCYCLOPAEDIA METROPOLITANA, the philosophical arrangement predominates and regulates; the alphabetical arrangement, and the references, whether to it or from it, are auxiliary. We never refer from the first and second Divisions to the fourth, or from the first to the second, for the explanation of a term, the establishment of a principle, or the demonstration of a proposition. The reference, whenever it occurs, unless it be *retrospective*, is not for the purpose of essential information, but for that which is collateral and subordinate. The theory of the *balance*, for example, is given where it ought to be, in the Treatise on Mechanics; but they who wish to acquaint themselves with the various constructions of balances for the purposes of commerce or philosophy, knowing that these cannot be introduced into a scientific treatise, without destroying the symmetry of its parts by a suspension of the logical order, will naturally turn, whether there be a reference or not, to the alphabetical department of the work. So again, the principles of the *telescope* are given in the treatise on Optics; the varieties of construction in the alphabetical department: the principles of the *thermometer*, when treating of the effects of heat; its varieties of construction in the alphabetical department. Practical detail, and niceties or peculiarities of construction, can seldom be interwoven with propriety among the regular deductions of a methodical treatise: in all cases where they cannot, our general principle, as it comprehends proportion, accuracy, utility, and convenience, demands a reference, whether expressed or not, to the appropriate place for all that is subservient; that is, to the fourth or alphabetical division.

This final division of our work will bring the whole into unison with the two great impulses of modern times, trade and literature. These, after the dismemberment of the Roman empire, gradually reduced the conquerors and the conquered at once into several nations and a common Christendom. The natural law of increase, and the instincts of family, may produce tribes, and under rare and peculiar circumstances, settlements and neighbourhoods: and conquest may form empires. But without trade and literature, combined, there can be no nation; without commerce and science, no bond of nations. As the one has for its object the wants of the body, real or artificial, the desires for which are for the greater part excited from without; so the other has for its origin, as well as for its object, the wants of the mind, the gratification of which is a natural and necessary condition of *its* growth and sanity. In the pursuits of commerce the man is called into action from without, in order to appropriate the outward world, as far as he can bring it within his reach, to the purposes of his corporeal nature. In his scientific and literary character he is internally excited to various studies and pursuits, the ground-work of which is in himself.

This, again, will conduct us to the distinguishing object of the present undertaking; in endeavouring to explain which we have dwelt long upon general principles; but not too long, if we have established the necessity of what we conceive to be the main characteristic of every just arrangement of knowledge.

Our method embraces the two-fold distinction of human activity to which we have adverted;—the two great directions of man and society, with their several objects and ends. Without advocating the exploded doctrine of *perfectibility*, we cannot but regard all that is human in human nature, and all that in nature is above herself, as together working forward that far deeper and more permanent revolution in the moral world, of which the recent changes in the political world may be regarded as the pioneering whirlwind and storm. But woe to that revolution which is not guided by the historic sense; by the pure and unsophisticated knowledge of the past: and to convey this methodically, so as to aid the progress of the future, has been already announced as the distinguishing claim of the ENCYCLOPAEDIA METROPOLITANA.

The principles of Method, developed in the preceding Essay, will, it is hoped, render perfectly intelligible the Plan of our whole work, which is comprehended under Four Divisions as follow:

FIRST DIVISION

PURE SCIENCES (2 Vols.)

{
  FORMAL {
    Universal Grammar and Philology: or the forms of Languages.
    Logic, particular and universal: or the forms of Conceptions and their combinations.
    Mathematics: (Geometry, Arithmetic, Algebra, &c.) or the forms and constructions of Figure and Number.
  }
  REAL {
    Metaphysics: or the universal principles and conditions of Experience, having for its object the Reality of our speculative knowledge in general.
    Morals: or the principles and conditions of the coincidence of the individual will with the universal reason, having for its object the Reality of our practical knowledge: (hence, in a lower stage, Politics and Human Law.)
    Theology: or the union of both in their application to GOD, the Supreme Reality.
  }
}

SECOND DIVISION

MIXED AND APPLIED SCIENCES (6 Vols.)

{
  MIXED {
    Mechanics.
    Hydrostatics.
    Pneumatics.
    Optics.
    Astronomy.
  }
  I. EXPERIMENTAL PHILOSOPHY. {
    Magnetism.
    Electricity, including Galvanism.
    Chemistry.
    Light.
    Heat.
    Colour.
    Meteorology.
  }
  II. THE FINE ARTS. {
    Poetry, introduced by Psychology.
    Painting.
    Music.
    Sculpture.
    Architecture.
  }
}

Manufactures.

IV.

NATURAL HISTORY.

Introduced by Physiology in its widest sense.
Inanimate:—Chrystallography, Geology, Mineralogy.
Insentient:—Phytonomy, Botany.
Animate:—Zoology.

V.

APPLICATION OF
NATURAL HISTORY.

Anatomy.
Surgery.
Materia Medica.
Pharmacy.
Medicine.

THIRD DIVISION

BIOGRAPHICAL
AND
HISTORICAL.
(8 Vols.)

Biography CHRONOLOGICALLY arranged, interspersed with introductory Chapters of National History, Political Geography and Chronology, and accompanied with correspondent Maps and Charts.

FOURTH DIVISION

MISCELLANEOUS
AND
LEXICOGRAPHICAL
(8 Vols.)

Alphabetical, Miscellaneous, and Supplementary:—containing a GAZETTEER or complete Vocabulary of Geography: and a Philosophical and Etymological LEXICON of the English Language, or the History of English Words;—the citations arranged according to the Age of the Works from which they are selected, yet with every attention to the independent beauty or value of the sentences chosen which is consistent with the higher ends of a clear insight into the original and acquired meaning of every word.

The INDEX.—Being a digested and complete Body of Reference to the whole Work; in which the known English name, as well as the scientific name, of every subject of Natural History, will be found in its alphabetical place.

Appendix 3 GENERAL BIBLIOGRAPHY

Bibliographien sind Eingeständnisse der Tatsache, dass uns die Bücherflut über den Kopf gewachsen ist.

Dr GERT A. ZISCHKA

N.B. The articles under the heading ENCYCLOPAEDIA in most encyclopaedias are disappointing, with some notable exceptions listed below. Nevertheless, these articles are well worth examining since they often throw light on the particular encyclopaedia being handled, and they sometimes record contemporary circumstances of publication, etc., long since forgotten.

Allgemeine Enzyklopädie der Wissenschaften und Künste, edited by Ersch and Gruber, pages 204–6 (article on 'Encyklopädie' in section 1, Theil 34). 1840

Ersch, Johann Samuel. *Literatur der vermischten Schriften . . . Neue fortgesetzte Ausgabe von Christoph Anton Geissler.* Leipzig, 1837

Encyclopédie Française, volume XVIII, pages 24–6 to 24–12 (article on 'Encyclopédie et encyclopédies'). 1939

Hammer-Purgstall, Joseph, Freiherr von. *Über die Encyklopädie der Araber, Perser und Türken*, Vienna, Gerold's Sohn, 1857

Jackson, Sidney L. 'What a history of the encyclopaedia could show.' *Library Review*, Volume 19, no. 6, pages 398–401. Summer 1964

Klinckowstroem, Carl, Graf von. 'Enzyklopädien: Bibliographie der ersten deutschsprachigen enzyklopädischen Werke.' *Philobiblon*, volume I, pages 323–7. 1957

Lawätz, Heinrich Wilhelm. *Handbuch für Bücherfreunde und Bibliothekare.* Halle, Gebauer, 1788. Part I, volume 2, pages 377*ff.*: 'Allgemeine gelehrte Wörterbücher'; *and*, 1st supplement, 2nd section (1791), pages 175*ff.* and 183*ff.*

Lewalter, E. 'Das Konversationslexikon und seine Vorfahren.' *Atlantis*, 1940, pages 298–9

Meusel, J. G. *Leitfaden zur Geschichte der Gelehrsamkeit.* Leipzig, Hahn, 1800. Part 3 (pages 1338*ff.*): 'Über das Streben nach Einheit und Zusammenhang in der Wissenschaften, oder Geschichte der Enzyklopädie' (edited by J. A. Ortloff)

Malclès, Louise-Noëlle. *Les sources du travail bibliographique*, volume 1. Geneva, Droz; Lille, Giard, 1950. Chapter on Encyclopaedias

Roberts, A. D. *Introduction to reference works*. Latest edition, edited by E. Dudley. London, The Library Association. Chapter on Encyclopaedias

Schaller, Karl August (died 1819). *Encyklopädie und Methodologie der Wissenschaften*. Magdeburg, Heinrichshofen, 1812

Schleiermacher, A. A. E. *Bibliographisches System der gesammten Wissenschaftskunde, mit einer Anleitung zum Ordnen von Bibliotheken, Musikalien, Kupferstichen, wissenschaftl. und Geschäftspapieren*. Brunswick, Vieweg, 1852. 2 volumes

Schmiele, W. 'Meditationen über das Lexikon.' *Neue literarische Welt*, no. 14, 25th July 1953

Schneider, Georg. *Handbuch der Bibliographie*. 4th edition. Leipzig, Hiersemann, 1930, pages 138–58: 'Allgemeinenzyklopädien'

Shores, Louis. 'The ideal encyclopedia.' *Wilson bulletin*, volume 11, June 1937, pages 68–81

Steinberg, S. H. 'Encyclopaedias.' *Signature*, new series, no. 12, 1951, pages 3–22 (an important, enthusiastic and very readable account of the development of the encyclopaedia)

Toro, M. de. 'Les encyclopédies à travers les âges.' *Le Portique*, no. 5, 1947, pages 65–92

Walford, A. J. (editor). *Guide to reference material*. London, The Library Association, 1959. (Supplement, 1963.) Sections on Encyclopaedias

Winchell, C. M. *Guide to reference books*. 7th edition. Chicago, The American Library Association, 1951. (4 supplements, 1954–63—new edition in preparation.) Sections on Encyclopaedias

Zischka, Gert A. *Index lexicorum: Bibliographie der lexikalischen Nachschlagewerke*. Vienna, 1959 (particularly the Introduction, pages xi–xliv—an excellent summary of the history of the encyclopaedia; and 'Enzyklopädien und Konversationslexika', pages 1–16)
'The uses of encyclopaedias; past, present, and future.' *The American Behavioral Scientist*, volume VI, no. 1, September, 1962, pages 3–40 (an important symposium, with contributions by Livio C. Stecchini, Jacques Barzun, Harry S. Ashmore, W. T. Couch, Charles Van Doren, Francis X. Sutton, David L. Sills, Carl F. Stover and Alfred de Grazia)

Appendix *4* LIST OF ENCYCLOPAEDIAS NOT MENTIONED IN THE TEXT

In a volume of this size it has not proved possible to include in the text details of all the encyclopaedias that have been issued. Below is given a list of works that have had to be omitted, together with explanatory notes where appropriate.

American (Robert Underbrinck's and James P. Walsh's bibliographies (see page 228) will be found of particular help with regard to current items)

Aiton's Encyclopedia: a practical work of reference for the home, school and library . . .
Minneapolis, Welles Bros. & Co., 1910. 5 volumes

American educator encyclopedia. Lake Bluff, Illinois, The United Educators Inc.,
1965. 14 volumes
Derives from the *New practical reference library* (1907). Published as the *American educator*, 1919 onwards. Previous edition: *The American educator encyclopedia* (1956. 10 volumes)

American Oxford encyclopedia for home and school. New York, Little & Ives, 1965. 14
volumes
Based on the *Oxford junior encyclopaedia* (see page 212), but 'modified and expanded to meet American needs and interests, but in the essential pattern it remains as Oxford made it'. Editor-in-chief: William T. Couch

The American peoples encyclopedia: a comprehensive modern-minded reference work.
Chicago, The Spencer Press, 1948. 20 volumes
Editor: Franklin J. Meine. Now issued, with *Yearbook*, by the Grolier Society of New York

The Anglo-American cyclopedia: a standard work of reference in art, literature, science, history, geography, commerce, biography, discovery and invention. New York, London, etc., Anglo-American Encyclopedia Co., 1911. 50 volumes (last two, Index)

Basic everyday encyclopedia. Prepared by the Reference Department of Random House, under the editorship of Jess Stein. New York, Random House, 1954

The book of knowledge: the children's encyclopedia. New York, The Grolier Society, 1912. 24 volumes
The American edition of Arthur Mee's *The Children's encyclopaedia* (London, 1910—see page 15). Now issued in 20 volumes with *The book of knowledge annual*, 1949 to date

The century dictionary and cyclopedia: a work of universal reference in all departments of knowledge, with a new atlas of the world. New York, The Century Co., 1901. 10 volumes. Supplement, 1909: 2 volumes
Edited by William Dwight Whitney (1827–94) and—for volumes 9 and 10—Benjamin Eli Smith (1857–1913)

The Columbia–Viking desk encyclopedia. 2nd edition. New York, Viking Press, 1960
Based on the *Columbia encyclopaedia* (see page 209). Editor-in-chief: William Bridgwater

The complete reference handbook. New York, Stravon Publishers, 1964

Doubleday's encyclopedia. Garden City, N.Y., Doubleday, Doran, 1931. 10 volumes
Edited by librarian Arthur Elmore Bostwick. Adapted from *Harmsworth's universal encyclopaedia* (see page 201). Now issued by the Grolier Society under the title *Grolier encyclopedia*, with the *Encyclopedia year book: the story of our time,* 1957 to date

Encyclopaedia international. New York, Grolier, 1963. 20 volumes
Edited by George A. Cornish

Encyclopedic dictionary of American reference. Boston, 1901. 2 volumes
Edited by John Franklin Jameson (1859–1937) and James William Buel (1849–1920). First published in 1894 under the title: *Dictionary of US history*

Everybody's encyclopedia. Chicago, De Bower-Chapline Co., 1909.
Issued also under the titles: *La Salle Extension University encyclopedia,* and *Webster's universal encyclopedia*

The everyday reference library: an encyclopedia of useful information. Chicago, J. G. Ferguson Publishing Co., 1961. 3 volumes
First published 1948 under the title: *Austin's new encyclopedia of usable information.* Edited by Lewis Copeland and Lawrence W. Lamm

Facts: the new concise pictorial encyclopedia. Garden City, N.Y., 1934. 4 volumes
Edited by Nella Braddy. Issued in a revised one-volume edition as *The new concise pictorial encyclopedia* in 1938; in 1941 in one volume as *Facts*; and since 1951 as *The world home reference encyclopedia* (Chicago, Consolidated Book Publishers, 4 volumes)

Funk & Wagnalls New standard encyclopedia of universal knowledge. New York and London, Funk & Wagnalls, 1931. 25 volumes
Known also as the *Standard encyclopedia.* Edited by Francis (Frank) Horace Vizetelly (1864–1938). Issued in 1949–50 in 36 volumes as *The new Funk & Wagnalls encyclopedia*; published under that title by Unicorn Publishers of New York, together with *Funk & Wagnalls new standard encyclopedia year book,* 1933 to date. Present title: *Funk and Wagnalls standard reference encyclopedia* (New York, Standard Reference Works Publishing Company, 1962. 25 volumes)

Golden book encyclopedia. New York, Golden Press, 1959. 16 volumes in 8
Edited by Bertha Morris Parker

The golden home and high school encyclopedia. New York, Golden Press, 1961. 20 volumes
Editor-in-chief: Virginia Sarah Thatcher

The golden treasury of knowledge. Revised edition. New York, Golden Press, 1961.
16 volumes
First edition 1958. Editor-in-chief: Margaret Bevans

Grolier universal encyclopedia. New York, Spencer International Press, 1965. 10
volumes
'Developed and published under the supervision of Dr Lowell A. Martin'

The home university encyclopedia: an illustrated treasury of knowledge. New York,
Books Inc., 1956. 12 volumes
Previously issued in 15 volumes in 1941. Edited by C. Ralph Taylor. Based
on *Nelson's new loose-leaf encyclopedia* (see page 205), *World wide illustrated
encyclopedia* (1935), and *University illustrated encyclopedia* (1938)

The human interest library, visualized knowledge. Chicago, The Midland Press, 1914.
4 volumes
Edited by the Right Rev. Samuel Fallows (born 1835) and Henry W. Ruoff
(born 1867). From 1928 onwards, issued as *The new human interest library,* in
6 volumes. (Revised edition. New York, Books Inc., 1962. 7 volumes)

Illustrated home library encyclopedia. Brooklyn, N.Y., Premiumwares Inc., 1954.
21 volumes
Issued in 1956 as the *Illustrated encyclopedia of knowledge.* Based on the latter,
the *Illustrated world encyclopedia* was published by the Bobley Publishing
Corporation of New York, in 21 volumes, in 1958, and *The illustrated encyclopedia* (1959)

*Library of universal knowledge: the practical self-educator, including Webster's compre-
hensive encyclopedic dictionary and all its supplementary parts.* Chicago, H. Ross,
1942
Editor-in-chief: Franklin Julius Meine. 1954 and later editions issued by the
Consolidated Book Publishers of Chicago

*The Lincoln Library of essential information: an up-to-date manual for daily reference,
for self-instruction, and for general culture* . . . Buffalo, N.Y., The Frontier
Press Co., 1924
Frequently revised and re-issued

The Little and Ives illustrated ready reference encyclopedia for home and school use. New
York, J. J. Little & Ives Publishing Co., 1962. 20 volumes
Editor-in-chief: Franklin Dunham

Modern encyclopedia: a new library of world knowledge. New York, Grosset, 1933
Edited by A. H. McDannald. Title changed to *The new modern encyclopedia:
a library of world knowledge,* from 1943 onwards. The present publishers,
William H. Wise & Co. of New York, also issued *The concise encyclopedia*
(8 volumes; 1937), based on this work

The national encyclopedia. New York, P. F. Collier, 1932. 11 volumes
Edited by Henry Suzzallo (1875–1933)

*The new American comprehensive encyclopedia: a complete encyclopedia of the arts,
sciences, history, biography, geography and general literature* . . . New York,
J. A. Hill & Co., 1906. 5 volumes
Issued in 1902 as volumes 1–5 of the *Anglo-American encyclopedia and dictionary*

The new American encyclopedia: a concise and comprehensive reference work especially planned, compiled and written for school, college, office and home use. Boston and New York, Books Inc., 1938
Edited by Charles Ralph Taylor. Based on this, and with the addition of new entries and illustrations from *Webster's New American dictionary,* the H. S. Stuttman Company of New York have published since 1953 *Webster's unified dictionary and encyclopedia: a concise and comprehensive reference work, completely new and up-to-date, planned and written by modern educators and lexicographers to serve the essential requirements of school, college, office, and self education at home.* The 1963 edition is called *The American family encyclopedia* (8 volumes)

New century book of facts. New York, Continental Publishing Co., 1965
First published 1909 as *Century book of facts*

The new golden encyclopedia. Revised edition. New York, Golden Press, 1963
Editor-in-chief: Jane Werner Watson

New masters pictorial encyclopedic. Washington, Publishers Co., 1955. 8 volumes

New pictorial encyclopedia of the world. New York, Pictorial Encyclopedia Co., 1954. 18 volumes
With the addition of a two-volume atlas and gazetteer, this work was issued in 1957 as the *Illustrated encyclopedia of the modern world.* Editor-in-chief: Franklin Dunham

The new standard encyclopedia. New York, The University Society, 1906. 12 volumes
Edited by William A. Colledge (1859–1927), Nathan Haskell Dole (1852–1935), and George Jotham Hagar (1847–1921). Now issued in loose-leaf form in 14 volumes by the Standard Edition Society of Chicago

The new wonder book encyclopedic of world knowledge: the thrilling stories of twentieth century industry, science, nature, transportation, communication, and other marvels of the world. Philadelphia, International Press, 1954. 12 volumes
Originally issued in 1953 for distribution to a Canadian chain of supermarkets

Our wonder world: a library of knowledge . . . Chicago & Boston, G. L. Shuman, 1914. 10 volumes
Changed title to: *The new wonder world: a library of knowledge.* Chicago, G. L. Shuman, 1932. 11 volumes; *New wonder world encyclopedia* (1959); and, *The cultural library* (New York, Parents' Magazine Cultural Institute, 1965. 10 volumes)

Our wonderful world: young people's encyclopedic anthology. Chicago, Spencer Press, 1955. 18 volumes
Edited, with annual supplement, by Herbert S. Zim

Pictured knowledge; the full color encyclopedia. New York, Little & Ives Co., 1956. 14 volumes

The progressive reference library; a new edition with extensive revisions, constituting a consolidation of the publications formerly on the market under the titles: International Reference Work and The New Teachers' and Pupils' Cyclopedia, a library

of history, geography, biography, biology, literature, economics, civics, arts, sciences, discoveries, explorations, inventions, commerce, etc., cyclopedia of general and recent information . . . Boone, Iowa, and Chicago, Ill., The Holst Publishing Co., 1928. 10 volumes

Edited by Bernhart Paul Holst. The *International reference work* and *The new teachers' and pupils' cyclopedia* were both published in 1927, in 10 and 8 volumes respectively (same editor, same publisher). *World-scope encyclopedia*, edited by B. P. Holst, was based on *The progressive reference library*, and issued, 20 volumes in 10, by the Readers League of America, in New York in 1945. *The standard international encyclopedia* (also published in cheaper form as *The New World family encyclopedia*, 1953), edited by William H. Hendelson, was also based on *The progressive reference library*, and issued in 20 volumes, by The Standard International Library, in New York in 1953. Later derivatives include: *The world university encyclopedia* (Washington, Publications Co., 1964. 12 volumes); *The new American encyclopedia* (Washington, Publications Co., 1963. 16 volumes); and, *World educator encyclopedia* (Miami, International Book Co., 1963. 16 volumes)

Richards cyclopedia . . . *Edited by Ernest Hunter Wright and Mary Heritage Wright* . . . New York, Richards, 1933. 24 volumes in 12

Systematically arranged, the last two volumes constituting an index and bibliography. Now issued, with a yearbook, as *Richards topical encyclopedia*, in 15 volumes

Twentieth century encyclopaedia: a library of universal knowledge . . . Philadelphia, Syndicate Publishing Co., 1901. 6 volumes

Edited by Professor C. S. Morris

The twentieth-century encyclopedia; . . . showing the most important events in history, science, literature, art, &c. . . . Cleveland, World Library Guild, 1930. 10 volumes

Edited by Francis J. Reynolds who extended the number of volumes to 11 in the 1934 edition. Also issued as the *American international encyclopedia*

The unified encyclopedia: a modern reference library of unified knowledge for the parent, student and young reader. New York, Unified Encyclopedia Press, 1960–62. 30 volumes

'Reprints the *Grolier encyclopedia*, unified with reading units from *Richards topical encyclopedia*.' Editor-in-chief: Ellen Veronica McLoughlin

Universal world reference encyclopedia: an authoritative compilation of knowledge. Revised edition. Chicago, Consolidated Book Publishers, 1961–62. 15 volumes

First published 1916. Editor-in-chief: Virginia Sarah Thatcher

The volume library: a concise, graded repository of practical and cultural knowledge designed for both instruction and reference. Chicago, The W. E. Richardson Co., 1911

Edited by Henry Woldmar Ruoff. Issued as *The volume library: an encyclopedia of practical and cultural information* by The Educators Association of New York, and later as *Cowles comprehensive encyclopedia* (New York, Cowles Educational Books, 1962)

Weedon's modern encyclopedia . . . Cleveland and Toronto, The S. L. Weedon Co.,
   1931–32. 8 volumes
   Edited by Garry Cleveland Myers

The wonderland of knowledge: the pictorial encyclopedia. Chicago, Wonderland of
   Knowledge Corporation, 1937. 14 volumes
   Edited by Harry Orrin Gillet; issued frequently. (Lake Bluff, Illinois,
   Tangley Oaks Educational Center, 1961. 12 volumes. Edited by Everette
   Edgar Sentman)

The world-wide cyclopedia: a complete library of reference . . . New York, Syndicate
   Co., 1919. 6 volumes
   Editor-in-chief: George Jotham Hagar (1847–1921). Founded on *Everybody's
   cyclopedia* (New York, Syndicate Publishing Co., 1911. 5 volumes); *People's
   cyclopedia*, edited by C. Leonard-Stuart and George Jotham Hagar (New
   York, Syndicate Publishing Co., 1914. 5 volumes); and, *The new world
   encyclopedia*, edited by George Jotham Hagar (New York, The Christian
   Herald, 1919. 6 volumes)

*The world-wide encyclopedia and gazetteer: compiled and revised to date from the leading
   encyclopedias of the world. A dictionary of arts, sciences and literature, to which is
   added biographies of living subjects* . . . New York, The Christian Herald,
   1908. 12 volumes
   Editor-in-chief: William Harrison De Puy (1821–1901)

World wide illustrated encyclopedia. Revised edition. New York & Boston, Books
   Inc., 1937. 15 volumes
   Revised edition of the *New York Post world wide illustrated encyclopedia* (1935).
   Also published under the title: *University illustrated encyclopedia.* Edited by
   Charles Ralph Taylor

Arabic

Hādjdjī Khalīfa (d. 1657). *Kashf al-zunūn ān asāmi 'l-Kutub wa'l-funūn* (bibliographical and encyclopaedic lexicon). Text edited by Gustav Flügel in
   the Oriental Translation Fund series (1835–58)

aṭ-Ṭabari, Muḥammad ibn Ǧarīr (838–923). *Annales quos scripsit Abu Djafar
   Mohammed ibn Djarir at-Tabari:* cum aliis edidit M. J. de Goeje, Th.
   Nöldeke, . . . Leiden, E. J. Brill, 1879–1901. 15 volumes (facsimile edition,
   1964–66)
   Essentially a universal history, though important also for its philological
   contribution

al-Zahrāwī, Abulcasis. *al-Tasrif.*
   One of the very earliest of the medieval encyclopaedias. It was written, in
   thirty treatises, in the second half of the tenth century

Australian

The Australian junior encyclopaedia. New Edition. Sydney, N.S.W., Australian
   Educational Foundation, 1956. 3 volumes
   Editor-in-chief: Charles Leslie Barrett

Austrian

Allgemeinnütziges Geschicht- und Staaten-Wörterbuch. Vienna, 1794. 4 volumes

Gutenberg Konversationslexikon. Vienna, Hamburg and Zurich, 1930–31. 6 volumes

Neues Welt-Lexikon. Vienna, Literaria Verlag, 1955. 2 volumes

Neuestes Conversations-Lexicon; oder, Allgemeine deutsche Real-Encyclopädie für gebildete Stände. Von einer Gesellschaft von Gelehrten ganz neu bearbeitet. Vienna, F. Ludwig, 1825–36. 19 volumes (the last, supplementary)

Österreichische National-Encyclopädie; oder, Alphabetische Darlegung der wissenswürdigsten Eigenthümlichkeiten des österreichischen Kaiserthumes ... Vienna, 1835–38. 7 volumes (the last, supplementary)

British

Black's Children's encyclopaedia. London, A. & C. Black, 1964
Edited by William Worthy and R. J. Unstead

Burrowes, Amyas Deane. *The modern encyclopaedia; or, General dictionary of arts, sciences and literature.* London, Richards & Co., 1816–20. 11 volumes. 4to

Cassell's Storehouse of general information. London, Cassell, 1891–94. 4 volumes
New edition issued under the title: *Cassell's Encyclopaedia of general information* (10 volumes; London, Cassell, 1908)

The Caxton encyclopaedia. London, Caxton Publishing Co., 1960. 6 volumes
Also published as: *The Caxton world of knowledge*

Child's first encyclopaedia in colour. London, Odhams Press, 1964. 6 volumes

The compact encyclopedia. London, The Gresham Publishing Co., 1929. 6 volumes
Based on *The new Gresham encyclopedia*, issued between 1921 and 1924, and edited by two of its editors—Richard F. Patterson and John Dougall. Rather less than half as long as its predecessor. Material revised to 1927. 'Compression, not amputation or excision, has been the watchword'

Great encyclopaedic dictionary. London, Reader's Digest, 1964. 3 volumes
Volumes 1 and 2 originally published as the *Oxford illustrated dictionary* (New edition. 1962). Volume 3 comprises 29 specialist dictionaries

Hunter, Robert (1823–97). *Encyclopaedic dictionary.* London and New York, Cassell, 1879–89. 7 volumes
Known as *Lloyd's encyclopaedic dictionary*, from the name of the publisher of the re-issue in 1895

Hutchinson's new 20th century encyclopaedia. New edition. London, Hutchinson, 1964
Edited by E. M. Horsley. Previously published as the *Twentieth-century encyclopaedia* (1955)

John Whethamstede *or* Bostock (d. 1465). *Granarium de viris illustribus.* c. 1420–40. 4 volumes
Pt. I: over 100 long articles on historical events and people especially contemporary happenings; Pt II: mainly ethical topics

Knowledge. London, Knowledge, 1963. 20 volumes

The modern encyclopaedia, illustrated. London, Odhams Press, 1961
General advisory editor: Lord Corell

The national cyclopaedia of useful knowledge. London, Knight, 1847–51. 12 volumes
New edition published by G. Routledge, in 12 volumes, 1856–59

*The national encyclopaedia: a dictionary of useful knowledge. The new national encyclo-
paedia atlas . . .* London and Glasgow, W. Mackenzie, 1867–68. 14
volumes. 8vo
This was a new edition of *The national cyclopaedia of useful knowledge*, with
additions. Later editions of *The national encyclopaedia* were published in
1875 (Glasgow, W. Mackenzie. 13 volumes); and in 1884–88 (Glasgow,
W. Mackenzie. 14 volumes) edited by J. H. F. Brabner

New age encyclopaedia; edited by Sir Edward Parrott. London and New York,
Nelson, 1920–21. 10 volumes

New age encyclopaedia, world atlas and sports supplement. New edition. London,
Collins, 1963
Edited by George F. Maine and J. B. Foreman. Previous edition 1957

Newnes Popular encyclopaedia. London, Newnes, 1962. 8 volumes

*The popular encyclopaedia; or, 'Conversations Lexicon'; being a general dictionary of arts,
sciences, literature, biography, history, ethics, and political economy; with dissertations on the rise and progress of literature by Sir D. K. Sandford, on the progress of
science by T. Thomson, and on the progress of the fine arts by A. Cunningham.*
Glasgow, Blackie, 1841. 7 volumes (last volume supplementary)
This and the seven-volume editions of 1862, 1867–82 and 1877–79 were
edited by A. Whitelaw. From 1882 the encyclopaedia was edited by C.
Annandale, the edition of 1890–93 being in 14 volumes. In 1901 it was taken
over by The Gresham Publishing Company of London, under the title: *The
new popular encyclopaedia*, and again changed its title to *The modern cyclopaedia
of universal information: a handy-book of reference on all subjects and for all readers;
a new edition* (8 volumes; London, The Gresham Publishing Co., 1906–07).
Charles Annandale also edited Ogilvie's *Imperial dictionary of the English
language*

Purnell's New English encyclopaedia. London, Purnell's New English Encyclopaedia, 1964–67. 12 volumes (and a two-volume Dictionary)
Issued in weekly parts. 'The only adult encyclopaedia illustrated in full
colour on every page.' Managing editor: N. J. Marshall

Wonder-world of knowledge in colour. London, Odhams Press, 1961

Bulgarian

Kratka Bălgarska entsiklopedija. Sofia, Bălgarskata Akademija Naukite, 1963–67.
5 volumes
Editor-in-chief: Vladimir Georgev. This dictionary is mentioned by the
English translation of its name only on page 225 (*Concise Bulgarian encyclopaedia*)

x

Canadian

Encyclopédie Grolier. Montreal, Société Grolier, 1958. 10 volumes
    First published in 1947. There is also a supplementary yearbook: *Le livre de l'année annuaire: de l'Encyclopédie Grolier*

Czech

Ottuv slovník naučný nové doby. Prague, J. Otto, 1930–43. Volumes 1–6 (not completed)
    Edited by B. Němec. Volumes 5 and 6 published by 'Novina'.

Danish

Nordisk conversations-lexicon; indeholdende en almindelig forklaring over alle rigtige navne, gjenstande og begreber, som forekomme i livet under laesning og i samtale. Copenhagen, Forlagsburean, 1858–63. 5 volumes. 8vo
    Edited by Christian Frederik Ingerslew. W. Mollerup took over the editorship with the 3rd edition (6 volumes; 1884–90). By the edition of 1944–50 the number of volumes had been increased to 14

Dutch

Buys, Egbert (died 1769). *Nieuw en volkomen woordenboek van konsten en weetenschappen.* Amsterdam, K. de Veer, 1769–78. 10 volumes
    This is more of a dictionary than an encyclopaedia

Oosthoek's geïllustreerde encyclopaedie. Utrecht, Osthoek, 1916–23. 11 volumes
    Edited by H. F. Nierstrasz and E. C. G. Brünner. 2nd edition (13 volumes; 1925–34). 3rd edition (14 volumes; 1932–39). 4th edition (16 volumes; 1947–1955), under the title: *Osthoek's Encyclopaedie*

Verschuerens Modern woordenboek. Turnhout, Brepols, 1933. 2 volumes
    Frequently revised and re-issued

Witsen-Geysbeek, P. G. *Algemeen nootwendig woordenboek der zamenleving.* Amsterdam, 1858–63

Zoek-licht: Nederlandsche encyclopaedia voor allen. Arnheim, Slaterus, 1922–31. 9 volumes (last volume supplementary)
    Edited by T. P. Sevensma

Estonian

Eesti entsüklopeedia. Tartu, K./Ü. 'Loodus', 1932–37. 8 volumes
    Edited by R. Kleis, P. Treiberg, and J. V. Veski

Eesti entsüklopeedia. Stockholm, Kirjastus Estonia, 1957– . Volume 1– (in progress)
    Edited by H. Meister

French

Encyclopédie internationale Focus. Paris, Bordas, 1963–64. 4 volumes

Encyclopédie Péreire
An encyclopaedia that was never published. Planned in 1862 and 1863 by the brothers Emile, Isaac and Eugène Péreire, and inspired by the economist Michel Chevalier, this could have been one of the greatest encyclopaedias of the nineteenth century. See Jean Bonnerot's fascinating article 'Sainte-Beuve et l'Encyclopédie Péreire' in the *Revue des sciences humaines*, Jan.–Mar. 1963, pages 39–58

Encyclopédie universelle. Verviers, Gerard, 1961–63. 8 volumes. (Collection Marabout Université)
General editors: Jean-Jacques Schellens and Jacqueline Mayer

Nouvelle encyclopédie autodidactique Quillet: l'enseignement moderne et pratique. Paris, Quillet, 1963. 4 volumes
Published in 1922 under the title: *Nouvelle encyclopédie autodidactique illustré d'enseignement moderne.* Assumed present title in the edition of 1956

German

Adelung, Johann Christoph (1732–1806). *Kurzer Begriff menschlicher Fertigkeiten und Kentnisse.* Leipzig, Hertel, 1778–81. Pts. 1–4

Allgemeine Realencyclopädie; oder, Conversations-Lexikon für das katholische Deutschland. Regensburg, Mainz, 1846–50. 14 volumes (last two, supplementary)
Edited by Wilhelm Binder. Known as the *Manz'sche Realencyklopädie.* Frequent new editions and revisions

Allgemeines Conversations-Taschen-Lexikon; oder, Realencyklopädie der für die gebildeten Stände nothwendigen Kenntnisse und Wissenschaften. Quedlinburg, 1828–32. 62 volumes

Allgemeines deutsches encyklopädisches Handwörterbuch; oder, Wohlfeilstes Taschen-Conversationslexicon für alle Stanze. Augsburg, 1828–31. 36 volumes

Allgemeines deutsches Sach-Wörterbuch aller menschlichen Kenntnisse und Fertigkeiten. Meissen, 1824–30. 10 volumes
Edited by Joseph Max von Liechtenstein and Albin Schiffner. 2nd edition (1834) enlarged to 11 volumes

Allgemeines Real-Handwörterbuch der gemeinnützigen Sachkenntnisse; oder, Encyklopädie der wissenswürdigsten Begriffe und Kenntnisse aus den ökonomischen, kaufmännischen, medicinischen, Chemischen, juristischen, kameralistischen und politischen, militärischen, naturhistorischen, mathematischen Wissenschaften und schönen Künste . . . Halle, Gebauer, 1793

Beckmanns Neues Weltlexikon, mit Weltatlas. Munich and Vienna, Beckmann, 19
Frequent reprints and new editions. Also a smaller version in two volumes issued from 1927 onwards: *Der kleine Beckmann*

Das Bertelsmann-Lexikon. Gütersloh, Bertelsmann. 4 volumes
Frequent editions. There is also the smaller *Bertelsmann Volkslexikon*, in one volume

Büsch, Johann Georg (1728–1800). *Encyklopädie der historischen, philosophischen und mathematischen Wissenschaften, grossentheils nach dem Grundrisse des sel. Reimarus ausgearbeitet* . . . Hamburg, A. Campe, 1775. 2 parts
Second edition issued in 1794

Deutsche Encyklopädie: ein neues Universallexikon für alle Gebiete des Wissens. Leipzig, Grunow, 1885–86. 8 volumes
Known as 'Grunow'

Habbels Konversations-Lexikon. Regensburg, Habbel, 1912–18. 5 volumes
New edition 1922–28

Heinsius, Otto Friedrich. *Encyklopädisches Handwörterbuch für Wissenschaft und Leben, zum Schul- und Hausgebrauch.* Berlin, Duncker, 1828

Hirzel, Heinrich. *Das Haus-Lexikon: Encyklopädie praktischer Lebenskenntnisse für alle Stände* . . . Leipzig, Breitkopf & Härtel. 6 volumes
Frequently re-issued

Hottinger, Christoph Georg. *Suchbuch: ein Nachschlagebuch für den täglichen Gebrauch. Konversationslexikon.* Strassburg, Hottinger
Frequently re-issued

Huhn, Eugen. *Topographisch-statistisch-historisches Comptoir-, Amts-, Post-, Reise- und Zeitungslexikon von Deutschland: eine vollständige deutsche Landes-, Volks- und Staatskunde.* Hildburghausen, Bibliographisches Institut, 1848–49. 6 volumes

Ife, August. *Der deutsche Polyhistor; oder, Universal-Handwörterbuch für häusliche und öffentliche Leben.* Berlin, Hayn, 1837

Illustrirtes Konversations-Lexikon: Vergleichendes Nachschlagebuch für den täglichen Gebrauch. Hausschatz für das deutsche Volk und 'Orbis pictus' für die studirende Jugend. Leipzig and Berlin, Spamer, 1869–82. 10 volumes, and Atlas (last two volumes, supplementary)
Second edition, 1885–91

Jedermanns Lexikon. Berlin, H. Klemm, 1929–34. 12 volumes (last two, supplementary)

Katholisches Universal-Volkslexikon für jedermann. Nordhausen, Vincentius, 1903–1912. 3 volumes
Edited by Nikolaus Thömes

Kiepen-Lexikon des Wissens und der Bildung. Cologne, Kiepenheuer, 1958. 2 volumes

Kirchner, C. *Akademische Propädeutik.* Leipzig, W. Vogel, 1842

Der kleine Pöschl: Kleines Sprach- und Wissenslexikon. Kassell, Hess. Druck- u. Verl.-Anst, 1952–53. 2 volumes

Das kluge Alphabet: Konversationslexikon. Berlin, Propyläen, 1934–35, 10 volumes
Post-war edition 1957 (3 volumes)

Knaurs Lexikon. Munich, Droemer, 1931
Frequently revised and reprinted

Kürschners Universal-Konversationslexikon

Lexikon A–Z. Leipzig, Enzyklopädie, 1956–57. 2 volumes
Edited by Gerhard Wahrig

Neues Conversations-Lexikon: Staats- und Gesellschafts-Lexikon. Berlin, Heinicke, 1859–68. 24 volumes (last one, supplementary)
Edited by Hermann Wagener

Neues Volks-Konversationslexikon. St Gallen, Scheiflin, 1869
Edited by Otto Henne-Am Rhyn. 2nd edition 1874 reached first 2 fascicules only

Oestergaards Lexikon. Berlin, Oestergaard, 1931–37. 20 volumes

Otto Wigands Conversationslexicon für alle Stände. Leipzig, Wigand, 1845–52. 13 volumes

Das Pfennig-Journal; oder, Universal-Lexikon und gedrängter, verständlicher Kürze in einem Bande. Herausgegeben von einem Verein Gelehrter. Breslau, H. Richter, 1835
2nd edition (Breslau, H. Richter, 1839) issued as the *General Conversations-Lexicon*

Reuss, Christian Frederik. *Encyclopädie.* Tübingen, 1783
This is devoted to medical sciences

Roth, Johann Ferdinand (died 1814). *Gemeinnütziges Lexikon für Leser aller Klassen, besonders für Unstudirte.* . . . Nuremberg, Grattenaur, 1788. 2 parts
2nd edition issued 1791; 3rd, 1806

Rotteck, Carl W. von *and* Welcker, Carl T. *Staats-Lexikon; oder, Encyklopädie der Staatswissenschaften.* Altona, Hammerich, 1834–43. 16 volumes (last, Index)
A four-volume supplement was issued 1846–48

Sanders, Daniel. *Moment-Lexikon mit Fremdwörterbuch.* Berlin, 1912
A miniature book, designed to be used with a magnifying-glass

Schelling, Friedrich Wilhelm Joseph von. *Vorlesungen über die Methode des academischen Studiums.* 3rd edition. Strassburg, 1830
First published 1803. 'In 1803 Schelling had noted that his *Vorlesungen* . . . might easily develop into a general encyclopaedia of the sciences' (Alice D. Snyder: *Coleridge's Treatise* . . ., pages xxii–xxiii)

Schmid, Carl C. E. *Allgemeine Encyklopädie und Methodologie der Wissenschaften.* 1810
An outline of the theory of encyclopaedia-making

Volkslexikon: Nachschlagebuch für sämtliche Wissenszweige . . . Nuremberg, Wörlein, 1894–98. 5 volumes (last, Index)
Edited by Emanuel Wurm

Das Weltall: ein geographisch-statistisch-naturhistorisches Handwörterbuch mit Berücksichtigung des Wissenswürdigsten aus der Weltgeschichte. Aus authentisches und den neuesten Quellen geschöpft und in alphabetische Ordnung zusammengestellt . . . Frankfurt, Friedrich, 1828–32. 16 volumes

Greek

Julius Pollux. *Onomasticon.* (2nd century.) 10 books. Dedicated to Pollux's former pupil, the Emperor Commodus. Systematically arranged. Of particular interest for its definitions of technical terms, and for its lavish use of quotations. Edited by Erich Bethe as vol. 9 in the series *Lexicographi graeci* (Leipzig, Teubner, 1900)

Hungarian

Uj idök lexikona. Budapest, Singer & Wolfner, 1936–42. 12 volumes

Dormándi, Lászlá *and* Juhász, Vilmossal. *Új lexikon: a tudás és a gyakarlati élet egyetemes enciklopédiájá.* Budapest, 1936. 8 volumes

A Franklin kézi lexikona. Budapest, 1911–12. 3 volumes

Közhasznu esmeretek Tára: a Conversations-Lexicon szerént Magyarországra alkalmaztatva. Pest, 1839. 12 volumes

Italian

Bazzarini, Antonio. *Dizionario enciclopedico delle scienze, lettre ed arti.* Venice, 1824–37. 16 volumes (last two, supplementary)

Dizionario enciclopedico Sansoni. Florence, Sansoni, 1952–55. 4 volumes
    Edited by Mario Niccoli and Guido Martellotti

Dizionario universale di scienze, lettere ed arti. 2nd edition. Milan, Treves, 1880–83. 2 volumes
    Edited by Michele Lessona and Carlo Avale. Later edition (Turin, Unione tip., 1905–19) in 6 volumes

Enciclopedia Curcio delle lettere, delle scienze, delle arti. Rome and Milan, 1950. 3 volumes
    Edited by Gennaro Vaccaro

Enciclopedia Hoepli. Milan, Hoepli, 1955– . (in progress)

Enciclopedia moderna e dizionario italiano della conversazione ad imitazione dell'Enciclopedia di Courtin, e degli analoghi dizionari e lessici tedeschi, inglesi e francesi più accreditati. Opera compilata dai signori dott. Albrizzi, dott. Asson . . . ed A. F. Falconetti pad., direttore. E corredata di tavole [2 volumes. 1847] . . . Venice, Tasso, 1837–53

Enciclopedia Pomba per le famiglie. Turin, 'Utet', 1948–50. 2 volumes

Grande enciclopedia popolare Sonzogno. Milan, Soc. Ed. Sonzogno, 1913–32. 24 volumes (last two, supplementary)
    A short revised version was issued in 3 volumes in 1954–57 under the title: *Nuova enciclopedia Sonzogno*

Griselini, Francesco *and* Fassadoni, M. *Dizionario delle arti e dei mestieri.* Venice, 1768–78. 18 volumes

Nuova enciclopedia popolare; ovvero, Dizionario generale di scienze, lettere, arti, storia, geografia, &c. . . . Turin, Unione tip., 1842–51. 14 volumes (last two, Indexes)
    Edited by G. Demarchi and F. Predari. Reached a sixth edition (Turin, Unione Tipografico-Editrice Torinese, 1875–88. 30 volumes in 32—of which the last 5 volumes (in 6) were supplementary), edited by Gerolamo Boccardo

Nuovissima enciclopedia illustrata. Milan, Ist. Edit. It., 1950–53. 5 volumes
   Edited by Giuseppe Maria Boccabianca

Piccola enciclopedia Garzanti. Milan, Garzanti, 1958. 2 volumes

Latin

Beyerlinck, Laurentius. *Magnum theatrum vitae humanae.* Leyden, 1678. 8 volumes

Desing, Anselmus (died 1773). *Index poeticus, exhibens compendio nomina propria, genealogiam, mythologiam, astrologiam, geographiam, et alia, ad eruditionem . . .* Amberg, N. A. Smaj, 1730; 3rd edition (Ingolstadt, Krüll, 1758)

Gesner, Johann Matthias (1691–1761). *Primae lineae isagoges in eruditionem universalem, nominatim philologiam, historiam in usum praelectionum ductae . . .* Göttingen and Leipzig, D. F. Rubler, 1756; 2nd edition in 2 volumes (Leipzig, C. Fritsch, 1774–75). 3rd edition (Göttingen, 1786)

Salomon, Bishop of Constance (d. 915). *Dictionarium Universale*
   Often called an encyclopaedia but, in fact, a glossary

Latin American

Fonseca, Simões da. *Novo diccionário enciclopédico illustrado da lingua portugueza.* Rio de Janeiro, 1926

Ramirez, J. *Diccionario enciclopédico.* Mexico City, 1855

Séguier, Jayme de. *Diccionário prático illustrado: novo diccionário enciclopédico luso-brasileiro.* Rio de Janeiro, 1910
   Frequent reprints and new editions

Zerolo, Elias. *Diccionario enciclopédico de la lengua castellana.* Paris, Garnier, 1895. 2 volumes

Latvian

Latvju enciklopēdija. Stockholm, Trīs Zvaigznes, 1950–53. 3 volumes (Supplement, 1962)
   Edited by Arveds Švābe

Latviešu konversācijas vārdnīca. Riga, A. Gulbis, 1927–40. Volumes 1–21 (not completed)
   Edited by Arveds Švābe, Alexandrs Būmanis, and Kārlis Dišlers

Latvju mazā enciklopēdija. Riga, 'Gramatu Draugs', 1936
   Edited by Alfreds Bīlmanis and Sigurds Melnalksnis

Lithuanian

Lietuviškoji enciklopedija. Kaunas, Leidéjas 'Spaudos Fondas', 1931–44. Volumes 1–10 (not completed)
   Edited by Valcovas Biržiška

Lietuvių enciklopedija. Boston, Mass., Lietuvių Enciklopedijos Leidykla, 1953–
   Volume 1– (in progress)
   Edited by Vaclovas Biržiška and partly based on his *Lietuviskoji enciklopedija*

New Zealand

The New Zealand junior encyclopaedia. Wellington, N.Z., Educational Foundation (Northern) Publications, 1962. 3 volumes
Edited by T. J. Dwyer

The Oxford New Zealand encyclopaedia. Oxford University Press, 1964
Edited by John Pascoe and Laura E. Salt. A companion volume to the *Oxford junior encyclopaedia*

Polish

Encyklopedja powszechna Ultima Thule. Warsaw, Wydawnictwo Ultima Thule, 1930–38. Volumes 1–9 (A–Spa)
Edited by Stanisław Fr. Michalski. Not completed

Gloger, Z. *Encyklopedia staropolska ilustrowana.* Warsaw, 1903. 3 volumes
New edition in 2 volumes (Warsaw, 1939)

Grande encyclopédie universelle polonaise. Warsaw, PWN, 1962. 10 volumes

Ilustrowana encyklopedia Trzaski, Everta i Michalskiego. Warsaw, Trzaska, 1925–1928. 5 volumes
Edited by Stanisław Lam. Supplement: *Encyklopedia XX wieku*, 1938

Podręczna encyklopedja powszechna: encyclopédie universelle. Paris, 1955
Edited by Stanisław Lam

Wielka ilustrowana encyklopedja powszechna. Cracow, 1930–38. 22 volumes

Portuguese

Encyclopedia e diccionario internacional, organizado e redigido com a collaboração de distinctos homens de sciencia e de lettras brasileiros e portuguezes. Lisbon, 1919. 20 volumes
Edited by W. H. Jackson

Encyclopedia portugueza illustrada: diccionario universal . . . Porto, Lemos, 1910. 11 volumes
Edited by Maximiano Lemos. Previously published in parts over a number of years

Pinheiro Chagas, Manuel (1842–95). *Diccionario popular: historico, geographico mythologico, biographico, artistico, bibliographico e litterario.* Lisbon, Lalleman frères, 1876–90. 16 volumes

Rumanian

Adamescu, Gh. *and* Candrea, A. *Dictionarul enciclopedic ilustrat.* Bucarest, 1932. 2 volumes

Russian

Berezin, Ilya Nikolaievich (1819–95). *Russkii entsiklopedicheskii slovar'.* St Petersburg, 1873–79. 16 volumes

Spanish

Diccionario enciclopédico ilustrado. Barcelona, Sopena, 1954. 3 volumes

Diccionario Salvat: enciclopédico popular ilustrado . . . Barcelona, Salvat, 1907–13. 9 volumes, + an Appendix
2nd edition in 12 volumes (1934–46); 3rd in 12 volumes (1955); 11th in 12 volumes (1964)

Enciclopedia ilustrada Seguí: diccionario universal con todas las voces y locuciones usadas en España y en la América latina. Barcelona, Seguí, 1907–28. Volumes 1–12 (A–Ll)
Issued in parts. A supplement, *Gran diccionario francés-español por Enrique Diaz-Retg*, was also issued. The encyclopaedia was not completed

Enciclopedia popular de las novedades: diccionario de la conversación y la lectura. Madrid, 1859–60. Volumes 1–2 (A–Gen)
'Redactado bajo la direccion de D. M. M. y G.' The encyclopedia was not completed

Gillman, F. *Enciclopedia popular ilustrada de ciencias y artes, formada con arreglo á la Enciclopedia iconográfica y el Conversations Lexicon de Alemania.* Madrid, Rubiños, 1882–86. 9 volumes

Larousse universal: diccionario enciclopédico en tres volúmenes. Adaptación hispano americana del Nouveau Larousse universel, dirigido por Claude y Paul Augé. Publicado baja la dirección de Miguel de Toro y Gisbert. Paris, Larousse, 1958. 3 volumes

Lexis: enciclopedia de las artes, ciencias, oficios, juegos y deportes, y diccionario de la lengua. Barcelona, Seix, 1952–55. 6 volumes

Universitas: enciclopedia de iniciación cultural. Barcelona, Salvat Editores, 1944–46. 20 volumes
Systematically arranged. Index in volume 20

Terreros y Pando, Esteban (1707–82). *Diccionario castellano, con las voces de ciencias y artes y sus correspondientes en las tres lenguas, francesa, latina é italiana.* Madrid, Impr. de la viuda de Ibarra, 1786–93. 4 volumes
Edited by Francisco Meseguer y Arrufat and Miguel de Manuel y Rodriguez

Swedish

Åhlén och Söners uppslagsbok: illustrerad konversationslexikon. Stockholm, Åhlen, 1931–34. 13 volumes. Edited by Helge Lindberg. Also known as *Hemmets Konversationslexicon*

Gjörwell, C. C. *Encyclopedie; eller franzyskt och svenskt real- och nominal-lexicon.* Stockholm, 1777

Kunskapens bok: illustrerade uppslagsverk. Stockholm, 1955. 9 volumes (last two, Index)

Svenskt Konversations-Lexicon. Stockholm, 1845–52. 4 volumes

Thai

Saranukromthai: rajabanditsathan. Bangkok, Runbruanbtham Publishing Co. 1956– (in progress).

INDEX OF NAMES, TITLES AND SUB-TITLES

A–Z̧ encyklopedia popularno PWN, 217
A.N̂.S.I.E., 214
Aalheim, T., 201
Abi Ghuddah, Ibn, 72
About encyclopaedias, 228
Académie des Sciences, 114–19, 125–26, 128, 132
Académie Française, 92–94, 95, 96
Acsádi, I., 194
Adamescu, Gh., 312
Adams, C. K., 193
Adelard of Bath, 54, 59, 60
Adelung, J. C., 307
Adler, A., 47
Aepitomae omnis philosophiae, 75
Åhlen och Söners uppslagsbok, 313
d'Ailly, P., 70
Aiton's Encyclopedia, 298
Akademische Propädeutik, 308
Albericus, 28, 54
Albertus Magnus, 68
Alcuin, 36
d'Alembert, J. le R., 116, 119, 121–22, 125–26, 132–36
Alexander Romances, The, 62
Alfonso X, 57
Algemeen nootwendig woordenboek, 306
Algemeene nederlandsche encyclopedie, 195
Algemeine nederlandse systematisch ingerichte encyclopedie, 214
Algemene Winkler Prins encyclopedie, 195
'Allam, Muhammad Mahdi, 206
Allamand, J. N. S., 107
Allbuch, 171
Allers illustrerede konversationsleksikon, 195
Alletz, P.-A., 107
Allgemeine
  deutsche Biographie, 225
  deutsche Real-Encyclopädie, 162–63
  Encyclopädie der Wissenschaften und Künste, 179–81, 296
  Encyklopädie und Methodologie der Wissenschaften, 309
  Hand-Encyclopädie, illustration Realencyclopädie, 307
Allgemeines
  Conversations-Taschen-Lexikon, 221, 307
  deutsches Conversations-Lexikon, 164
  deutsches encyklopädisches Handwörterbuch, 307

deutsches Sach-Wörterbuch, 307
  historisches Lexikon, 101, 102
  Lexicon der Künste und Wissenschaften, 102
  Real-Handwörterbuch, 307
  Real-Wörterbuch, 110
Allgemeinnütziges Geschicht- und Staaten-Wörterbuch, 304
Almqvist & Wiksell, 216
Alsted, J. H., 85–86
Alte und neue musikalische Bibliothek, 223
Ambrose, St, 59
American
  annual cyclopedia and register, 187–88
  cyclopaedia, The, 187–88
  dictionary of the English language, 183
  educator encyclopedia, 298
  family encyclopedia, 301
  international encyclopedia, 302
  Oxford encyclopaedia, 298
  peoples encyclopedia, The, 298
American Library Association, 227, 228
Amundsen, L., 208
An-ch'i, Yü, 86
Anatomia ingeniorum et scientiarum, 84–85
Anatomy of melancholy, 20
Anaxagoras, 68
Ancona's Dictionnaire des miniaturistes, 225
Angelo, Michel, 69
Anglo-American
  cyclopedia, The, 298
  encyclopedia and dictionary, 300
Annales quos scripsit . . . at-Tabari, 303
Annandale, C., 305
Anselm, St, 52
Ansley, C. F., 209
d'Antin, Louis, duc, 116
Apacius, J., 87
Apáczai Cseri, J., 87
Apparatus eruditionis, 88
Appian, 79
Appleton's annual cyclopedia and register, 187–88
Apuleius, 270n
Aquinas, St Thomas, 65
Arendt, R., 167
d'Argenson, le comte, 120, 121, 124
Aristophanes, 266
Aristotle, 22, 31–32, 67, 68
Armao, E., 98n
Armitage, J., vii

315

Artes, 24–25
Aschehougs konversations-leksikon, 201
Asson, Dr, 310
Athenaeum kézi lexikona, Az, 194
Augé, J. C., 190–91, 313
Augé, P., 191, 313
Augustine, St, 32–34, 44, 49, 52, 68, 77
Aurelianus, Caelius, 34
Austin's new encyclopedia, 299
Australian encyclopedia, The, 225
Australian junior encyclopedia, 303
Avale, C., 310
Averroes, 68
Avicenna, 68

Babbage, C., 235
Bacon, F., 82–84, 115, 124, 238, 245, 253, 268–77
Baird, S. F., 187
Baker's Biographia dramatica, 225
Baker's Biographical dictionary of musicians, 225
Baldensperger, F., 197
Baldwin, J. M., 220
Balfour, E. G., 225
Bandini, D. & L., 70–72
Barnhart, C. L., 218
Barratt, T. J., 196
Barrett, C. L., 303
Barrow, J., 105
Bartholomaeus Anglicus, 57–59, 60, 69
Baruch, B., 152
Basic everyday encyclopedia, 298
Basler Lexikon, 102–03
Basnage de Beauval, H., 95, 98
Bastard, comte Auguste de, 55
Bateson, F. W., 113
Bayle, P., 89, 94–97, 101, 105–07, 115
Baynes, T. S., 144
Bazzarini, A., 310
Beach, F. C., 184
Beardsley, A., 131
Beaumont, C. de, 124
Beauvais, Vincent of, 52, 60–63, 68
Beck, J. C., 103
Beckmanns Neues Weltlexikon, 307
Bede, 52
Beer, R., 35
Bekker, I., 46
Belcazer, V., 58
Bell, A., 138–41, *illustration*
Bell, C. M., 146
Benedict of Nursia, 30
Bentley, R., 262
Bequemes Correspondenz- und Conversations-Lexikon, 103
Bercheure (Berchorius), P., 58, 69, 76
Berei, A., 216

Berezin, I. N., 312
Bergelin, S.-E. S., 193
Bernis, l'abbé de, 129
Berryer, N. R., 120–21, 128
Bersuire, P., 58, 69, 76
Bertelsmann-Lexikon, Das, 307
Berthelot, A., 194
Berthier, G.-F., 124
Besselaer, J. J. van den, 30*n*, 31
Bethe, E., 310
Bettesworth, J., 112
Beuchot, A. J. Q., 97
Bevans, M., 300
Beyerlinck, L., 311
Bibliographisches Institut, Leipzig, 198, 208
Biblioteca universale sacro-profano, 98
Bienemann, F., 168
Bilder-Atlas, 168
Bilder-Atlas zum Conversationslexikon, 166, 187
Bilder-Conversations-Lexikon, 165
Billy, A., 137
Bīlmanis, A., 311
Binder, W., 307
Binzer, A., 182
Biographia dramatica, 225
Biographie universelle, 225
Biographie universelle des musiciens, 223
Biographisches Lexikon der hervorragenden Ärtzte, 225
Birch, T., 105
Biržiška, V., 311
Black, A. & C., 143–47, 304
Blanck, J., 197
Blangstrup, C., 196
Blom, E., 223
Boccabianca, G. M., 311
Boccaccio, 28*n*, 62
Boccardo, G., 310
Boeke, H. van der, 75
Boethius, 28, 30, 32, 34, 49, 68
Böhner, P., 80
Boissevain, U. Ph., 39
Bokor, J., 195
Bol'shaia entsiklopediia, 200
Bol'shaia sovetskaia entsiklopediia, 206
Bonilla y San Martín, A., 78
Bonnerot, J., 307
Bonniers Folklexikon, 206
Bonniers Konversations lexikon, 205–06
Book of knowledge, The, 298
Book of the moralities of great natural things, 67
Booklist and subscription books bulletin, The, 227, 228
Boor, C. de, 39
Bossuet, J. B., 93
Bostock, J., 304
Bostwick, A. E., 299

Boswell, H., 112
Bosworth, N., 176
Boüard, M. de, 67n, 81
Boumphrey, G., 212
Boyer, A., 190
Boyle, A., 202
Brabner, J. H. F., 305
Brack, W., 74
Braddy, N., 299
Brasch, M., 169
Braulio, Bishop, 33
Braun, H., 160
Brethren of Purity, The, 41–42
Brewster, Sir D., 175–76
Briasson, C., 117, 118, 131, 132, 133
Bridgwater, W., 209, 299
Britannica
  book of the year, 149–50, 153–54
  junior, 150, 153
  year book, 150
British Academy, 26
British
  cyclopaedia of arts and sciences, The, 136
  encyclopaedia, The, 175
  encyclopaedia of medical practice, 222
  universities encyclopaedia, 189
Brockelmann, C., 38
Brockhaus, A. E., 170
Brockhaus, D. A. F., 156–73
Brockhaus, Friedrich, 162
Brockhaus, Fritz, 170
Brockhaus, F. A., 156–73, 229
Brockhaus, Hans, 170
Brockhaus, Heinrich, 163
Brockhaus, Heinrich Eduard, 173
Brockhaus, 5, 7, 16, 17, 156–74, 184, 187, 192, 199, *illustration*
Brockhaus & Efron, 170, 172, 194
Broissinière, D. de J., 79, 86–87
Brosseus, Petrus, 31
Brothers of Purity, The, 41–42
Browne, J., 143
Brunet, J. C., 134
Brünner, E. C. G., 306
Buch de natur, 59
Buddeus, J. F., 89, 101
Buel, J. W., 299
Buffereau, F., 63
Buffier, C., 98, 115
Buffon, G. L. L., comte de, 120, 133
Bulgarian Academy of Sciences, 225, 305
Būmanis, A., 311
Burgos, Fr V. de, 58
Burke, E., 109
Burma Translation Society, 214
Burney, Dr C., 104, 109, 110
Buron, E. J. P., 70
Burrowes, A. D., 304
Burton, R., 20

Büsch, J. G., 307
Bustani, Butrus al-, 193
Bustani, Fuad Aram al-, 214
Buttimer, C. H., 49
Buttner-Wobst, I., 39
Buxtorff, A. J., 103
Buys, Egbert, 306
Byron, Lord, 138

Cabeen, D. C., 113
Cabinet encyclopaedia, The, 182–83
Cáceres, F. de, 73, 88
Caelius Aurelianus, 34
Caesalpinus, 256
Caesar, Julius, 244, 248
Calovius (Calan), A., 87
Campe, J. H., 160
Cañal, C., 34n
Candrea, A., 312
Cantimpré, Thomas of, 59–60
Capella, Martianus Minneus Felix, 27–28, 44, 73
Cappelli, L. M., 80
Carlquist, G., 208
Carlsson, J., 208
Carlyle, T., 174
Carmody, F. J., 65
Carnap, R., 19
Caroillon de Vandeul, A.-F. N., 133, 136
Cassell's Concise cyclopaedia, 194
Cassell's Encyclopaedia of general information, 304
Cassell's Storehouse of general information, 304
Cassiodorus, Flavius Magnus Aurelius, 28–31, 49
Catherine II, 129, 132, 133
Catholic encyclopedia, 218
Cato, Marcus Porcius, 23
Cavalcanti, G., 63
Caxton, W., 63
Caxton Encyclopaedia, 304
Caxton World of knowledge, 304
Celsus, Aulus Cornelius, 24–25
Centro di Studi Filosofici di Gallarate, 220
Century book of facts, 301
Century dictionary and cyclopedia, 299
Cesckloslovenska Akademie Věd Encyklopedický Institut, 216
Ceylon Department of Cultural Affairs, 217
Chabaille, P., 65
Chalcidius, 68
Chambers, E., 103–04, 108–09, 112, 115–18, 121
Chambers, W. & R., 188–89
Chambers's Encyclopaedia, 188–89

Chambers's Encyclopaedia world survey, 189
Champion, A.-A., 117
Chang Hua, 26
Chang Huang, 79
Chao-ch'un, Tai, 197
Charles V, 58
Chauffepié, J. G. de, 106
Chauvin, E., 95
Ch'ên, Yang, 197
Ch'ên Jen-hsi, 86
Ch'ên Wei, 113
Ch'ên Yao-wen, 78–79
Ch'eng, Kao, 46
Chêng Ch'iao, 46
Ch'êng-lieh, Wang, 113
Chénier, A. de, 136n
Cherwell, Lord, 151
Chevalier, M., 307
Chevigny, Sieur de, 100–01, 107
Ch'i, Wang, 65, 86
Ch'i ming chi shu, 113
Chi tsuan yü an hai, 57
Chia-pin, Wang, 57
Chiao, Chêng, 46
Chien, Hsü, 35
Ch'ien ch'io chü lei shu, 86
Ch'ien Lung, The Emperor, 66
Child's first encyclopaedia in colour, 304
Children's Britannica, 155
Children's encyclopaedia, The, 15, 298
Chin hsiu wan hua ku, 57
Ch'in Ting, 36
Chin Tsao, Liu, 197
Ch'ing ch'ao hsü wên hsien t'ung k'ao, 66,
　　197
Ch'ing chao t'ung chih, 46
Ch'ing chao t'ung tien, 36
Ching chuan I I, 113
Chisholm, H., 146–47, 150
Chitwood, J. R., 155
Chiu t'ung, 36
Chiu tung ch'uan shu, 36
Chomel, N., 115, 116
Christian, Abbot of St Jacob, 52
Ch'u hsüeh chi, 35
Ch'uan, K'ung, 36
Chü'i, Po, 36
Chung-yu, T'ang, 57
Cicero, 65, 68
Clark, S., 108
Clarke, J., 145
Clement XIII, Pope, 127
Cobbett, W. W., 224
Cochin, C.-N., 124
Coetlogon, Chevalier D. de, 106
Coggeshall, Ralph de, 56
Cohn, T., xi, *illustration*
Colbert, J. B., 114
Colby, F. M., 200–01
Coleridge, S. T., 20, 179, 229–95, 309

Coleridge, Mrs H. N. (Sarah), 237
Collectanea rerum memorabilium, 26, 28
Colledge, W. A., 233
Collier, J., 97
Collier's encyclopedia, 213
Colonna, 62
Columbia encyclopaedia, The, 209, 228, 299
Columbia Viking desk encyclopaedia, 299
Columbus, Christopher, 70, 249–50
Comenius, J. A., 85
Comité de l'Encyclopédie française, 209
Commentariorum urbanorum libri xxxviii,
　　77
Compact encyclopedia, The, 304
Comparison of encyclopaedias, 228
*Compendious dictionary of the English lan-
　　guage, A*, 183
Compendium philosophiae, 67
Complete dictionary of arts and sciences, The,
　　107–08
Complete reference handbook, 299
Compton, F., 205
Compton yearbook, The, 205
Compton's Pictured encyclopedia, 205
Conches, William de, 22
Concise Bulgarian encyclopedia, 225, 305
Concise encyclopedia, The, 300
Condillac, E. B. de M. de, 278
Condorcet, M. J. A. N. C., marquis de,
　　115–16, 136, 278
Congrès Mondial de la Documentation
　　Universelle, 228
Conrad, J., 221
Constable, A., 141–43, 229
Constantine VII (Constantine Porphyro-
　　genitus), 38–39
Constantino, Michael, 45–46
Copeland, L., 299
Copernicus, 28n
Coplestone, F., 80
Corbichon, J., 58, 65
Corneille, T., 95–96, 115, 116
Cornish, G. A., 299
Coronelli, V. M., 98
Cortés y Góngora, L., 35
Couch, W. T., 298
Coulomb, C. A. de, 252n
Cowles comprehensive encyclopedia, 302
Cox, R., 143
Cramer, W., 167
Crane, R. S., 113
Crawford, J. P. W., 74
'Creutzberg, A.', 99
Croce, N., 73
Croker, T. H., 108
Cseri, J. A., 87
Cubas, A. G., 226
Cultural library, 301
Cunningham, A., 305
Curie, Mme, 152

Curieuses Natur-, Kunst- . . . und Handlungslexikon, 100
Cursus philosophici encyclopaedia, 85
Curtis, S. & T., 179, 182, 231–37
Cuvier, L. C. F. D., 254
Cyclopaedia (E. Chambers), 103–04, 108–109, 112, 116–18
Cyclopaedia of India, 225
Cyclopaedic survey of chamber music, 224

Dahl, J., 201
Daily Mail, 145
Daily Mail year book, 196
Da'irat al-Maarif, 193, 206, 214
Damiens, R.-F., 126
Dana, C. A., 187
Dante, 63, 76
Dār al-kutab al-Misrāya, 66
Daremberg, C. V., 25, 42, 222
Daubenton, L. J. M., 120, 136
ad-Dauwānī, 74
David, M.-A., 118
Davy, Sir H., 257, 287
De artibus, 78
De causis corruptarum artium, 78
De chorographia, 27
De diversis artibus, 50–51
De disciplinis, 77–78
De doctrina christiana, 32–33
De expetendis, 75–76
De l'esprit, 126–27
De l'esprit des loix, 120
De natura rerum, 59–60
De naturis rerum, 54–55
De omnifaria doctrina, 45–46
De originibus rerum libellus, 69
De proprietatibus rerum, 57–59, 69
De Puy, W. H., 303
De studio legendi, 47–49
De tradendis disciplinis, 78
De universo, 36–37
De viris claris virtute aut vitio, 72
Delfino, D., 73, 79, 88
Delineatio sapientiae universalis, 86
Delisle, L., 50
Demarchi, G., 310
Dennert, E., 200
Derenbourg, H., 194
Des arts de construire les caractères, 115
Descartes, R., 119
Descriptio totius urbis, 56–57
Description et perfection des arts et métiers, 114–16, 128, 132
Desing, A., 311
Desmaizeaux, P., 96–97
Despréaux, N. B., 93
Detlefsen, D., 26
Deutsch-amerikanisches Conversations-Lexicon, 192–93

Deutsche
    Encyklopädie (Köster & Roos), 110
    Encyklopädie (Grunow), 308
    Polyhistor, Der, 308
    Revue der Gegenwart, 168
Deutsches Bildwörterbuch für Jedermann, 172
Deutsches Kolonial-Lexikon, 225–26
Dewey, J., 152
Diaconovich, C., 195
Diaconus, Paulus, 26
Díaz-Plaja, G., 197
Diaz-Retg, E., 313
Diccionario
    . . . de El Salvador, 226
    enciclopédico, 311
    enciclopédico hispano-americano, 195
    enciclopédico ilustrado, 313
    enciclopédico U.T.E.H.A., 213
    geográfico . . . de Cuba, 226
    geográfico . . . de los Estados Unidos Mexicanos, 226
    prático illustrado, 311
    Salvat, 313
Dick, A., 28
Dictionarium
    historicum, 89
    historicum, geographicum et poeticum, 79, 87, 89
    polygraphicum, 105
    propriorum nominum, 79
    universale, 311
Dictionarul enciclopedic ilustrat, 312
Dictionary of
    American biography, 225
    applied physics, 221
    arts and sciences (Nicholson), 175
    arts and sciences, A (Gregory), 175
    arts, sciences and literature, 178
    Christ and the Gospels, A, 219
    gardening, 224
    music and musicians, 223
    national biography, 225
    philosophy and psychology, 220
    political economy, 220–21
    the Apostolic Church, 219
    the Bible, A, 219
    the sciences and arts, 176
    United States history, 299
Dictionnaire
    complet de la langue française, 190
    d'archéologie chrétienne, 219
    de biographie française, 225
    de la conversation et de la lecture, 184–85
    de la langue française, 190, 191
    de droit canonique, 219
    d'histoire et de géographie ecclésiastiques, 219
    de la Bible, 219
    de la spiritualité, 219
    de théologie catholique, 219
    de Trévoux, 95, 98–99, 115–16, 124–25

Dictionnaire—contd.
  des antiquités grecques et romaines, 222
  des arts et des sciences, 95–96, 116
  des miniaturistes, 225
  domestique portatif, 107
  historique, 107
  historique et critique, 96–97
  historique-portatif, 107
  oeconomique, 115, 116
  théologique, historique, poétique, cosmo-graphique . . ., 79, 87
  universel des arts et des sciences, 17, 94–95, 116
  universel françois et latin, 95, 98–99, 115–16
  universel géographique et historique, 96
Didascalicon, 47–49, 74
Diderot, D., 51, 84, 104, 110, 114–38, 208, 229
Diderot, M.-A., 125, 133, 136
Didot, A. F., 184–85
Dieckmann, H., 137
Dieterici, F. H., 42
Diodati, O., 127
Disciplinae, 27–28
Disciplinarum libri IX, 23, 28
Dišlers, K., 311
Dizionario
  delle arti e dei mestieri, 310
  enciclopedico delle scienze, lettere ed arti, 310
  enciclopedico italiano, 214
  enciclopedico Sansoni, 310
  generale di scienze, lettere . . ., 310
  universale delle arti e delle scienze, 103
  universale di scienze, lettere ed arti, 310
Dodwell, C. R., 51
Dolce, L., 73
Dole, N. H., 301
Dolenský, A., 207
Dolphin, A. E., 154
Dormándi, L., 310
Doubleday's encyclopedia, 299
Dougall, J., 304
Dreyfus, F. C., 194
Du Cerceau, J. A., 115
Duchesne, A., 56
Duckett, W. D., 185
Duden pictorial encyclopaedia, 208
Dudley, E., 297
Dulles, J. F., 152
Dunham, F., 301
Dunton, J., 96
Durand, L., 118, 119n, 121
Dutt, R. P., 151
Dwyer, T. J., 312
Dyche, T., 117, 120, 121

ENSIE, 211–12
Edinburgh encyclopaedia, The, 175–76

Eerste nederlandse systematisch ingerichte encyclopedie, 211–12
Eesti entsüklopeedia, 306
Eesti üleüldise teaduse raamat ehk encyklo-pädia, 200
Egyetemes magyar encyclopaediá, 189
Eisler, R., 220
Elémens des connoissances humaines, Les, 107
Eleutheroudaké enkyklopaidikon leksikon, 207
Elucidarium carminum et historiarum, 75
Elvin, A., 205
Enciclopaediae praemessum, 86
Enciclopedia
  Barsa, 155
  cattolica, 218–19
  Curcio, 310
  dell'arte antica, classica e orientale, 222
  dello spettacolo, 224
  filosofica, 220
  Hoepli, 310
  italiana, 207
  labor, 215–16
  larense, 226
  moderna, 310
  Pomba, 310
  popular de las novedades, 313
  popular ilustrada de ciencias y artes, 313
  Română, 195
  Românĭei, 210–11
  universal ilustrada europeo-americana, 201
  universale dell'arte, 222
  yucatense, 226
Enciklopedičeski rečnik, 195
Enciklopedija Jugoslavije, 214
Enciklopedija leksikografskoy Zavoda, 214
Encyclopaedia, septem tomis distincta, 85–86
Encyclopaedia, seu Orbis disciplinarum, 80
Encyclopaedia/Encyclopedia
  Americana, 184
  Britannica, 17, 104, 106, 138–56, 174, 178–79, 184, 189, 199, 229, *illustration*
  Burmanica, 214
  Canadiana, 225
  e diccionario internacional, 312
  Edinensis, 178, 183
  Hebraica, 213
  international, 299
  Judaica, 220
  metropolitana, 20, 178–83, 229–95
  of Canada, The, 225
  of chemical technology, 222
  of Islam, 206, 220
  of religion and ethics, 219
  of sports and games, 224
  of the social sciences, 221
  of world art, 222
  portugueza illustrada, 312
  Perthensis, 177–78
  year book, 299
Encyclopaedias disciplinarum realium ideae, 87

Encyclopaedic dictionary, 304
*Encyclopaedic dictionary of American refer-
ence*, 299
Encyclopaedic dictionary of physics, 221
Encyclopaedie van Nederlandsch-Indië, 226
Encyclopedie (Gjörwell), 313
Encyclopédie
  (de Diderot), 84, 104, 107–08, 110,
   114–38, 141n, 208, 229
  balkanique permanente, 211
  belge, 225
  coloniale et maritime, 226
  de famille, 185
  de la musique, 224
  de la Pléiade, 214–15
  de pensées, 107
  des beaux esprits, 87–88
  des sciences ecclésiastiques, 219
  des sciences mathématiques, 221
  du jeune âge, 190
  française, 209–10
  Grolier, 306
  internationale Focus, 306
  Larousse des enfants, 192
  méthodique, 110–12, 135, 200, 231
  Péreire, 307
  universelle, 307
  universelle du XXe siècle, 202
Encyklopädie
  (v. Klügel), 110
  *der historischen, philosophischen und mathe-
matischen Wissenschaften*, 307
  der mathematischen Wissenschaften, 221
*Encyklopädische Darstellung der neueren
Zeit*, 168
*Encyklopädisches Handwörterbuch für Wissen-
schaft und Leben*, 308
Encyklopädisches Wörterbuch, 182
Encyklopedia staropolska ilustrowana, 312
Encyklopedia XX wieku, 312
Encyklopedja powszechna, 188
Encyklopedia powszechna Ultima Thule,
  312
Endres, J., 52
Engelhardt, C. M., 55
Engelmann, W., 42
Engelstoft, P., 195
English encyclopaedia, 185
Enkuklopaideia de Politis, 194
Enquire within upon everything, 196
Ensiklopedia Indonesia, 213–14
Entsiklopedicheskii slovar', 195, 213
Entsiklopedicheskogo leksikona, 186
*Enzyklopädie der gesammten musikalisches
Wissenschaften*, 224
Enzyklopädie der technischen Chemie, 222
Erasmus, 77
*Erh shih ssu shih chiu t'ung chêng tien lei yao
ho pien*, 197
Ersch, J. S., 161, 179–80, 296
  Y

Ervine, St J., 151
Eschenburg, J. J., 112
Espasa, the, 201
Espe, K. A., 165–66
l'Esprit de l'Encyclopédie, 133
Essais d'un Dictionnaire universel, 94
Estienne, C., 79, 87, 89
Etrennes des esprits forts, 127
Etymologiarum libri XX, 33
Euclid, 39
Eurymedon, 22
Evangelisches Kirchenlexikon, 219
Everybody's cyclopedia, 303
Everybody's encyclopedia, 299
Everyday reference book, 299
Everyman encyclopaedia, 202
Excerpta historica, 39
Excerpta Peiresciana, 39
Exley, T., 176
Eyssenhardt, F., 28
Ezhegodnik Bol'shoi sovetskoi entsiklopedii,
  206

Fabricius, J. A., 45, 90
Facts, 299
Falconetti, A. F., 310
Fallows, S., 300
al-Fandi, Muhammad Thabet, 206
Fang, Li, 40–41
Fant, C., 63
Farid Wajdi, M., 206
Farinator, M., 67
Farrington, B., 82
Fassadoni, M., 310
Fejér, G., 100
Felice, F. B. de, 133
Fellowes, B., 233
Fêng-chieh, Wang, 39
Fêng-tsao, Lu, 113
Fenner, R., 230–37
al-Fergani, 68
Ferrarius, P., 89
Festus, Sextus Pompeius, 26
Fétis, F.-J., 223
Findlater, A., 188, 193
Finley, J. H., 205
Flaccus, Marcus Verrius, 26
Flores, M. H., 155
Floridum, 49–50
Florilegium, 84
Flörke, F. J. & H. G., 108
Flügel, G., 303
Focus uppslagsbok, 216
Fons memorabilium universi, 70–72
Fonseca, S. da, 311
Fontenelle, B. le B. de, 116
Ford, C. A. & G. S., 205
Foreman, J. B., 305
Formey, J. H. S., 126

Fornerius, G., 31
Foster, E. D., 202
Foundations of the unity of science, 19
Fox, C. J., 109
Franke, C. W., 156–57, 161
Franklin kézi lexikona, A, 310
Franz, A., 31
Frauenzimmer-Lexikon, 156
Frederick II, 129, 132
Fréron, E.-C., 125
Freud, S., 152
Frick, J., 90
Friederich, W. P., 197
Fromageot, l'abbé, 135
Fulgentius Planciades, Fabius, 27
Funk & Wagnalls New standard encyclopedia, 299
Funk & Wagnalls Standard reference encyclopedia, 299
Furetière, A., 17, 92–95, 98, 116

Galletti, A., 198
Gallucci, G. P., 75
Gāmi' al 'ulum, 54
García, M. A., 226
Garcia Cubas, A., 226
Garetius, J., 31
Garvin, J. L., 152
Garzanti, Enciclopedia, 311
Gathy's Musikalisches Conversationslexikon, 224
Gautier de Metz, 63
Geddie, W., 188
Gegenwart, Die, 166, 168
Geillustreerde encyclopaedie, 192
Geissler, C. A., 296
Gemeinnütziges Lexikon, 309
Gemüths Vergnügendes historisches Handbuch, 105–06
General
　Conversations-Lexicon, 309
　dictionary, historical and critical, A, 105
　encyclopedias in print, 228
Gentile, G., 207
Geoffrin, Mme M.-T., 128
Georgiev, V., 305
Gerber, E. L., 223
Gervase of Tilbury, 56–57
Gesner, J. M., 256, 311
Geyer, B., 80
al-Ghazzālī, 73
Giamboni, B., 65
Gibbon, E., 104, 109
Gilbert, W., 268
Gillam, S., vii
Gillen, O., 56
Gillet, H. O., 303
Gillman, F., 313
Gillman, J., 232

Gilson, E., 80
Gjörwell, C. C., 313
Glanville, Bartholomew de, 57
Glazebrook, Sir R., 221–22
Gleig, G., 141
Globe encyclopaedia, The, 188
Globe encyclopaedia of universal information, The, 193
Gloger, Z., 313
Glossaria latina, 26
Goedeke, K., 113, 197
Goeje, Michiel J. de, 38, 303
Golden
　book encyclopedia, 299
　home and high school encyclopedia, 299
　treasury of knowledge, 300
Golding, A., 27n
Goldschmidt, A., 37
Goldsmith, O., 103, 104, 109
Góngora, L. Cortés y, 35
Good, J. M., 176–77
Gooding, L. M., 155
Goodrich, C. A., 183
Goodwin, R. M., vii
Gordon, D. H., 130
Gorell, Lord, 305
Gossuin, 63
Gottschall, R. von, 168
Gottsched, J. C., 97, 105, 160
Gove, P. B., 183
Gower, J., 35
Grabmann, M., 80
Granat's encyclopedia, 195
Grand
　dictionnaire historique, Le, 88–89
　dictionnaire universel du XIXe siècle, 190
　Larousse encyclopédique, 191
　mémento encyclopédique, 191
　vocabulaire français, 132
Grande
　e general estoria, 57
　enciclopedia popolare Sonzogno, 310
　enciclopédia portuguesa e brasileira, 209
　encyclopédie, La, 194
　encyclopédie de la Belgique, 226
　encyclopédie universelle polonaise, 312
Great encyclopaedic dictionary, 304
Great instauration, The, 82–84
Greet, W. C., 218
Gregorii, J. G., 105–06
Gregory, G., 175, 176, 177
Gregory, O. G., 176–77
Gregory of Tours, 28n
Grente, G., 113
Gresham encyclopaedias, 305
Griffin, Messrs, vii, 236, 237
Griggs, E. L., 237
Grigson, G., 21
Grisellini, F., 310
Grolier encyclopedia, 299, 300, 302, 306

Groseclaude, P., 137
Grosse Brockhaus, Der, 170-71, 172, 173
Grosse Conversations-Lexikon, Der, 186
Grosses vollständiges Universal-Lexikon, 104-105
Grove, Sir G., 223
Gruber, J. G., 161, 179-80, 296
Grunow's encyclopedia, 308
Gua de Malves, l'abbé J.-P. de, 119
Gulielmus Pastregicus, 69
Gurlitt, W., 223
Gutenberg Konversationslexikon, 304
Guy, A., 38
Gyldendals leksikon, 208

Habbels Konversations-Lexikon, 308
Hadjdjī Khalīfa, 303
Hadley, A. T., 146
Hagar, G. J., 301, 303
Hagerups Illustrerede konversations leksikon, 195
Hai lu sui shih, 46
Hain, L., 161
Hammer-Purgstall, J., Freiherr von, 236
al-Ḥanafī, 77
Handbuch der Altertumswissenschaft, 223
Handbuch des Wissens, 170, 171
Handwörterbuch
    der Sozialwissenschaften, 221
    der Staatswissenschaften, 221
    der Wissenschaften und Künste, 175
Hansteen, C., 176
Harless, G. C., 45
Harmsworth encyclopaedia, The, 201
Harmsworth's universal encyclopaedia, 299
Harris, G. E., vii
Harris, J., 17, 51, 97, 99, 103, 115-16, 118, 121
Harris, W. T., 183
Hart, L. H., 228
Hasse, F. C., 161, 163, 165
Hastings, J., 219
Hatchett, C., 257
Haus-Lexikon, Das, 308
Hawthorne, J. G., 51
Haydn, J., 262
Heaton, W., 194
Heck, J. G., 166, 187
Heckscher, W. S., vii
Hedwig, J., 256
Heinsius, O. F., 308
Helm, R., 31
Helmarshausen, Roger of, 50-51
Helvétius, C.-A., 126-27
Hemmets Konversations-lexikon, 313
Hendelson, W. H., 302
Hendrie, R., 51
Henne-Am Rhyn, O., 309
Herders Konversations-Lexikon, 187, 199

Herman, K. A., 200
Herrad, Abbess of Hohenburg, 55-56
Herschel, Sir J., 235
Herzog, J. J., 219
Hesychius, 47
Hettiaratchi, D. E., 217
Hill, J., 103
Hippocrates, 52
Hirzel, H., 308
Histoire générale des dogmes et opinions philosophes, 133
Historia naturalis, 21, 25-26, 28
Historisch-biographisches Lexikon der Ton-künstler, 223
Historisch-politisch-juristisches Lexicon, 101
Historisches und critisches Wörterbuch, 97
Hobbes, T., 115
Hoefer's Nouvelle biographie générale, 225
Hoffmann, C. O., 109
Hoffmann, J. J., 89
d'Holbach, P. H. D., baron, 136
Holmesland, A., 201
Holst, B. P., 302
Holtzmann, M., 169
Home university encyclopedia, The, 300
Homer, 52
Honorius Inclusus, 51-53, 63
Hooke, R., 269, 273-74
Hooper, F. H., 146-53
Hooper, H. E., 145-51
Horace, 52, 262
Horder, Lord, 222
Hormayr, J., Freiherr von, 161
Horsley, E. M., 304
Hortus deliciarum, 55-56
Hottinger, C. G., 308
d'Houry, L., 117
Howard, G. S., 112
Hrabanus Maurus, Magnentius, 36-37, 50, 52
Hsi-min, Hua, 39
Hsiao chih lu, 113
Hsieh Wei-hsin, 65
Hsin chien chueh k'o ku chin yüan liu chih lun, 65
Hsin pien ku chin shih wên lei chü, 65
Hsü Chien, 35
Hsü kuang shi lei fu, 39
Hsü T'ien-lin, 59
Hsü t'ung chih, 36, 46
Hsü t'ung tien, 36
Hsü wên hsien t'ung k'ao, 36 65-66
Hsün ou-yang, 33
Hua, Chang, 26
Hua Hsi-min, 39
Huang, Chang, 79
Huang ch'ao hsü wên hsien t'ung k'ao, 197
Huang ch'ao san t'ung, 36
Huang ch'ao t'ung chih, 36, 46
Huang ch'ao t'ung tien, 36

Huang ch'ao wên hsien t'ung k'ao, 36, 66
Huang ian, 26
Huang Pao-chên, 39
Huang Shu-lin, 197
Hübner, J., 100, 105, 157
Hübscher, A., 173
Hugh of St Victor, 22, 32, 45, 47–49, 54, 74
Hugh of Strasbourg, 67–68
Huhn, E., 308
Hui yao, 37
Human interest library, The, 300
Hung, W., 41
Hunter, J., 252
Hunter, R., 304
Hutchinson's New twentieth century encyclopaedia, 304
Hutchinson's Technical and scientific encyclopaedia, 221
Huxley, Sir J., 152
al-Ḥwarizmī, 39–40, 54
Hyginus, 52

I lin hui k'ao, 86
I see all, 208
I shih chi shih, 197
I wên lei chü, 33
Ibn Qutaiba, 37–38
Iconographic encyclopaedia, 187
Idea methodica, 83
Idée générale des études, 100–01
Ife, A., 308
Ikhwān al-Safā', 41–42
Ikonographische Encyklopädie der Wissenschaften und Künste, 168
Illustrated
  encyclopedia, 300
  encyclopedia of knowledge, 300
  encyclopedia of the modern world, 301
  globe encyclopaedia, The, 193
  home library encyclopedia, 300
  world encyclopedia, 300
Illustreret konversations leksikon, 195
Illustreret norsk konversations-leksikon, 201
Illustriertes Haus- und Familien-Lexikon, 167
Illustrirtes Konversations-Lexikon, 308
Ilmer, K. C., vii
Ilustrowana encyklopedia Trzaski, Everta Michalskiego, 312
l'Image du monde, 63
Imago mundi (Honorius), 51–53
Imago mundi (d'Ailly), 70
Imperial dictionary of the English language, 305
Imperial encyclopaedia, The, 176
Index poeticus, 311
Information please almanack, 196
Ingerslew, C. F., 306

Inönü ansiklopedisi, 211
Institut de France, 114
Institutio oratoria, 21
Institutiones divinarum et humanarum lectionum, 28–31
International
  dictionary of the English language, 183
  encyclopaedia of unified science, 18–19
  reference work, 302
Iselin, J. C., 89, 102–03
Isidore, St, 27, 33–37, 50, 52, 54, 60, 68, 73
Istituto della Enciclopedia italiana, 207, 214, 222
Istituto per la Collaborazione Culturale, 220, 222
Ivigné-Broissinière, D. de, 79, 86–87

Jablonski, J. T., 102
Jackson, W. H., 312
Jackson, W. M., 146
Jahrbuch zum Conversations-Lexikon, 168
James, R., 118
Jameson, J. F., 299
Jaucourt, Chevalier Louis de, 128, 130
al-Jauzī, 54
Jedermanns Lexikon, 308
Jellicoe, Lord, 152
Jên Kuang, 46
Jên-hsi, Ch'ên, 86
Jenner, E., 141
Jerome, St, 34
Jewish encyclopedia, The, 220
John of Trevisa, 58
John the Scot, 49
John Whethamstede, 304
Johnson, A. J., 193
Johnson, Dr S., 104, 109
Johnson, W. M., 176
Jones, J. M., 203
Jones, L. W., 31
Jones, Sir W., 109
Jones, W. H. S., 26
Josephus, 52
Joyce, J., 176, 177
Juhász, V., 310
Juigné Broissinière, D. de, 79, 86–87
Julius Caesar, 244, 248
Julius Pollux, 309–10
Junior Britannica, 150, 153
Jussieu, A. de, 256

Kaiser, A., 165
Kalan (Kalau), A., 87
al-Kalkashandī, 66, 72
K'ang Hsi, The Emperor, 102
Kant, I., 112, 231
Kao Ch'eng, 46
Kasarov, L., 195

Kashf al-zunūn 'an asāmi 'l-kutub wa'l-furūn, 303
Katholisches Universal-Volkslexikon, 308
Kaufmanns-Lexikon, 105
Kay, J., *illustration*
al-Kazwīni al Shāfi'i, 53–54
Keller, G., 56
Kent, C. H. W., vii
Kent, F. L., vii
Khalīfa, Hādjdjī, 303
Khorshid, Ibrahim Zaki, 206
al-Khwarizmi, 39–40, 54
Kiepen-Lexikon, 308
Kingsley, C., 144
Kirchner, C., 308
Kirk-Othmer Encyclopedia of chemical technology, 222
Kitāb
  al-ma'ārif, 38
  al mudhis, 54
  al muqābasāt, 45
  al-sharāb 38
  al-shi'r, 38
  ta'wil al-ru'ya, 38
  'uyūn al-Akhbār, 38
Klapp, O., 113
Kleine
  Beckmann, Der, 307
  Brockhaus, Die, 170, 172
  Enzyklopädie, Die, 172
  Pöschl, Der, 308
Kleines Brockhaus'sche Conversations-Lexikon, 167
Kleis, R., 306
Klinckowstroem, C., Graf von, 296
Kluge Alphabet, Das, 308
Klügel, G. S., 110
Klussmann, R., 42
Knaurs Lexikon, 308
Knight, C., 185, 305
Knowledge, 305
Kober encyclopaedia, 189
Kogan, H., 146, 155
K'o-i, Liu, 197
Konversations-Lexikon (Herder), 187
Koo, W., 152
Körner, J., 113
Korth, J. W. D., 108–09
Kossarski, L., 109
Köster, H. M. G., 110
Közhasznu esmeretek Tára, 310
Kratka Bălgarska entsiklopedija, 225, 305
Krause, K. C. F. 161
Krleža, M., 214
Krogvig, A., 201
Krug, W. T., 161
Krünitz, J. G., 108–09
Ku chin ho pi shih lei pei yao, 65
Ku chin shih wên lei chü, 65
Ku chin yüan liu chih lun, 65

Kuang, Jên, 46
Kuang kuang shih lei fu, 39
Kuang po wu chih, 26
Kuang shih lei fu, 39
Kuang-t'ao, K'ung, 33
K'ung Ch'uan, 36
K'ung Kuang-t'ao, 33
Kung Mêng-jên, 102
Kunskapens bok, 313
Kürschner, J., 182
Kürschners Universal-Konversationslexikon, 308
Kurtzel, A., 166, 168
Kurzer Begriff aller Wissenschaften, 106
Kurzer Begriff menschlicher Fertigkeiten, 307
ibn Kutaiba, 37–38

La Fontaine, J. de, 93
La Laurencie, L. de, 224
La Pezuela y Lobo, J. de, 226
La Porte, l'abbé J., 133
La Rivière, B. de, 95
La Salle Extension University encyclopedia, 299
La Torre, A. de, 72–74, 79, 88
La Tour, M.-Q. de, 125
Labeo, Notker, 28
Labriolle, P. de, 42
Lactantius, 34
Ladies' dictionary, 96
Ladvocat, J. B., 107
Lalande, A., 220
Lam, S., 312
Lambert of St Omer, 9–50, 51
Lambrino, S., 42
Lamm, L. W., 299
Lang, J., 76, 84
Lang, P. L. F., 22
Lanson, G., 197
Lardner, D., 182–83, 235
Larousse, P. A., 171, 184, 189–92, 198, 199
Larousse
  du XXe siècle, 191
  mensuel illustré, 190–91
  pour tous, 191
  universal, 198, 313
  universel, 191, 198
Latini, B., 21, 63–65, 75
Latviešu konversācijas vārdnīca, 307
Latvju enciklopēdija, 311
Latvju mazā enciklopēdija, 311
Lavignac, A., 224
Law, M. D., 189
Lawätz, H. W., 296
Le Bouvier de Fontenelle, B., 96
Le Breton, A.-F., 117–20, 128–35, 229
Le Fanu, W. R., vii

Le Mangeor, Pierre, 61
Leander, Archbishop, 33
Legras, J., 137
Lehman, B. P., 63
Lehmann, E. H., 173
Lehrbuch der Wissenschaftskunde, 112
Leibnitz, G. G., 56
Leibniz, G. W., 28n
Leipziger Lexikon, 101
Leiste, C., 51
Leksikon rossiiskoi, 112
Lemos, M., 312
Lenin, 5, 195
Leo VI, The Emperor, 38
Léon de Saint-Jean, Fr, 86
Leonard-Stuart, C., 303
L'Escalopier, Charles, comte de, 51
Lessing, G. E., 51, 112
Lessona, M., 310
Lettres sur les aveugles à l'usage de ceux qui voyent, 120
Leupold, F. A., 157
Levaré, H. de, 119
Lewalter, E., 296
Lexicographi graeci, 310
*Lexicon
  rationale*, 95
  technicum (Harris), 17, 51, 97, 99, 103, 116, 118
  universale, 89
Lexikon A–Z, 308
Lexikon für Theologie und Kirche, 219
Lexis, 313
Li Fang, 40–41
*Liber
  de mirabilibus mundi*, 56–57
  de nuptiis Mercurii et Philologiae, 27
  excerptionum, 54
  floridus, 49–50
Library of universal knowledge, 300
Libro intitulado Visión deleytable, 73
Lichtenstein, E., 97n
Licinianus, Marcus Porcius, 23
Lieber, F., 184
Liebesny, F., vii
Liebrecht, F., 56
Liechtenstein, J. M. von, 307
Lietwiškoji enciklopedija, 311
Lietuvių enciklopedija, 311
Light of the soul, 67
Lille Salmonsen, Den, 196
Limiers, H. P. de, 100–01
Lincoln, A., 187
Lincoln library of essential information, The, 232
Lindau, W. A., 164
Lindberg, H., 313
Lindsay, W. M., 26, 35
Linnaeus, 255–56, 287–88
Linnean Society, 109, 110

Little & Ives Illustrated ready reference encyclopedia, 300
Liu Chin Tsao, 197
Liu K'o-i, 197
Liu T'ung, 36
'Living encyclopaedia, The', 18
*Livre
  de clergie, Le*, 63
  de l'année annuaire, Le, 306
  des cérémonies, Le, 39
Livres dou trésor, Li, 64–65
Lloyd, N., 89–90
Lloyd's Encyclopaedic dictionary, 304
Löbel, R. G., 156–57, 159, 161, 169, 229
Locke, G. H., 202, 203
Locke, J., 97, 115
London encyclopaedia, The, 182
Long, E. G., 185
Louis I of Bavaria, 36
Louis XV of France, 126
Lu Fêng-tsao, 113
Lucan, 52
Lucidarius, 53
Lucretius, 34, 136n
Lucubrationes, 78
Ludendorff, E. von, 152
Ludewig, J. P. von, 105
Ludovici, K. G., 105
Lumen animae, 66–67
Luneau de Boisjermain, P.-J.-F., 131, 132
Lütken, G., 195
Lyall, W. R., 235

Ma Tuan-lin, 65
Ma'aseh Tobiyyah, xi, *illustration*
MacArthur, D., vii
Macaulay, Lord, 144
McDannald, A. H., 184, 300
Macé, Jean, 86, 115
Macfarquhar, C., 138
McGraw-Hill Encyclopedia of science and technology, 221
Maclaren, C., 142
Maclise, D., 183
McLoughlin, E. V., 302
Macrobius, 49
Mader, J. J., 56
Maerlant, J. van, 59
Mafātīḥ al-'ulum, 39–40
Maffei, R., 77
Magma' multaqat az zuhūr birauḍa min al manzūm wal mantur, 77
Magnon, J. de, 88
Magnum theatrum vitae humanae, 311
Magyar encyclopaedia, 87
Maidment, W. R., vii
Maine, G. F., 305
al-Majrīṭi, 42

Mała encyklopedia powszechna PWN, 217
Malaia sovetskaia entsiklopedia, 206
Malclés, L.-N., 296
Malesherbes, C. G. de L. de, 125
Mallet, l'abbé, 125
Malý, J., 189
Mandeville, Sir J., 35, 59, 62
Manuel y Rodriguez, M. de, 313
Manz'sche Realencyklopädie, 307
Mappemonde, 27, 63
Maqālatar radd 'alā unmūdag al 'uιūm, 74
Marbach, O., 165
Marchand, P., 96, 106-07
Margarita philosophica, 21, 74-75
Mariétan, J., 32n
Marklot, A. F., 158, 164
Marmontel, J. F., 135, 136
Marperger, P. J., 100, 105
Marshall, N. J., 305
Martellotti, G., 239
Martianus Capella, 27-28, 44, 73
Martin, L. A., 300
Martini, M., 83
Marx, F., 25
Masaryk, T. G., 151
Masarykuv slovník naučný, 207
Mason, H. A., 80
Matritensis Codex, 35
al-Maula, Muhammad Jao, 206
Maurus, Magnentius Hrabanus, 36-37, 50, 52
al-Mawsou'at al'arabiyyah, 214
Mayhoff, K., 26
Mee, A., 15, 298
Megalē hellenikē enkyklopaideia, 207
Magenberg, Konrad von, 59
Meijer, B., 193
Meine, F. J., 298, 300
Meister, H., 306
Mela, Pomponius, 27
Mélange curieux de l'histoire, Le, 88
'Melissantes', 105-06
Melnalksnis, S., 311
Mémoires critiques et littéraires, 107
Mendel, H., 224
Mendelssohn-Bartholdy, F., 224
Mêng-jên, Kung, 102
Mentz, G., 198
Meseguer y Arrufat, F., 313
Messie, P., 79
Métraux, G. S., viii
Metz, Gautier de, 63
Meusel, J. G., 296
Mexia, P., 79
Meyer, J., 5, 186, 198, 199
Mézières, A., 202
Michael VII Ducas, The Emperor, 45
Michalski, S. F., 312
Michaud's Biographie universelle, 224-25
Michel, H., 171

Mien, Su, 37
Migne, J. P., 31, 35, 37, 45, 53
Millar, J., 142, 178
Mills, J., 117-18, 122
Milton, J., 262
Mirabellius, D. N., 76-77
Mirbel, C. F. B. de, 256
Mirrour of the world, The, 63
Moberly Bell, C., 146
Modern
    cyclopaedia of universal information, The, 305
    encyclopaedia, The (Burrowes), 304
    encyclopaedia (Gorell), 305
    encyclopedia (McDannald), 300
Moivre, A. de, 104
Moller, J., 90
Mollerup, W., 306
Moment-Lexikon, 309
Momigliano, A., 30
Mommsen, T., 27
Monceau, D. de, 128
Montaner & Simón, 195
Monte Cassino, 37
Montesquieu, C. de S., baron de, 120, 125, 136
Moratori, A., 103
Moréri, L., 88-90, 97, 101, 107n
Morhof, D. G., 90-92
Morley, J., 137
Morris, C., 19
Morris, C. S., 302
Mozart, W. A., 262
Mufīd al 'ulūm wamubīd humūm, 53-54
Muirhead, L. R., v
Muller, K. O., 26
Multifarium, 68
Murray, Sir J., 257
Musik in Geschichte und Gegenwart, Die, 223
Musikalisches Conversations-Lexikon, 224
Musikalisches Lexikon, 223
Musiklexikon, 223
Mussolini, B., 5
Myanma swezon kon, 214
Myers, G. C., 303
Mynors, R. A. B., 31
Myrrour and descrypcyon of the worlde, The, 63

Nani-Mirabelli, D., 76-77
Napier, M., 142-43
Nastol'nyi slovar', 189
National
    cyclopaedia of American biography, 225
    cyclopaedia of useful knowledge, 185, 305
    encyclopaedia, The (Mackenzie), 305
    encyclopedia, The (Suzzallo), 300
Necker, J., 136

Neckham, A., 54–55
Nehring, J. C., 101
Nelson's Perpetual loose-leaf encyclopaedia, 205, 300
Němec, B., 306
Neu vermehrtes historisch- und geographisches allgemeines Lexikon, 101, 102–03
Neue
  Brockhaus, 170, 171, 173
  deutsche Biographie, 225
  Folge des Konversations-Lexicons, 163
Neues
  Conversations-Lexikon (Wagener), 309
  elegantes Conversations-Lexicon, 185–86
  historisch-biographisches Lexikon der Tonkünstler, 223
  Volks-Konversationslexicon, 309
  Welt-Lexikon, 304, 307
Neuestes Conversations-Lexicon, 304
'Neufville, Louis de', 128, 130
Neurath, O., 18–19
New
  age encyclopaedia, 305
  American comprehensive encyclopedia, 300
  American cyclopaedia, The (Dana), 187–188
  American encyclopedia, The, 302
  American encyclopaedia, The (Taylor), 301
  century book of facts, 301
  concise pictorial encyclopedia, 299
  cyclopaedia, The, 109–10
  Funk & Wagnalls encyclopedia, The, 299
  general English dictionary, A, 117, 120
  golden encyclopedia, 301
  Gresham encyclopedia, 304
  international dictionary of the English language, 183–84
  international encyclopaedia, 200–01
  international year book, 201
  Masters pictorial encyclopedia, 301
  modern encyclopedia, The, 300
  pictorial encyclopedia of the world, 301
  popular encyclopaedia, The, 305
  practical reference library, 298
  royal cyclopaedia, 112
  Schaff-Herzog encyclopedia of religious knowledge, 219–20
  standard encyclopedia, The, 301
  standard encyclopedia of universal knowledge, 299
  teachers' and pupils' cyclopedia, The, 301
  universal encyclopaedia, 193
  wonder book encyclopedia, The, 301
  wonder world, The, 301
  world encyclopedia, 303
  world family encyclopedia, The, 302
  York Post World wide illustrated encyclopedia, 303
  Zealand junior encyclopedia, 312

Newman, L. F., 26
Newnes Family encyclopaedia, viii
Newnes Popular encyclopaedia, 305
Newton, Sir I, 99, 115
Niccoli, M., 310
Nicholson, W., 175, 177
Nichomacus, 39
Nierstrasz, H. F., 306
Nieuw en volkomen woordenboek, 306
Nieuwenhuis' Woordenboek, 192
Nöldeke, T., 303
Nordisk conversations-lexicon, 306
Nordisk familjebok, 193
Norsk allkunnebok, 212
Norsk konversasjonsleksikon, 208
Norstedts Uppslagsbok, 208
Northcliffe, Lord, 147
Notker Labeo, 28
Nouveau
  dictionnaire historique et critique, 106–07
  Larousse illustré, 190
  Larousse universel, 198
  petit Larousse, 191
  petit Larousse illustré, 191
Nouvelle biographie générale, 225
Nouvelle encyclopédie autodidactique Quillet, 307
Nouvelle encyclopédie portatif, 107
Novo diccionário enciclopédico, 311
Novy veliký ilustrovaný slovník, 207
en-Noweiri, 66
Nihāyat al-Arab fī funūn al-aabab, 66
Nuevo pequeño Larousse ilustrado, 192
Nuova enciclopedia popolare, 310
Nuova enciclopedia Sonzogno, 310
Nuovissima enciclopedia illustrata, 311
Nuovo dizionario, scientifico e curioso, 106
al-Nuwairi, 66
Nye Salmonsen, Den, 196
Nyhuus, H., 201

Oekonomisch-technologische Enzyklopädie, 108–09
Oersted, H. C., 176
Oestergaards Lexikon, 309
Onomasticon, 309–10
On divers arts, 51
Ontañon, J., 78
Oosthoek's Geïllustreerde encyclopaedie, 306
Orbis disciplinarum, 80
Orevalo, F., 35
Orgelbrand, S., 188
Originum, seu Etymologiarum libri XX, 33
Orosius, 34, 52
Ortloff, J. A., 296
Osborn, G. F., vii
O'Shea, M. V., 202
Österreichische National-Encyclopädie, 304
Otia imperialia, 56–57

Otto IV, 56
Otto Wigands Conversationslexicon, 309
Ottuv slovník naučný, 194, 306
Ou-yang Hsün, 33
Our wonder world, 301
Our wonderful world, 301
Ovid, 52, 68, 69
Oxford
    dictionary of the Christian Church, 220
    illustrated dictionary, 217–18, 304
    junior encyclopaedia, 212, 298
    New Zealand encyclopaedia, 312

Pafford, J. H. L., vii
Palgrave, Sir R., 220–21
Pallas nagy lexikona, A, 195
Palme Dutt, R., 151
Pamelius, Jacobus, 31
P'an Tzŭ'mu, 57
Panckoucke & Agasse, 110–12, 132, 134–135, 200
Panofsky, E., 81
Panstwowe wydawnictwo naukowe, 216–17
Pantologia, 176–77
Pao-chên, Huang, 39
Pascoe, J., 312
Paulus Diaconus, 26
Parallèle des anciens et des modernes, 114
Pardon, W., 117
Parker, B. M., 299
Parrott, Sir F., 305
Partington, C. F., 186
Pastrengo, G. di I. da, 69
Patrick, D., 188
Patterson, R. F., 304
Pauly, A. F. von, 42, 222
Pavlenkov, F., 195
Pears cyclopaedia, 196
Pei t'ang shu chao, 33
P'ei wên yün fu, 102
P'êng Ta-i, 79
Penguin encyclopaedia, viii
Penny cyclopaedia, The, 185
Pensées philosophiques, 119
People's cyclopedia, 303
Pequeño Larousse ilustrado, 191–92
Pera librorum juvenilium, 96
Péreire family, 307
Perrault, C., 114
Petit Larousse illustré, 191
Petite encyclopédie, 107
Petrarch, 69, 70, 77
Petrus de Aliaco, 70
Pexenfelder, M., 88
Pfannkuch, K., vii, 171
Pfennig-Encyklopädie, 185–86
Pfennig-Journal, Das, 309
Phenomena of the universe, The, 82–84
Phillips, W. A., 147

Philo, 39
Piccola enciclopedia Garzanti, 311
Pictured knowledge, 301
Pien Chu, 33
Pien tzŭ lei pien, 102
Pieper, J., 30, 80
Pierer, H. A., 167, 182
Pierre's Mappemonde, 27, 63
Piltz, O., 168–69
Pinheiro Chagas, M., 312
Pirenne, H., 151
Pitras, J. B., 60
Pivati, G., 106
Planciades, Fabius Fulgentius, 27
Plato, 21, 49, 52, 68, 266–67, 271, 273
Pléiade, La, 214–15
Pliny the Elder, 21, 25–26, 28, 34, 59, 82
Pliny the Younger, 25
Plotinus, 32
Po Chü'i, 36
Po k'ung liu t'ieh, 36
Po shih liu t'ieh shih lei chi, 36
Podręczna encyklopedja powszechna, 312
Pölitz, K. H., 161, 175
Pollux, Julius, 309–10
Polyanthea nova, 76–77, 84
Polyhistor, 27, 52
Polyhistor literarius, philosophicus et practicus, 90–92
Pomba enciclopedia, 310
Pompadour, Mme de, 125, 129
Pomponius Mela, 27
Popowitsch, J. S. V., 160
Popular encyclopaedia, The, 305
Porphyry of Tyre, 32
Porter, N., 183
Portrait de la sagesse universelle, Le, 86
Pos, H. J., 211
Pöschl, Der kleine, 308
Potone, 22
Prades, l'abbé J.-M. de, 124
Praecepta ad filium, 23
Predari, F., 310
Prévost, B.-L., 124
Primae lineae isagoges, 311
Prior, O. H., 63
Příruční slovník naučný, 216
Progressive reference library, The, 301–02
Psellus, Michael, 45–46
P'u, Wang, 37
Puisieux, Mme de, 120
Pulitzer, J., 196
Pure and Faithful, The, 41–42
Purnell's New English encyclopaedia, 305
Pythagoras, 68

al-Qādirī, 77
al-Qazvini, 53–54
Quillet Encyclopédie, 307

Quintilian, 21, 80
ibn Qutaiba, 37–38

Rabanus Maurus, Magnentius, 36-37, 50, 52
Rabelais, 80
Racine, J., 93
Rameau, J. P., 126n
Ramsay, A. M., 116, 117
Rand, E. R., 31
Rasā'ulu Ikhwan al ṣafā, 41–42
Raunkjaers Konversations leksikon, 212
Ray, J., 99, 256
ar-Rāzī, 54
Real-Encyclopädie der classischen Altertums-wissenschaft, 222–23
Realencyklopädie für protestantische Theologie, 219
Reales Staats- und Zeitungs-Lexikon, 99–100
Reallexikon für Antike und Christentum, 222
Réaumur, R. A. F. de, 116, 125–26, 128
Reductorium, repertorium et dictionium morale, 69, 76
Rees, A., 104, 109–10, 174, 229
Regensburg, 52, 53
Reimar, H. S., 307
Reinhard, Bishop of Halberstadt, 47
Reisch, G., 21, 74–75
Reissmann, A., 224
Religion in Geschichte und Gegenwart, Die, 220
Remigius of Auxerre, 49
Rerum divinarum et humanarum, 23–24
Reuss, C. F., 309
Révai nagy lexikona, 202
Reynolds, F. J., 302
Reynolds, Sir J., 109
Rheinische Konversations-Lexikon, 164
Rhondda, Lady, 152
Richard of St Victor, 54
Richards encyclopedia, 302
Richards topical encyclopedia, 302
Richelieu, Cardinal, 92, 114
Rieger, F. V., 189
Riemann, H., 223
Rihani, A., 214
Rines, G. E., 184
Ringelbergh, J. S. van, 78, 80
Ripelin, H., 67–68
Ripley, G., 187
Roberts, A. D., 297
Roger of Helmarshausen, 50–51
Rolle, R., 59
Roman de la rose, 62
Roos, J. F., 110
Rørdam, E., 195
Rose, Henry John, 179, 199, 235
Rose, Hugh James, 179, 235
Rosenkjaer, J., 208

Ross, J. M., 188, 193
Roth, J. F., 309
Rother, J. H., 105
Rotteck, C. W. von, 309
Rousseau, J.-J., 126, 136
Roux, A., 107
Royal Geographical Society, 185
Royal Horticultural Society, 224
Royal Society, The, 97, 99, 103, 109
Rüder, F. A., 100
Ruoff, H. W., 300, 302
Russell, B., 152
Russkii entsiklopedicheskii slovar', 312

Saeland, S., 201
Saglio, E., 42
St Clair, G., 203
St Evrémond, C. M. de St D., seigneur de, 96
St-Jean, Fr Léon de, 86
St Victor, Hugh of, 22, 32, 45, 47–49, 54, 74
St Victor, Richard of, 54
Ste Beuve, C. A., 307
Sallust, 34
Salmonsen Leksikon tidsskrift, 196
Salmonsens Konversations leksikon, 195
Salmonsens Store illustrerede konversations-leksikon, 195
Salomon, Bishop of Constance, 311
Salt, L. E., 212, 312
Salutati, C., 70
Salvat diccionario, 313
San Gimignano, G. G. da, 76
San kuo hui yao, 197
San ts'ai t'u hui, 86
San T'ung, 36
Sandeman, G., 201
Sanders, D., 169, 309
Sandford, Sir D. K., 305
Sandys, Sir J. E., 43, 81, 113
Sanford, E. M., 50, 53
Saranukromthai, 313
Sartine, A.-R. de, 128, 132
Sarton, G., 81
Satiricon (Capella), 27–28
Satyra, 27–28
Saunderson, N., 120
Saunier, Le Sieur, 87–88, 115
Savadjian, L., 211
Saxl, F., 37
Scalich (Scaliger), P., 79–80
Scalitzius, Count, 79–80
Schaller, K. A., 297
Scheer, R., 152
Schelling, F. W. J. von, 231, 309
Schem, A. J., 192
Schiffner, A., 307
Schilling, G., 223–24

Schlegel, K. W. F. von, 262, 263
Schleiermacher, A. A. E., 297
Schmid, C. C. E., 231, 309
Schmiele, W., 297
Schnee, H., 225
Schneider, G., 297
Schütz, M. C. von, 109
Schwabe, J. J., 102
Schweizer-Lexikon, 172, 211
Science des personnes de la cour, 100-01
Science universelle, La, 88
Scientiae sermocinales realesque, 44
Scientiarum omnium encyclopaediae, 86
Scientific American, 184
Scientific method, 20
Scott, G. L., 104, 109
Scribe of Khwarazm, The, 39-40
Segui enciclopedia, 313
Séguier, Jayme de, 311
Seligman, E. R. A., 221
Sellius, Godefroy, 118, 122
Sentman, E. E., 303
Serís, H., 197
Sevensma, T. P., 306
Shaftesbury, Lord, 97, 119
Shakespeare, W., 259-65
Shan t'ang ssŭ k'ao, 79
Shaw, G. B., 152
Shên Tzŭ-nan, 86
Sherwood, E. J., 209
Shi lei fu, 39
Shi lei fu t'ung pien, 39
Shi wê lei chü, 65
Shi wu yüan hui, 112-13
Shih-chan, Wu, 39
Shih-nan, Yü, 33
Shih wu chi yüan, 46
al-Shinshanari, Ahmad, 206
Shores, Dr Louis, vii, 213, 297
Shu, Wu, 39, 40
Shu hsü chih nan, 46
Shu-lin, Huang, 197
Sichardus, Johannes, 31
Sijthoff's Woordenboek, 195
Silva Uzcátegui, R. D., 226
Simón-Diaz, J., 113
Simpson, E., vii
Sincere Brethren, The, 41-42
Sinclair, R., 212
Sinhalese encyclopedia, 217
Sinold von Schütz, P. B., 99-100
as-Sīrazī, 74
Skalich, P., 79-80
Slovnik naučný, 189
Smedley, E., 179, 235
Smellie, W., 138-39, *illustration*
Smith, A., 109
Smith, B. E., 299
Smith, C. S., 51
Smith, G. C. E., vii, 205

Smith, Sir J. E., 110
Smith, R., 213
Smith, R. A., 1, 18, 228
Smith, W., 256
Smith, W. R., 144
Snyder, A. D., 309
Société nouvelle de l'Encyclopédie française, 209
Society for the Diffusion of Useful Knowledge, The, 185
Solatio imperatoris, 56-57
Solinus, Gaius Julius, 26, 28, 34, 52, 59
Sommario di tutte le scientie, 79
Sommerfelt, A., 201
Sonzogno enciclopedia, 310
Southey, R., 229, 231
Speculum
    doctrinale, 61-63
    historiale, 61-63
    maius, 60-63, 68
    morale, 60-63
    naturale, 60-63
    vel Imago mundi, 60
Spenser, W. G., 25
Speusippos, 22
Spies, O., 72
Sprach-Brockhaus, 171, 172
Spravochnii entsiklopedicheskii slovar', 187
Ssu shu wu ching lei tien chi ch'êng, 197
Ssŭ-chang, Tung, 26
Ssŭ-i, Wang, 86
Staats-Lexikon, 309
Standard encyclopedia, 299
Standard international encyclopedia, The, 301-02
Stanyan, T., 117
Starchevskii, A., 187
Statius, 52
Steenberghen, F. van, 81
Stein, J., 298
Steinberg, S. H., 160, 297
Stephanus, Carolus, 79, 87, 89
Stockmann, G., 169
Stoddart, Sir J., 233
Stoddart, J. M., 184
Stonehouse, F., 112
Stopes, M., 151
Storia letteraria d'Italia, 113, 198
Størmer, L., 201
Stoupe, J.-G.-A., 134
Strasbourg, Hugh of, 67-68
Straub, A., 56
Student's encyclopaedia of universal knowledge, The, 193-94
Su Mien, 37
Subḥ al-ashʾā fi ṣināʾat al-inshā, 72
Suchbuch, 308
Suchodolski, B., 216
Sudmann, A., 212

Suetonius, 34
Suffolk and Berkshire, The Earl of, 224
Suidas, 46–47, 94
Sulzer, J. G., 106
Summa totius de omnimoda historia, 53
Summa de exemplis, 76
Summerscale, Sir J., viii
Sung, Wei, 197
Suzzallo, H., 300
Švābe, A., 311
Svensk uppslagsbok, 207–08
Svenskt konversations-lexicon, 313
Sylva sylvarum, 54

aṭ-Ṭabari, Muhammad ibn Ġarīr, 303
Tableau général des connoissances humaines,
   107
Ta-i, P'êng, 79
Tai Chao-ch'un, 197
T'ai p'ing kuang chi, 41
T'ai p'ing yü lan, 40, 41
T'ai Tsung, The Emperor, 40
T'ang Chung-yu, 57
T'ang hui yao, 37
T'ang lei han, 86
T'ang sung po k'ung liu t'ieh, 36
Taschen-Brockhaus zum Zeitgeschehen, 171
al-*Tasrif*, 303
Tatischev, V. N., 112
at-Tauḥīdī, 45
Taylor, C. R., 300, 301, 303
Taylor, J., 49
Technical and scientific encyclopaedia, 221
Templeman, W. D., 198
Terreros y Pando, E., 313
Tesoretto, 64
Teuffel, W. S., 222–23
*Teutsch-orthographisches Schreib- . . . und
   Sprüch-Wörter-Lexicon*, 101–02
Thackeray, W. M., 183
Thatcher, V. S., 299, 302
Themistius, 258n
Theobald of Monte Cassino, Abbot, 37
'Theophilus', 50–51
Thesaurus philosophicus, 95
These eventful years, 151–52
Thieme, H. P., 198
Thomas of Cantimpré, 59–60
Thomson, J., 104
Thomson, T., 305
Thorbecke, A., 31
Thorndike, L., 81
Thorpe's Dictionary of applied chemistry, 222
Thyselius, 193
Ti wang ching shih t'u p'u, 57
T'ien chung chi, 78–79
T'ien-lin, Hsü, 59
Times, The, 145–47
T'ing-kuei, Yeh, 46

Tirpitz, A. P. F. von, 152
Titus, The Emperor, 25
Toletanus Codex, 35
Toll, F. G., 189
*Topographisch-statistisch-historisches Comp-
   toir- . . . und Zeitungslexikon*, 308
Toro, M. de, 297
Toro y Gisbert, M. de, 191, 313
Torrentius, H., 75
Torrey, N. L., 130
Tournefort, J. P. de, 256
Tournemine, J. R., 98, 115
Towards a living encyclopaedia, 228
Traill, T. S., 144
Transylvanian Association for the En-
   couragement of Rumanian Litera-
   ture and Culture, 195
Treccani, G., 207
Treiberg, P., 306
Trésor qui parle de toutes choses, Le, 65
Trevisa, John of, 58
Trévoux, Dictionnaire de, 95, 98–99, 115–
   116, 124–25
Trygvason, Olaf, 53
Trzaski, Everta i Michalskiego encyklopedia,
   312
Tsao, Liu Chin, 197
Ts'ê fu yüan kuei, 41
Tsëng pu shih lei fu t'ung pien, 39
Tu shu chi shu lüeh, 102
T'u shuh pien, 79
Tu Yu, 35–36, 65
Tuan-lin, Ma, 65
T'ung chi, 36, 46
Tung han hui yao, 59
T'ung k'ao, 65
Tung Ssǔ-chang, 26
T'ung tien, 35–36, 65
Turgot, A. R. J., 136
Türk ansiklopedisi, 211
Twentieth century
   encyclopaedia (Hutchinson), 304
   encyclopaedia (Morris), 302
   encyclopedia (Reynolds), 302
   encyclopedia of religious knowledge, 219
Tytler, J., 139–40
Tzǔ-mu, P'an, 57
Tzǔ-nan, Shên, 86
Tzǔ shih ching hua, 102

Uj
   idok lexikona, 310
   lexikon, 310
   magyar lexikon, 216
Ullmann, F., 222
Ulman, B. L., 63
Ultima Thule encyklopedja, 312
al-'Umari, 66
Underbrink, R. L., 228, 298

Unified encyclopedia, 302
Unity of Science, First International
    Congress for the, 1935, 18; 1937,
    19
Universal
    cyclopaedia, 193
    dictionary, 176
    dictionary of arts and sciences (Goldsmith),
    109
    dictionary of arts and sciences, An (Chambers), 103–04
    dictionary of knowledge, 177–78
    dictionary of science, art, . . ., 182
    dictionary of the arts, sciences, . . ., 173
    history of arts and sciences, 106
    Jewish encyclopedia, The, 220
    Lexikon, 211
    Lexikon (Pierer), 167, 182
    world reference encyclopedia, 302
Universitas, 313
University illustrated encyclopedia, 300, 303
Unmūdag al 'ulūm, 74
Unsere Zeit, 168
Unstead, R. J., 303

Vaccaro, G., 310
Valla, G., 75–76
Van Nostrand's Scientific encyclopedia, 221
Variae, 30
Varro, Marcus Terentius, 23–24, 28, 34,
    44
Verschuerens Modern woordenboek, 306
Verthamon de Chavagnac, M., 124
Veski, J. V., 306
Vincent of Beauvais, 52, 60–63, 68
Vinogradoff, Sir P., 151
Virgil, 52, 68
Visé, D. de, 95
Visión deleytable, 72–74, 79, 88
Vitruvius, 34
Vitry, J. de, 59
Vivats Geillustreerde encyclopedie, 200
Vives, J. L., 77–78
Vizetelly, F. H., 299
Vloten, G. van, 40
*Vocabulaire technique et critique de la
    philosophie*, 220
Vocabularius poeticus, 75
Vocabularius rerum, 74
Vogt, A., 39
Volaterranus, R., 77
Volks
    Brockhaus, 171, 172, 173
    Lexikon, 309
    Universal-Lexikon, 200
Vollständiger Handatlas, 166
Voltaire, F. M. A. de, 114, 124, 125, 128,
    132, 136, 265
Volume library, The, 302

Vorlesungen über die Methode des academischen Studiums, 309
Vvedenskii, B. A., 206, 213
Vyver, A. van de, 31

Wagener, H., 309
Wagenseil, J. C., 96
Wahrig, G., 308
Wajdi, Muhammad Farid, 206
Walford, A. J., 297
Wallace, A. R., 141
Wallace, Sir D. M., 146
Walsh, J. P., 228, 298
Walter, J., 56
Walther, J. G., 223
Wang Ch'êng-lieh, 113
Wang Ch'i, 65, 86, 112–13
Wang Chia-pin, 57
Wang Fêng-chieh, 39
Wang P'u, 37
Wang Ssŭ-i, 86
Wang Ying-lin, 66
Watson, F., 78
Watson, J. W., 301
Watts, R., 269n
Webster, N., 26, 183
Webster's
    Comprehensive encyclopedic dictionary, 300
    *International dictionary of the English
        language*, 183–84
    New American dictionary, 301
    Unified dictionary and encyclopedia, 301
    Universal encyclopedia, 299
Weedon's Modern encyclopedia, 303
Wei, Ch'en, 113
Wei Sung, 197
Wei-hsin, Hsieh, 65
Welcker, C. T., 309
Wellmann, M., 25
Wells, H. G., 17–19, 152, 209, 228
Weltall, Das, 309
Wên hsien t'ung k'ao, 36, 65
Werenskiold, W., 201
Westerink, L. G., 45–46
Whethamstede, John, 304
Whibley, L., 43
Whitaker's Almanack, 196
Whitelaw, A., 305
Whitney, W. D., 299
Wielka encyklopedia powszechna PWN, 216–
    217
Wielka ilustrowana encyklopedja powszechna,
    312
Wigand, O., 309
William de Conches, 22
Williams, Talcott, 201
Williams, Thomas, 108
Winchell, C. M., 297
Winkler Prins, A., 192

Winkler Prins Boek van het jaar, 192
Winsnes, A. H., 201
Winston, Richard and Clare, 30
Wissowa, G., 42, 223
Witsen-Geysbeek, P. G., 306
Wolff, O. L. B., 186
Wollaston, W. H., 257
Wonder-world of knowledge in colour, 305
Wonderland of knowledge, The, 303
Woodward, L. J., vii
World
  almanac, The, 196
  book, The, 202–05
  book encyclopedia dictionary, 218
  brain, 17, 209, 228
  educator encyclopedia, 302
  home reference encyclopedia, The, 299
  scope encyclopedia, 302
  university encyclopedia, 302
  wide
    cyclopedia, 303
    encyclopedia and gazetteer, 303
    illustrated encyclopedia, 300, 303
'World encyclopaedia', 17–18, 228
Wörterbuch der philosophischen Begriffe, 220
Worthy, W., 304
Wrangham, F., 232
Wright, A., 198
Wright, E. H., 302
Wright, M. H., 302
Wright, T., 55
Wu Shih-chan, 39
Wu Shu, 39, 40

Wu tai hui yao, 37
Wulf, M. de, 81
Wurm, E., 309
Wüstenfeld, H. F., 38, 72

Yang Ch'ên, 197
Yao-wên, Ch'ên, 78–79
Yeh T'ing-kuei, 46
Ying-lin, Wang, 66
l'Ymage du monde, 63
Yu, Tu, 35–36, 65
Yü An-ch'i, 86
Yü hai, 66
Yü Shih-nan, 33
Yuan liu chih lun, 65
Yüan Yüan, 41
Yün fu shih i, 102
Yung lo ta tien, 70
Yunis, Abdul Hamid, 206
Yushakov, S. N., 200

al-Zahrāwī, Abulcasis, 303
Zakī Pasha, Aḥmad, 66
Zara, Antonio, 84–85
Zedler, J. H., 104–05
Zerolo, E., 311
Zim, H. S., 301
Zischka, G. A., 296, 297
Zoek-licht, 306
Zotov, V. R., 189